THE HIDDEN WHITE HOUSE

ALSO BY ROBERT KLARA

FDR's Funeral Train: A Betrayed Widow, a Soviet Spy, and a Presidency in the Balance

THE HIDDEN WHITE HOUSE

HARRY TRUMAN AND THE
RECONSTRUCTION OF AMERICA'S
MOST FAMOUS RESIDENCE

ROBERT KLARA

THOMAS DUNNE BOOKS
ST. MARTIN'S GRIFFIN   NEW YORK

THOMAS DUNNE BOOKS.
An imprint of St. Martin's Press.

www.thomasdunnebooks.com
www.stmartins.com

Photograph on page 1 courtesy of the Smithsonian Institute Libraries, Washington, D.C. Photographs on pages 8, 21, 32, 42, 53, 65, 106, 130, 150, 173, 186, 199, 229, 240, and 251 by Abbie Rowe, National Park Service, courtesy of Harry S. Truman Library. Photograph on page 74 courtesy of the Harry S. Truman Library. Photograph on page 85 courtesy of the D.C. Public Library, Washingtoniana Division. Photograph on page 95 courtesy of The State Historical Society of Missouri. Photograph on page 113 courtesy of *Trinity and Beyond*, VCE, Inc. Photograph on page 118 courtesy of Hagley Museum and Library. Photograph on page 141 by Abbie Rowe, National Park Service, courtesy of the New Haven Museum & Historical Society Library. Photograph on page 164 by William F. Carnahan, Silver Spring, Maryland. Photograph on page 180 courtesy of U.S. Government Printing Office: 1952. Photograph on page 209 from the author's collection. Photograph on page 219 reprinted with permission of the D.C. Public Library, Star Collection, © *The Washington Post*.

The Library of Congress has cataloged the hardcover edition as follows:

Klara, Robert.
    The hidden White House : Harry Truman and the reconstruction of America's most famous residence / Robert Klara.
        p. cm.
    Includes bibliographical references and index.
    ISBN 978-1-250-00027-9 (hardcover)
    ISBN 978-1-250-02293-6 (e-book)
    1. White House (Washington, D.C.)—History—20th century.
2. Truman, Harry S., 1884–1972.   3. Public buildings—Repair and reconstruction—Washington (D.C.)—History—20th century.   I. Title.
    F204.W5K55 2013
    975.3'042—dc23

                                                        2013020952

ISBN 978-1-250-05393-0 (trade paperback)

First St. Martin's Griffin Edition: October 2014

10   9   8   7   6   5   4   3   2   1

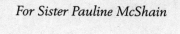

For Sister Pauline McShain

CONTENTS

THE HIDDEN WHITE HOUSE

PROLOGUE

With one accord, they raised their eyes to the ceiling and uttered a terrible cry. The chandelier, the immense mass of the chandelier was slipping down, coming toward them.

—Gaston Leroux, *The Phantom of the Opera*

*D*espite the forty-six years of wear on its floor, the six years since its draperies had been replaced, and the more than seven since the public had even been permitted inside, the White House's Blue Room was, on a winter afternoon in early 1948, still arguably the most beautiful chamber in the United States.[1]

If there was one thing more remarkable than the endless details required to serve a White House tea, it was that the White House was serving tea at all; it had been a long time since the old place had seen any guests.[2] The protracted, painful years of World War II and the American blood it had spilled on the soils and seas of two hemispheres had made it unseemly (if not outright crass) to host lavish state dinners and breezy luncheons on the lawn. In December 1941, shortly after he'd gone up to Capitol Hill to declare war on Japan, President Franklin D. Roosevelt had returned to the White House and declared the party over.

But the war was a memory now, and even with thousands of servicemen still stationed in Europe's ruins, Harry S. and Bess Truman had decided by the fall of 1946 that it was appropriate, both politically and symbolically, to resume the executive mansion's long tradition of having a few—or a few hundred—people over. And so it was that the members of the Daughters of the American Revolution, the tradition-bound women's organization headquartered over on 1776 D Street, had come to the Blue Room for a little socializing.

The largest White House events had always been held in the East Room, a neoclassical cavern of plaster whose near eighty-foot length permitted seven hundred emissaries and other swells to rest their elbows on the state table linen. But the "Oval Reception Room"—first done up in blue by Martin Van Buren in 1837—had long been considered the house's aesthetic centerpiece and, as such, the perfect space for intimate gatherings. "The gem of the White House," *Century* magazine had called it back in 1903, "one of the most finely proportioned rooms in this country."[3] Journalism of the early 1900s was known for leaking enthusiastic gases, but in this case there was no exaggeration: The Blue Room had been designed to enchant visitors and now, in 1948, as it neared its sesquicentennial, it was still doing precisely that.

A perfect ellipse girdled by a chair rail in white enamel, the room's walls were as dark as a captain's uniform. A suite of white-and-gold French Empire chairs—upholstered in silk and carefully copied from those in the Château de Compiègne, outside Paris—stood sentry along the wainscoting, opening up an uninterrupted expanse of oaken herringbone parquetry glistening from its latest coat of floor polish. Offering a commanding view of the South Lawn as it tumbled down toward the distant shimmer of the Potomac, three tall windows opened off the Blue Room's far side. Gilt eagles perched high on the casing, their talons clutching drapery rods from which spilled a profusion of folds, fringes, tassels, and valences of white stars.

Off to the left of the room's main entrance, a fireplace mantel hewn from slabs of milk white marble and accented by arrows tipped in bronze stood flush to the wall, surmounted by a gilded clock. Luxuriating across the clock's top, Minerva, the Roman goddess of wisdom, rested her right elbow just above the number 12 and cast a languid stare across the room. She'd been holding this lazy pose—bare-chested—since 1817.[4]

None of the room's fineries, however, exceeded what dangled from its ceiling. Suspended on a heavy chain was a chandelier so large and dazzling, it looked as though a tree had been felled from a forest of crystal and strung up as a prize. The fixture, crafted in the Manhattan workshops of Edward F. Caldwell & Co., boasted eighteen gilded-bronze arms that stretched out like goosenecks to support as many electric candlesticks. Snaking between them were twelve additional arms, each of them topped with a turned-glass finial shaped like a perfume bottle. From tiny hooks along all of the arms dangled hundreds of Baccarat crystal prisms that formed a shimmering bouquet of rosettes, faceted knobs, and French drops.

The Blue Room's chandelier—numbered 11836 and labeled "Pende-loque" in Caldwell & Co.'s surviving records—represented the lighting firm's best handiwork, and among its largest. From shackle to finial, the mighty Pendeloque stood at five and a half feet, its arms spreading forty-two inches across.[5] It was anyone's guess what this gargantuan fixture weighed, but its stature was comparable to the trio of tent-and-bowl chandeliers that Caldwell & Co. had made for the East Room—and each of *those* monsters tipped the scales at twelve hundred pounds.[6]

The architectural firm of McKim, Mead & White had commissioned the Blue Room's chandelier as part of Theodore Roosevelt's sweeping renovation of the mansion back in 1902. Workmen had evidently screwed the hook for the Pendeloque's thick chain into one of the heavy wooden beams just above the plaster ceiling. The beam crossed the Blue Room laterally, mortised into the brick walls on the east and west sides. The beam also did the work of holding up the Oval Study on the second floor—the president's private office, which contained, among other things, a Victorian carved oak desk, six chairs, a couch, two large tables, Truman's book collection, several lamps, a thick woolen carpet, and a Steinway concert grand piano. That this accumulated weight might be a grave burden to be putting on an old wooden floor joist was a thought worth considering. Not that anyone had. The beam up there was a good foot thick, and the mighty Pendeloque had been hanging from it for the preceding forty-six years. If its hundreds of pounds' worth of finger-thick crystal slabs might be putting undue strain on the lumber, well, nobody appeared much aware of it.

Another thing nobody was aware of was that, on this afternoon, as the Daughters of the American Revolution milled merrily about below, the beam holding the chandelier above their heads had just about reached its breaking point. The beam's red-tinted pine, felled in the virgin forests of Virginia, was now 131 years old. The wood had never been treated or sealed, and the passing of 524 seasons had left it bone-dry, brittle, and laced with cracks. Carpenters had first laid the beam down back in 1817 during a rebuild of the house after the British army had set fire to it. By the time architect Charles Follen McKim began renovating the mansion for Theodore Roosevelt in 1902, the beam was already in bad shape. The architect should never have left it in place, but Teddy had rushed him, and he'd had no choice. McKim tried to mitigate the second floor's problems by socketing steel beams into various trouble spots, but it wasn't enough. A brittle lattice of timber was still working overtime in the Blue Room ceiling. It was a miracle that the old crosspiece had held, a second miracle that it had shown no signs of distress. It was about to.

Standing just beneath the Pendeloque's faceted finial ball was Bess Wallace Truman. Clad in white gloves and a boxy two-piece suit, maintaining her straight posture and looking (as *Time* magazine would rather indelicately put it) like one of the shoppers at the local A&P, the First Lady smiled broadly as she shook the hands of her guests.[7] She was miserable. Few members of the public were privy to the fact, but Mrs. Truman detested official events like this one. Though hardly as formal as a state dinner, a White House tea could be every bit as taxing, an interminable sentence of polite smiles and vapid small talk. It was the last way the president's wife wanted to spend this, or any, afternoon.[8]

Though Bess Truman had been First Lady for longer than two years, she'd never gotten over her dread of the social obligations that came with the post. To say she was shy would understate the matter; when it came to facing the public, Bess Truman was usually terrified.[9] "We felt sorry for Mrs. Truman at every reception she gave, knowing her agony," recalled Lillian Parks, whose years working as a seamstress behind the White House's storied stone walls had turned her into a sharp observer of human character, especially that of Harry Truman's wife. "She was so timid about people and crowds," Parks remembered, "that her hands perspired when she had to stand in the receiving line."[10] That, not fashion, was the real reason the First Lady was wearing those white gloves.[11]

Milling about in their pearls and horn-rims, the ladies of the DAR were thrilled to have been invited to the country's most famous home, and even more thrilled to meet its hostess. Their hands shot forward like daggers. Bess Truman smiled, grasped each one, and shook. So nice to see you. Thank you for coming. She was slogging it out at what

Margaret Truman laughingly called "First Ladying," but only Margaret thought that joke was funny.[12] In later years, Bess Truman would complain that all the handshaking had made "a wreck" out of her arm, swelling her glove size from a six to a six and a half. Eventually, the president would have to instruct her on the right way to shake hands—firmly, but with a quick release—so as to leave her phalanges no worse for wear.[13] But that lesson was still years away on this afternoon, and so Bess Truman clasped one hand after another, shook painfully, and kept smiling.

The ritual also revealed a dreary truth about the White House itself, one that wide-eyed visitors somehow never guessed, but one that the mansion's longtime staffers had known for years: For all the history in its walls, the place was rather a haggard old heap, more a banquet hall than a home. Usher J. B. West had seen countless teas like this one, the Blue Room packed with nattering old biddies. They had "purple" hair, he recalled, those "berouged Washington ladies who came through our reception lines."[14] Social secretary Edith Helm herded the women through like cattle, a skill that butler Alonzo Fields quietly admired. "Mrs. Helm could pour a cup of tea, keeping up a conversation with a guest who was dead set on a prolonged conversation, give her the tea and then get rid of her and continue the same running conversation with the next guest faster than anyone I have ever seen," he said.[15] Helm was indeed a pro. She'd been getting rid of guests since the Wilson administration. But even President Truman had learned the White House social drill pretty quickly. As he'd later sum up the ritual of having guests over: "Go on into the dining room and have some cookies and punch and then go away."[16]

It would be speculative to say that Bess Truman was hoping for some reason—any reason—to escape the Blue Room at this moment, to slip away and leave all those hands for someone else to shake. But if she was indeed hopeful for such an excuse, she was about to get one. A tinkling sound—faint at first, then more persistent—drew her eye up into the forest of crystals in the chandelier overhead. The pendants, for some reason, were all trembling.[17] No breeze could be at fault here; it was wintertime in the capital city, too cold for open windows. Nonetheless, hundreds of crystals were dancing in place, splashing light around the room as the party continued below, the participants oblivious. A few tense moments passed and then, glancing up again, Mrs.

Truman noticed that the entire fixture had begun to swing. This was serious business. The Pendeloque was bigger than a kitchen refrigerator: If the thing came down, it was likely to squash at least one Revolutionary daughter, perhaps two. The First Lady gestured for a nearby aide to summon J. B. West. When the assistant usher presented himself, Bess whispered urgently in his ear, "Would you *please* find out what is going on upstairs?"[18]

What was going on upstairs was this: Harry S. Truman, the thirty-third president of the United States of America, was enjoying a vigorous splash in the bathtub. Just to the west of the Oval Study stood the president's bedroom, which included a small bathroom. Truman liked to take naps in the afternoon and, sometimes, baths, too. The tea going on downstairs was his wife's affair, not his, so what was the harm?

J. B. West raced up the stairs, trying to remember if he'd given orders to move any heavy furniture around on the second floor that day. As he reached the Oval Study, he bumped into Fields, the butler, who was strolling out of the president's bedroom. Indignant with fright, West yelled at him, "What's going on up here?" Fields stopped, confused by the question. "The boss is taking a bath," the butler said, "and he asked me to get him a book."[19]

Fields was a handsome black man with a gracious and dignified bearing. He stood six foot three and weighed 250 pounds. Over the years, West had grown accustomed to the dishes in the pantry rattling as Fields clomped past. But this time, things were different. Downstairs, a chandelier big enough for the Fox Theatre was threatening to drop on the holy heads of the DAR. West had been charged with finding out what was causing it, but he had no idea. Everything up here seemed in perfect order. As the butler continued on his way, West could feel the floor trembling beneath the thick carpeting. He looked up in alarm, but Fields just shrugged.

"This place," the butler said, "has been squeaking like this for years."

⊹⇌ ⇌⊹

Later, after the last Daughter of the American Revolution had been given her coat, thanked, and whisked out the door, Bess Truman returned to the Oval Study upstairs. West and Fields accompanied her. One by one, they tramped across the floor in an attempt to re-create the shaking that West had felt. It wasn't difficult. The floor, as Truman himself later described it, "vibrated when any group of people walked up the stairs and it made the great crystal chandelier tinkle in the Blue

Room below."[20] It was, in other words, a condition that the president was apparently familiar with already.

But the swooping of the chandelier over guests' heads? That was something new. "I was afraid," Bess announced, "the chandelier was going to come right down on top of all those people!"[21]

At this, Truman burst out laughing, conjuring the image of his bathtub—with him inside of it—falling through the floor, allowing him to salute the Daughters of the American Revolution wearing nothing more than his reading glasses.[22] "That would have been something!" the president exclaimed, chuckling on.[23]

Bess Truman was not amused. (Sometime afterward, the president admitted that his bawdy joke had "shocked the madam."[24]) For his part, Fields felt guilty about the whole thing, especially later on, when the mansion's structural problems became public. "I was so big, with my flat feet," Fields said. "The White House was falling down under my weight."[25]

The butler turned out to be correct about one thing: The White House *was* falling down, though it had nothing to do with his feet. Its moment of humor past, the president's joke about streaking the DAR—as one of Truman's architects later put it, "to descend in the tub among the ladies"[26]—left the room in an uncomfortable silence. The truth was, even in his joking, Truman had been harboring anxieties of his own. The trembling floor had been going on for some time now. "Not an easy man to scare," *Collier's* magazine would report a few months hence, Truman had to admit that the noticeable swaying of the Blue Room's chandelier had "made him nervous."[27] The president quickly shifted into decision mode, searching for a course of action that would both address the problem and calm the agitation of those around him. "You'd better get some engineers in here," Truman said to West. "They might have to shore up the floors."[28]

At that moment, none of those assembled in the study above the Blue Room could imagine that the house they stood in would, within a year's time, send them running for their lives.

ONE

MOVING DAY

I pray heaven to bestow the best of blessings on this house, and all that shall hereafter inhabit it. May none but honest and wise men ever rule under this roof.

—letter from President John Adams to his wife;
quote chiseled into the State Dining Room's mantel

*T*here is a story about President Calvin Coolidge taking a walk around the White House grounds one evening with Missouri senator Selden P. Spencer, who pointed to the luminous mansion of carved sandstone and remarked, jokingly, "I wonder who lives there." The lugubrious Coolidge responded, "Nobody. They just come and go."[1]

Indeed they do, and no two stories of how a new president and his family come to live in America's most famous house are alike. Most, however, share a common trait: The White House is a prize that candidates fight for, often for years. But a handful of others gain admittance by fate alone, and this was the case with Harry S. Truman. "If there ever was a man who was forced to be President," Truman once said, "I'm that man."[2] The news reached him and his family on the afternoon of April 12, 1945. It struck them like a bolt of lightning. It came, fittingly, in the middle of a rainstorm.

In those days, the Trumans lived in a second-floor apartment at 4701 Connecticut Avenue, in a quiet neighborhood tucked into the city's northwestern quadrant, not far from Rock Creek Park. On that April afternoon, Bess glanced out the window at moody gray skies over the city and did not like the looks of them. Her husband—a last-minute choice to be Franklin Delano Roosevelt's vice president—was scheduled to fly up to Rhode Island to deliver a speech. Air travel frightened Bess Truman; many things did.

Down the hall, the Trumans' daughter, Margaret, was primping in her bedroom mirror. The twenty-one-year-old college junior was preparing for a date that evening. A few feet away sat the cantankerous Madge Wallace, Bess's eighty-two-year-old mother, who was visiting from Missouri. Grandma Wallace hurled one probing question after another about the evening's suitor, while Margaret, dabbing on her makeup, minted perfect responses. She knew the drill by now. Nearly twenty-six years earlier, Madge Wallace had lost Bess at the altar to that "dirt farmer" Harry Truman, and she was bent on assuring that her lovely granddaughter didn't wind up with a bum, too.[3]

Harry Truman was far from being a bum, but his salary as public servant had never amounted to much. In the eleven years since Harry's narrow election to the Senate in 1934, the Trumans had lived in a series of tiny apartments. Back home in Independence, the Wallace family home was a fourteen-room Victorian with stained-glass parlor windows. But Washington was a big town. Beginning with the family's first flat—a cramped price gouger at $150 a month—getting by had been difficult.[4]

It was why the Trumans adored 4701 Connecticut Avenue so much. They'd chanced on their two-bedroom apartment in 1941, and the onset of the war would show them just how lucky they'd been. World War II brought a scarcity of everything, especially housing. In 1942, Washington's population swelled by a quarter of a million people, all of whom went looking for apartments. Soon, ten thousand boardinghouses were operating in the capital city, many filled with young women from

the hinterlands, "government girls" who'd arrived to push the paperwork of war.

⁜⟺ ⟺⁜

In a city of old row houses and overcrowded hostelries, the Trumans'
building was a vision from a fairy tale—a white brick prewar of five
stories embracing a leafy courtyard trimmed with flower beds. Apartment 209 faced the front and took in the morning sun. It had two
bathrooms, a sleeping porch, and even enough space for Margaret's
Steinway baby grand. For all this, the family paid $120 a month. Tru-
man's recent elevation to the vice presidency had bumped his monthly
take-home pay to exactly $982.45, making their apartment an out-
right steal.[5] And yet the attachment they'd formed with their apartment had since run deeper than the family budget. As solid Missouri
stock, the Trumans lived modestly. Ostentation made them uncomfortable. So far as they cared, FDR was welcome to the carved paneling and marble fireplaces of the White House; the Trumans were
perfectly happy with their rental.[6]

At 6:00 P.M., the telephone rang. Margaret walked over and answered
it. It was her father calling. Margaret began her usual kidding with
him—telling him she had a date and wouldn't be home for dinner—
but Truman cut her off and demanded to speak with "Mother."[7] Confused and hurt over her father's uncharacteristic "voice of steel,"
Margaret surrendered the phone and trooped back to her room.[8] Bess
Truman took the receiver and nestled it into her graying curls.

"Bess," Truman barked, "I'm at the White House. President Roosevelt died about two hours ago. I'm sending a car for you and Margaret.
I want you here when I'm sworn in."[9] And then he hung up.

In their nearly twenty-six years of marriage, Bess Truman had never
heard a tone in her husband's voice quite like the one that echoed in
her head now as she put the receiver back on the hook.

⁜⟺ ⟺⁜

It's not known whether the Truman women said anything to each
other as the heavy black limousine thrummed the cobblestones on its
way down to the White House, but they didn't have to. Already, the
realization was dawning that the lives they'd known for the past eleven
years had been swept away in the time it took to answer a phone.
Moments after the conversation had ended, a reporter from the As-

sociated Press raced up the stairs to knock on the apartment door. Still in her slip, Margaret opened it without thinking—only to slam it back shut in the reporter's face. Bess and Margaret tried to sneak out of the building through the back door, but the press had already staked the whole place out, leaving them to run a gauntlet of photographers before reaching the limousine. This, they knew, was only the beginning.

They'd been so lucky up to now. Until a cerebral hemorrhage felled him in his cottage retreat down in Warm Springs, Georgia, FDR had been the most captivating president of the twentieth century. His laughter, his crafty storytelling, that thousand-watt smile—all of it kept the newsmen in a permanent state of distraction. It permitted the Trumans to live as ordinary people. Margaret pursued her B.A. in history at George Washington University. Bess would slide behind the wheel of her '41 Chrysler Windsor to visit the stores downtown, where, to her enduring delight, nobody recognized her.[10] Bess's shock and grief over Roosevelt's passing were genuine, but before long it became clear to her that she was actually mourning not one loss, but two—a president, and her privacy.[11]

Now the news of FDR's death cut into radio broadcasts and spread in whispers down the sidewalks. Traffic on Connecticut Avenue knotted between Cumberland and Chesapeake streets as drivers slowed up to rubberneck at the building where the new president lived.[12] Or *used* to live. What were the chances the Trumans could ever go back there now?

As the crow flies, the White House stood only four miles from 4701 Connecticut Avenue. To Bess's mind, the place might as well have been on the moon. Decorum would, of course, require her to feign happiness over the chance to live in the executive mansion. Privately, though, she made her true feelings about the White House clear. "I just dread moving over there," she said.[13]

⋯⋯ ⋯⋯

The White House wasn't ready to take them anyway, at least not yet. The days following FDR's death had plunged the usual efficiency of the mansion into chaos. No sooner had Harry Truman been sworn in than the planning for Roosevelt's funeral began. The Roosevelts' things had to be packed up. FDR and Eleanor had lived in the White House for twelve years. Their Victorian love of clutter had, by the end, left the mansion looking like a Paris flea market. Truman took it upon himself to ease the strain on Mrs. Roosevelt. "Now don't you be in any hurry to leave the White House," he told her. "Take all the time you need in the world."[14] What the new president failed to understand was that hurrying was one thing Eleanor Roosevelt *liked* to do. On Monday, April 16, the day after her husband was laid in his grave, she pulled on an old pair of shoes and a tattered housedress and began tagging furniture, oil paintings, ship models, and barrels of china. "The amount of packing to be done was appalling," Elliott Roosevelt remembered, but his mother refused to slow down. "I'll be out by Friday," she warbled, and she meant it.[15]

As the movers came and went, usher J. B. West decided all the activity was good cover for a personal mission. Taking a notebook in hand, he quietly slipped out of the mansion, crossed the street, and climbed the steps of the yellow town house just off Lafayette Square. He wanted to meet Mrs. Truman, his new boss.

The door on which West was knocking belonged to Blair House, the White House's official guest residence. The Secret Service had decided to install the Truman family there immediately after FDR's funeral. The agents had learned by degrees what Bess had probably suspected from the start: A president simply cannot live in an apartment building. The Trumans' neighbors at 4701 Connecticut Avenue had been good sports about it all—the security checkpoint hastily set up in the lobby, the demands for identification. But, as Margaret remembered, "it was obviously impossible for us to stay."[16]

West was led up to a room on the fourth floor that Mrs. Truman had selected as her temporary office. He could see immediately that the new First Lady was buckling under the strain. The Secret Service had given the Trumans their own private Pullman aboard the Roosevelt funeral train, but "sleep was practically impossible," Margaret remembered.[17] The trip had exhausted her mother. Among Mrs. Truman's many worries, one was especially sinister. Though FDR had suffered from coronary disease, it was the presidency that had really killed him. Now she dreaded the "terrific load on Harry"—the Oval Office moving on to its next victim.[18]

Bess Truman put on the best face she could as she looked at the usher. West had come to get a sense of her requirements, which was ludicrous on its face: Bess Truman *had* no requirements. "I'm afraid I don't know much about the operations of the White House," she said. "You can appreciate how sudden this is for us."[19]

West could appreciate that. The usher was Iowa-born, educated no further than high school. As he gazed at this Missouri homemaker seated across the desk, he recognized a lot of himself: an ordinary person thrust without warning onto the public stage. Bess Truman hadn't chosen the White House, and neither had West. The vagaries of the civil service system had transferred him there in 1941, for no other reason than the ushers' office needed help and West happened to know shorthand. Since then, he had learned that, for as glamorous and beautiful as the mansion seemed to the public, the old house could be a cruel place. It excelled at plunging its occupants into depths of confusion, loneliness, and fear—the very things already apparent in the pale blue eyes of Bess Truman.

West noticed something else. Despite her obvious distress, the First Lady had smiled, offered him a comfortable chair, and addressed him informally. It was the sort of respect rarely shown to the help. "I felt at ease and I liked her immediately," West later said.[20] At this moment, a friendship began to form between Bess Truman and the White House usher. Considering what the house across the street held in store, both of them would need it.

On Wednesday, April 18, another pair of feet scurried up the steps to Blair House's front door, but this time the sensible shoes and toothy smile belonged to Eleanor Roosevelt. Surprised and flattered by the visit, Bess and Margaret invited FDR's widow to come in.

Like everything else Mrs. Roosevelt did, she paid this call in haste and seemed to be anxious to get to her next engagement—even though that was little more than a long automobile ride to upstate New York, where retirement awaited her at Val-Kill, her rambling cottage in the Hyde Park woods. Finally crated up, the Roosevelts' possessions had filled no fewer than twenty army trucks, which had already left as a northbound convoy. Mrs. Roosevelt had beaten her own move-out deadline by two full days.

The ostensible purpose for her stopping by was to wish the Trumans well, but it soon became clear that Mrs. Roosevelt had a second reason: She wanted to warn the incoming family about the White House. "[She] was somewhat apologetic about the [building's] condition," Margaret recalled. "The war and her heavy travel schedule had never given her time to do much decorating or housekeeping."[21]

That sounded reasonable enough. Who couldn't cut Eleanor Roosevelt, the busiest First Lady in history, some slack over a little dusting and vacuuming? Then, just before she left, she let drop another detail. The whole house, Mrs. Roosevelt said, was "infested with rats."[22] She recounted the story of how an especially fat rodent had shown up at a luncheon on the terrace some weeks before, winning the instant and undivided attention of the guests. With that, FDR's widow wished the Truman family luck, clattered back down the steps, and disappeared into history.

⊷ ⇌ ⇌ ⊷

The following day, propelled by their curiosity, Margaret and her mother donned their dresses and hats and made their way across Pennsylvania Avenue. Passing through the guard booth at the northwest gate, they started up the sweeping semicircular drive that led to the White House. For all their dread of moving here, it was difficult even for Bess and Margaret Truman to deny the beauty of the place. Gnarled boughs of oaks and elms twisted overhead, their canopies already coaxed into leaf by the warm spring breezes. To the left, near the circular pool, the tulip trees, silver bells, and forsythia had burst into bouquets of pink, white, and yellow.

And then suddenly, there it was. Rising from a nest of bushes just ahead, a tetrastyle portico of Ionic columns reared skyward from an Anglo-Palladian palace of white sandstone. The mansion soared to nearly sixty feet, its roof balustrade enclosing a forest of chimneys. Dotted by tall and slender windows, the facade erupted with carvings— griffins, garlands, rosettes, and swags tooled into the soft sedimentary rock. The house was massive, stunning, and also somewhat haunting. Its intricate stone blocks had been carved by Scottish masons, then hoisted into place by slaves. So many lives had been lived within its walls, yet the house had belonged to none of them. Like an old hotel—or a reusable coffin—it was simply cleaned and shined up for the next occupant. Now, as Bess and Margaret drew closer, they could see that the beautiful white frontage visible from the avenue was actually faded, cracked, and peeling. The painters, they would later learn, had not visited since the Great Depression.[23]

Six stone steps rose from the curbstone beneath the North Portico and there, at the top, stood J. B. West. He'd been expecting them. The purpose of this visit, as Margaret later put it, was to have a peek at "our new quarters."[24] West would see that they got that peek, though inwardly he'd probably worried about this visit. Though the usher was proud to work at the mansion, he was ashamed of what had become of it. The public rooms downstairs were dignified and beautiful, with their billowing draperies, polished parquet, and antique clocks ticking quietly on the mantelpieces. But the Truman women had come to see the *second* floor, where they'd be living. That was a different story.

The moment that Margaret Truman stepped into the family quarters, "what we saw made me yearn to stay in Blair House," she said.[25] The floor looked, West admitted, "like a ghost house."[26] The usher led the women through a warren of deserted rooms, their feet stepping across mangy, threadbare carpets. Cracked and yellow with neglect, the walls bore the dusty outlines of where hundreds of the Roosevelts' framed pictures had hung. Remnants of draperies clung to the curtain rods like rags, bleached and brittle from the sun. What furniture that remained lay strewn about the rooms, its upholstery faded and torn, "like it had come from a third-rate boarding house," Margaret said.[27] Many of the chairs and tables were literally falling to pieces. The usher explained that upkeep had not been a priority during the war years, but the excuse felt hollow. "What little was left of the White House," he said, "gave it the appearance of an abandoned hotel."[28]

At first, Bess could muster no response. Her frozen expression was "a paragraph of exclamation points," Margaret recalled.[29] Margaret herself struggled to reconcile what she'd seen down in the public rooms with the ruins at the top of the stairs. She marveled that the public had no idea what squalor existed in the White House. "The areas seen by tourists were kept freshly painted and decorated," she said. "But . . . the private quarters [were] dingy."[30]

Dingy wasn't the worst of it. The disrepair reached beyond the aesthetic and into the far more serious realm of the structural. Cracks several feet long cut across the walls in all directions. Overhead, the plaster ceilings sagged like tent canvas.[31] But the Truman women did not ask about the house's architectural integrity, and the usher did not mention it.

After a while, Bess Truman finally spoke up. "How much redecorating can we do?" she asked. West's reply was the first good news the women had heard since coming in the front door. The usher explained that Congress appropriated a yearly allowance of fifty thousand dollars for the mansion's upkeep (funds that Eleanor Roosevelt had left wholly unspent) and that this money could at least buy some paint and drapery fabric, for starters. Margaret remained sullen. "She assured me that the old place would look a lot better once we got some fresh paint on the walls," Margaret recalled, and she'd almost believed it.[32]

The broken furniture presented another problem because the Trumans had no furniture of their own to replace it with. "We'd planned to use what's already here," Bess explained to West.[33] In view of the facts, that plan now felt absurd and embarrassing. But time was short and alternatives few. As the three continued their tour of the family quarters' maze of bedrooms and parlors, Bess Truman motioned toward whatever items looked salvageable—a chair here, a bed there—as West compiled a list of pieces to be rounded up and reconditioned.

The night of April 19, Margaret Truman sat in her room in Blair House, opened her diary, and recounted the sad little tour of earlier in the day. "The White House upstairs is a mess," she wrote. "I was so depressed when I saw it."[34]

Had Harry Truman not been a man who'd sweated in the mail room of the *Kansas City Star*, steered a horse-drawn plow through the Missouri dirt, and lost his haberdasher's shop in the recession of 1922—had he not, in other words, been a tireless worker with no use for the conceits of the upper classes—he might have been upset to learn that the executive mansion was in such rotten shape. But the new president was unruffled. He'd lived in old houses his whole life, and what farmer hasn't seen a few rats?

In fact, the rodent story his wife recounted with horror left Harry Truman tickled. "Mrs. Roosevelt told Bess and me that it [the White House] is infested with rats!" Truman wrote in a letter to his ninety-two-year-old mother a few days later. "Said she was giving three high-hat women a luncheon on the south portico when a rat ran across the porch railing."[35]

Still, the main reason that the dilapidated White House didn't trouble him was this: Harry Truman was a man with more important things on his mind. Foremost was how to perform in a job he had never wanted nor, thanks to a horrendous oversight by Franklin D. Roosevelt, ever been groomed for. Senator Harry Truman had never planned on being *vice* president, let alone president. In the teeth of the 1944 Democratic National Convention in Chicago, as the party threatened to split over Roosevelt's potential running mates, James Byrnes and Henry Wallace (men too far to the right and the left, respectively, to carry a delegation vote), Truman's name had been trotted out as a compromise. Most everyone liked the idea except Harry Truman. Citing the senator's refusal to join the ticket, DNC chairman Robert Hannegan referred to Truman as "the contrarianist Missouri mule I've ever dealt with."[36] The mule held his hoofing until a long-distance call came in from a furious FDR. "You tell the senator," the president boomed, "that if he wants to break up the Democratic party in the middle of a war, that's his responsibility!" Roosevelt slammed the phone down. Truman, who'd overheard the call, blanched. "Oh shit," he said.[37] Then he accepted the nomination.

But during the eighty-three days that Harry Truman served as vice president, Franklin Roosevelt—exhausted by the war, his heart steadily failing—had met with Truman only twice, and those meetings were mainly photo ops. Figuring he needed the Missourian only as a bridge to the Senate when the war ended and the peace needed ratifying, FDR neglected to include Truman in any policy discussions. It was a rare oversight for an otherwise-brilliant president, who then died suddenly and left his VP in "almost complete darkness," as press secretary Jonathan Daniels later wrote.[38]

Now, Truman logged inhuman hours in the West Wing as he attempted to crash-learn the world's most difficult job. Truman's diary shows that in the first two days of his presidency, he met with no fewer than forty-one senior officials, including the secretaries of state, war, and treasury; three admirals, two generals, and one colonel; FDR's closest confidants, James Byrnes and Harry Hopkins; and eighteen senior members of Congress. What secrets they shared, Truman remembered; what counsel they offered, he accepted.

But mainly, Harry Truman read. Adm. William D. Leahy recalled massing a "sizeable stack" of official memoranda generated by the Joint Chiefs of Staff and leaving them on Truman's desk. "In a few days," Leahy said, "he had digested them."[39] Years later, Daniels would recall, Truman "lifted his hand higher than table level to indicate the pile of documents, agreements, conference minutes, cables which he had to read in trying to understand the problems and responsibilities he had assumed."[40]

And so Harry Truman had little time to worry about a few dingy rooms in the White House, the cracked walls and cobwebs and whatever else was up there. He had a country to run, a war to win. It would take nineteen days before Truman finally found a few minutes to wander down the West Colonnade and poke his head into the mansion.

The visit came on May 1, 1945. That morning, the radio crackled with news intercepted from a German broadcast: Hitler was dead. West assumed that this was the probable reason that the president was in a "jaunty" mood, an observable bounce in his step.[41] Then again, the usher also discovered that Harry Truman pretty much had just one speed: fast. The man didn't walk so much as march. And now that he'd finally gotten around to visiting the mansion he would call home, he had no shortage of comments about the place. "When you think of all the great men who've lived in this house," Truman chirped to the usher, his owl eyes blinking at West through thick eyeglasses, "you can't help but feel a sense of awe."[42]

Maybe. West's days of awe had ended sometime back during the Roosevelt administration. At the moment, he was most likely feeling a sense of dread. After all, Truman wanted to go upstairs to see "where Mrs. Truman is going to put us all."[43] Fortunately, the painters and maintenance men had been put to work, and the rooms had shaken off the derelict look that had so horrified Truman's wife and daughter. For a solid week, West recalled, "[o]ur staff [had] painted, hung draperies, cleaned, upholstered, and rearranged the White House for the Trumans."[44]

As the president soon learned, where his wife would "put" the family was where First Families ended up anyway: the western side of the second floor. Holding to tradition, the president would take the bedroom just off the Oval Study, and with a quick walk through an adjacent sitting room, he could reach Mrs. Truman's bedroom in the southwest corner. As for Margaret's quarters, well, West figured it was a good thing the president had come by, because there was an executive decision to be made.

The second floor had plenty of room down on the eastern side of the house. Either the Blue or Rose bedroom, large and private, would have been perfect for Margaret. The Trumans were an unusually close family, however, and the president wanted them all to be together. The only available bedroom was one in the northwestern corner that Eleanor Roosevelt had used for her overnight guests. It was filled with the brooding furniture that Mary Todd Lincoln had bought in New York back in 1861, including an eight-foot-long rosewood bed with a headboard that resembled nothing so much as a tombstone. This crypt of a room was no place for a college girl who still loved to pile her pillows with stuffed animals. "The dark, clunky furniture that was cluttering up my sitting room had to go," Margaret said, "preferably as far away as possible."[45]

Yet here the president paused, seeing the problem. "Would we dare move Mr. Lincoln out of here?" the president asked his usher. "Would that be tampering with history too much?"[46]

Those big eyes were looking at him again. West later learned that the president had been born with a structural astigmatism—or, as Truman called it, "flat eyeballs."[47] In 1889, the family doctor had warned a five-year-old Harry that that roughhousing with his friends outside would get his eyes "knocked out."[48] Petrified into staying indoors, Truman discovered the Independence Public Library. By the time he turned fourteen, the story goes, he had devoured all three thousand books in it.[49] The doctor's advice had been misguided, but it had inadvertently forged a true intellectual. One of Truman's passions was reading history, and one of his favorite topics was Abraham Lincoln.

Luckily for Truman, J. B. West knew some history, too. The usher explained that Lincoln had probably slept in several different rooms on the second floor. What's more, Lincoln's office had been down the hall in the southern corner, over the East Room. It was there where, on January 1, 1863, he'd signed the Emancipation Proclamation.[50] That was all that Truman needed to hear. He immediately ordered Abe's ponderous furniture trundled down the hall, starting in motion a process that would culminate with a new name for the Blue Bedroom: the Lincoln Bedroom.[51]

Truman's combination of forethought and rapid, decisive action impressed the usher. "Harry Truman was his own man," West said. "There was no pomp or pretense about him. . . . We were going to enjoy working for this family, I decided."[52]

When the Trumans' moving van lurched to a halt beneath the North Portico on May 7, West realized that Bess Truman hadn't been kidding: They really *didn't* own any furniture. About all that lay in the dark of the trailer were clothing and books. There hardly seemed a need for a truck at all, until West noticed one huge object inside—the sinuous black Steinway.

According to Margaret, it took block and tackle to finesse the instrument through a second-story window. West would recall the movers manhandling the thing through the front door.[53] Maybe they were remembering different pianos, because there would be three of them in the family quarters alone: the baby grand in Margaret's room, a concert grand in the Oval Study, and an upright Gulbransen in one of the sitting rooms.[54]

The upright's purpose was to be wheeled around, because dueling pianos were inevitable in a family in which two-thirds of the members were accomplished at the ivories. Truman had played since he was five years old. "My choice early in life was either to be a piano player in a whorehouse or a politician," Truman often deadpanned to male visitors. "To tell the truth, there's hardly a difference."[55] Truman could still dash off some bars of Beethoven's Piano Concerto no. 4 or Chopin's A-flat waltz, but Margaret was accomplished enough as a vocalist and performer that she was thinking about turning professional after college.

While it was a matter of little concern at the time, all of those pianos were adding an enormous amount of weight to the house's 128-year-old beams. Margaret's Steinway was most likely a Model S, a "baby" that weighed a not-so-cuddly 540 pounds.[56] Her father's Steinway, a monster of mahogany crafted in 1937, came in somewhere between six hundred and eight hundred pounds.[57]

But the floor held, and the White House accepted the country's thirty-second presidential family with a tired embrace. Margaret remained sullen, ruminating that the house "looked so shabby and second rate."[58] Her father proved far more adaptable. That night, Harry Truman tucked into his bed delighted as a schoolboy, later joking that he'd "slept in the President's room."[59]

THE GREAT WHITE JAIL

Well I'm here in the White House, the great white sepulcher of
ambitions and reputations. I feel like last year's bird's nest which
is on its second year.
                    —Harry Truman, letter to Bess, December 28, 1945

H *arry Truman turned* sixty-one years old on the morning he
awoke from his first night in the big old house, and a suitable
birthday present was waiting for him: The war in Europe was
over. From the White House, he noticed a crowd of jubilant people
raising righteous hell out front, surging against the front lawn's high
iron gate. When Truman emerged from the mansion with his arms
raised in victory, the crowd went wild. They cheered so long and loud
that he came out and did it again.

He looked so presidential at that moment, sporting a tailored suit
and a grin wider than the Mississippi. No doubt it would have surprised many people in that crowd to know how much Truman wished
he were one of them—an ordinary citizen on the *other* side of that
fence. "He did not want to become president at the time and in the

manner that he inherited the job," Margaret said of her father years later. "He did not want it because he knew Bess did not want it."[1]

Truman regarded the presidency as a job that had to be done, and it was a task to which he devoted himself wholly. But that is not the same thing as choosing it. And since the mansion was, among many things, the physical symbol of the presidency, Truman's family seemed to take a parallel view: It was their duty to live in the White House, which is also not the same thing as choosing it. Around this time, Bess Truman's childhood friend Mary Paxton received a letter from her that summed up the dichotomy neatly and sadly. "We are not any of us happy to be where we are," Bess Truman wrote, "but there's nothing to be done about it except to do our best."[2]

For the sake of a First Family he was beginning to genuinely like, J. B. West had done his best, too. Under his direction, the mansion's small army of handymen had descended on the second floor like infantry. Soon the threadbare carpets and rotten drapes were gone and a fresh coat of paint glistened on the walls. Broken furniture disappeared somewhere into the bowels of the house (probably the carpentry shop below the front steps), where the workmen did emergency surgery, swabbing paint and stain on the scratched-up wood, setting wobbly chair legs with glue and clamps. From another room came the sounds of shears and whirring sewing machines as the seamstresses transformed bolts of fabric into draperies, slipcovers, and dust ruffles.

It was probably no coincidence that Bess Truman turned the White House's second floor into a space that bore an uncanny resemblance to the family's old apartment, at least as far as the drapes and upholstery went. Up on Connecticut Avenue, Bess had indulged her love of big floral prints. Now, down on Pennsylvania, she did the same. Yard after yard of gigantic blossoms in lavender, mauve, and gray spilled down the windows and wardrobe doors of her bedroom. Margaret got to decorate her own room, but she went with chintz flowers, too. (The president's bedroom, done up in solid blue and green pastels, escaped this floral fate.)

West watched with muted amazement as the thrifty First Lady picked out pieces of salvaged furniture—a huge four-poster bed for her husband, a marble-topped Victorian table to hold vases of roses—and created room after room that, while hardly fancy, exuded a kind of secondhand stateliness. When she confessed to the usher that she had no art to hang, West made some calls. Soon the curators from the National Gallery came by with crates of oil paintings hauled out of their vaults. They let the Trumans pick out whatever they wanted (on loan, of course). It was, West would recall, "one grand, art-filled evening."[3]

To the outsider, all the economizing might have seemed beneath the dignity of the presidency, but to those who understood the family's modest background and aversion to pompousness, it somehow all fit. One of these people was Truman's assistant Clark Clifford. At first, the family quarters struck him as "rundown and dowdy," but the young attorney quickly revised his view. "At the time, the White House just seemed simple and informal," he said, "like the Trumans themselves."[4]

Simplicity and informality were so intrinsic to the family's sense of self that, though they willingly lived in the old stone mansion, they refused to permit it to change life as they knew it. The Trumans, West said, "lived as simply at 1600 Pennsylvania Avenue as they had [on] Connecticut Avenue or in Independence, Missouri."[5] Each evening, they gathered in the same room to read, listen to 78 records, or just talk. Few diversions made Harry Truman happier than sharing the piano bench for a duet with his daughter. The Roosevelts' status-conscious housekeeper, Henrietta Nesbitt, sniffed that the Trumans "were not much given to company," reading their remove as a lack of social grace.[6] But Lillian Parks knew better. "There was nothing impersonal about it," she said, "each [merely] had a great interest in everything the others did."[7] It was as though the family believed that, by maintaining their old habits, they could will the White House into being a backdrop to otherwise-unaltered lives. And for a while, it actually worked.

Harry Truman still rose religiously at 5:30 each morning. Just because he was now president of the United States, he saw no reason to desist in his habit of putting on the underwear that he'd washed in the sink himself.[8] The onetime Kansas City haberdasher had always dressed impeccably seven days a week. Truman owned no fewer than 489 neckties and seemed bent on bringing the bow tie back into style—a task at which, as president, he largely succeed.[9] By 6:00 A.M., fitted out with his fedora, bentwood cane, and a few splashes of Revlon's Top Brass aftershave, he was ready to go.

Whether it was a warm spring day or five inches of frozen slush buried the sidewalk, the president began each morning with a brisk walk of 120 steps per minute.[10] On his first day as the White House's official resident, Truman skipped down the stairs and, seeing nobody around, strode right out the front door. Truman made it all the way to Fifteenth Street before his Secret Service detail came pounding up the pavement behind him. "Well now, it's nice of you to join me," Truman said, smiling at the panting men. "Beautiful day, isn't it?"[11]

Breakfast was at 8:00 A.M. sharp, when the president ate his customary fare of oatmeal, two pieces of whole-wheat toast, orange juice, buttermilk, and coffee. Truman was proud of the fact that he could still fit into the suits he'd bought in 1935, and he was not about to let the caloric extravagances of the White House kitchen swell his waistline. At times, such determination could be fanatical. Being hypertensive, Bess Truman could have no sodium; when Truman discovered that the White House had a water-softening system, he had it ripped out.[12]

Truman grudgingly accepted the custom that butlers wait on presidents, but being served by liveried pantrymen still made him squirm. He found ways to compensate. Truman never failed to introduce butler Alonzo Fields to his lunch companions, startling kings and prime ministers who'd probably never met a black man before.[13] Washington might have been a martini town, but the Trumans liked their bourbon and drank it every night before dinner. Bess liked her old-fashioneds dry as wood and the president took his I.W. Harper straight, no chaser. They might as well have been on the front porch back home.

The privileges of White House life have been known to taint some First Ladies. Mary Todd Lincoln went on shopping sprees that sent the taciturn Abe into rages. Florence Harding covered the tracks of her husband's corrupt administration by burning his papers in the Oval Study's fireplace. But the house did nothing to alter Bess Truman's moral polarity. A closetful of colorful gowns could have been hers for the asking, but Bess stuck with the basic black outfits she'd always worn. That a periwinkle dress might have better set off her blue eyes was a gentle suggestion seamstress Lillian Parks tried again and again— always to receive the same response: "Well, Lillian, you can't go wrong with black."[14] Despite the ample supply of hired help, Bess Truman still cooked, cleaned, kept the budget, and answered each and every letter by hand. "We tiptoed around [her] and marveled," Parks recalled.[15]

But the real marvel of Bess Truman was the shrewd politician who lurked beneath those boxy black skirts. For the decade Truman had been a senator, his wife had served as his Dutch uncle. She read every page of the *Congressional Record*, composed his floor speeches, and even counseled him on his votes.[16] In fact, Clark Clifford believed that Bess Truman's political sense was sharper than her husband's. "President Truman was not always analytical or sufficiently detached in evaluating the people around him," Clifford said. "Mrs. Truman often had better insight."[17]

Now, at the White House, the president made it clear to the staff that he and his wife were not to be disturbed after dinner. Each night at nine o'clock, Truman would take his wife by the arm, lead her into the Oval Study, and close the door. For the next two hours, the couple talked shop. They worked on his statements, on his policies, on "designing his politics," as West put it. "Few people knew," said the usher, "that she was his full partner in every sense of the word."[18]

But as time went on, the family discovered that the White House could never be just a backdrop to the life they had known before; that that life had changed inexorably, and the mansion was now a central force within it—limiting it, controlling it. The first troubling evidence appeared as a rift in the Truman marriage. Bess Truman had every intention of maintaining her advisory role in her husband's presidency. But gradually, steadily, she found herself pushed aside.

The eighteen-hour days of the West Wing began chipping away at what had been the couple's private time. Truman also discovered there were many state secrets he had to keep from his wife. Meanwhile, the only thing available to replace the consultative role that Bess cherished was the mindless work of playing hostess—donning those white gloves and standing beneath that ridiculous chandelier in the Blue Room. In time, Margaret recalled, her mother was "forced to face a very unpleasant fact. She had become a spectator rather than a partner in Harry Truman's presidency. That made her very, very angry."[19]

She might have endured the affront were it not for the fact that the White House had already killed off every little pleasure she'd come to know. Bess was forced to give up her cherished Chrysler because driving on her own, the Secret Service warned, was too dangerous.[20] A trip to the shops? A stroll in the park? Out of the question. About all there was to do outdoors was take a walk on the White House's South Lawn. But what fun was that? Secret Service men tagged along just feet behind, while tourists lining the fence hooted and yelled as though the Trumans were animals in a zoo.[21]

Margaret, too, had watched as the doors closed on her personal life. A fetching young woman with auburn curls and green eyes, Margaret had her pick of the lads. But the White House scared them off one by one. "I ask you to consider," she said, "the effect of saying good night to a boy at the door of the White House in a blaze of floodlights with a Secret Service man in attendance. There is not much you can do except shake hands, and that's no way to get engaged."[22]

The cruel dichotomy of the White House was that, with its swimming pool, flower shop, movie theater, and twenty-four-hour room service, the mansion boasted every amenity a family could want—except for the privacy and intimacy a family needs. The *New York Times'* long-time D.C. man Cabell Phillips put it this way: "However one looks at the White House, enchanted or in awe, one must know that in its most essential character it is a goldfish bowl—the most ornate, complex and inescapable goldfish bowl in all the land. For the men and women who live there renounce, once they have passed its portals, all claims to a life of their own."[23]

For Bess and Margaret, there was only one recourse. When the summer arrived, they boarded a Baltimore and Ohio train and returned to Missouri. Back in Independence, in the family's old Victorian at 219 North Delaware Street, Truman's wife and daughter pretended that the White House did not exist.[24] Over the ensuing weeks, Bess would communicate with her husband by letter; sometimes, not even that.

It's impossible to understate how traumatic this event—one Margaret would tactfully refer to as "an emotional separation"—was for the president.[25] Truman always said he'd been in love with Bess Wallace since first laying eyes on her in 1890 (he was six). As a young man, he'd courted her for nine years. He'd carried her photograph across the battlefields of France. And while Harry Truman was never especially talented with money, the gold band he'd bought at Tiffany & Co. in 1919 with his saved-up army pay proved to be the best investment he'd ever made: The Truman marriage was now in its twenty-fifth year.

Harry Truman's bond with his daughter was equally unbreakable. While the topic was never spoken of, the White House staff learned that, back in 1930, a stranger had attempted to kidnap Margaret from her grade school. "Ever since that time," Parks said, "she was never out of their sight."[26]

But now, thanks to the White House, *both* Truman's wife and daughter were out of his sight, hiding out in Missouri. In their absence, the president simply wilted. "Just two months ago today, I was a reasonably happy and contended Vice President," Truman wrote his wife on June 12, 1945. "Maybe you can remember that far back too. But things have changed so much it hardly seems real."[27]

Bess's resolve to stay out of Washington would hold until August, when she softened and made a reluctant return. But her method of coping would be permanent: For each year to follow, Bess and Margaret would abandon Truman to the White House for the entire summer. "I sure hated to see them go," the president would write in his diary one sweltering night after watching the St. Louis–bound National Limited disappear down the track. "It is hot and humid and lonely. Why in hell does anybody want to be a head of state? Damned if I know."[28]

As his unwanted solitude altered Truman's view of the presidency, it radically darkened his feelings about the house that came with it. Only days into his term, Truman had brimmed with a "sense of awe" as he toured the White House with J. B. West. Now, Truman found himself hardening to the place, even starting to hate it. In time, he would dismiss 1600 Pennsylvania Avenue as "the taxpayers' house," "the great white sepulcher of ambitions," and—perhaps thinking about that tall iron fence out front—"the great white jail."[29]

It was during Bess and Margaret's first extended absence that the president became acquainted with the White House ghosts. Introductions took place on a balmy night in June 1945, a little more than a month after the family had moved in. Alone in the big house, Truman sat down to write a letter to his wife. That night, the president was most likely working in the Oval Study upstairs, even though the room (unlike the bedrooms) had no air-conditioning. But Truman's books were in the study, as was his piano and his desk. The desk was no ordinary piece of furniture. A lavishly carved oaken relic presented to President Hayes in 1879 by Queen Victoria, it had been handcrafted from the timbers of the HMS *Resolute*, a British expeditionary vessel abandoned in an ice field by its crew in 1854. *Resolute* had been adrift for a year by the time the American whaler *George Henry* had found her. The desk was, in other words, made from a ghost ship. Did Harry Truman believe in ghosts? He was about to.

He sat in a huge swivel chair, its leather soft from use, its casters coasting softly on the carpet as Truman slipped his legs into the knee-hole. The desk's broad surface was a muddle of books and papers, ephemera of every kind encroaching on the blotter like an invading army: paperweights, pens, and picture frames, a black telephone at his left elbow and a chrome pitcher of ice water off to his right. His pen scratched quietly on the paper below the banker's lamp.

It was then that he heard them—the ghosts—shuffling up and down the empty corridor outside. By the time Truman finished writing his first paragraph, he decided to tell Bess about his unexpected visitors: "I sit here in this old house and work on foreign affairs, read reports, and work on speeches—all the while listening to the ghosts walk up and down the hallway and even right in here in the study. The floors pop and the drapes move back and forth."[30]

Had the windows of the study been open that night, a breeze might have explained the movement of the curtains. But what of the sound of footfalls outside the study door? Only three people lived on the White House's second floor; at this moment, two of them were nine hundred miles away.

The second-floor corridor ran the length of the house. It was also wide enough to function as a kind of living room. Bookcases, wing-back chairs, and side tables lined both walls of the 170-foot passageway, which enjoyed the civilizing touches of a few Oriental rugs and antique oils in heavy gilt frames. At night, a few of the silk-shaded floor lamps might be left on, bathing the hallway in a soft, gauzy light. Tonight, however, all of the wing-back chairs were empty, as were the bedrooms: The president was the only man on the floor.

Truman sat alone at his desk while the strange sounds grew more plentiful. There were groans, creaks, thumping noises. What—or who—could be causing all of it? Truman paused, decided on a possible reason, and continued his letter: "I can just imagine old Andy [Andrew Jackson] and Teddy [Theodore Roosevelt] having an argument over Franklin [FDR]," he wrote.[31] To this gathering of the departed, Truman added James Buchanan and Franklin Pierce, and then Millard Fillmore and Chester A. Arthur. And why not? It sounded like he had a houseful of company: ". . . the din is almost unbearable," he wrote. "But I still get some work done."[32]

Harry Truman would not be the first to suspect that the mansion's odd noises were evidence of restless spirits. During the Harding administration, maid Maggie Rogers had once heard "a terrible, ghostly groaning" as she made her way up the back stairs between the second floor and the attic.[33] Years later, during FDR's presidency, Parks was in the northwest master bedroom—which at the time still contained Presi-

dent Lincoln's old rosewood bed—when she swore she heard "footsteps coming right through the door." But "when I looked that way,"
Parks said, "I never saw anyone." Later on, she decided to confide her
story to one of the butlers. "That was Abe you heard," he told her.[34]

There was the night in 1941, just before Roosevelt's mother died,
when the staff heard "a scuffle of footsteps" in the Blue Room. Investigating, they found no one there. From time to time, the Rose Room
was said to erupt with phantom laughter. The butlers could relate how,
in several different rooms in the house, paintings "would fall off the
wall for no apparent reason." Even in the president's own Oval Study,
visitors had reported hearing a strange voice that seemed to be coming
from the ceiling, groaning the same sentence over and over: "I'm Mr.
Burns, I'm Mr. Burns . . ."[35]

The stories were nothing new. Yet as Truman's first term progressed,
it did seem as though the ghosts—that is, the unexplained thumps and
knocks and creaks—made more frequent appearances.

One night in 1946 (Bess and Margaret had, once again, decamped
to Missouri), Truman was sound asleep in his big four-poster bed. His
bedroom had two doors. One of them led to the study. The other, situated at the end of a short passage, opened onto the second floor's main
corridor. At precisely 4:00 A.M., Truman jolted awake. Someone was
pounding on the door—the *outside* door. He remembered "three distinct knocks." Whoever or whatever was pounding had to be out in the
hallway. Truman could have been forgiven for hiding under the
covers—even hiding under the bed itself. Instead, he wrote in a subsequent letter to Bess, "I jumped up and put on my bathrobe [and] opened
the door."[36] The corridor was empty.

The president had grown accustomed to the ghosts making a racket
while he tried to work, but this time the spooks had the nerve to awaken
him. He decided to investigate. Truman eased his way out into the hall,
eyeing the empty chairs in the distant shadows. No one was about. Just
then, he heard another sound—footsteps. They were coming from
Margaret's room. He crossed the corridor and peered inside. Nobody.
"The damned place is haunted sure as shootin'," he thought, returning
to his room.[37]

Was the White House haunted? Possibly. But even the sort of people
who believe in ghosts would have had a hard time accepting that so
many of them had chosen to haunt the same house, and make such a

consistent racket. In *A Christmas Carol*, Charles Dickens's Ebenezer Scrooge was haunted by four ghosts in a single evening, but Harry Truman appeared to be racking up scores of them. "This old place cracks and pops all night long," Truman complained.[38] No, something else had to be behind the "din" of noises, the drapes swishing, the floors popping, the phantom fists pounding on the old mahogany doors—but what?

The question eventually found its way to Lorenzo Winslow, a man in a good position to answer it. Ensconced in a small office on the second floor of the East Wing, Winslow was the White House's resident architect, and he'd been studying, measuring, drawing (and apparently listening to) the executive mansion for the last twelve years. "The sounds aren't hard to explain," the affable Winslow opined, a slight North Carolina accent sugaring his stiffer Boston one. "There are hundreds of tons of wood in this house, and at night, when the air cools off, the wood has a tendency to snap."[39]

Winslow was absolutely certain of one thing: The sounds were *not* the work of ghosts. It wasn't that the architect didn't believe in spirits—he did. But the haunting just wasn't logical, and Winslow was happy to explain why. "No president who passed away would come back to the White House to haunt it," he joked, "considering what he went through while he lived here."[40]

Lorenzo Winslow listened patiently to the complaints. His equanimity was a good foil for Truman's increasingly tempestuous head. A courtly man of fifty-three, descended from affluent New England stock, Winslow puffed a corncob pipe, dressed in tweeds, and tooled around town in an old MG roadster. An MIT-trained engineer and architect, Winslow had made his name building palatial homes in the suburbs of Greensboro, North Carolina, until the Great Depression forced him to seek the safety of a civil service job in Washington.[41] In 1933, Winslow entered a competition to design a West Wing lap pool for Franklin Roosevelt. (Swimming, the president hoped, might restore movement to his polio-stricken legs.) FDR was so taken by Winslow's "excellent taste" that he immediately created the post of architect of the White House and installed Winslow in it.[42]

As the holder of what the *Washington Post* called "the Nation's No. 1 architectural job," Winslow knew the way around the old mansion better than anyone. But his breezy dismissal of the White House's disturbing noises left Truman less than satisfied, especially since there were more noises all the time. Just to be prudent, the president quietly went over Winslow's head, asking the commissioner of public buildings to have a look at the place. Her father knew, Margaret Truman said, "that any building as old as the White House needed to be inspected at regular intervals to make sure it was structurally sound."[43]

Weeks passed—and then a month, and then a year—with no word from back the commissioner.[44] Meanwhile, the strange noises continued.

THREE

THE PORCH

A second story Balcony
It seemed a simple plan
To give a quiet breathing space
To such a harried man.
Yet no sooner was it mooted
Than a fierce attack began . . .
—William Adams Delano

Early one evening during the second week of February 1946, assistant usher J. B. West and chief usher Howell Crim appeared in the doorway of the Oval Study, where the president had summoned them a few minutes earlier. Truman sat alone at the Resolute Desk, and the ushers could tell right away he was in a smoldering mood. As West would later recall, "He looked weary. But he was ready to do battle."[1]

Truman had swiveled around in his chair to look out the windows along the study's bow-shaped southern wall. The South Portico's enormous Ionic capitals were just a few feet away up here, close enough to read the fine detailing in the stone roses and volutes. The portico's six smooth stone columns, eight and a half feet apart, carved the view into slender rectangular slices. Below the house, the South Lawn descended gradually in the growing shadows until, just beyond the craggy tree line, the spindle of the Washington Monument bisected a pink-and-blue sunset. Farther in the distance, on the other side of the Tidal Basin, the dome of the Jefferson Memorial floated like the temple of a lost city. The three men in the room had seen this view many times. That still didn't stop them from admiring it.

"That's a magnificent sight, isn't it?" the president asked, breaking the silence.

Crim nodded in assent. "It certainly is," he said.

Truman was obviously leading up to something. "I'd like to be able to take better advantage of that view," he continued, then proceeded to reveal a plan that he'd apparently been considering for a long while: He wanted to add a balcony to the White House—right there, on the second floor, within the South Portico. Not only was there a commanding view from up here but, for the sake of the White House overall, "it would be far more architecturally correct to have a balcony up here," the president declared.[2]

To appreciate the gravitas of what Truman was proposing, it bears mentioning that no president had touched the White House's facade since 1824, when James Monroe had added the semicircular South Portico, and five years later, when Andrew Jackson had built the tetrastyle one on the north side. Even so, those classical additions had been envisioned by Thomas Jefferson in 1807—far enough back that one could argue (and many did) that they were part of the White House's original design.[3]

But a *porch*? Truman was off on his own with that one.

He did have a good logistical reason at least. A second-floor balcony would eliminate the need for the seven canvas awnings that had been rigged up lower down on the portico columns in an effort to keep sun out of the Blue Room. Truman bristled at the very sight of those big tents of fabric, complaining that they "put the beautiful columns out of proportion" and trapped half the dirt in D.C.[4] Each year, the federal treasury expended two thousand dollars to buy new awnings for the White House. A nice concrete balcony, declared Truman, would solve that problem permanently.

If the president's justifications for altering the White House's appearance for the first time in 117 years still felt a little flimsy, it may have been because his real reasons for wanting a balcony were ones he was playing closer to the vest.

The first had to do with his wife. Crushed over Bess's determination to flee Washington for Missouri every summer, Truman hoped that giving her a private perch at the White House might convince her to remain. He'd already tried to get her to stay put by installing powerful new air conditioners in her bedroom and sitting room, but the tactic had failed.[5] Perhaps a balcony would do the trick.

The idea wasn't as nutty as it sounded. "One of the chief pleasures of 219 North Delaware Street were its porches, particularly the back porches, where the family whiled away more than one summer afternoon or evening, secure from prying eyes," Margaret said. "Dad hoped Mother would spend more of her summers in Washington, [so] he decided the White House ought to have a back porch." It was, he hoped, something that would "make Mother feel more at home."[6]

The other reason Truman wanted the White House to have a porch had nothing to do with his sweetheart and everything to do with his temper. Congress had humiliated him publicly several weeks before, and the president was hungry for a piece of revenge. A balcony, he decided, would be perfect.[7]

⊷═ ═⊷

The fight with Congress had begun innocently enough. On December 12, 1945, Truman had sent what looked like an ordinary request up to the Hill for funds to do a little work around the house: "alterations," "furnishings"—that sort of thing.[8] It was, as South Dakota representative Francis Case would later recall, "a simple little statement that [the funding] was for some improvements or some additional facilities down there."[9] Even though the president was asking for a lordly $1.6 million, Congress didn't bother to question it. After all, Christmas was two weeks away and everybody was eager to get home. Without a peep of protest in either House or Senate, Congress quietly attached Truman's request to the First Deficiency Appropriations Act, voted him the money, and split.

Only when laborers arrived during the first week of January 1946 to begin demolition work did Congress realize exactly what it had paid for. On Truman's orders, Lorenzo Winslow had drawn up plans for an addition to the West Wing that would graft another 145 feet of stucco-covered brick onto the building, turning it into an enormous L shape.

Workmen had already begun demolishing the place, ripping up the grounds and the fencing, and punching the windows out of the building.

To Truman's mind, none of this work was unreasonable. The White House had always been short on office space. Wasn't that why Teddy Roosevelt had built the West Wing in 1902? Had anyone given hell to FDR when he added an East Wing during the early days of World War II? Everyone knew that it took a town's worth of administrators to run the executive branch. Space was so tight that Truman had begun to quarter some of his assistants down in the basement.[10] The time had come to build. It was that simple.

Or not. When news broke about Truman's "urgently needed," fifteen-thousand-square-foot addition to the White House, the public promptly lost its mind.[11] "Newspapers, some architects, and virtually all Republicans rushed to the rescue of the historic house at 1600 Pennsylvania Avenue," *Newsweek* later reported.[12] Few would have begrudged the president a little more wiggle room for his staff, but Winslow's plans for the White House looked more like Speer's plans for Berlin. His addition would nearly *double* the size of the West Wing, adding a second story and ramrodding the building another 155 feet to the south, devouring all the grass and trees in the way. The size of the new structure was alarming enough, but what truly galled the public was Truman's definition of "urgently needed" facilities. These included a cafeteria, a recording studio, and a 375-seat theater complete with a stage elevator.[13]

Calling the extension a "mutilation" of the house, the *Washington Post* accused Truman of keeping his scheme a "secret until the last possible moment."[14] It also accused Winslow of having drawn a building so imperiously ugly that it resembled "something about midway between a large and pretentious railroad depot and the clubhouse of a very expensive Long Island golf club."[15] In fairness to Truman and his architect, their plans would never have touched the historic mansion proper, only the forty-four-year-old West Wing. But would the public have changed its mind had it known that the blueprints were technically just *an addition to an addition* to the White House? Probably not.[16] The whole thing was too big, too expensive—and too sneaky. Capitol Hill was fuming.

So was Truman. Calling the outcry a "tempest in a teapot," the president invited all members of Congress who wished to protest to come down to the South Lawn and chain themselves to the bush or tree of their choice.[17] Nobody came. Instead, Congress saved itself the mile-and-a-half walk and voted to revoke every penny of the $1.6 million in funding. It was February 7, 1946, and the president of the United

States, like a boy dipping into the cookie jar, got his hand smacked while an entire country looked on.

⊢⇌ ⇌⊣

This, then, was the mood Truman was in on that February evening of 1946 as he stared out the Oval Study's windows and talked to his ushers. The memory of the scuttled expansion plans was still fresh in his mind, and to the president—whose happiest years had been spent as a United States senator—Congress's actions had felt like a personal rejection. He was hurt. More to the point, he was mad.[18]

The fact has been largely forgotten, but behind Truman's folksy manner and whistle-stop smile, there burned a temper hotter than a blast furnace. Few men would cross Harry Truman and not come to regret it. "When the 'feuding blood' of his Kentucky ancestors was allowed to get the upper hand," recalled an old friend from Missouri, "Harry Truman was a man to be avoided."[19] David Lilienthal, chairman of the Atomic Energy Commission, actually worried that Truman's hotheadedness might inadvertently trigger World War III.[20] Moreover, once an inflamed Harry Truman had decided on a particular course of action, no force in the universe could sway him. "I have not always agreed with Truman's policies," adviser and friend George Allen once said, "nor have I ever made the mistake of trying to talk him out of them."[21]

In this instance, the "policy" was the balcony, and it was plain to assistant usher J. B. West that it would be the president's way of hitting back.[22] In rejecting Truman's West Wing expansion plans, Congress had self-righteously declared that its cause was "to preserve the general architectural scheme" of the White House. Now, addressing Crim and West, Truman declared, "I'm going to preserve the general architectural scheme of the White House any damn way I want to!"[23]

To achieve his coup de théâtre, Truman knew he'd have to fund the balcony without the help of Congress. Seated at his old oak desk piled high with books and papers, Truman pressed usher Crim on the numbers. "Can we get this out of our own budget?" he asked. Squirming under Truman's gaze, Crim raced to figure the numbers in his head.[24] A moment passed. Then Crim told Truman that if the balcony would not cost more than ten thousand dollars, there would be enough money left in the White House's operating budget for the year to pay for it.[25] The money could be discreetly set aside, and nobody in Congress had to know. West watched as a "gleeful smile" spread across the president's face.[26]

Truman would end up mulling the idea over until the middle of 1947 before quietly setting his balcony plans into motion. He might have done it sooner, but human events do not wait for a man to plan a balcony, even if he is the president, and Truman had plenty of events to contend with in 1946. Though a dreaded postwar depression did not materialize, consumer-goods shortages and a spike in the cost of living had chewed away at whatever goodwill most Americans had felt for the haberdasher president who'd replaced FDR. By year's end, American voters had handed control of both houses of Congress back to the Republicans.

Truman's concerns about the mansion itself intruded on his balcony plans, too. Just as the year 1946 drew to a close, the ghosts decided to up their game.

Starting in 1947, Truman noticed something distressing on the mansion's main floor. The chandeliers—first in the Blue Room, then in the East Room—had this way of swaying on their own. That summer, the White House's chorus of eerie sounds began to grow louder and more diverse. "The ghosts walked and walked last night," Truman wrote in a June letter to his wife. "I left all the doors open," he continued. "That gave me a chance to hear all the pops and creaks in your room."[27] The president's July 16 letter to Margaret also contained a mention of expanded ghost activity upstairs. They had begun "to walk up and down the hall and around the study" also, Truman said.[28] Margaret probably didn't notice it, but her father had put the word *ghosts* in quotation marks in his letter to her. Perhaps the punctuation was simply inadvertent. Or maybe it signaled that, when it came to the eerie happenings at the White House, Harry Truman no longer believed—even in jest—that spirits were the cause.

The month of August 1947 was just a few days old when a letter from the White House slipped through the mail slot of 126 East 38th Street in the Murray Hill neighborhood of Manhattan. Years earlier, a gut renovation had turned the former carriage house and milk depot into a sumptuous palazzo. The transformation was the handiwork of the architectural firm of Delano & Aldrich, for which the building presently served as a headquarters. Only families with names like Mellon and Rockefeller could afford the services of William Adams Delano, but an envelope from 1600 Pennsylvania Avenue would, of course, have received prompt attention.

Inside it was a letter from Truman's appointments secretary, Matthew

Connelly, who explained the president's desire to affix a balcony to the White House. Connelly also informed Delano that the president would view it as "a special favor" if he took on the project, which at that point was still a secret from the public. Not only was Delano a man of "outstanding professional attainments," Connelly's letter petted and cooed, but "your acceptance of this assignment would go a long way toward appeasing the small group who invariably oppose any additions or changes to the Executive Mansion."[29]

Connelly wasn't naming names, but he didn't have to: It was clear he was referring to Washington's haughty Fine Arts Commission. The seven-member body had been created by Congress in 1910 to "preserve the dignity of the nation's capital"—whatever that was supposed to mean.[30] In terms of regulatory power, the seven-member commission was toothless. But it enjoyed de facto power over the White House where aesthetic matters were concerned. If the president wanted his porch—at least, if he wanted it without a public-relations disaster—he'd have to "ask" the commission if it was okay.

The very idea of supplicating to those "high hats" made Truman's blood boil.[31] It also made Delano his only ticket. Not only had the seventy-three-year-old Manhattan architect put on a new roof for Calvin Coolidge back in 1927; Delano had himself chaired the Fine Arts Commission and was friendly with the group's current chairman, Gilmore D. Clarke. Truman had tried to get his balcony idea past Clarke, but the stuffy Cornell professor seemed more likely to approve a moat and drawbridge. Clarke, however, made one icy concession: If Truman could get William Adams Delano's approval for the balcony, the commission would yield. It was an underhanded offer. Clarke was certain that Delano would dismiss Truman's crazy porch scheme. He was also in for a big surprise.

Behind the French doors of his office in the old milk depot, Delano considered the letter carefully. Just to see how a balcony might look, he dipped his pen in white ink and drew one right onto a black-and-white photograph of the house. Delano decided that the addition "will be rather a fussy piece of work, requiring a good deal of study in order to achieve a satisfactory result."[32] But, to the president's delight and Clarke's horror, he also decided a balcony idea wasn't half bad.

Delano took the job.

⊹══▶ ◀══⊹

Fortunately, Delano had held on to his set of White House blueprints from the Coolidge work twenty years before, and he got started right away. By the end of September, he had drawings ready. He also had some advice for the president: Get ready for the mud to fly. "Since the Fine Arts Commission has not given this project its benediction, and because the many patriotic societies are self-appointed guardians of The White House," Delano wrote, "we shall have to expect a good deal of adverse publicity."[33]

Truman needed no reminding. In fact, Winslow had tried to brace the president even before Delano did. "I told him there would be an outburst of feeling—sort of warned him," the White House architect remembered. But Truman couldn't have cared less about a backlash at that point. "I'll take it!" he said.[34]

The balcony would consist of steel girders fanning out from the White House wall like wagon-wheel spokes, supporting a series of cast-concrete slabs above.[35] Viewed from below, it would resemble a halved slice of orange, filling in the ten-foot space between the White House's outer wall and the convex line of portico columns. The addition would be nothing more than a narrow, curved slab of cement canted ever so slightly off horizontal to allow rainwater to run off its floor.[36] Anchoring the balcony's steel beams into the house's 150-year-old sandstone wall would not be easy, but Delano left the messy affairs of engineering and construction to Winslow. "He knows far more about the White House than I do," Delano asserted.[37]

When it came to giving the balcony ornamental flourishes to match those of the mansion's facade, Delano did nothing of the sort. He'd long been wary of "overloading . . . facades with superfluous ornament," claiming the practice was "as vulgar as rich women who wear all their jewelry in the street."[38] He kept the balcony simple, functional. Its sole decorative flourish was a lintel with a lower band slightly recessed from the one above—a subtle but elegant nod to the portico's architrave. Wisely, Delano also designed the balcony so that it could be taken apart in just ten days' time, should a future president decide he no longer wanted it there.[39]

Despite Delano's imprimatur, the Fine Arts Commission never did approve the balcony, a fact Truman lost no sleep over. "To Hell with them," he said.[40] When the president got wind of Gilmore Clarke's duplicity—granting the commission's conditional approval based only on his presumption that Delano would reject the job—Clarke's head rolled, as did those of three other commissioners.[41] "That was the way Harry Truman was," J. B. West later said, not without admiration.[42] Delano, too, enjoyed a client who had guts. "I loved Truman," said the architect. "He knew exactly what he wanted."[43]

The public got its first look at what Harry Truman wanted on January 2, 1948, when the White House press secretary, Charlie Ross, formally presented the balcony plans at a press conference. Ross kept it brief. The balcony—whose price had risen to fifteen thousand dollars in view of the complexity of the job—would furnish the Trumans "outside breathing space without being subjected to public view," he said.[44] Ross hastened to add that the porch would save two thousand dollars of taxpayer money a year, the money it had cost previously to replace the unwieldy awnings. The briefing wrapped and the reporters left. In private, Truman had his fingers crossed. "I hope," he'd told Delano, "everything works out without too much turmoil."[45]

The turmoil began in the next day's papers. The *New York Times* accused Truman of trying to "desecrate the noble old mansion."[46] The Colonial Dames of America decried the balcony as "a defacement of an historic shrine."[47] In Congress, Pennsylvania Republican Frederick Muhlenberg decried that Truman's building project was "illegal,"[48] while some right-leaning publications reminded Americans that Hitler and Mussolini had liked balconies, too.[49]

Meanwhile, the White House mail room filled with furious missives. "You have some nerve, don't you?" sputtered one woman from Savannah, Georgia, who told Truman to go "botch up your own home." A telegram from a Colorado woman was a bit more artful: "YOU QUOTED AS SAYING THE WHITE HOUSE A PRISON. PRISONS DON'T HAVE BALCONIES."[50] One man mailed in a piece of asphalt siding stamped with an imitation brick pattern, pointing out that since the cheap cladding was so popular in Missouri, perhaps the president would like to cover the White House with it.[51]

It's inevitable that a president's decisions will always anger someone. But Truman had dropped atomic bombs on two foreign cities to comparatively little protest, yet now the public was berating him over a porch? Truman felt as though "he had been accused of interfering with the natural order of the universe," Clark Clifford recalled.[52] Still, he stuck to his guns. If he got nowhere with his architectural argument that a balcony would make the South Portico "look right," he'd simply default to his presidential prerogative.[53] "This old barn called The White House," Truman said, "should be arranged for the President so he could live like other people."[54]

He got his wish. Winslow let the construction contract to Washington's F. H. Martell Co. and by March 1948 the balcony was nearly finished. The structure's final cost came in at $16,050.74, a figure that did not include the administrative costs borne by the United States Treasury, whose engravers had to redo the printing plates for the twenty-dollar bill so that the rendering of the White House would show the south facade with a balcony.[55]

In the end, for all the trouble it caused, the balcony was a disappointment. Bess ventured out onto it every now and then to sit and read. If an amateur baseball game sprang up on the Ellipse, the First Lady (who never missed a home game of the Washington Senators) would sit and watch. But, ironically, the balcony that was intended to give the Trumans more privacy had only wound up making them more visible. "Crowds would gather at the end of the south lawn and gape at them as they sat there," West remembered.[56] In time, the family retreated back indoors, Bess continued retreating to Missouri, and the porch sat empty.

For all the congressmen, editors, cartoonists, architects, and ordinary citizens who wished the balcony hadn't been built, there was also a document whose contents suggested that it *shouldn't* have been built—at least not so hastily. The document, a confidential report, appeared on Truman's desk on January 30, 1948, not long after Martell's workmen had begun cutting notches in the stone to receive the balcony's steel supports. The report was from W. E. Reynolds, commissioner of public buildings, whom Truman had asked to look into the strange noises that the mansion's "ghosts" were making every night.

Truman kept the report's contents secret, but he slipped up once and mentioned it in a letter he wrote to his cousin Ethel Noland in Missouri. After running through the usual news of his busy week and the hullabaloo that his balcony was causing, Truman dropped an astonishing bit of news. "I've had the 2nd floor where we live examined," he wrote, "—and it is about to fall down!" Truman told Noland that the government engineer had also discovered that the ceiling of the State Dining Room (located directly beneath the First Lady's bedroom and sitting room) was about to collapse, too. The floor would need to be shorn up, and probably replaced. Then the president wound up his letter. "Take care of yourself," Truman bid his cousin, "and don't mention what I've told you."[57]

FOUR

"LIKE A SHIP AT SEA"

It's a shame the old White House had to fall down. But it's a
godsend it didn't when we had 1,500 people in it.

—Harry Truman

*T*he entire second floor of the White House—about to fall down?
It was a tidy piece of news to tuck into the end of a letter. Truman
had chattered on line after line, asking cousin Ethel about her
new bathtub, wanting to know if that photo album she'd lost had
turned up.[1] And only then did he mention—oh, by the way—that the
floor where the family lived was about to collapse. What could account
for his apparent nonchalance? Perhaps this: Truman had already harbored doubts about the old house's stability for all of 1947, and he
could point to signs of trouble that had appeared long before that. It's
quite possible that the structural report's findings weren't so much a
surprise to the president as a confirmation of his suspicions.

The nightmarish quarters that J. B. West showed the Truman women
during that first tour in April 1945 had obviously not decayed to that
condition overnight. As it turned out, Franklin Roosevelt had forsaken
the house's upkeep for most of the Depression, and then for most of
World War II, as well.[2] It wasn't that the government lacked funds to

maintain the house, but the maxim of those lean years—"Use it up, wear it out, make it do, or do without"—was one that FDR adopted publicly. He'd refused to have the White House painted, a noble gesture that saved three hundred gallons of paint each year, even if it did result in the popular joke that the president lived in the "Off-White House."[3]

Had their shock over the second floor's decrepitude prompted them to ask around, Margaret and Bess Truman might have discovered that they were hardly the only ones who thought the house was in appalling shape. Lorenzo Winslow might have told them (as he would later tell Congress) that he thought the family quarters looked "like a run-down Chautauqua hotel."[4] He also might have mentioned that elsewhere in the mansion, the rot ran deeper. Wooden window frames, reduced to splinters, had weathered down to the putty. Iron railings bristled with rust. Cracks meandered through the marble floors.[5]

From any of the older servants, the Trumans might have heard how the mingy Calvin Coolidge had obtained the White House plumbing secondhand from Maryland's Fort Meade army base, and about how those pipes had sprung countless leaks ever since.[6] Had the Trumans chanced to speak with anyone who'd stayed at the White House during the war years—when the strange creaking and popping noises were already evident—they might have heard about the standard assurances the staff used before tucking in overnight guests. "You may think someone is knocking on your door in the middle of the night," the servants would say, "but don't pay it no mind. Nobody will be there."[7]

Had Truman not been so overwhelmed with being a president and ending a war, and had his curiosity been piqued as to why J. B. West had led his wife and daughter around quarters befitting a Kansas City flophouse, then the dust might have blown off some very interesting papers hiding in file cabinets around Washington. At the Public Buildings Administration, for example, were many old reports on the White House's buckling floors, on the large chunks of plaster that had routinely fallen from its ceilings, and on pipes discovered *physically bent* from the shifting weight of the house as it settled in the soft ground. "The old Federal Works Agency, Public Buildings Administration, had long been aware of the construction shortcomings of the White House," Gen. Jess Larson would admit many years later.[8] There was also an Army Corps of Engineers' inspection paper, presented to FDR in 1941, that warned of brittle, dry wood and mortar crumbled to dust—a report that had called the White House a "firetrap"—a report that President Roosevelt had dismissed.[9]

Had Eleanor Roosevelt's rat story troubled President Truman instead of tickling his funny bone, he might have discovered that rodents essentially had their run of the White House—and had enjoyed the privilege since the 1890s at least. A veritable rat battalion had once chased off Mrs. Benjamin Harrison,[10] and it was not uncommon for Theodore Roosevelt to interrupt his meals to chase rats from the dining room. Usually, his sons helped.[11] The record also shows that FDR's Public Works Project No. 634, which converted the White House from DC to AC current in 1935, had a rat-eradication initiative discreetly tacked onto it.[12]

When the Trumans moved in, J. B. West's small army of carpenters and painters patched up the second floor in record time, but the house's problems quickly bled through the bandages. Truman was barely settled in the Oval Study when the maintenance men discovered termites in the baseboard and had to rip it all out.[13] The chandeliers began to tremble and the ghosts visited each night, coaxing those eerie sounds out of the walls and floors. "The White House building seemed to have it in for the Trumans," Lillian Parks remembered of those early days. "It seemed as if the building were creaking and groaning and making the family unwelcome."[14]

Things worsened. By the time Truman's first year in office drew to a close, the parquet floors were a mess of worn-down grooves and missing tiles. That winter, Coolidge's secondhand plumbing hissed and clanged inside the walls as though a locomotive were passing, and then the house's heating system finally collapsed.[15] The ushers and maintenance men could no longer conceal the house's problems from the visiting public. Down on the State Floor, the silk damask of the Green Room's walls hung in tatters from water damage.[16]

Even though Congress quashed Truman's $1.6 million appropriations request over his disastrous West Wing expansion plans, living conditions inside the mansion itself had grown so bad by February 1946 that a House-Senate conference committee quietly slipped the Truman administration $780,000 to make the place livable.[17] The congressional gift basket included $59,000 for a new furnace, $22,000 for new floors, and enough money to replace the damaged wallpaper, drapes, and carpeting.[18] Readers of the *Washington Post* were no doubt surprised to see the word *hazardous* used to describe conditions within the White House.[19] Not long after, surprise grew to anger when the public read that the White House Easter egg hunt, a cherished tradition for children since 1878, was to be cancelled. The official reason given was "the necessity for food conservation," but the real reason was that the maintenance scaffolding set up around the White House had torn up too much of the lawn.[20]

Workmen were busy with the emergency repairs when, one day in June 1946, Truman walked out of the Oval Study on the second floor and found, much to his surprise, that he could look straight down and see the *first* floor. "They are fixing a hole in the middle of the hallway, opposite my study door," the president wrote. "All the rugs are rolled back and a great scaffold has been constructed under the hole." Truman quipped that it "looks like they intend to hang a murderer."[21]

The men finished up their work in time for Edith Helm to send out her invitations for the 1947–1948 social season. Only later would Truman look back at this period and realize that all of the hasty repairs were too little, too late. "In 1947," he said, "the old house began to fall down."[22]

The first sign of serious trouble began during one of the state dinners early that year.[23] Following protocol, the butlers would circulate among the arriving guests downstairs and discreetly escort cabinet members and their wives up to the second floor for a private audience with the president. The tradition was not only a show of respect for the inner circle but also the means of assembling a procession. Just before dinner, the Marine Corps Color Guard—the four-man detail charged with carrying the U.S. and presidential flags—would "remove the colors" from their stanchions in the Oval Study, then escort the entire party down the grand staircase as the band struck up "Hail to the Chief."

Everything went according to plan until 8:45, when the heavy clomp of marines in dress uniform thundered across the study floor. Seated at his desk, Truman glanced up and noticed something amiss with the chandelier. It was swaying back and forth, free as a porch swing.[24] Margaret happened to look up at the same moment. The sight of the ornate old fixture in motion, its ropes of tinkling lead crystal so close to the scalps of the cabinet members, froze her in fear. Decades later, she could still feel the chill of that moment. "It looked," she remembered, ". . . as though [the chandelier] would collapse on the heads of everybody present."[25]

Truman pretended not to notice. He rose, calmly took Bess by the arm, and marched downstairs—his officials tottering behind him and none of them the wiser. It had been a near thing, and the boss was not pleased as he reported the incident to the Public Buildings Administration the first chance he got. The close call was all the more upsetting because this would be the second time Truman had asked the PBA to take a look at the house. "For more than a year he had been prodding the Commission . . . to take a good look at the place," Margaret said.[26]

As things turned out, it was to be a season of misbehaving chandeliers. Next up was the center fixture in the East Room.

The night of February 11, 1947, had begun without a hint of trouble. The State Dining Room hummed with conversation and the clinking sounds of flatware on the presidential china. After the dessert course, the guests rose and promenaded down the Cross Hall's red carpeting, past the Istrian stone planters and the sprays of fern, and into the East Room. The mansion's largest room glowed like a treasure chest that evening. Thick wall mirrors tossed the candlelight out over an expanse of parquet trimmed in red Numidian marble. From their gilded frames high on the walls, George and Martha Washington looked out over the vases of Talisman roses and the rows of chairs arranged for that evening's recital. A grand piano with carved eagles for legs stood in the center of the floor. Directly above the piano hung a chandelier. At eleven feet tall and nearly six feet wide, the chandelier was bigger than the piano.[27]

At the ivories that night was twenty-eight-year-old Eugene List, riding high on the outrageous fortune that had tapped him on the shoulder during the summer of 1945. It had happened at the Potsdam Conference, held in a lakeside villa just outside the ruins of Berlin. Truman needed some entertainment for the dinner he was hosting for Stalin, with whom his dealings had been strained and frustrating. The young List, plucked from a U.S. Army Special Services unit in Paris, was the nearest concert pianist Truman could find.

That night at No. 2, Kaiserstrasse, with the president himself turning the sheet music pages, List rendered Chopin's Waltz in A Minor so beautifully that the Bolshevik man of steel, nearly moved to tears, rose to his feet and raised his tumbler of vodka in tribute. Though the evening of Paderewski and Shostakovich had bored Winston Churchill into a stupor ("I can't stand this noise," he moaned), Truman succeeded in building a bridge—however temporary—to the perplexing Soviet leader. While the president basked in his cleverness, List gained an imprimatur that would change his life. Back in the States, the pianist traded his drabs for a tailcoat and was soon pulling in $2,500 per concert. Wisely, he also kept his talents on call for President Truman.[28]

List began to play. As the Steinway's velvety tones enveloped the room, chief usher Crim and Agent Jim Rowley, the Secret Service man charged with the White House detail, emerged from the shadows and threaded their way through the rows. Neither man would have disturbed the president at a time like this unless it was an emergency. Crim and Rowley had decided that it was. One of them crouched down and whispered something into his ear. The exact words of this exchange are unknown, but two things about it are clear. First, here was a piece of news that *should* have been imparted to the president earlier—hours or even days earlier—but for some reason had not been. Second, the situation at hand was, without question, dire.

It was this: After endless months of procrastination, the Public Buildings Administration had finally sent some men over to take a look at the house. At most, it seems, they'd taken a rather cursory look around. Still, they'd found something amiss with the East Room's center chandelier, and the ushers had failed to tell Truman about it. And so now—*now*, during a state dinner, as List played a Honduran mahogany Steinway below six thousand prisms of Bohemian crystal—Crim and Rowley decided the president should know that the chandelier's chain was, well, "stretching."[29] "It was a nice time to tell me," Truman later jabbed.[30]

As he sat there, Truman considered what would happen if a half-ton chandelier were to come crashing down atop the piano, atop Mr. List, and atop "the customers"—his private term for White House guests.[31] Truman had been president nearly two years, and if he hadn't quite mastered the tact required by the job, he'd excelled at its demand for quick decisions. "If the facts available justify a decision at the time," Truman later said, "it will also be correct in future time."[32] And so Truman made a quick decision based on the facts he had at the time—which, according to Margaret, were these: "Dad decided that if the chain hadn't broken yet, it would probably hold up for a little while longer."[33] With that, Truman kept his attention trained on his favored pianist, and the concert continued.

"If [the chandelier] had fallen," Truman admitted later, "I'd have been in a real fix. But it didn't."[34] It wasn't going to, either. The next day, he ordered the behemoth of gilded brass and Austrian crystal slipped from its hook and safely lowered to the floor.[35]

⊶⇒ ⇐⊷

For the time being, this was all he would do. Truman would probably have acted more decisively over the troubled house in February 1947, but the weight of world affairs was pulling harder than the weight of chandeliers.

Stalin had turned his back on the West following the war's end. The dictator's string of broken diplomatic promises, his publicly blaming World War II on "monopoly capitalism" (meaning: the United States), and his obvious desire to turn Eastern Europe into a buffer of puppet states—all of these developments had frightened and preoccupied Truman by early 1947. Just weeks after the East Room chandelier incident, Truman made an impassioned plea to Congress for $400 million to prop up the tottering governments in Greece and Turkey, lest the Soviet boot plant itself in the center of the Middle East. Within four months, Secretary of State George Marshall would warn that if the United States did not do more to aid in the rebuilding of Europe (the Marshall Plan, as it would become known), it, too, would not remain standing.

Then there was the bomb. By 1947, the U.S. nuclear arsenal stood at thirty-two plutonium-implosion weapons—a tripling of the stockpile from the previous year.[36] Alarmed by the question of who'd control all of these bombs, Truman had already created the Atomic Energy Commission (AEC). Now, in the summer of 1947, the Joint Committee on Atomic Energy would grapple with the question of what number of bombs was needed to defend the country.[37]

But defend it against what? The Soviets did not possess the atomic bomb. Still, the confidence in America's atomic monopoly was crumbling, and this was still another of Truman's worries. Just weeks after the war's end, the U.S. embassy in Moscow had warned Washington that the Soviets were going all out in their effort to construct an A-bomb. Then, on Christmas Day of 1946, the USSR triggered its first nuclear chain reaction. As 1947 rolled nervously ahead, some voices were warning that the Russians were much closer to producing a nuclear bomb than many of Truman's own advisers were telling him.[38]

Not that Stalin would be sending Truman a birth announcement once he had the thing. Throughout 1947, AEC commissioner Lewis Strauss would argue that the Americans should start using some of their leftover B-29 bomber fleet—the WB-29s, as they were called, refitted as weather-observation planes—to fly reconnaissance missions over the Arctic Circle. "Continuous monitoring of the radioactivity in the upper atmosphere," Strauss said, "would perhaps be the *only* means that we would have for discovering that the test of an atomic weapon had been made."[39]

Strauss's idea was a fine one, but it would remain mired in bureaucracy for at least another year while the AEC (which oversaw the nation's tiny nuclear stockpile), the Joint Committee on Atomic Energy (which oversaw the AEC), and the president and his generals wrestled with the question of how to manage the most horrifying weapon in history. "No one seems to have thought the thing would work out as it has," Truman complained in his diary early in 1947. "So I am the heir to a hell of a mess."[40]

The crumbling White House was another of his messes but, as a decidedly smaller one, it would have to wait.

Credit for the fact the White House eventually received the serious attention it deserved must go to the house itself. No matter how thoroughly the nascent Cold War dominated Truman's attention, the mansion insisted on its own share. Invariably, Truman's long hours at the Oval Office would be met at day's end by news of the house's latest malady. One day, the Red Room's plaster had begun to crack, even though it had just recently been patched. On another, a burst pipe shorted out the circuitry and forced tourists to evacuate the house. At one point, Truman cast a wary look at the second floor and noted that it was visibly sagging.[41]

Then, one morning after his walk, the president asked Fields to bring his oatmeal and toast to his desk in the Oval Study. "The big fat butler brought me my breakfast," he said, "and the floor shook."[42] Truman didn't mean the usual quiver coaxed by the butler's heavy step; he meant the floor was truly moving.[43] "Fields is a big man—and a grand man too," Truman later wrote. But "the floor sagged and moved like a ship at sea."[44] Even Fields himself, accustomed to setting the china cabinets clattering as he strode past, marveled that the floor had seemingly detached itself, "as if floating in space," he said.[45]

By the early weeks of 1948, the White House had served up a full year's worth of alarming events, which by this time also included the Blue Room chandelier's *danse macabre* over the heads of the Daughters of the American Revolution. Truman's suspicions were fully awakened now. One day, the president borrowed a stethoscope from the White House physician, pressing its diaphragm flush against the plaster. Then he listened as the groans of the old timber whispered to him from inside the walls.[46]

Alarming as all of these warning signs were, Truman apparently did not regard them as sufficient reason to postpone his balcony project. Nor, apparently, did Winslow, who supervised as workmen rammed fourteen steel beams into the outer masonry wall, then poured a foot and a half of concrete over the formwork. The porch heaped another sixty-two tons of weight onto the old house's foundations.[47]

To date, there had been three close brushes with the White House's aberrant chandeliers. It would take a *fourth* before everyone finally woke up to the danger they were in.

On January 13, 1948, the Social Office held a reception for the heads of the federal departments. In the Blue Room, the president and his wife took their usual post in the middle of the oval chamber, where the receiving line could file past them. It was a delicious bit of coincidence that one of the federal agencies being feted that evening was the Public Buildings Administration, which put commissioner W. E. Reynolds in the receiving line.

As the queue inched its way past the Trumans, an eerie, tinkling sound rose over the din of conversation. Gradually, the guests became aware of the noise and looked around for its source. The Trumans, of course, knew exactly what it was. Spotting Reynolds in the line, the president made his way to the commissioner's side, as if to say, Now, watch *this*.

The Pendeloque filled the room with the chimes of colliding crystals while the whole of the five-and-a-half-foot fixture danced an aerial Charleston. It was an impressive performance, and not a little terrifying: The guests cleared out from beneath the possessed fixture, pressing their bodies up along the walls. The party, now in the shape of a doughnut, soldiered on. But somewhere in the tangle, Truman was able to get Reynolds alone. Then and there, the president made it clear to his buildings commissioner that he wanted something done about the house.

It wasn't a hard sell. Reynolds had just seen with his own eyes what the old place was capable of. Sobered and shaken, he acted without delay.[48]

In the Oval Study, Reynolds and two of his men began poking around. Lorenzo Winslow was on hand to help. They knocked on the walls and checked the doors. When the house yielded none of its secrets this way, the men began cutting through the floor. What they discovered beneath the parquet left them wide-eyed. Cracks cut long and deep through the floor beams. The engineers also discovered mysterious notches hacked into the old Virginia pine, some of them five inches deep. The notches crippled the beams' strength, yet they'd been deliberately cut. Who would have done such a thing? The men expanded their investigation throughout the whole of the second floor. They found the same conditions everywhere.

One thing was clear: The split and gouged-out beams explained why the second floor heaved when people walked across it. The engineers could also account for the quivering chandeliers, since the heavy fixtures had been screwed into those same beams from below. Charles Barber, chief structural engineer for the PBA, later recalled how disturbed his men were over what they'd discovered. "We found surprising structural conditions which could have, without exaggeration, led to disaster," he said.[49]

W. E. Reynolds reported the findings to Truman on January 29. The commissioner advised the president to permit no more than fifteen people in his study at one time, and to relieve the Marine Corps Color Guard for the foreseeable future. "I can only believe," a shaken Reynolds wrote, "that the beams are staying up there from force of habit only."[50]

The Public Buildings Administration was not an especially large or lavishly equipped agency, but Reynolds's men did what they could. The engineers raised temporary steel supports in the mansion's bedrooms, sitting rooms, and bathrooms.[51] Chief structural engineer Barber ordered steel collars tightened around the beams. The men reached down into the floors' freshly sawed holes and shackled as many joists as possible. But there was only so much they could do as long as the First Family was still calling the White House home.

"Shoring up the second floor was no small job," Margaret recalled. "It resulted in a forest of steel pipes running through the private rooms.

To get in and out of Dad's study, my sitting room, and mother's bedroom you had to wend your way through a metal maze."[52]

After telling Ethel Noland that the family floor was "about to fall down" in his letter of January 30, 1948, Truman also mentioned the steel braces, probably to keep his cousin from worrying. "I'm having [the floor] shored up," he wrote, before telling her to keep this to herself.[53] Cousin Ethel obeyed. The newspapers hadn't the slightest idea of the drama unfolding behind the walls of 1600 Pennsylvania Avenue.

But Commissioner Reynolds did, and it ate at him. The White House "wouldn't pass the safety standards of any city in the country," Reynolds would soon say.[54] Though he'd only laid eyes on a few sections of cracked beam, the commissioner would have known that his PBA deputies were facing a problem bigger than they could handle on their own. They were going to need outside help, men who were the best in their fields, and especially men who could be trusted to keep a secret.

On February 3, 1948, Truman's secretary sent out a pair of letters.

FIVE

THE INSPECTION

When the President asked for an investigation, he did so rightly.
Why so long delayed has always puzzled me.

—Douglas Orr

*D*ouglas William Orr, fifty-five years of age, recognizable by his bow ties and round spectacles, had a saying: "To specialize is to fossilize."[1] The draftsmen of Orr's small New Haven architectural office had heard this mantra so many times that Orr had begun to seem like their father. But, like a father, Orr led by example. And he did not specialize. Though the tweedy Yale-bred architect personally favored the Federal and Colonial styles, a few strokes of his pen could conjure the Beaux Arts or Art Deco just as easily. Orr had designed the majestic New Haven Lawn Club and a soaring white-limestone skyscraper for New England Telephone. The American Institute of Architects (AIA) had recently asked him to be its president.

On a chilly morning in early February 1948, Orr arrived at his office at 96 Grove Street and discovered a letter from the White House.[2]

At roughly the same time, sixty-seven miles down the Atlantic coastline, Richard E. Dougherty was beginning his own workday, heading down into Manhattan from his home in White Plains, New York. At sixty-eight years of age, Dougherty was still a man in demand. He'd retired from the New York Central Railroad that same year, but he had scarcely loosened his necktie before the American Society of Civil Engineers voted him in as its president. Gray-haired and tall as a lamppost, Dougherty had the kind of wry smile that mathematicians wear when they solve problems—and during his forty-six years with the railroad, Dougherty had solved plenty of them. In 1929, he'd hoisted the dangerous street-level freight tracks on Eleventh Avenue onto an iron viaduct thirty feet in the air. The structure's ingenious shock-absorbing cushions allowed trains to pass straight through Manhattan skyscrapers without shaking them.[3]

On a chilly morning in early February 1948, Dougherty arrived at his office at 230 Park Avenue and discovered a letter from the White House.[4]

Between them, Orr and Dougherty had spent nearly seven decades listening to the peculiar, complex, and at times near-impossible demands of those who wanted structures erected. But it's unlikely either man had ever beheld a request as startling as this one.

"It will be appreciated if you could find it possible to come to the White House at 10:00 a.m., February 25, 1948, for a meeting," read the letter from Matthew Connelly, Truman's secretary. "The purpose of this meeting is to make a structural survey of the safety of the White House."[5]

On the appointed day, a Wednesday, Orr and Dougherty arrived at the White House together below a gray Washington sky threatening rain. Head usher Crim, with his shiny pate and impeccably knotted tie, invited the Yankee architect and the civil engineer from Manhattan to step in from the cold. With the usher was Winslow, the White House architect, and Commissioner Reynolds from Public Buildings. Professionally, having reached the tops of their respective fields, the five men shared much in common, though there was one important thing they did not: Orr and Dougherty were the first—and, for the time being, the only—two nongovernment men whom Truman entrusted with the secret that the White House was in danger.

The president himself was not at home. With his face already pink from the sun, Truman was relaxing in the cool leather-paneled cabin of the *Sacred Cow*, the unofficial name for the C-54 Skymaster that Douglas Aircraft had refitted for President Roosevelt's use. (Truman's own plane, a beautiful new DC-6, to be dubbed *The Independence*, was not yet ready.) The president had lifted off from Washington on February 20, paying a diplomatic call first in Puerto Rico and then at the naval station in Cuba's Guantánamo Bay before commencing the trip's real purpose: a few days of R&R at the submarine base in Key West, Florida.

There, in the empty commandant's house expropriated as a presidential retreat, the drink was whiskey, the exercise was poker, and—as Truman once put it—"I can do as I please and let 'em all go to hell."[6] A glorious 1,029 miles from the political double-dealing of Washington, Key West was the only place where Truman willingly ditched his gray suits in favor of his treasured floral-print tropical shirts—suitable, if hideous, attire for the eighty-degree breezes that slipped through the jalousies of the house's porch. The president also liked a particular pair of bright red pants—ones Bess Truman hated so much, she'd once told her husband that either the trousers would be boarding the plane for Florida or she would. Truman relented, but on his subsequent trip to Key West, he took the pants.[7]

This trip to the "Little White House" would be the fourth in the Truman presidency, and one he had truly earned. Having decided to make a run for the Oval Office in the 1948 election, Truman had drawn the battle lines against the Republican-controlled Congress in his January seventh State of the Union address by tacking hard left: demanding a minimum-wage increase, a "poor man's" tax cut, and even nationalized health insurance.[8] Then he surprised even liberals by calling for a sweeping package of civil-rights legislation. It was a move that so outraged his once-loyal base of southern Dixiecrats that Mississippi senator James Eastland publicly accused Truman of trying to "secure political favor from Red mongrels in the slums."[9]

Eastland's vitriol touched on both sources of conflict that Truman faced at the start of 1948, the political ones at home and the military ones across the Atlantic. By now, many Americans were worried about new terms that had worked their way into the vernacular—*Iron Curtain*, *Cold War*—and the lengthening shadows they cast over what was supposed to be a peaceful future.[10] The Soviets were bent on expanding their borders. Poland, Bulgaria, Romania, Czechoslovakia—Stalin had already stuffed all of them into his socialist rucksack. The only thing that would stop the Red advance was the Marshall Plan. It would send $16.5 billion to prop up what remained of free Europe, but Congress hadn't voted on it yet. Truman had taken it upon himself "to save the world from totalitarianism," working until 4:00 A.M., driving his sixty-three-year-old body to the brink of collapse.[11] Bess tolerated it only for so long. "Harry," she finally said, "it's time for a vacation."[12]

Truman, then, was nowhere in evidence on the overcast February morning as usher Crim led the architect Orr and the civil engineer Dougherty through the hushed opulence of the White House. Few details survive from that fateful first assembly of "the committee," as this pioneering group would later be called. But the brief recollections penned by Dougherty and Orr both make clear that Truman, through his emissaries, made his fears about the White House understood.

"The President had become alarmed at the increased effects of vibrations in the second floor," Dougherty recalled, "manifested by the tinkling of the huge crystal chandeliers, [and] the ominous creaking of the timbers."[13] For his part, Orr remarked that Truman's anxieties pertained mainly to the second floor "but [were] not confined to it."[14] After the briefing, the two guests were invited to inspect the family quarters. Winslow had brought blueprints over from his East Wing office for the men to look at, but Orr and Dougherty seemed to want to knock around the place on their own.[15]

From the outset, the two realized there was only so much inspecting they could really do, since, as Dougherty later put it, "the essential structural portions of the building [were] shrouded in plaster and building finish."[16] But Orr and Dougherty did take advantage of the holes that the PBA men had cut in the floor a few weeks earlier, and what they saw was enough to convince them that the White House was a dangerous building.

"Even . . . from its first observations, the committee was greatly concerned with the conditions of the structure," Orr later said.[17] What load-bearing wood the men could inspect was very old and very dry. Some of the beams, they already knew, were cracked, sagging, and riddled with those notches. The place was unquestionably a firetrap, and that was the least of it.

Though Truman would not return for another week, the men completed a fact-finding report that same day. "The second floor should be reconstructed at the earliest practicable date," Orr and Dougherty concluded.[18] They signed the bottom of the report, and Reynolds added his name below theirs. Their duty now dispatched, the men departed.

A week later, on the afternoon of March 5, the president's silver bird touched down at Washington National Airport. As the four Double Wasp engines whirred to a stop, Truman—rested and red as a tomato— sprang from the aft port hatch to kiss Bess and Margaret. Then the family slipped into the heavy limousine parked and purring nearby.

Preoccupied as Truman was with what looked to be a looming war with the Soviets, he was still very interested in what the experts from New Haven and New York had concluded about the White House. His calendar for this first day back in Washington was solid with appointments, but Truman pried open a pocket of time long enough for Crim to brief him on Orr and Dougherty's report. Truman's reaction has gone unrecorded, but the poor prognosis evidently troubled him enough that he'd mentioned it to the assistant press secretary, Eben Ayers. "The President said he had received a report from Crim," Ayers wrote in his diary. "The second floor . . . had been found unsafe and almost in danger of falling down."[19]

Actually, Orr and Dougherty's report never stated flat out that the house was in danger of collapse. Having noted that the main floor had been rebuilt in 1902 and the attic floor in 1927, the committee pointed out that the second floor was the only one left that wasn't fire-resistant— in other words, it was made of wood. The wood was "very dry," posed "a definite fire hazard," and, sooner rather than later, "the second floor should be reconstructed," the report said.[20]

That was enough for Truman, who dispatched a memo to Maj. Gen. Philip B. Fleming, administrator of the Federal Works Agency, parent of the Public Buildings Administration. The president informed the agency, in the words of the White House's correspondence log, that "they should take some concrete action" on the house.[21]

For all of Orr's and Dougherty's alarming conclusions, it's surprising what still *wasn't* being said at this point—at least officially. The report made no mention of the fact that the floors heaved like the deck of a schooner. Nor did any of the men venture the observation that, if the White House's second floor was in this much trouble, the causes might lie in the rest of the house, above or below the second floor. The hastily written report had also left unstated another disquieting fact:

Replacing the middle floor of a three-story building would be as messy as removing the cream filling from a layer cake.

Douglas Orr knew it. At one point during his visit, the Connecticut architect had wandered downstairs to the State Floor. There, he had looked up at the heavy plaster ceilings and noted how they hung from rods driven into the second floor's beams—beams showing a perceptible sag. "Even the reconstruction of the second floor only," Orr reflected, would constitute "a major operation."[22]

News that the house he'd tended so carefully was, in fact, a danger to the First Family left J. B. West deeply shaken. "It was a wonder that we hadn't burned to the ground," the usher fretted.[23] Edmund R. Purves, an architect who knew Winslow and worked as the AIA's public-relations man, was equally disturbed: "I was appalled by the realization that the President and his family were living unnecessarily dangerously."[24]

The committee's report had identified fire as the greatest danger in the house, and it upset Purves especially that, with the exception of a small service stairway tucked behind the usher's office on the east side of the house, the main staircase was the only way for the Trumans to escape if the house were to catch fire. The danger had been even greater for the late Franklin Roosevelt, a fact that had stupefied Dougherty during his visit. "I inquired as to how, in the event of fire or other emergency, they had expected to get a crippled president out," the civil engineer related. "The response was that a canvas chute had been constructed outside of his bedroom window on which he would be placed, in the event of trouble, by one of his husky bodyguards—then he would slide to the lawn where an automobile stood ready."[25] It was no wonder that FDR often practiced crawling.[26]

Meanwhile, West followed Orr and Dougherty's interim suggestions and cut down the wattage in the family quarters. Told that she could no longer plug in her vacuum cleaner, Bess Truman held up her hands in surrender. On his part, Truman reduced the "live weight" on the second floor by limiting the number of friends he invited up to his study for a bourbon and a story.

But it was the report's "Recommendation C" that would prove to be the study's most valuable finding. It hinted—ever so slightly—that fire hazards might *not* be the White House's worst ill; that the replacement of the second floor might not be enough. "The situation," Orr, Dougherty, and Reynolds had written, "should be carefully watched and further investigations conducted."[27] Perhaps it was just pro forma language, but the committee of Orr, Dougherty, and Reynolds had nevertheless made it clear to the president that they considered their work unfinished.

In fact, around this time one of the men (probably Reynolds) mentioned to Truman that the entire mansion might even have to come down. "Before that happens," Truman shot back, "I'm going to have the most thorough study ever made of every nook and cranny, beam and pipe in this old house."[28]

He was serious, too. Such a study, however, would take money— money from a Senate still angry at a president who'd just pulled that little trick with the balcony in January. But Truman understood how the wheels turned in Washington. Now that Reynolds had a dossier of alarming discoveries about the White House, Truman sent him up to the Capitol. When the Senate Appropriations Committee gave Reynolds an April first hearing, he spooked them by trotting out his best line: that the mansion's "second floor was staying up there purely from habit." It worked. The senators scooped fifty thousand dollars out of the federal coffers to fund a more aggressive investigation.[29] Later, West marveled that Congress had "suddenly got generous."[30]

With money in the kitty to pay for a serious structural survey, the president picked his dream team. Characteristically loyal to men who'd done him a service, Truman began by asking Orr, Dougherty, and Reynolds to come back. New invitations went out—to the National Bureau of Standards, to the Forest Products Laboratory, and to Edward F. Neild of Shreveport, Louisiana. Fourteen years earlier, as the presiding judge of Jackson County, Missouri, Truman had supervised the building of a four-million-dollar Art Deco courthouse in downtown Kansas City. Neild had been his architect.

Also summoned was Charles B. Spencer of the Manhattan firm of Spencer, White & Prentis. Since 1919, the contracting company at 10 East 40th Street was, as *The New Yorker* magazine would later describe it, "a firm of foundation experts that is almost always called in whenever architects and builders think anything complicated or unexpected may occur below ground."[31] It was the magazine's genteel way of saying that Spencer's company took on work that sensible engineers ran from.

When the builders of the Bank of Manhattan Trust Building discovered in 1928 that the lot on which they planned to raise a seventy-two-story skyscraper was "quicksand to 49 feet below the street level," as *Fortune* magazine put it, Spencer, White & Prentis drove in the footings that let them build it.[32] And when vibrations from subway trains rumbling below Broadway cracked the foundation walls of Trinity Church, built in 1846, it was "the knowledgeable fellows from the offices of Spencer, White & Prentis," wrote *New York Times* folklorist Meyer Berger, who shoveled straight down through the churchyard's terrene of coffins and bones and propped the church back up.[33]

Knowing that the work on the White House would mean noise, dust, and craters appearing in the walls and floors, Truman asked his new team to hold off their assault until June; Bess and Margaret would be gone for the summer by then. Orr was pleased that he and his cohorts would be laying waste to the house "with a minimum of inconvenience to the President and his family."[34] Winslow concurred. "You just can't barge into the president's bedroom at any time," he said.[35]

As things turned out, there was little chance of disturbing the president, either. He'd planned a long campaign trip, by train, for an election he hadn't a prayer of winning.

If one thing in Washington was crumbling faster than the White House, it was the popularity of its tenant. The president's 1945 approval rating of 87 percent had plummeted to a dismal 35 percent by early 1947, as Americans blamed every postwar problem from inflation to a shortage of housing on the man from Missouri.[36] Truman jokes tumbled across dinner tables: "I'm just mild about Harry" and "To err is Truman."[37] The GOP's primped and prized nominee, Thomas Dewey, was believed to be such a shoo-in that pollster Elmo Roper assured the country that "no amount of electioneering" would stop Dewey from claiming the Oval Office.[38]

Truman disagreed. At 10:45 P.M. on Thursday, June 3, a sixteen-car train slipped away from the iron gates of Union Station. The Truman Special would call on forty cities during its 8,500-mile meander to Los Angeles. Just before the president left for the station, J. B. West had warned him that the expanded team of architects and engineers would be making a serious mess of the White House this time. "They'll be drilling into the walls, tearing off plaster, and we'll have to put scaffolding in the East Room," West said. Truman waved him off. "Don't worry about us," he replied.[39]

⊶⇌ ⇌⊷

As June's heat baked Washington and Truman tongue-lashed the Republicans at every whistle-stop, the troupe of engineers and architects cracked the White House open like a walnut.

Though Orr and Dougherty were nominally in charge, they were also based in cities to the north, so it would be Winslow and Reynolds who'd get the plaster dust in their hair.[40] Helped by a team of assistants, the men bored holes in the walls to inspect the studs, pried up baseboards and flooring, and chipped away the stucco over the interior brick walls to see where all the cracks originated. Most everywhere they looked, the men discovered something that disturbed them. And then, days or hours later, they'd find something that disturbed them even more.

With the rugs rolled back and the furniture moved aside, the men could finally get a good look at the floors. As West recalled, "the floors sagged and sloped like a roller coaster."[41] As workmen chipped the plaster off the brick walls, the usher also noticed that "many walls were cracked on the inside"—meaning that the cracks were not cosmetic, but structural. In the northwest corner of the West Sitting Room, engineers followed the zigzagging path of one crevice right up through the ceiling: The crack was two stories tall.[42]

The men proceeded slowly, not only because they'd begun to fear the frailty of the house but also because they were working blind. Apart from the drawings Winslow had (which he'd apparently made himself), most all the blueprints for the house had vanished years or decades before. The White House was the nation's most important dwelling, but almost no documents had survived to show how the place had been put together.[43]

Peering into the dark cavity below the floors, the men discovered splits that had worked their way clear through some of the support beams. They found more of those deep notches, too, which "caus[ed] the uncut portion to receive many times its normal stress," a later report said.[44] Winslow's men discovered careless and foolish maneuvers that a first-year architecture student would never have made, including doors cut carelessly through load-bearing walls, and horrifying relics entombed inside the walls themselves.[45] There were wood shavings and sawdust—decades-old detritus from one alteration or another—piled high between the studs. The highly combustible sawdust sat just inches from the electrical wiring, some of which had no insulation.[46] There were pipes in those walls, too: thousands of pounds of abandoned lead pipe, the remnants of the first gas lighting from 1848, and a hot-air heating system installed in 1872. None of these systems worked any-more, and yet nobody had thought to remove the scrap metal that collectively heaped thousands of pounds of needless weight atop the foundation.

Then there was the foundation itself, down to which the inspection eventually led. What the men discovered there could explain just as much of the trouble upstairs as the cracked beams could. The White House's lowest level was its ground floor. From this depth, the house's outside walls of stone extended down some five feet and rested on spread footings eight feet across. It was very good engineering, especially for the late 1700s.

The house's interior structure, however, was a different story. Criss-crossing the ground floor was a grid of brick walls, many of them tak-ing the form of four-foot-thick piers that supported a system of arches and groin vaults. These walls and piers were meant to share, with the outer walls, the burden of holding up the house. But so far as the engi-neers could tell, the interior walls had no footings to speak of. They appeared to sit right on the ground—ground that consisted of moist sand and clay. This kind of earth could never support a structure as heavy as the White House, and, in fact, it wasn't: The mansion's brick interior walls were sinking as untold tons of presidential house pressed down from above, and cracking all the way up through three floors as they did.

It would take a subsequent survey by Spencer, White & Prentis to confirm these early findings, but if they were correct, they would solve many mysteries: why the ceilings sagged and the parquet undulated like prairie hills, why the entire ceiling of the Green Room had pulled away so far from the wall that only two nails were left keeping it there, and why the butlers could never seem to keep the drafts out of the rooms upstairs.

It also explained all of the creaking and knocking and groaning that the "ghosts" had been blamed for. As L. C. Martin, an official of the Bureau of the Budget, would later appraise this period, "The character and extent of the structural weakness was found to be truly appall-ing."[47]

It was around this time that the investigation took a critical and permanent turn away from talk about preventing fires to a fevered discussion about how to stabilize the entire house.[48] Shaken awake to the fact that the mansion's problems were no longer confined to the second floor, Reynolds, Winslow, and their men now faced a task exponentially larger than the one they'd been discussing only a few weeks before. One afternoon, as the group pondered its limited options around the big table in Truman's Cabinet Room, Purves, the AIA's public-affairs man, turned to Reynolds with a question. "I asked him if he, as the Commissioner of Public Buildings, would certify the White House as safe for public occupancy." Reynolds sputtered no, of course he would not. Purves then reminded the commissioner—reminded the whole group, in fact—that "we had the President of the United States living in it."[49]

A silence fell over the room.

One of the cracked beams on the White House's second floor happened to run beneath Margaret Truman's sitting room, a pretty little retreat with a marble fireplace and walls of robin's egg blue. That June, Margaret had left not one but *two* pianos in that room. The First Daughter, who'd launched a singing career the previous March when she soloed with the Detroit Symphony, practiced on her Steinway religiously. But she was fond of four-hand compositions, too—accompanied by her father or by her friend Annette.

The assistant usher would later recall the First Daughter's pretty voice, which was still echoing in his head. "Mr. West, do you think we could roll the little spinet piano into my sitting room just for tonight? Annette Wright is coming over to spend the night and we'd like to try a duet."[50]

Just for the night? No. Housemen had trundled the Gulbransen upright in and out of Margaret's room for years now, fitting it snugly alongside the baby grand—and adding perhaps as much as a thousand pounds to the beam's burden below.[51] No apparent harm had come of it—except on one recent night.

Annette and Margaret had been deep into a classical duet when, sight-reading their sheet music, they came to a movement marked with an "*ff*"—fortissimo. The girls had let it rip, leaning hard into the keyboards and hammering at the ivories with all the might in their young fingers. Suddenly, Margaret had felt vaguely dizzy. It had almost seemed like the floor beneath them was rising and falling in time to the music. It had taken the girls a moment to realize that, in fact, that was exactly what was happening. "The two young ladies and the pianos were to all intents and purposes bouncing up and down rhythmically on an impromptu springboard—the split beam beneath them," Purves later explained.[52]

It had been a warning sign, and a big one at that. Had the warning been heeded, the two pianos would never have been left in Margaret's sitting room that summer. But they had been left there. And now, in June of 1948, the house could stand it no more.[53]

Exactly what happened next will probably never be known, for the versions varied widely and took on new colors with each telling.[54] This much is certain: Straining under the enormous weight of two pianos, a portion of the sitting room's dry-rotted flooring split, opening a rift big enough to swallow one of the pianos' legs.[55] Down it went—plunging through the parquetry, through the subfloor, and punching through the plaster ceiling downstairs. It must have made quite a noise, that falling piano—230 strings opening up in a hellish chorus as the instrument staggered to its knees, then the dead thud of hardwood on hardwood. In the room below, a shower of splinters and plaster dust fell twenty feet to the floor.[56]

Margaret would later remember that it was the spinet that took the plunge.[57] Nevertheless, for the rest of his life the venerable Theodore E. Steinway would love telling the story of how he took a phone call from the White House not long after this incident. It was a young Margaret Truman on the line, asking for a man who could come over to rescue a piano.[58]

SIX

THE EVICTION

[A] foolish man, which built his house upon the sand . . . And the rain descended, and the floods came, and the winds blew, and beat upon that house; and it fell: and great was the fall of it.
—Matthew 7:26–27

When Truman returned from his whistle-stop tour on June 18, 1948, news of the falling piano hit him with the force of, more or less, a falling piano. His fury over the incident would burn for years. He insisted that the accident would have "killed" Margaret had she been at the keys.[1] But what had struck Truman even deeper was a realization. Until this point, he had regarded the crumbling White House with a mixture of wariness and wit. Now, as his aide Robert Landry recalled, Truman "decided that the place was getting dangerous to live in."[2] Margaret, too, recalled this shift in her father's thinking. "If any further evidence was needed that the White House was falling apart," she said, "it came . . . when the piano in my sitting room broke through the floor."[3]

The incident was more than just a personal turning point for Truman; it became the defining symbol of the mansion's plight for recorded history. In the 1979 NBC miniseries *Backstairs at the White House*, Harry S. Truman (neatly turned out in a bow tie and gray suit by actor Harry Morgan) hears the piano's crash and rushes into Margaret's room, where the stricken baby grand—its pedals snapped off—lies at a forty-degree angle to the floor. "That does it!" Morgan yells. "This place is a national disaster! We're getting the hell out of here!"[4] It is a corker of a scene, but pure Hollywood nevertheless. Not only were the Trumans not even home when the piano fell; it would take several more mishaps to force them finally to flee the doomed house.

Dramatic license aside, the piano incident raised an unavoidable question: Why, after the instrument fell, did Truman stay? And why did he continue to risk the lives of his wife and daughter by allowing *them* to stay? The answer was sad and simple. Election day hovered a little over four months off, and Truman's odds of reelection were already long. If word got out that the White House was disintegrating, "can you imagine what the press would have done with this story?" Margaret later wrote. "The whole mess would have been blamed on Harry Truman. The White House would have become a metaphor for his collapsing administration."[5]

And so everyone in the know kept quiet. Though the papers had written off and on about the occasional problem in the mansion, the real story of what a disaster the place actually was remained—incredibly—a secret. But the secret was getting harder to keep with each passing day.

⊹⇌ ⇌⊹

When the architects finally ripped up enough of the floor to get a good look at the beam below Margaret's sitting room, they found it completely split—"broken in half," as structural engineer Charles Barber recalled.[6] The discovery was a harbinger. By now it was August, and Washington's hellish heat and humidity were at their worst. The soft ground skirting the Potomac seemed to awaken to the primordial memory of having once been a swamp, and the White House submitted to its mucky grasp. Astonished engineers discovered that Margaret Truman's room was slipping away from them. "The floor just sunk in," Landry remembered.[7] The men scrambled into the Family Dining Room directly below to measure the ceiling. It had dropped by eighteen inches.

Winslow sprang into action, fastening Margaret's room to the floor above it with steel rods. But it was useless: The entire west side of the mansion was on its way down. Across the hallway, the president noticed one morning that his bathtub—the one he'd joked about riding down onto the heads of the DAR—had begun to sink into the Red Room. Later, a story would circulate that the president's own foot plunged through the floor. That account proved apocryphal, but Truman did later admit to looking at his toilet and thinking, "One day, I'm going to flush this thing during a diplomatic reception and wind up in the Red Room while the band plays 'Hail to the Chief.' "[8]

When the *Titanic* sank in 1912, doomed passengers who saw the bow slipping below the ocean ran for the stern. It was a useless, if understandable, response—and its corollary now took place inside the White House. Helpless to stop the west side of the mansion from sinking, Winslow moved the president to the east side of the mansion.

"The White House Architect and Engineer have moved me into the . . . Lincoln Room—for safety—imagine that!" Truman wrote in his diary on August 3.[9] A little over three years earlier, Truman had told J. B. West to move all of the Mary Todd Lincoln's gloomy rosewood furniture down the hall into the Blue bedroom. Now he was living there.

Not long after, Truman decided to update his sister, Mary Jane, on what now passed for normal life at the executive mansion. "The White House is still about to fall in," he wrote. "Margaret's sitting room floor broke in two but didn't fall through the family dining room ceiling. They propped it up and fixed it. Now my bathroom is about to fall into the red parlor. They won't let me sleep in my bedroom or use the bath. I'm using Old Abe's bed and it is very comfortable."[10]

When Truman's wife and daughter returned at summer's end, they found even more steel pipes bracing the ceilings of their rooms. "They were particularly thick in Dad's study, my sitting room, and Mother's bedroom," Margaret recalled. "You had to walk around them to get out of the doors. It was not what I called gracious living."[11] New bracing had been put in place alongside the old bracing, which effectively united the mechanisms for keeping the third floor from falling into the second with the ones meant to keep the second from falling into the first—or something like that.[12]

Climbing around all the rigging was a nuisance, but seamstress Lillian Parks found herself oddly grateful for all the steel supports around her sewing machine. "After the piano incident," she wrote, "the men came running immediately with a pole to hold up my linen room, the ceiling of which, they said, was about to collapse." Ugly as all the braces were, Parks believed they had saved her life.[13]

$$\text{⊹} \text{⊹}$$

When September arrived, the committee gathered for its second, all-hands meeting. With Orr and Dougherty present, the men easily agreed that they were no longer dealing with a crumbling floor, but a crumbling house. "A major operation would be required," Dougherty recalled, "not merely a reconstruction of the second floor."[14] Orr believed that only "heroic remedies" could save the mansion now.[15]

If the conclusion was obvious, deciding what to do with it was not. The committee's members were in more of a political bind than an engineering one: Releasing news of this magnitude before the election would surely doom Truman, but sitting on it for too long might incur later accusations of concealment. The public sense of the problems in the house was wildly out of sync with how bad things really were. The *Washington Post* had reported, for example, that the funds from Congress would be used to "take the shimmy out of the floor"—as though a few good nails would do the job.[16] What's more, the clock was ticking. Five long months had elapsed since Congress had granted fifty thousand dollars to fund a structural survey of the house. The legislature would not wait forever for a report. The men would have to say something.

Deciding what to say fell to Lorenzo Winslow, who'd worked in the government long enough to know how to wrangle these things. The White House architect decided that he would deliver the bad news—just not all of it.

On September 30, 1948, the affable, chain-smoking Winslow faced a clutch of reporters and explained the findings of the government's fifty-thousand-dollar foray into the quivering White House. While pencils flew on notepads, the architect claimed that the house's "structural nerves" (whatever those were) had been damaged. Then he announced the solution: The second floor would need to be rebuilt.

This, of course, was the very remedy that the committee had discarded earlier in the summer as patently inadequate. But, technically, Winslow wasn't lying. The second floor would indeed be rebuilt—just in the course of rebuilding the entire mansion. That latter detail the architect omitted.

No doubt conscious of Truman's political future—which had direct bearing on his own—Winslow was determined to focus on good news, even if he had to tiptoe across a rhetorical minefield to reach it. Winslow told the reporters that, on the whole, the White House "probably is good for another 25 years without any repairs at all, but the work ought to be done on the second floor." The work might take six months, Winslow allowed, and it might even cost a million dollars. But overall, the architect concluded, the White House was in "good shape."[17]

One wonders if his dreams that night were troubled.

Whatever Winslow's sins of omission might have been, they bought Harry Truman some time—which is all that the president needed. On the day that the White House architect faced the press in Washington, the president was a third of the way across America on his *second* national whistle-stop tour, this one to last forty-five days and cover 21,928 miles. Buoyed by the unexpected success of his earlier railroad junket, Truman was convinced he could clinch the presidency if only he could get out and speak to enough ordinary people. And, he promised, "I'm going to give 'em hell."[18]

He did: a hell of a knock to the Republicans, and a hell of a show for anyone who stopped by the depot when the president's campaign special chuffed in. Truman predicted his railroad excursion would be "the greatest campaign any President ever made," and he wasn't off by much.[19] Before the junket was over, Truman would deliver a total of 275 speeches (on one day, he delivered 16 in a row) to a total of fifteen million Americans. The Truman Special of the previous June was now the Victory Special, and as the train snaked its way across the country— drawing crowds often double the size of the ones that Thomas Dewey's train was getting—Americans saw a Harry Truman they hardly recognized. He was seething and merciless, eloquent and hilarious; a dapper-looking family man who could charm like a preacher and hit like Joe Louis. Republicans gasped as Truman delivered the gut blows. He called them "bloodsuckers with offices in Wall Street"[20] and warned the working-class crowds "if the Republicans win, they'll tear you to pieces."[21]

One of the millions of spectators to witness Truman's trackside bravado was John Hersey, a writer for *The New Yorker* magazine. Hersey had gone to the train station in Norwalk, Connecticut, expecting to see only "the hack politician who succeeded the great F.D.R."[22] He came away amazed instead—at the size of the crowds, as well as the eloquence of the speaker. "I went home convinced that this man would be hard to beat," the writer said. Hersey also decided that, if he could get the necessary clearances, he would go to Washington to profile the man himself.

⊹⊱⊰⊹

While Truman click-clacked his way across the country, the White House began its final slide to the bottom.

On October 26, usher Crim discovered "a considerable amount of fallen plaster" on the floor of the East Room—a floor that had just been swept a short time earlier. This was a strange thing. Then Crim looked up and noticed a crack in the ceiling that had not been there the last time he'd looked. The crack was twelve feet long. Once more, the engineers came running. They discovered that the ceiling had dropped by half a foot. Here was proof that the *east* side of the house was sinking now, just like the western half had been since August. Where would Crim put the president when he got back? None of the rooms upstairs was safe now.

Soon the clap of hammers echoed up and down the Cross Hall. When it ended, an ugly contingent of wooden X-braces eclipsed the East Room, their raw timber limbs slashing across the once-beautiful space like knives stabbing a cake. It was a painful sight, but nobody would be seeing it anyway. As soon as the carpenters left, Crim sealed off the East Room permanently. "The situation as it exists now is extremely dangerous," the head usher wrote three days later in a report to the president.[23]

That same day, Reynolds finished his own memo to Truman, one with its own pieces of bad news. Engineers nosing around below the grand staircase had found cracks riddling the brick supporting pier on the west side of the steps. Load tests had proved that the masonry was fracturing under weight far greater than it could handle. "The margin of safety," wrote Reynolds, "is a minimum."[24]

It was an alarming discovery, but the next would be stupefying. A few days after Reynolds wrote his memo, engineers peered into another hole they'd sawed in the floor and discovered a beam blackened and eaten down by scorch marks. Before long, Winslow men uncovered burned timber lurking all over the house. The only blaze that could have left scars like that was the arson fire that British admiral Sir George Cockburn set during the War of 1812. Here, then, was unimpeachable evidence that the carpenters hired to rebuild the White House in 1817 had taken shortcuts by leaving singed beams in place.[25]

Worse, it was proof that the workmen hired to renovate the mansion back in 1902 had taken the same shortcuts. "The old burned and scorched timbers were put back into the building," a flabbergasted Truman later said. "Teddy [Roosevelt] was evidently using his Big Stick somewhere else."[26]

Meanwhile, outside, sandhogs from Spencer, White & Prentis were digging. Charles Spencer was out to make a conclusive inspection of the house's foundation walls. The committee had already discovered that the White House's interior brick walls "had settled to an alarming extent," but since none of the original plans for the house had survived, only Spencer could tell them what the mansion's structure actually looked like below the ground.[27]

Spencer wrote to Winslow with his findings on November 10, 1948. The tiny bit of good news was that the White House's exterior sandstone walls, eight feet wide at their lowest point, seemed to be holding their own. The interior brick walls, however, were as bad as the committee had feared. Actually, they were worse. Spencer found these to be only four feet thick, resting on "rubble masonry laid up in inferior mortar."[28] Four feet might sound like a substantial wall, but not when twenty tons of White House were pressing down on *each linear foot*, and not when there was nothing but soft, sandy, clay-streaked ground below it all. "This unit loading is approximately double that usually considered safe on soil of this character," Spencer wrote.[29] His tone was clinical, but it was still a death sentence: The house would sink until it tore itself apart. The only real question was how much time was left.

By now, some of the men were scared of simply entering the White House, for fear that it would cave in and bury them. The mansion's interior brick walls were actually pulling away from the outside walls of stone, leaving gaps big enough to put an arm through. Engineers warned that even a slight seismic tremor would be enough to cause the mansion to fall.[30] J. B. West carried this knowledge around in his head as he mustered the courage to keep working in the White House. "Any collapse of the interior walls," he later wrote, "would plunge everything into the basement."[31]

Truman's Victory Special chuffed into the depot at Independence, Missouri, on the afternoon of November 2. Truman had done more to win back his office than any president who'd preceded him. Still, the man kept his head down on the way back to 219 North Delaware Street. He was afraid that the sight of him would only force his neighbors to wish him luck with an election that was still, obviously, not his to win. The sixty-four-year-old president was exhausted. Never good at reading typed manuscripts aloud, Truman had winged it through three hundred speeches. He'd shaken more than thirty thousand hands.[32] Aboard the "Ferdinand Magellan," FDR's trusty Pullman, Truman manned the open vestibule in the wind and the cold on a few hours' sleep. Truman had narrowed Dewey's margin but, he was sure, not by enough.

That night, while the confident New York governor backslapped his way across the plush carpeting of the Roosevelt Hotel in Manhattan, Truman took a bath in Missouri. "I had my sandwich and a glass of buttermilk, and went to bed at six-thirty," Truman recalled later. When he woke up and flicked on the radio around midnight, he listened as NBC assured its listeners that "Mr. Truman will be defeated by an overwhelming majority."[33]

At ten o'clock the following morning, a telegram arrived at 219 North Delaware, announcing the unthinkable: The election was over—and Truman had won it. All the fearsome talk of Republican Wall Street bloodsuckers had worked: Union men and residents of the the farm states had turned out in force at the polls, delivering 303 electoral votes to Truman and leaving Dewey with only 189. As *Time* magazine later said, "He had humbled the confident, discomfited the savants and the pollsters, and given a new luster to the old-fashioned virtues of work and dogged courage."[34]

Ecstatic, almost disbelieving, Truman grabbed Bess and Margaret, boarded his train, and hurried back to Washington.

Waving from the backseat of FDR's old '39 Lincoln as he drove away from Union Station, Truman guzzled the energy from the cheering crowds. The moment he pulled up to the White House, he scampered up the steps to deliver an impromptu victory speech. The president's buoyancy left him totally unprepared for J. B. West's grave countenance waiting just inside the front doors, away from the cameras and microphones. "I'm afraid you're going to have to move out right away," the usher told him by way of a greeting.

At first the president didn't seem to understand. He responded with a joke. "Doesn't that beat all!" he barked. "Here we've worked ourselves to death trying to stay in this jailhouse and they kick us out anyway!"[35] It would take a meeting with Crim and the committee to convince the president that West had been quite serious: This was no homecoming, it was an eviction.

Chairing the closed-door session was Gen. Philip Fleming, administrator of the Federal Works Agency. "Mr. President," Fleming said, "I am going to do something to you that the Republicans couldn't. I am going to move you out of the White House."[36] Whatever the others present told Truman (and there is no reason to believe it was nothing but the worst) turned him "sober," as West recalled.[37] Truman might have kept the presidency, but he would not be keeping the address that went with it.

"The White House [is] in one terrible shape," Truman recorded in his diary later on, after taking a long, contemplative walk around the dying mansion. "There are scaffolds in the East Room, props in the study, my bedroom, Bess' sitting room, and the Rose Room."[38] Margaret, too, stood slack-jawed over what their home had turned into. "The first and second floors were in a precarious state," she recalled. "A swarm of construction workers had already put up scaffolds in the East Room and propped up most of the second floor."[39] Margaret, like her mother, had never wanted to move to the White House in the first place, but it was still a shock to be ordered out of the place. "The engineers and architects had concluded," Margaret later wrote, "that it would be dangerous for us to live there."[40]

The engineers had also found, oddly enough, that the only safe place left in the house was none other than Truman's controversial balcony—probably because the house's thick outer walls, and not its sinking inner ones, were still holding up.[41] None of the structural men knew it yet, but the outer walls were actually not stable, either.

Truman must have understood that his family had pressed their luck by staying in the White House as long as they had, even if the gamble had helped him win a second term. In time, he would grow reflective about the chances he'd taken. "My heart trembles when I think of the disasters we might have had—big receptions we used to hold, of fourteen hundred and sixteen hundred people, downstairs, none of them knowing that a hundred and eighty tons might drop on their heads at any moment," he'd tell a guest in the coming months. "All I can say is God must have been looking out for us."[42]

SEVEN

THE SLOW MURDER

Great architecture has only two natural enemies: water and stupid men.

—Richard Nickel

*B*oth *usher Crim* and Commissioner Reynolds had been urging the president to shutter the White House indefinitely. On November 7, 1948, it finally happened.

That Sunday, Americans who fetched the papers from their front stoops were in for a surprise. "White House Is Closing as Unsafe; Usual Social Season Is Canceled," blared page one of the *New York Times*. The *Washington Post* consigned its story to the metro section, but slugged the White House as a "Shaky 132-Year-Old Firetrap" right over the headline. Details that followed came from a press conference held by the assistant press secretary, Eben Ayers, and the social secretary, Edith Helm. Truman was nowhere in evidence, nor would he be. He'd slipped out of Washington early that morning for a two-week vacation down in Key West.

News of the White House's closing caught the public off guard.

After all, hadn't Winslow *just* assured the press that the house was in "good shape" not a month ago, saying that the problems were those of the second floor alone? He had. But the structural survey was now complete, the officials said, and explained that, as reported in the *Washington Post*, "hazards have been found in other parts of the building also."[1] Now the papers carried stories of the horrors that had been kept secret for months—how the Pendeloque in the Blue Room shook menacingly over the heads of guests, how the brick pier holding up the main staircase was crumbling to pieces. Now it emerged, finally, that the pristine White House viewed from the iron gates was very different from what actually lay inside. "Tourists see it as a monumental shrine with the ghosts of history in its rooms," wrote Milton Lehman in a tell-all that *Collier's* published in mid-November. "But for the men who have lived there, the White House has been more of a nightmare than a dream mansion."[2]

Across the country, the question was the same: How was it that the most storied, treasured, and fussed-over residence in the entire nation could be—so suddenly—on the verge of ruin?

One night several weeks after the White House had been closed, presidential assistant John R. Steelman gathered his notes and ascended the rostrum at the Mayflower Hotel. This night, the seats below the ballroom's long barrel vault were filled with members of the Columbia Historical Society, assembled to celebrate the group's fifty-fifth anniversary by tucking into a dinner of sherried terrapin soup and a half chicken with asparagus tips. As a keynote speaker, Steelman didn't exactly radiate star quality, but he'd nevertheless made the stuffy Columbia dinner a hot ticket in town. Steelman would be confronting a question that everyone in the room—indeed, everyone in the nation—wanted answered.

"People all over the country are asking, 'Why is the White House suddenly so unsafe?'" Steelman intoned over the sea of heads and linen tablecloths. "The answer," he said, "is simple. The White House has not *suddenly* become unsafe. It has *been* unsafe for many, many years."[3]

The president's assistant went on to explain that the troubles with the White House had been brewing for many decades and were the result of many factors. Some of them, including the soft ground beneath the mansion, were the consequence of well-intentioned but misguided decisions made during the planning of the city itself. But other problems were not so easy to excuse. These were the decades' worth of so-called improvements that had not just taxed the structure beyond capacity but had been planned and executed by men who should have known better. In short, the White House was not dying because it was old; it was dying because generations of its custodians—from carpenters to presidents—had killed it. Steelman was too polite to put things this way, but *Architectural Record* was not. What had happened to the White House, the magazine said, was nothing less than "the slow murder of the original building."[4]

There was no question that the soil below the White House was poor, but it was difficult to fault the two men who'd chosen the site: a French art-school dropout named Pierre Charles L'Enfant and a certain president named George Washington.

In 1777, L'Enfant, the twenty-three-year-old son of a royal court painter, abandoned his studies at Paris's Royal Academy of Painting and Sculpture to cross the Atlantic and enlist in Gen. George Washington's Revolutionary army. L'Enfant chanced upon Washington himself in the winter of 1778 and, fatefully, sketched his portrait. Later, with independence won and an actual country to put together, President George Washington remembered the artistic young Frenchman and enlisted him to develop a master plan for his new federal city.

The "city" was really nothing more than ten square miles of farm, woodland, and low-lying mire wedged between the Potomac and Anacostia rivers, but George Washington envisioned a great capital rising from the tidal marsh. So did L'Enfant. In 1791, the designer—no doubt influenced by a childhood spent at Versailles—sketched out a metropolis of carved stone buildings and broad public promenades. Though the tempestuous Frenchman made the wrong enemies and lasted barely a year in his post, George Washington was smitten by his plans and kept the basic vision intact. That included the spot that L'Enfant had chosen for the President's Palace, as the White House was known originally. L'Enfant had worked by choosing the locations of the most important buildings first, then connecting them hub-and-spoke-style with wide boulevards. His scheme had already situated the Capitol and the presidential mansion on the two highest geographical points in the city.

As the nation's first president and as a former land surveyor, George

Washington possessed both the civic authority and the technical skill to change the mansion's location had he wanted to. He chose not to. L'Enfant had thrummed the president's heartstrings by assuring that a commanding view of the river Washington loved would unfold from the mansion's southern windows—"facing," the Frenchman rhapsodized, "on the grandest prospect of both branches of the Potomac."[5]

When it came to the ground beneath the mansion, however, there was nothing grand about it. The soil was what architects call "compressible"— a sophisticated way of saying that whatever you put on it tended to sink. In fact, the earth all over the neighborhood was bad. "As you know, much of downtown Washington was marshy in the early days," Steelman told his audience, "a fact that even now complicates the problems of construction."[6] It had complicated the construction of the very hotel that Steelman's audience was sitting in. Workers digging the foundations of the Mayflower back in 1922 had run into "dark swamp muck about eight feet thick," rich with the decayed remains of smartweed, beggar-tick and cocklebur from the Pleistocene era. Put another way, the neighborhood just north of the White House sat on a bed of 100,000-year-old decayed plant goo.[7]

But none of this would have given pause back in the 1790s. The study of soil mechanics would not emerge until the nineteenth century, long after the White House's completion. It was unfair to accuse L'Enfant—much less the father of our country—of poor planning.

The same held true for James Hoban, the Irish-born architect who'd won the competition to design the executive mansion in 1792. Hoban, whose winning submission was a close copy of Leinster House in Dublin, designed an uncommonly strong building by the standards of the day, especially when it came to its thick outer stone walls with their broad subterranean footings.

"Unlike many 18th century buildings, in England particularly, that were so poorly built that they had to be torn down," said *Architectural Record*, "the White House shows that our ancestors built well."[8] Douglas Orr concurred. "If any fault can be attributed to the original structure," he wrote, "it was founding it on compressible soil."[9] True, Hoban's interior brick walls had been erected without footings to anchor them, but the practice wasn't unusual for the time. The interior walls were adequate to carry the customary weights imposed by a Federal-era gentleman's house.

Yet that was the rub. The White House was no longer just a gentleman's house, and it had not been one for a century or more. As Steelman told his audience, the mansion "was designed as a comfortable late Eighteenth Century home. It has become the nerve center of the world."[10] Transforming it into that nerve center had meant adapting the house, altering it, updating it. And that was where the real troubles began.

Every president has ordered changes of one kind or another to the White House, but for the first three decades of the mansion's existence, these changes had not overburdened the structure itself. That changed starting in 1833. Workmen arrived to lay piping so Andrew Jackson could enjoy running water, and then returned in 1848 to lay eight hundred more feet of pipe so President Polk could dine by gaslight. Plumbers wrestled a half-ton zinc and mahogany bathtub up to the second floor for Millard Fillmore in 1850, and Franklin Pierce filled it with hot water three years later, courtesy of a heavy new furnace with heat-exchanger coils. Industrial-age technologies muscled their way into the old house next: a telegraph for Andrew Johnson in 1866 and the first telephone for Rutherford Hayes by 1879. Soon after, carpenters cut a vertical shaft down through the house's floors for a hydraulic elevator. By 1891, Benjamin Harrison was reading by the light of carbon filament, courtesy of the mansion's new electrical system.

And on it went. Each administration ordered workmen to install something new, from Chester Arthur's ice-fed air-conditioning system to a top-floor kitchen that allowed FDR to escape the bland cooking of his housekeeper. But each new "improvement" meant more holes to be drilled in the wood, more walls to be moved or knocked down, and more weight heaped upon the house.

Born in an age of whale-oil lanterns and outdoor privies, James Hoban had designed the house with none of these advancements in mind. The Irish architect with the frilly cravat could never have foreseen a technological future in which men summoned hot water from a tap or communicated through electric wires. Logically, then, the responsibility for assuring that the old house could physically support all of these new accoutrements fell to subsequent generations of its keepers. But those keepers had let the house down.

Always laboring under tight deadlines, with orders to minimize any inconvenience to the president, the plumbers and carpenters and electricians who'd made alterations to the White House worked in haste and worked blind: Floor plans and wiring schematics that might have helped them had been long before lost or thrown away.[11] The result was nearly always a rushed and sloppy job. Each time workmen laid in new piping for water, steam, or sewerage or routed wire through the house for electricity, telegraph, and telephone, they'd bored or hacked straight through the wall studs and floor beams, seldom checking to see what those structural members might be supporting.[12] They were turning the house into a block of Swiss cheese.

In some cases, tradesmen were so bent on ramming their conduits through that it hardly mattered what was in the way. The AIA's Purves later recalled finding a brick archway in the basement whose keystones had been hammered to pieces so that a hot-air duct could pass straight through. Purves seethed at the "utter disregard of those who had made [these] changes," but it was insult added to injury: Not only had the fool who'd done this work undermined the structural integrity of the house; the air duct he'd installed had long since been abandoned.[13]

The abuses perpetrated on the mansion's floors were even worse. When the plumbers or electricians required a right-of-way, they had simply pried up the floorboards and sawed out huge U-shaped channels through the supporting beams below, laying their pipe or wire into the trough. This practice accounted for the strange notches that Orr, Dougherty, Winslow, and Reynolds had found hacked into the joists beneath the parquet. "There is scarcely a beam in the entire building," reported *Architectural Record*, "that has not been bored or cut through dozens of times."[14] Noted another observer, "Termites running entirely amok could hardly have been as destructive."[15]

The mortal wounds ran wide and deep. Most of the White House's beams had started out life as substantial pieces of wood—twelve-by-twelves or even fourteen-by-twelves. But as Fine Arts Commission member Felix de Weldon later recalled, hatchet-happy workmen had reduced them to trellis sticks. "In many cases," he said, "there were only 2×2s left."[16] How long could a stick of wood like that possibly hold up a grand piano, a Victorian oak desk, or a twelve-hundred-pound crystal chandelier? "Mr. Winslow can point out," Steelman told his astonished audience, ". . . many places [where] two or three tons of materials is supported by wood only two inches thick."[17]

And still the abuse of the mansion's structural components did not stop. Over the years, carpenters had also changed the floor plan upstairs, moving walls and doors at the whim of whatever First Family was in residence.[18] Apparently, no one ever found the nerve to tell a president that the wall he wanted a door cut through might be better left alone—for example, because it happened to be holding up the roof. But nothing was said, and walls shuddered under the assault of saws and sledgehammers. In the East Room alone, along one twenty-eight-foot length of wall, no fewer than five doors had been cut through at one time or another, each of them in turn shifting the weight of the house above to the smaller and smaller stretches left of the supporting wall.[19] During the 1948 inspections, Winslow's and Reynolds's men had peered behind some plaster on the second floor and discovered one wall stud that had been sawed off several feet above the floor and simply left hanging there.[20]

"It was quite natural and desirable that as the mechanical age came and grew, the building be provided with modern conveniences," Douglas Orr would say, trying to be philosophical about the abuses he'd seen. "But each time such improvements were added, something was subtracted from the structure itself. Doors, openings and chases were cut through and into walls, floor joists were bored, cut and altered with complete abandon, apparently with the idea that there always would be enough structure left to support the loads."[21] By 1948, there was barely enough structure left to support anything.

Complicating the problem were the mansion's interior brick walls, which sat right atop the soft ground. As the years passed and the weight of the house increased, the interior walls had started to sink. No better example of overloading existed than the notorious Taft bathtub. Forged at the J. L. Mott Iron Works in the Bronx (the same foundry that had cast the Capitol dome), the tub, large enough to hold the 332-pound president, was seven feet long and weighed a ton—and that was a *dry* ton, with no water and no Taft.[22] In 1909, plumbers installed the tub in the presidential bathroom, which lay nearly at the exact center of the house—exactly where the interior brick walls, unable to share the burden with the stronger stone walls on the mansion's exterior, were least capable of holding it up.[23]

Again and again, Truman's experts anguished over the damning fact that those brick walls rested on little more than shallow rubble-work bases that barely penetrated the loamy soil.[24] Army Corps engineer Douglas H. Gillette: "The interior walls . . . all lack the wide footings that characterize the . . . exterior walls."[25] Engineer Richard Dougherty: "The interior walls [stood on] inadequate foundations."[26] Architect Douglas Orr: "These walls and piers [were] without adequate or even reasonable footings, bearing on compressible soil."[27] Chief structural engineer Charles W. Barber: "the original builders . . . put *no* foundations under the interior walls."[28]

Had the White House's brick walls been thicker, deeper, and better anchored, they might have been up to meeting the weighty demands of the nineteenth and twentieth centuries. But they were not, and the inevitable had occurred: As the weight of the house exerted itself on the sandy ground beneath it, the center of the mansion sank more than did the perimeter, which stood on, one might say, bigger feet. As the plunge continued, the house began to pull itself apart: Walls cracked, floors buckled, and ceilings worked themselves loose. The White House was a sinkhole.[29]

The story of why the executive mansion nearly collapsed around Harry Truman has one last pair of culprits, their complicity all the more surprising because they were presidents. Earlier in the century, both Theodore Roosevelt and Calvin Coolidge ordered major renovation projects. Although both men intended to improve the White House, they only hastened its demise.

By the time Theodore Roosevelt assumed the presidency in 1901, the White House had suffered from a century's worth of careless remodeling and the accumulation of tons of excess weight. Before long, Roosevelt began noticing the same warning signs that would discomfit Harry Truman six administrations later. Dishes in the china cabinets rattled as the butlers walked past. During receptions, the overloaded floors groaned like the decks of a brigantine, forcing the butlers to wedge temporary supports beneath the beams.[30] Clearly, something had to be done.

Enter Charles Follen McKim, partner in the New York firm of McKim, Mead & White, who found himself testing the White House floors with his own weight on a summer afternoon in 1902. The droopy-mustached McKim was among the most famous and accomplished architects in the United States (he would soon design Manhattan's legendary Pennsylvania Station), but the White House job haunted him. McKim had discovered deep cracks and burned timbers in the walls, and an East Room that was clearly sinking. The project assured prestige, but McKim's career had advanced beyond the point of his needing that. He hesitated. "It was not without many misgivings," the architect later told Roosevelt, "that we accepted at your hands the task of restoring the White House."[31]

McKim had made it clear that "radical steps should be taken to relieve the beams from the weight they have carried too many years," and he assumed he'd be allowed the time and resources to take those steps.[32] Instead, Roosevelt overwhelmed his architect with a litany of cosmetic demands—including redesigning the house's interiors and constructing a new West Wing—and gave him just four months to finish the whole contract. The pressure nearly broke McKim. A few weeks into the hellish job, the architect confided to a friend, "The house is torn to pieces, and all of the trades are working in there at once, for dear life, with night shifts." Time, McKim agonized, "is terribly short."[33]

All McKim could really do was stabilize the house and hope it would buy time. He slammed steel I-beams across the State Floor, brought the wiring up to code, and covered it all back up with ornate plaster and paneling. He had no practical chance to correct the faulty construction on the second floor, much less address the White House's tragic flaw—the lack of foundations below its interior walls.[34] In the end, a dispirited McKim called his own work nothing more than a "nip and tuck."[35]

McKim's triage kept the house quiet for another three administrations, but by 1925 the familiar problems were back, this time on the watch of Calvin Coolidge. Engineers had nosed around the third floor and returned with the news that unless Coolidge replaced it, the roof would cave in. The cause of these latest troubles, the engineers concluded, was none other than Theodore Roosevelt's wife.

During McKim's renovations of 1902, Edith Roosevelt bemoaned the fact that the State Dining Room could fit only sixty guests. (The First Lady thought that 107 was a bit more like it.) Edith complained to Theodore, and Theodore complained to McKim. Ordered to enlarge the dining room, the architect had only one option: tearing out its northern wall and the old wooden staircase behind it.

The pity was that the wall McKim was removing happened to be holding up a good portion of the White House's western side. Because he could now no longer support the second floor from below, McKim decided to *hang* it from above, using a series of steel trusses that he integrated with tie-rods into the third floor's old wooden superstructure.[36] It was a tricky bit of engineering, but it held. And it surely would have held for longer had it not been for the meddling of yet another First Lady. In 1913, Woodrow Wilson's wife Ellen ordered a suite of new guest rooms and bathrooms constructed on the top floor, adding tons' worth of timber, porcelain, and cast iron, elements that McKim had never factored into his truss assembly. Charles McKim might have warned how dangerous the Wilsons' third-floor renovation would be, but he had died in 1909. Before long, his truss began to expire, too.

"We had not lived in the White House very long," First Lady Grace Coolidge recalled, "when we were told that the roof over our heads was unsafe, and that its condition was becoming serious."[37] At first, the parsimonious Coolidge refused to spend the money on repairs. "If [the roof] is as bad as you say," he challenged Public Buildings officer Col. Clarence O. Sherrill, "why doesn't it fall down?"[38]

Sherrill didn't have to answer, because the roof did. A chunk of it broke off and bonked President Coolidge in the head.[39] Cal signed the papers.

On November 19, 1926, the Office of Public Buildings issued a request for bids. The winning architect was one William Adams Delano, who'd created an office in an old milk depot in Manhattan. Work started in March 1927. Twenty years before Delano would add the White House balcony for Truman, he'd replace the roof for Coolidge.

Delano's spatial work was inspired. By simply changing the pitch of the roof and dropping the floor by sixteen inches, he transformed the stooped old garret into a proper third floor without touching the roof-line's profile. Delano expertly multiplied seven bedrooms into fourteen, added seven bathrooms, and even installed a glass-walled "sky parlor."[40] He would build everything out of concrete and steel, which at first blush seemed to solve all the old problems, but a fatal engineering mistake lay hidden in his plans.

Delano's rebuilding of the third floor upset a critical balance that James Hoban had put into place way back in 1792. Hoban had designed such extraordinarily thick stone perimeter walls so that they could carry most of the mansion's weight, laying his slate roof over ten wooden trusses that spanned the entire breadth of the house—outer wall to outer wall. While the interior walls of brick shared the burdens of carrying the White House's first and second floors, Hoban had sensibly spared them from holding up the crushing tonnage of the top one, blanketed by all those stone shingles. But now Delano's design changed that.[41] Delano decided to anchor some of his new roof trusses to those interior brick walls—the ones with no foundations beneath them.[42] This disastrous arrangement shifted the mansion's enormous loads away from the stronger walls and onto the weaker ones. In time, it would crush the family floor below it like a paper cup.[43]

How could an architect of Delano's caliber have made a mistake so serious? Actually, he didn't: Delano was simply following the job specifications issued by the Office of Public Buildings.[44] In other words, the government blew it. Whatever civil servant drew up the specs for the job evidently believed that the White House's old brick interior walls were up to the task of shouldering the top floor's 360,000 pounds of steel and concrete. They weren't.

Once Delano's new construction was in place, no force on earth could save the White House. The doomsday clock ticked inexorably, until time ran finally out in 1948. In the end, the president's army of architects and engineers concluded, it was a century's worth of ignorance, mistakes, and oversights that had conspired to assure the house's doom. But only the eloquence of Harry Truman could sum it all up in a single line: "Coolidge put a concrete 3rd floor on top of Teddy's botched rebuilding," he said.[45]

EIGHT

WANTED: HOME FOR PRESIDENT

Gracious my lord, hard by here is a hovel;/Some friendship will it lend you 'gainst the tempest . . .

—Shakespeare, *King Lear*

With his four Double Wasp Pratt & Whitney engines cranked to 1,500 rpm, pilot Francis Williams tore down Washington National's runway until *The Independence* hit 110 knots and he lifted her nose up into the chilly November sky. Boeing had delivered Harry Truman's new plane about a year earlier. She had elk-hide upholstery on her chairs and fire in her pistons. Though the modified DC-6 cruised at 320 mph, Williams could push her to 360 if he wanted. But on this morning, no speed was fast enough for the president. Harry Truman wanted out of Washington.[1]

Back in the cabin, Truman sat back in his recliner and talked with his men. He was still happy about winning the election, but the long weeks of campaigning had left him drained and brittle. A two-week vacation at Key West lay at the end of the 1,109-nautical-mile flight path on the navigator's chart up front, and Truman could hardly wait to get there.

By now, the president's inner circle knew the dress code expected of them in the Keys—Hawaiian shirts, swimming trunks, pith helmets—and had packed accordingly. Since it was a Sunday, Truman told Captain Williams to drop the bird down in New Bern, North Carolina, so he could go to church. After that, he could break out the bourbon and the playing cards for two weeks and get down to some sinning.

Even as Washington disappeared in the slipstream, the situation with the White House weighed on Truman. The past few months of living in a house that was sinking into the ground had been as rough on his family as it had been on him. He'd been careful not to let his agitation show, "but he was afraid of it falling down," as one observer would later note.[2] The move from the White House would take place in two weeks, on November 21, 1948, the day *The Independence* would return from Florida. As to where they'd all be moving to, Truman had no idea. Back in 1946, he'd joked with Bess that if he could have his way, he'd turn the White House into a museum, "giving the President a rent allowance [so] we could go back to 4701 [Connecticut Avenue.]"[3] But even a president's power, he knew, could never make that happen.

The Independence's 2,400-horsepower engines droned outside the fuselage. The plane would make Key West by 4:00 P.M. Margaret and Bess had decided not to join the flight, but they'd be traveling down in a few more days. Meanwhile, Truman had packed enough of his loud tropical shirts to keep them both annoyed.[4]

—◦═══ ═══◦—

Bess Truman had a good reason for staying behind in Washington: She'd taken it upon herself to hunt down a new home for the family. Her husband had no preferences, save for one: "Wherever we go, it has to be a government house," Truman said.[5] He didn't want any grief from the newspapers for accepting the hospitality of a rich friend who'd put the family up on some estate, thereby leaving the president in a position—however implied—to pay back a favor.

The First Lady and J. B. West climbed into one of the White House fleet cars. Motoring around the city, they checked out each of the government-owned houses that West had put on a list. Much as they'd feared, the options were institutional and depressing. Only one place stood out: Winona, a gorgeous 1873 stone manor house on the campus of the National Institutes of Health in Bethesda, Maryland. But the NIH was busy putting up new buildings (a contractor named McShain was doing the work) and a convoy of dump trucks enveloped the house in noise and dust. Winona lost.

At length, the pair found themselves standing in a familiar place: Blair House, the pale yellow Federal where the assistant usher and Bess Truman had first shaken hands more than three years before. In light of the other options, Blair suddenly looked perfect. It was historic and beautifully furnished. Best of all, it was mere steps from the White House. This was no accident. Eleanor Roosevelt had prodded her husband into acquiring an adjacent guest house after she grew sick of Winston Churchill's smoke-filled, booze-soaked stays. Thanks to Blair's location, Truman could reach the Oval Office by simply trotting across the street. The decision seemed to have been made before anyone said anything: The Truman family would be returning to 1651 Pennsylvania Avenue.

Blair was not without its liabilities. Its plumbing was antediluvian, the cook still shoveled coal into an iron stove, and the place was tiny as a dollhouse. There would be room only for the family and a few servants. Entertaining large parties would be out of the question. J. B. West shook his head over these shortcomings, but Bess Truman could hardly conceal her glee. When West reminded her that a diplomatic attaché from Brazil had already been invited to Washington and was *supposed* to be staying at Blair, she tooted, "We'll just have to put the President of Brazil and the other visitors someplace else!"[6]

The official orders for the move came on November 9, two days after the president left for Key West. Even years later, the back-stairs staff would remember this time with astonishing clarity, and with good reason: The move was pure chaos. Only two weeks to relocate the First Family? The deadline was so tight that Crim put a call in to the Carlton Hotel to reserve several suites for the Trumans just in case.[7]

As far as a master plan for the move, there wasn't one. The butlers grabbed what they thought they'd need and walked it out the front door.[8] Alonzo Fields packed up anything he could lift: china, silver, linens, even kitchen equipment. Housekeepers unhooked the curtains, rehemmed them, and hung them back up across the street. To Lillian Parks, it was an embarrassing spectacle and clearly beneath presidential dignity. She winced at the sight of her fellow maids and butlers "stagger[ing] across Pennsylvania Avenue with a bunch of pots and pans in their arms, or armloads of pillows."[9]

The staff worked quickly, not just because of the tight schedule but also because they feared the White House itself had little time left. "I don't want the house to fall down on the president," said one mover, hefting an oil painting out of the Green Room. "But I don't want it to fall down on me, either."[10]

West had known from the start that Blair House alone was too small for a presidential entourage, so he'd talked Truman into appropriating Lee House, the town house that stood next door and, luckily, also belonged to the government. But while the opulent domicile of Francis Preston Blair could be used as is, Lee House could not. The building had until recently housed offices and a commercial laundry. West conscripted a small army of carpenters, electricians, plumbers, and painters. He sent them in and told them to hurry.

Lee House was also empty as a cavern, but that was fine with West: With Blair House already filled with its original Aubusson rugs, French antiques, and brocaded sofas, the usher would need someplace to put all the furnishings on their way over from the White House. Alonzo Fields recalled that "most of the White House things which we took were put in the Lee House."[11] Soon, with a little substituting and rearranging, West was able to create a surrogate White House. One of the tiny chambers could harbor the treasures of the Green Room, another those from the Red Room. The staff even gave Truman a new study just inside Lee's House's front door, though the space (a former cloakroom) would never fit his grand piano.

Late at night, as the lights around the capital city clicked off one by one, Blair and Lee became twin beacons on Lafayette Park as the painters worked around the clock, the sounds of their brushes slapping the baseboards and stairway spindles filling the house like an otherworldly conversation.

Over at the White House, Crim faced a nightmarish task. The head usher knew that only a fraction of the White House's furnishings would be needed across the street. What remained—every painting, mantel mirror, and vase; every Chippendale chair and Adam secretary; every tapestry and carpet, candelabra and chandelier—had to be carefully removed and put into storage . . . where? That was Crim's problem. And he had just a few days to solve it. The chief usher figured he'd need a miracle. Then the miracle knocked on his door.

His name was Charles T. Haight, and he ran the interior-design department at the B. Altman & Co. department store in New York. Altman's had been recently commissioned to redecorate the Green Room, and the designer had nearly finished the job when the order had come down to vacate the White House. Haight was in a pickle, but he could see that Crim was in a far bigger one. The usher needed not only thousands of square feet of storage space but also men experienced in moving antiques. "Certain of the furnishings required storage in air-conditioned vaults," read a subsequent report on the matter, "and there was a considerable amount of repair required for some of the rugs and draperies."[12]

Fate smiled on the careers of both Mr. Crim and Mr. Haight on this day, for it just so happened that B. Altman & Co. offered all of these services. Of course, Crim knew that the government required competitive bidding for a job of this scale. He also knew that now was no time for paperwork. With the White House groaning and creaking over their heads, the two men made a gentleman's agreement. Haight would tag, crate, ship, catalog, repair, and store everything up in Altman's climate-controlled vaults in New York. And for all of these services, the patriotic Haight charged the U.S. government eighty-five dollars per month—the at-cost rate, with no profit whatever for his employer.[13]

Peter Minuit had scarcely scored a better deal in 1626, when he bought Manhattan for twenty-four dollars' worth of trinkets. But Haight was no fool. He likely sensed that this bit of diplomacy now would put B. Altman in a good position later on, when the government would doubtless need help decorating a rebuilt White House. And if Haight did indeed sense this, he would prove to be entirely correct.

Crim was an usher and not a curator, but he divvied up the house's contents as best he could. A few pieces of furniture would go across the street for the Trumans to use. Altman's would get the large or delicate stuff—draperies, carpets, upholstered pieces. A few hasty calls found temporary homes for everything else. The Library of Congress offered shelf space for books, and the Smithsonian agreed to take what it could. The National Gallery of Art generously offered Crim the use of a storage room, provided Crim put no wool rugs in it. Old canvas paintings, the curators explained, are a delicacy for moths.[14]

As men tagged the items, took inventory, and hefted the furniture out to the moving vans, the executive mansion emptied out. A crumbling White House had been a bad thing, and yet one devoid of the First Family and all of its beautiful interiors was tragic in a different way. Lillian Parks may have been a seamstress and maid, but she had the eye of a writer—and it was she who noticed that, as the moving men did their work, the mansion seemed to be dying.

"The house began to take on a sad look," she recalled. "Every room was empty." Haunted by the changes around her, Parks began to think that perhaps it was time for her to be moving on herself. She told Reynolds to be sure to label everything well, since she might not be around when the time came to move back in. Reynolds smiled and dismissed the idea. "Lillian, you are going to be the first person to come into the new house," he said. So it was that the two made a tiny, informal wager.[15]

Meanwhile, staffers slowly settled into their new positions in a house that was a fraction of the size they were used to. In some ways, life would be easier. Alonzo Fields noted with some relief that the Lee House dining room (where the entertaining would be done) could fit no more than twenty-two people—easy as pie for a butler of his experience. Other surprises were less pleasant. "The quarters where we butlers changed our clothes had been the slave quarters where [they] were locked in at night," he remembered. "The bars were still on the windows."[16]

As Lillian Parks explored Blair House (an expedition that did not take long), she was struck by how different it was from the White House. Mainly, the place was just smaller. But there was something else—a sense of encroachment, almost, from the outside. Then it hit her: While the White House sat deep within a verdant park, surrounded by a high iron fence and watched by sentries posted to a guard booth, this was just an ordinary row house skirted by a sidewalk. "Blair House was so close to the street, that I could see it right out the window," she said. It was true: Anyone could just walk up the front steps, open the door, and be inside.[17]

As the workmen upstairs relieved the White House of every stick of furniture, Winslow and Reynolds and their men stayed busy, having worked their way down to the ground floor, where they were ripping the plaster off the interior walls and brick piers flanking the mansion's axial corridor. If things had not looked good upstairs, they were especially bad down here. One of the walls was literally listing toward the center of the building as its base slowly disappeared into the soft earth below.[18]

Alarming as this was for the government engineers and architects, they'd at least earned the right to feel some sense of accomplishment. By impressing the dark facts on Truman, they had finally compelled him to vacate the mansion—and probably saved his life in the process. At the same time, the work of 1948 had been only diagnostic. To determine that a house is unsafe is one thing; figuring out what to actually *do* with it is another thing altogether. Their work had really only just begun.

Winslow's last public statement regarding the White House on November 7 had been bold but unspecific: He'd stressed that "extensive repairs must be made," and "started at the earliest possible date."[19] But now that the house lay empty and stripped like an etherized patient on an operating table, what exactly was Winslow to do?

The architect had three options sitting on his desk. The first had arrived in early November from Spencer, White & Prentis. Charles Spencer wanted to double the strength of the mansion's interior walls and proposed inserting needle beams. These were I-beams that would penetrate the walls laterally and then be attached to a solid anchorage in new foundations poured on either side of the wall.[20]

The second suggestion had arrived on November 17 in a letter from Charles Barber, structural engineering chief with the Public Buildings Service. Barber, too, emphasized the need to strengthen the house's interior walls, but he wanted to drive supporting columns deep into the ground and then fuse the walls to them.[21]

In case neither of these plans won Winslow's favor, Spencer had advanced another scheme—one he seemed to like better anyway. "We feel," he wrote, "[that] more positive results will be accomplished by extending the foundations downward to a superior material below."[22]

The firm had discovered this material after sinking its test pits near the house's foundations. It was a stratum of gravel thick and stable enough to carry all the mansion's weight. The catch was that this layer sat another twenty feet below the bottom of the house.

Thus dig a 20-foot-deep hole beneath a sandstone mansion that's already 168 feet long and 55 feet high, pour a new concrete foundation down there while you balance the house above, then cement the whole thing together. That was what the structural engineer from New York was proposing.

It was strong medicine, but all of the proposed solutions were. What's more, none of the plans bothered to mention something that nobody wanted to think about: that saving this doomed, iconic house—assuming it could be saved—would probably mean gutting it. Not only did the interior brick walls lack foundations; Barber's tests showed that the bricks themselves had "very little strength" left, maybe 40 percent of what masonry should offer. As for the timber, sixty years of sawing and gouging and boring had pretty much destroyed it.[23] Regardless of what sort of new foundations the men opted for, it was looking increasingly likely that the inside of the house would have to be torn out.

For now, Winslow was off the hook. The final decision of what to do with the house would be a fiscal as much as an architectural one. Money for work on this scale would have to come from Congress, and Congress was in recess until January 3, 1949. Meanwhile, Winslow's and Reynolds's men busied themselves knocking around the walls on the ground floor. If either man privately favored the less intrusive solutions, his hopes were fading fast.

Then, just after Christmas, hope died completely. Engineers working on the ground floor discovered cracks in the mansion's outer walls—the thick ones of solid stone previously believed to be impervious.[24] The finding transformed the crumbling White House from a serious problem into a catastrophe. It meant that *none* of the structure could be trusted now. All of it was sinking. All of it was in danger of collapse. "Conditions appear to be far more serious than originally expected," read the memo that went out to the president on December 27, 1948. The document went on to explain that the estimated cost of repairing the White House had just jumped from one million to four million dollars, that new foundations would be needed for the entire mansion, and that "everything below the third floor . . . must be removed."[25]

Winslow and Reynolds broke the news to the press two days later.

"We have been opening up White House walls and floors, and we do not like what we have found," Reynolds told the reporters. The previous press conference in early November, at which it was announced that the mansion would be closed, had held bad news aplenty, but now every problem is "quite beyond what we expected," the public buildings chief said. "The White House really is in a terrible fix."[26] As usual, the papers found a way to add a zinger to the copy. The following morning, the *New York Times* ran the headline PRESIDENTS' HOME CALLED A WRECK.

As the wind whipped through the bare branches on the front lawn, Lillian Parks stepped into the drafty, echoing White House. She had known the place perhaps better than any staffer, for she had walked its plush carpets even as a little girl, back in the days when her mother had been a White House seamstress, as she herself now was. But Parks had never imagined she'd see the great house looking like this. "I have never forgotten," she would recall years later, "how the White House looked stripped of everything. I guess I am the only person who will carry this picture in my mind always."[27]

She'd taken her life in her hands merely by walking in the front door, but she could not stay away. Perhaps, in a sense, she'd come to say good-bye. The old place was empty now. Its heavy tasseled draperies and festive swags, the rugs and hallway runners, the mahogany chairs and inlaid-marble tables and bookcases heavy with leather-spined volumes—all had been taken down or taken up, wrapped and rolled, and driven away. Gone were the electric lights, from the tiny table lamps to the bronze sconces to the great tent-and-bowl chandeliers. The sideboards had vanished from their stations against the walls, as had the great beveled mirrors over the mantelpieces. Missing were the oils of glowering presidents and the sylvan landscapes reposing inside heavy gilt frames. The grand pianos had been wrapped in tarpaulins and trundled off. Gone were the napkins, silverware, and gravy boats; gone were the pots and pans, the candlesticks and serving tongs. There were no more mantel clocks or potted palms or cut-crystal bowls that had burst with the fat yellow heads of Mrs. Truman's Talisman roses. Everything—every sign that people had once treated this warren of rooms and corridors as a home—was gone.

It was nearly too painful to look at now, even though Parks did look. She marveled at how the place could be so completely empty, until she noticed that one room had been used as a trash dump.[28] Such disrespect, she thought.

Parks remembered the first days of the move, weeks before. Clearing off the high, dusty shelves of the linen room, she'd discovered a flag that turned out to be from the Lincoln administration. Usher Crim had it sent to the museum in Springfield, Illinois, with the White House's compliments.[29] It would not be like Parks to simply take a souvenir for herself, and yet she had one. Just before Mrs. Truman left to join her husband in Florida, she'd donned a pair of old gloves and set up a Christmas giveaway table, heaped with treasures that she'd dug out of the closets. Bess Truman gave Lillian a little silver evening bag. Already, Parks treasured it.[30]

The seamstress had been climbing the stairs and now she was all the way up on the third floor. In its center, the workmen had left another pile of garbage. Parks sat down on top of the refuse. When her tears landed on it, she decided that she did not care.[31]

NINE

"THE PEOPLE WANT A
NEW BUILDING"

At issue is the question of whether the building is to be rebuilt
inside while keeping the historic walls, or completely razed.
—*Washington Post*, April 29, 1949

*A*s the year 1949 dawned over the United States, RCA introduced the 45 rpm record, snow fell in Los Angeles, and the
inaugural parade of Harry S. Truman—the first one ever to be
broadcast on television—did not return its victor to the White House.
"That old wreck is vacant now," Truman said.[1] Ever since the cold-
water talk that Reynolds and Winslow had delivered four days after
Christmas, the administration had abandoned all pretense of under-
playing the severity of the White House's condition, and the public felt

the full blow of the truth. As the *Washington Post* would tell its readers
that January, "The White House may collapse at any time."[2]

After the swearing-in ceremony, Truman, resplendent in his silk
top hat and striped trousers, stepped into "4X"—the Secret Service's
code name for the president's 6,163-pound Lincoln Cosmopolitan—
and joined the inaugural parade. Though he'd done an impromptu jig
when the brass band played "I'm Just Wild About Harry," there would
be no dancing at Blair House that night. The big bash would have to be
held at the National Gallery of Art, just down the hall from the room
holding hundreds of pieces of the White House furniture.

For her part, Bess Truman was all too happy to let the National Gallery and the caterers deal with the tuxedoed hordes; she would serve
finger sandwiches for a smattering of family and friends in Blair House's
tiny dining room. "Make it simple," she told J. B. West, though she
didn't have to. Bess Truman never wanted things any other way.[3]

The next general meeting of the committee of engineers and architects
appeared on the official calendar for January 14, but Lorenzo Winslow
had already been busy at his drafting table for weeks. He was working
on sketches for a fully and elaborately renovated White House, even
though Congress had not yet decided what to do with the place. Harry
Truman didn't care. As William Adams Delano had learned with the
balcony, the president already knew exactly what he wanted—and
Truman not only wanted to save the White House; he intended to involve himself in every step of the process.[4]

On January 11, 1949, three days before the committee's meeting,
Lorenzo Winslow slipped into the Oval Office a few minutes after
noon, accompanied by Public Buildings Commissioner Reynolds, usher
Crim, and consulting architect Edward F. Neild. The gathering was officially off the record. But Winslow had begun keeping a daily journal
in a little pocket pad. "Met with H.S.T. and started on the report of
W.H. condition, etc.," Winslow penciled. "Gave H.S.T. drawing of the
new stair design. O.K."[5]

In other words, Truman was already working hand in glove with
Winslow on the renovation plans—right down to details like the stairs.
In the coming weeks, Winslow would make repeated notations in his
journal that Truman had "approved" various drawings, even though
Truman wasn't officially in charge of the project.[6]

It's tempting to conclude that the president was playing puppeteer here, and perhaps he was. But Truman was nothing if not a realist. It was obvious that saving the White House would require an enormous amount of work—work that Congress would have to fund. Getting a renovation plan as elaborate as Winslow's over on the Hill would require all of the government architects and engineers to stay in lockstep, and a president's influence was good at that kind of thing. At its January fourteenth meeting, the committee met, rubber-stamped Winslow's plans, then snapped the ball to Reynolds to prepare the official report and cost estimate. Congress had all the paperwork by February 8. Team Truman had its plays down.

Reynolds's report made for quite a read. Declaring the mansion to be "unsafe" and "grossly inadequate," the buildings commissioner made it plain that the only options left were the drastic kind. To keep the mansion's historic facade standing, the report stated, the house's existing foundations would have to be driven down another twenty feet until they found surer footing on gravel. Meanwhile, everything inside the house—brick walls, timber floors, windows and doors, plaster and plumbing—would have to be ripped out. In their place would rise a skeleton of steel anchored to deep concrete piers. "The architectural rehabilitation," Reynolds's report read, "will, to all intents and purposes, start from the naked exterior walls."[7] Another way of putting it: This would be a gut job.

That the famous white walls would survive was the best that the house's advocates could hope for. While later critics of the effort would condemn it as a poor effort at conservation, in early 1949 this plan *was* conservation. To the thinking of the times, "saving" an old building meant keeping its facade, nothing more.[8] Of course, there were plenty of fittings left inside the White House that were both beautiful and historic. This material existed in a kind of limbo, however. If Lorenzo Winslow cared enough to pry loose and save any of that stuff, well, he was welcome to do so. But the other officials washed their hands of it. Building the new infrastructure would be hard enough.

It would be costly, too. Though Reynolds had penned his report and estimate for the Congress, it would fall to the president to make the formal request for the money. This he did on February 16, 1949. Two months shy of a year earlier, Congress had grudgingly parted with fifty thousand to pay for an investigation of the mansion's creaks and groans. Now it would learn that fixing the causes of those creaks and groans would cost no less than $5.4 million.[9]

Realizing that he'd be picking a political dogfight by proposing to supervise the project himself, Truman sent a letter to Congress on

March 25, encouraging the legislators to create a special commission to do it. "The people of this country expect this major undertaking to be accomplished by the best qualified architects, engineers and craftsmen available," he wrote.[10] For the president—who could always exert his influence behind the scenes—it was a smart tactical move. Politics was what Truman knew best.

In response, Congress did what *it* knew best: It scheduled a hearing.

At first, the odds looked good for the plan. On March 23, the *New York Times* reported that Truman's $5.4 million plea had been "favorably reported to the floor" by the Senate Appropriations Committee and that "reconstruction . . . is one step nearer to the excavation stage."[11] But that step went right over the edge of a cliff in the House, which routed Truman's request to its Committee on Public Works. Though the committee's hearing on March 30 was intended solely to consider a bill "to provide for a commission on renovation of the Executive Mansion," the proceedings quickly devolved into a free-for-all over whether renovating the White House was even a good idea.

The trouble came from George Anthony Dondero, a sixty-five-year-old Michigan Republican who'd worked out some figures and determined that the renovation would cost five dollars per cubic foot. That would put the price of fixing up the East Room alone at $440,000. "The thought has occurred to me," Dondero said, "would it be cheaper to spend a lesser sum of money on preserving the building and build a modern structure or White House for the President . . . and keep that one as a museum?"[12]

Two other members moved quickly to keep the proceedings from skidding into this ditch. Representative J. Harry McGregor pointed out that he'd already raised the idea of building a new house with the president. "In no uncertain terms," McGregor said, Truman "was in favor of remodeling the same one regardless of cost." Representative Morgan M. Moulder pressed further: "It should actually be renovated as proposed and actually occupied by the President in order to preserve the spirit that the people expect to see when they see the White House."[13]

Dondero surrendered. But the demon seed of an idea had been planted—and soon it would start to grow.

Clarence Cannon was a character straight out of a Dick Tracy comic. Short and wrinkled, perennially clad in a black suit, the seventy-year-old conservative Democrat tottered about with thick horn-rims balanced atop a bulbous nose. Cannon could easily have been a figure of ridicule had every legislator on Capitol Hill not been so scared of him. As chairman of the all-powerful House Appropriations Committee, Cannon determined the way Congress spent the taxpayers' money, and his consuming passion was assuring that as little of it was spent as possible.[14] To advance his agenda, Cannon was known to scream, wave his arms, and, when necessary, punch adversaries in the mouth.[15] Little wonder that when spotted eating a sandwich in a cafeteria near the Capitol, Clarence Cannon was invariably dining alone. When the little budget hawk caught wind that Harry Truman's renovation was going to cost over five million dollars, he was having none of it.

On April 15, 1949, Cannon announced to the press that the government should spare itself the expense and trouble and just bulldoze the White House instead.[16] Cannon proclaimed the White House's walls were "fragile as an egg shell" and would crumble in fifty years no matter what was done, though he never revealed the source of this intelligence.[17] An April nineteenth statement from the White House engineers that the exterior walls were "in perfect shape" did nothing to quiet him.[18] Tear the place down, Cannon insisted, and build a cheaper one. "The people want a new building," Cannon wrote, and he told Truman this himself.[19]

Had Cannon not held the congressional purse strings, his prognostications about architecture would likely have been laughed at. But when the *Washington Post* actually published an editorial in favor of razing the White House ("if the old walls are likely to crumble," the paper said, "there is no valid reason for delaying the inevitable work of demolition"), Truman realized that Cannon was winning converts.[20]

Down at Blair House, the president began to worry. "I'll do anything in my power to keep them from tearing down the White House," he told J. B. West, who himself could not fathom a modern White House. It would, the usher thought, "become just another brand-new office building."[21]

What about the idea of moving the chief executive elsewhere and turning the White House into a museum? While demoting the home of thirty-two presidents to an unoccupied display for tourists would have at least saved the building from the wrecking ball, more philosophically inclined legislators demurred. "It is my opinion," said Missouri representative Morgan Moulder, "such an idea would convert the White House into a dead, ghostly museum of the past."[22]

Yet as the days passed and Congress failed to move on the issue, it became clear that the White House needed a few more prominent friends to speak out. From her cottage in the upstate New York town of Hyde Park, one old friend did. On May 18, 1949, via her syndicated newspaper column "My Day," Eleanor Roosevelt put herself squarely behind the White House's old sandstone walls. "I feel strongly that, as far as it is humanly possible, the outer shell should be preserved," FDR's widow wrote. "No new design or new house could possibly have the historic interest of the old one." Be careful, Mrs. Roosevelt cautioned the Congress; a nation's history "should not be lightly thrown away."[23]

But it was not history that conservatives in Congress believed they might be throwing away; it was money, and the Truman/Winslow/Reynolds plan was going to cost plenty of that. To his credit, the president never denied the point. "It will be no small task to renovate and modernize the structure," Truman wrote to Congress, adding, "It perhaps would be more economical from a purely financial standpoint to raze the building and to rebuilt [sic] completely. In so doing, however, there would be destroyed a building of tremendous historical significance in the growth of the Nation."[24]

While officials skirmished on Capitol Hill, an unlikely crusader for the White House was eyeing the proceedings from down the Mall. Until now, other than advising her husband, Bess Truman had kept herself out of the political fray. Mrs. Truman's opinion was that she *had* no opinion. But as she listened to the rhetoric of those who would actually pull down the house that George Washington had built, she found that she could not just sit with her knitting. Bess Truman didn't like living in the White House, but that didn't mean she wanted it destroyed.

According to Margaret Truman, her mother believed that "no matter how thoroughly the old building might have to be gutted, some of it should be preserved."[25] Like millions of Americans, Bess Truman had witnessed how Eleanor Roosevelt had turned the position of First Lady into a political platform of sweeping visibility and influence. Unlike them, however, she had those tools now arrayed before her. It was simply a matter of picking them up and using them.

She acted behind the scenes at first, placing calls to the wives of powerful senators and congressmen—even firebrand fiscal conservatives like Ohio senator Robert Taft ("Mr. Republican," as he was known). "Browbeating was not her style," Mrs. Taft remembered, having received one of Mrs. Truman's calls, "but she let it be known that the building had to be saved at all costs."[26]

Once she reached the bottom of her call list, Bess donned her public attire and marched up to Capitol Hill herself. An uncharitable journalist had once written that, with her little black hat pushed too far onto her forehead, Mrs. Truman resembled "a little Missouri sidewheeler going full steam ahead."[27] But now, navigating the corridors of power, she was a battleship. Years of reading the *Congressional Record* had taught her which legislators wielded the most influence. She cornered them and argued her case as well as a lobbyist from a white-shoe firm. As a final salvo, the First Lady spoke to the media—a thing she'd refused to do until now—telling the broadsheets that "the White House walls should be kept intact as they now stand."[28]

"Most people think it was only Harry who had a deep sense of history," Treasury Secretary John Snyder later recalled. "It was also Bess. She took great pride in time-honored American institutions. Especially the White House. The country should be eternally grateful to her for the persuasive part she played in keeping it in one piece."[29]

Perhaps some of what motivated Bess Truman to launch her campaign to save the White House was her loneliness at Blair House. At the same time the debate over the executive mansion was heating up in Congress, Margaret moved away to New York. Metropolitan Opera soprano Helen Traubel had agreed to mentor her, and Margaret could not pass up the opportunity. Bess surrendered Reathel Odum—her irreplaceable buffer during all those dreadful teas in the Blue Room—to room with Margaret in Manhattan. "Now that we're going to be living a quiet life in Blair House," the First Lady told J. B. West, "I can manage without her."[30] It almost felt like the truth.

Slowly, the president and his wife adjusted. Bess didn't much care for the newfangled contraption called the television, which had recently shown its ugly face in the house. She read Westerns instead. Frequent spikes in her blood pressure would force her to lie on the couch until her heart calmed itself. When Truman wasn't toiling away at a stack of documents, he and Bess would have lunch in the garden. In keeping with Truman tradition, the presidential lunch was seldom fancier than fish salad and potato chips.[31]

The privacy made possible by Margaret's absence also allowed the president and his wife—now ages sixty-five and sixty-four, respectively—to reignite the romance of their youth. Often, they'd ask the maids to stay downstairs, and then the door to the president's bedroom would click shut. The staff began to refer to the president and Mrs. Truman as the "lovebirds."[32] It was a nickname they would live up to before the year was out. One morning, the First Lady took West aside and asked if one of the handymen could repair the president's bed. "Two of the slats broke during the night," a blushing Mrs. Truman explained.[33] Though handyman Traphes Bryant later deadpanned that the broken slats "couldn't have happened from lying there like a log,"[34] J. B. West effortlessly diffused Bess Truman's embarrassment by faulting the furniture. "It's an old antique bed anyway," he reassured her. Well, of *course* that must have been it.

This was not the first time that Bess Truman would regard J. B. West as the worker of small but significant miracles. The usher was the very soul of discretion. Perhaps this was because the unfortunate West was the keeper of his own secrets, too. Though he was married and had two daughters, West was a gay man. Every day of his life, the usher lived with the knowledge that if the Secret Service chanced to discover this part of his life, it would lead to his immediate dismissal.[35]

Lorenzo Winslow had also come to understand that he could not stand passively by while the White House's future hung in the balance. Combining his professional credentials and his affable manner, Winslow fashioned himself as a kind of architectural impresario, taking men of influence on house-of-horrors tours of the collapsing mansion. Winslow was alone in appreciating that the best advocate for the White House's preservation might just be the White House itself.

Winslow led the D.C. chapter of the American Institute of Architects through the place first. Then he took a group of sixteen reporters. When photographers wanted to come along to record the damage, Winslow took them, too.[36] Despite the very real dangers of being inside the house, the architect did not rush these excursions. Instead, he took his time (up to two hours) pointing out the crumbling bricks and sagging beams, explaining what was wrong and why it would cost nearly five million dollars to make it right.

A particular highlight of the tour was those spots where negligent carpenters had long ago left heaps of sawdust and wood shavings be-

tween the plaster walls, piled mere inches below the frayed electric
wiring—a fire hazard so horrifying that some insurance adjustors (yes,
they came along for the tours, too) rewrote their building standards
right then and there.[37]

As a finale, Winslow led his charges down to the ground floor and
pointed out the spot where the house *should* have had a foundation but
did not have one.[38] The mere sight of the once-proud mansion in its
decrepitude proved to be deeply affecting for many visitors, but not
always in a good way. By far the most influential of these were members
of the House Appropriations Committee itself. Representative Louis
C. Rabaut was among that group on the day of its visit. As Winslow led the congressmen to a spot where the plaster had been chipped
away to reveal the mansion's exterior walls, the sixty-two-year-old
Detroit attorney picked off a chunk of the sandstone. When he pinched
it between his fingers, it disintegrated in his hand.[39]

For much of that spring of 1949, deadlock prevailed. A House-Senate
conference committee postured over whether the house should be
saved or, as the *Washington Post* wrote, "completely razed and rebuilt."[40]
Funding was still an issue, too. After the Senate approved the $5.4
million in funding that Truman had requested, it kicked that ball back
over to the House. The lower chamber wasn't especially good at getting
anything accomplished, but its floor show was usually pretty good, and
June 2, 1949, was curtain time.

On that Thursday, the House Appropriations Committee invited
White House architect Lorenzo Winslow and the PBA's chief structural engineer, Charles Barber, up to the Capitol to have them defend
their complicated plan to save the house's outer walls. During the preceding weeks, Clarence Cannon had stood tirelessly atop his soapbox,
most recently proclaiming that knocking down the White House
would save taxpayers $700,000.[41] Well, now they would see. At the
long baize-covered table in the hearing room, Winslow and Barber took
their seats.

It was painful from the start. The congressmen were still confused
over how the Public Buildings Administration proposed to save the
house's facade, and so Winslow explained the plan again. Incredibly,
Clarence Cannon himself was absent from the hearing room that day,
but his colleagues were cantankerous in his place. That the legislators
knew essentially nothing about architecture or engineering did not

stop them from preaching to Winslow and Barber as though they were schoolboys. After grousing, "I think it is a mistake to do this patch job on such an enormous scale," Michigan representative Louis C. Rabaut warned that "when you start going under all those old walls, you will have a ticklish job"—as though the engineers had never considered that.[42]

Having recently joined one of Lorenzo Winslow's White House tours, Rabaut remembered how easy it had been to grind the sandstone to dust in his own hand. That appeared to be Rabaut's true jeremiad: He simply didn't think the walls were worth saving. In fact, Rabaut dismissed the mansion's exterior—one it had taken Scottish stonemasons four years to carve, one George Washington himself had approved—as "just . . . some sandstone that formed a wall and some windows."[43]

When Frank B. Keefe took his turn, the Wisconsin representative railed against the proposal to save the White House's third floor. In his report, Reynolds had recommended keeping the 1927 addition because it was already made of steel and concrete. Keefe, however, referred to it as an "antiquated, architectural abortion."[44] The congressman could also not get his arms around the concept of propping up the outer walls while workmen dug an enormous pit beneath them. And he was especially agitated, as the entire committee was, about the $5.4 million cost of the project—a number that Cannon assured the *Washington Post* would really turn out to be $10 million.[45]

Winslow had heard enough. Fortunately, he was able to use his time at the microphone to give the lie to most of Cannon's agitprop. Knowing that Cannon had referred to the mansion's outer walls as eggshells, Winslow testified that "the exterior walls will last as long as the steel in the building will last."[46] Winslow also explained why the purportedly less expensive alternatives on the table were no better than the PBA's plan, and, in fact, were probably worse. Preserving the White House as a museum would cost $3.5 million on its own—hardly pocket change—but would get the country no closer to a habitable home for its president. What about the idea of taking apart the outer walls, erecting the new interior, then remortaring the original blocks back in place—wouldn't that save money? No, Winslow said. The stone sure to be damaged in the disassembly would *add* $200,000 to the cost.

The fact of the matter was that the House Appropriations Committee wanted a cheap and easy way out of the problem, and there simply wasn't one. The exchange between Winslow and Representative Richard B. Wigglesworth of Massachusetts best illustrated the Hobson's choice before the committee.

MR. WIGGLESWORTH: Do I understand from what you have said, that in your opinion, if you took down temporarily the present outside walls and replaced them it would cost as much or more than the plan now recommended by Mr. Reynolds?
MR. WINSLOW: I fully believe so.[47]

And that was the end of it. While the U.S. Senate had no qualms about voting the full $5.4 million to renovate the White House, the House of Representatives had held two separate committee hearings, commenced a battle royal in the press, deadlocked on two deficiency supply bills, wasted sixty-four days of time, and finally given up.[48]

The special commission that Truman had recommended to administer the White House's fate—whatever it might turn out to be—had come into existence just a few weeks earlier. Now, as the *Washington Post* put it, the House of Representatives "tossed the decision of how the White House should be repaired into [its] lap."[49]

TEN

THE VERDICT

These old buildings do not belong to us only. They have belonged to our forefathers, and they will belong to our descendants. They are not in any sense our property, to do as we like with. We are only trustees for those that come after us.

—William Morris

The fate of the most famous house in the United States now rested with six men, known collectively as the Commission on the Renovation of the Executive Mansion. This was the group that Truman had recommended Congress create back in March and, in a refreshing departure from its usual recalcitrance, Congress had agreed—probably because it would be a power-sharing exercise. Two of the commission's members were to be chosen by the Senate, two by the House, and two by the president. The commission would possess enormous power; in every legal sense, it would *be* the federal government.[1] To it would fall complete responsibility for the White House and the seventeen acres on which it stood—a parcel valued at sixty million dollars at the time, but in reality priceless. "As the symbol of democracy," said *Holiday* magazine, "it is the most important piece of property on earth."[2]

Truman had submitted his two delegates right away: Douglas Orr and Richard Dougherty, the two men who'd answered his mysterious letter more than a year earlier to come and investigate the strange noises at the executive mansion. As private citizens, Orr and Dougherty would receive fifty dollars a day to work for Uncle Sam. The Senate sent down two old hands: Republican Edward Martin, former governor of Pennsylvania, and Kenneth Douglas McKellar, an eighty-year-old Tennessee Democrat who'd used some creative accounting during the war to keep the Manhattan Project funded. Despite McKellar's self-described "pow'ful tempuh," neither senator was likely to cause the architects and engineers much grief.[3]

The delegates from the House were a different story. The lower chamber sent over Representatives Rabaut and Keefe—the two men who'd just assailed the PBA's renovation plan during the Appropriations Committee hearing. Keefe, a former schoolteacher, was the legislator who'd likened the White House's top floor to an abortion. Democrat Louis C. Rabaut, a builder of suburban subdivisions outside of Detroit, was in favor of putting up a new White House.[4] In fairness, Rabaut had never advocated demolishing the mansion as Clarence Cannon had. But he did believe that "we would get into it quicker than we would if we try to save the old building."[5]

Assembled behind the commission was a large group of consulting engineers and architects who, though they lacked a vote in the proceedings, threw around the weight of their enormous reputations. William Adams Delano was part of this group. So was Ernest Howard, who'd built no fewer than twelve bridges across the Mississippi, and Emil H. Praeger, whose design for floating concrete breakwaters had enabled the Allied invasion of Normandy. If the senators and congressmen who sat on the commission did not happen to know much about architecture or engineering, their consultants certainly did.

Despite its commanding name, the Commission on the Renovation of the Executive Mansion got off to a clumsy start. Its first meeting, on June 3, 1949, was an informal gathering, whose accomplishments, if any, remain a mystery because there was as yet no stenographer to take the minutes.[6] What is known is that the men gathered in Truman's own Cabinet Room, where the president just happened to stop by to share his personal views on the project.

Fortunately, stenographers Helen Ganss and Bernice Tidwell were on hand to keep the minutes at the June fifteenth meeting, but little got done then, either. The men voted in Senator McKellar as chairman and Orr as vice chair, then spent the balance of their time fretting over their lack of facilities. Ironically, the commission set up to give the president of the United States a home was, itself, homeless. Until suitable quarters could be found, McKellar volunteered his own office in the Senate Office Building on Constitution Avenue, near Union Station. There, the men sat one and a half miles away from the mansion they were supposed to be looking at.

The sum total of accomplishments at the commission's second official meeting, on June 20, was an agreement on a regular time for future meetings (Tuesdays at 10:00 A.M.) and to have an official group photograph taken. Not only did the men believe a photo was a sensible use of their time; they picked as their backdrop the White House—the building that they possessed full legal authority to destroy. Rabaut took a philosophical view: "Whatever happens to the White House," he said, "we will have that for the background."[7]

The men picked a spot just below the South Portico, where President Truman joined them, dapper in a double-breasted summer suit, bow tie, and two-tone oxfords. Dougherty towered over the group like a sequoia. Orr crinkled his brow against the sunlight and smiled. The image suggests old college chums at a reunion; there's not a whiff of tension to the photo, no suggestion that the fate of the house behind them hung in the balance.[8]

In a sense, the White House's future was actually in the hands of two different groups. While the commissioners had the official power, Winslow and the Public Buildings Administration men who worked behind the scenes held nearly as much sway, not least because Winslow enjoyed entrée to the Oval Office.

This chummy little world of professional men operated largely behind the scenes of the official commission meetings, and Winslow's diary affords glimpses of it.[9] On the night of Wednesday, July 6, while the fate of the mansion still hung in the balance, Winslow bundled up his drawings and caught the train for New York. He slept on the Pullman and, after a quick breakfast at Grand Central Terminal, headed for Dougherty's office at 230 Park Avenue. There, nearly all of the men tapped to work on the White House thus far—the Public Buildings Administration engineers and foundation-digging wizard Charles

Spencer among them—convened in private. High up in the opulent skyscraper, the men reviewed Winslow's drawings again, solidifying their agreement that the mansion's outer walls should be kept at all costs.

After lunch at the Biltmore Hotel, Winslow headed down to Thirty-eighth Street to seek the additional benediction of architect William Adams Delano. Satisfied that all the professional men were of a single mind about the house's preservation, Winslow hopped the afternoon train back to Washington. "Home for dinner," he penciled in his neat, compact handwriting.

The commission could debate all that it wanted, but so far as the architects and engineers were concerned, the preservation plan drawn up by Winslow, adopted by the Public Buildings Administration, and backed by Truman was the only one that really existed.

As the summer wore on, the commission realized that, whatever course of action it decided on, the actual work would require a supervisor— not another congressman or even another architect, but an experienced project manager who could keep the shovels digging and the concrete pouring. The commission found that man in Maj. Gen. Glen Edgerton.

Born in the Kansas town of Parkerville in 1887, Edgerton possessed a remarkable intellect. He was a college student by the time he turned thirteen, earned a B.A. degree in engineering, then headed off to West Point. Compact in stature but polite and likable, Edgerton survived the wrath of the upperclassmen by tutoring the duller ones—one of whom was a youth by the name of George S. Patton.[10] Edgerton left West Point in 1908, graduating first in his class.

From that point until his appointment to the White House job, Edgerton lived the life of a swashbuckling corpsman all over the world— usually in its most exotic and inhospitable corners, where he smoked cigars and demonstrated a general attitude of fearlessness. Edgerton's exploits included plotting the Panama Canal route through the jungle, ramrodding the Alaska Highway through the Yukon, chasing Pancho Villa through Mexico, and directing postwar relief efforts in China. Edgerton was a born leader. As his son would later write, while the general's friends called him by his nickname, "Spec," most people—his son included—knew him only as "yes, sir."[11]

In 1949, Edgerton had just retired from the army at the mandatory

age of sixty-two. But instead of kicking back, he opened up a consult-
ing practice and immediately took a job in the Kingdom of Iraq. Edger-
ton was happily engaged in diverting the courses of the Tigris and
Euphrates when word reached him of a job offer back in Washington.
Would he be interested in supervising work on the White House?
Edgerton accepted immediately and arrived in the capital on July 22.
When the commission held its next meeting six days later, the general
was at the head of the table.[12]

Edgerton had arrived just in time. Both the public and the president
were feeling antsy that this much-vaunted commission, now on the
eve of its fifth meeting, had yet to decide on the fate of the mansion.

The *New York Times* had already pointed out on July 1 that the
White House had been vacant for seven months already, while the
president lived "in exile in Blair House."[13] The full appropriation of
$5.4 million had also, finally, come through the Congress. Truman had
signed the measure and placed the cash into the commission's hands.[14]
It was time to figure out what to do.

For weeks, the commission had been weighing the merits of three
options. The first was the original Winslow/Reynolds plan: Retain the
outer walls, take the foundation down twenty feet, and raise a steel
frame within. The second course involved the same steps for the foundation and interior, but it called for dismantling the outer walls while
the work went on, then reassembling the stone blocks. Finally, there
was option three, the doomsday button: "Razing the complete building
and erecting a new replica of the existing building," as the commission
phrased it.[15]

Some observers believed that the commission's path was all but pre-
ordained. In mid-June, the *Washington Post* had reported that the commission "is believed to be weighted in favor of preserving the White
House in its present form"—likely because of Truman's influence.[16]
But the other factor nudging the commission toward the preservation
plan was a logistical one. If the men voted to knock the house down,
Winslow would have to start drawing all over again, and that would set
the project back ten months.

Nevertheless, the commissioners were not figureheads. They really
did debate what to do with the White House, and they believed that
"all of these three methods are feasible."[17] In the unpublished memoirs

he wrote later in his life, commission chairman Kenneth McKellar revealed that, for a time, the group gave serious consideration to building "a white marble palace" for the president somewhere in the suburbs of Maryland.[18] Schemes like that aside, the commission really had just one big decision to make: whether to save the White House's outer walls or destroy them forever.

For architect Douglas Orr, the mere possibility that the White House might be brought to the ground frightened him so much that he wrote secretly to William Adams Delano. The famous architect who'd built the Truman balcony responded right away. "I feel so strongly on this matter that I cannot forbear writing you this letter," Delano told Orr. Using his reputation to try to save the house, Delano furnished Orr with a diktat—one that Orr immediately put into the commission's record. Delano warned that he would not abide the removal of a single stone from the White House facade—nor, he said, would the country. "The moment demolition of the exterior walls was begun," Delano declared, "I believe there would be a howl from the American people which could be heard from afar. There is too much sentiment connected with this building in the mind of the American public."[19]

It all came to head at the August 2, 1949, meeting. McKellar's "tempuh" was starting to show; he wanted to announce a decision. One by one, the six commissioners submitted their votes. Richard Dougherty read the verdict: "It is the considered conclusion of the Commission that is perfectly feasible and economical, and much more in keeping with the retention of what one writer characterized as the 'symbolic shrine of American Democracy' if the old walls were to be retained."[20]

And there it was: The original White House would remain standing.

The vote had been nearly unanimous; Rabaut alone dissented. "I have repeatedly said that I oppose the retention of the old walls," the congressman said, "but rather favor reconstruction of the White House from the ground up—a new building."[21] Rabaut could take some pride in standing by his convictions, but a single nay wasn't going to change anything. Indeed, even Congressman Keefe, no friend of the renovation plan initially, had experienced a surprising change of heart. "I have endeavored to sample the attitude of the American people to which this historic building belongs," Keefe told his colleagues. "I may say that in the hundreds of letters received, with few exceptions, the people of this country have indicated a clear desire to retain the exterior of this building."[22]

The commission's decision hit the papers the next morning. McKellar delivered a simple statement to the press. "We agreed on renovating the present building and leaving the walls as they are," he said. The *New York Times* led its story with the declaration "Tradition has prevailed."[23] Lorenzo Winslow, whose months of exhausting work on the plans would not go to waste after all, penciled only half a line in his diary: "Everything nice."[24]

Also relieved, yet shaken by the entire experience, Orr lamented the six months that had been wasted arguing over a plan that, to his mind, never had any viable alternatives anyway. "Sentimentally and historically there could never have been an ersatz White House," Orr said, "—it would have been indefensible."[25] Orr also fought off a slight shiver as he read the editorial in the *Herald Tribune*, a copy of which he possibly picked up at Union Station on his way back to New Haven. "The Commission have done well," said the paper. "Heaven alone could have offered safe refuge had they done otherwise."[26]

ELEVEN

"SHOOT IT"

... and these atomic bombs which science burst upon the world
that night were strange even to the men who used them.
—H. G. Wells, *The World Set Free*, 1914

At the same time the commission was debating the White House's fate in Washington, another group of men—these on the other side of the world—were hard at work on their own project. In time, the fates of the two would intersect.

Some of the men had nicknamed the device "Tatyana." Others called it Tykva—meaning "pumpkin"—no doubt because it was fat and round. It had taken two years to construct it at a place called Arzamas-16, a secret city rising within the old monastery town of Sarov, which had officially disappeared from maps in 1946. When the device was finished, it was moved by rail more than fifteen hundred miles to the east, to a test site designated Semipalatinsk-21, where men had constructed a 104-foot steel tower anchored by a trapezoidal base of steel-reinforced concrete. The extreme secrecy was probably not necessary; the tower—known as Poligon 2—stood some one hundred miles southwest of the

river Irtysh on the steppes of the eastern Kazakh Hills. The train journey to Novosibirsk (itself several hundred miles to the north) took
nearly a week from Moscow. A windswept plain caked with clots of
scrub grass, this was among the most desolate places in the Soviet
Union, and the world.[1]

At 5:00 A.M. on August 29, 1949, the device rode to the top of the
tower on a freight elevator. The plutonium core had been added to the
interior assembly the previous night. Once the detonator caps were attached, the engineers and physicists cleared out.

The countdown began just before 7:00 A.M. local time—eleven
hours ahead of eastern standard time in the United States. Back in
Washington, it was still 8:00 P.M. on Sunday, the twenty-eighth. The
presidential calendar for that day says only that Harry Truman took his
usual brisk walk in the morning, then returned to Blair House, where
he spent the rest of the day. Often, Truman would use these rare hours
of leisure to catch up on his reading. Sometimes, he played the piano.
But while Sundays were downtime for Truman, he was seldom without his "homework": sheaves of documents—sometimes up to six
inches thick—that needed reading before the next morning's briefing.[2]

Right around this period, *Washington Post* reporter Dorothea Andrews filed an exclusive on how the president spent his average day—
which always included a morning briefing on "problems that may
develop that day in the world." Wrote Dawson, "By 10 a.m. each day,
the President knows more than anybody else in the world about what
the domestic and world situation is."[3]

Except for what was happing on this day on a windswept steppe
called Semipalatinsk-21, where the countdown had already begun:
Desyat, devyat, vosem, sem, shest, pyat, chetyre, tri, dva . . . raz.

The flash was as bright as the sun.

There was so much that Truman would not learn until it was too late.
Back in July 1945 at the Potsdam Conference, when he decided to let
Stalin in on the secret that the Americans had developed a bomb "of
unusual destructive force," Stalin—taking the advice of his KGB chief
Lavrenti Beria—simply pretended not to understand.[4] But the man of
steel understood everything perfectly. "Stalin knew almost as much
about the bomb as they did," Margaret Truman would write, thanks to
the Soviets' efficient spy network, which had infiltrated the Manhattan Project, revealing to the Soviets the American plans for both a

uranium gun-type bomb and plutonium-implosion bomb.[5] Later, after the British and American diplomatic attachés had left Potsdam for home, Stalin would tell his foreign ministers that the two countries "are hoping we won't be able to develop the Bomb ourselves for some time. Well, that's not going to happen."[6]

Truman did not know that the Soviets' haste to reach a collapsing Berlin in the spring of 1945 involved more than just Stalin's prior agreement with the Americans that Berlin would fall within the USSR's postwar zone of control. Beria had dispatched a secret team to scour the ruins of the city for uranium. In the remains of the Kaiser Wilhelm Institute—where German physicists had been the first to split the atom by bombarding it with neutrons in 1938—the KGB operatives stumbled on two tons of uranium oxide, 550 pounds of metallic uranium, and a little more than five gallons of heavy water. These treasures (along with an undetermined number of captured German physicists) ended up on trucks that trundled back deep into Soviet territory, to secret cities that appeared on no maps.

As the chief of the most notorious secret police organization in the world, Lavrenti Beria was a man who did not waste his time. Early on, he'd informed the ranks of physicists under his command that a successful test of a nuclear weapon would mean medals of honor, and failure would mean the firing squad.[7] To motivate his men to work harder, Beria—himself laboring under a certain death sentence if the project failed—would employ cold little quips such as "Don't forget, we've plenty of room in our prisons!" By contrast, Igor Kurchatov, the bearded and brilliant Russian physicist and the brains behind "Task Number One," as the Soviet bomb project was known, took a fatherly stance with his men. Stalin himself was indifferent to the method of management, so long as the scientists delivered. Don't worry, Stalin reassured Kurchatov, "we can always shoot them later."[8]

Owing to the difficulty of obtaining uranium-235, Kurchatov had understood early on that he would have to follow the Americans' blueprints for the plutonium bomb. By the spring of 1949, the Soviet reactor at Chelyabinsk-40 had produced enough plutonium to form a critical mass of it into a smooth spherical core. Kurchatov and his physicists took it to the Kremlin so Stalin could inspect it himself.

The office was a large room girdled by coffered wainscoting. A baize-covered conference table dominated one side and diagonally across by a large window overlooking the Muscova River was the generalissimo's desk.[9] Dwarfed by the enormous portrait of Lenin on the wall behind him, Stalin was a diminutive man with a crippled left arm. His right one still worked fine, and that was the hand he used to sign the innumerable death orders of his countrymen. Now aged seventy, threads of silver in his bushy mustache, Stalin was mistrustful and paranoid to the point of near psychosis.[10] The men set the sphere down before him. Stalin regarded his visitors with his yellow eyes.

"How can one be sure," he demanded, "that it's plutonium and not a mere glittering piece of iron?"[11] Kurchatov was flabbergasted. What would men facing firing squads if the chain reaction failed possibly have to gain by passing off a dud? Worse, there was no hope of explaining the complex physics of a nuclear chain reaction to a zealot who lacked even a basic understanding of the sciences. Fortunately, Kurchatov remembered one thing that Stalin could understand—that plutonium's alpha decay makes it warm. "Put your hands around it, comrade," the bearded physicist advised, "and feel its heat."[12]

The details of this story vary (in one version Stalin touches the core, while in another he orders a guard to do it)—so much so that one must conclude at least part of the incident is apocryphal—the part about the plutonium core making the trip to Moscow.[13] But Stalin's grilling of his scientists was real. So was the threat of death if they failed him. And so was the order that the Soviet man of steel issued once he was satisfied that RDS-1, as the device would be called, was worth trying. "Shoot it," he said.[14]

The steel tower anchored to its concrete base evaporated in a millionth of a second. As the blast wave pulsed out of the epicenter, an orb of white light shot upward, turning angry shades of red and orange as it twisted into the shape of a column. When the shock wave passed, the energy dispersion reversed and the mounting column of fire became a vortex, sucking tons of earth and rock up into its fiery throat as the inferno clawed its way up through layers of cloud. Up it went—20,000 feet, then 26,000—dark streaks threading the shaft of fire, until the inferno finally slammed into the top of the atmosphere, where it retched its radioactive vapor and earthen debris into a mushroom top that spilled out, black and ugly, over the thinning neck of the flames below.

From a bunker several miles from ground zero, Kurchatov saw the flash of light and began shouting, "There it is! There it is!"[15] Beria—the KGB chief who preferred to torture his victims personally—rushed over to Kurchatov and kissed him. "It would have been a great misfortune if it hadn't worked!" he said.[16]

"It," the plutonium-implosion bomb they had just detonated, was nearly an exact copy of the "Fat Man" bomb that the United States had dropped on Nagasaki some four years earlier. Amid the chaos and celebration inside the bunker, Beria did not notice when one of Stalin's moles managed to get a call through to the leader and inform him of the news that the KGB chief had wanted to deliver first: The Soviet Union was now, officially, the world's second nuclear power.

In time, this fact would have serious consequences for the reconstruction of the White House.

TWELVE

THE SHOVEL IN THE EARTH

I would rather break even on a monument than make a million
on a warehouse.

—John McShain

*A*fter a contentious run of meetings leading up to the August 2,
1949, vote to save the White House's outer walls, the commission deferred any other serious business until the fall. The
bloodhounds from the papers had moved on to other stories and would
not return to the White House until the commission was ready to hire
a contractor. Meanwhile, Winslow finished up his last drawings.

Most who regarded Winslow from a distance saw only a tweedy bon
vivant with the best architecture job in the world. At his brick cottage
on Volta Place, he'd don a paint-stained smock and build furniture,
weed his garden, and lavish hours on his temperamental MG. "Stayed
home all day," he penciled in his pocket diary one late-summer night,

"and worked on car door frame."[1] Winslow was eccentric, gifted, and, as architect of the White House, at the apogee of his career.

Only those on the inside realized the crushing pressures he was under, especially now that the renovation would soon be under way. Though it would fall to the engineers to figure out how to balance a stone house in the sky while men dug a new foundation beneath it, most every other detail of the project would be on this one architect's shoulders. "Mr. Winslow's job [is] as difficult as Hoban's," said the *Washington Star*, "for he has the task of preserving the original walls, removing and re-installing as much of the original materials as possible, installing the latest conveniences and planning a decorating scheme to satisfy a multitude of tastes."[2]

Winslow had produced two hundred drawings of the renovated White House thus far. He'd drawn fine lines, and he'd walked them, too. Winslow had figured out how to keep the residential floor plan intact, even as he nudged the walls to make the guest rooms a bit bigger, furnish each bedroom with a bath, and (for the first time in the mansion's history) provide built-in closets. On the State Floor, where the layout was sacrosanct, Winslow's touch was harder to detect, but it was there. He would, for example, swap out plaster for white marble in the entrance foyer. It would make it easier for the maids to clean the public's fingerprints off the walls.[3]

Winslow had solved countless problems like these, but his biggest one still shadowed him. Once all the renovation work was completed, Americans trusted that their "original" White House would be returned to them. It was up to Lorenzo Winslow to determine what "original" was supposed to look like.

By the time the Trumans moved out, the White House had stood for 148 years. Most everything between its outside walls had been rebuilt twice, first in 1817 and again in 1902. Its rooms had endured thirty-two redecorations—one for each president. What look, then, reflected the authentic White House? Was it the way the mansion had appeared on opening day in 1800, the unfinished East Room showing walls of bare stone? Or was it in the high classicism of McKim's renovations for Theodore Roosevelt? Was the mansion any *less* the White House after Mary Todd Lincoln had stuffed it with Victorian pieces from New York than when James Monroe had stuffed it with overpriced treasures from

Paris ("pictures, candelabras, vases, stuck about in fifty places," as one observer had joked)?[4] Unless the renovated White House was to wind up like the public rooms of an ocean liner, each chamber aping a different period in history, Winslow knew he could select only one style.

On August 4, 1949, he announced his choice. "White House Going Back to Olden Day," said the *New York Times*, revealing that the interiors would be brought "back into the period of 1810."[5] It made sense. The White House of James Madison, filled with neoclassical furnishings bought in Philadelphia and New York, represented the Georgian-flavored, early-Federal style at its ideological best: stateliness without vulgar ostentation—"a very agreeable country residence," as Thomas Jefferson put it.[6] Just to make life a little easier, Winslow permitted himself a bit of latitude. He'd told Congress that his design would conform to the building's original architectural period—"which is 1800 to 1810."[7] To a friend, Winslow wrote that he planned to bring the mansion back "to the original design of about 1820."[8]

But even by allowing that twenty-year window, Winslow had set himself up with a monstrous job—in fact, an impossible one. He would have to accept or reject each and every interior furnishing on the basis of whether it was "within the period" or not.[9] But since the fire of 1814 had incinerated most everything that *was* of the period, he would need to improvise. Fortunately, much of the mansion's interior woodwork from 1902 could be kept (McKim's refined classicism fit comfortably into Winslow's vision of a Madisonian White House). Nevertheless, Winslow was in for some excruciating choices. His own rules would obligate him to discard antiques that didn't fit the period in favor of reproductions that did.

Winslow also realized that his aesthetic goals could not interfere with building a suitable home for a president. He was not about to ask Harry Truman to do without electricity or crouch over a chamber pot just so everyone could live authentically in 1810. It was why Winslow would lower the ceilings in the Red and Green Rooms so the air-conditioning ducts could slither through, and why electrical outlets would poke out from the oak paneling.[10]

Cutting his way through these contradictory brambles, Winslow was only facing what every designer must face on a restoration job: He was not really restoring the house so much as selectively rebuilding it, setting the dial on his time machine to whisk the edifice back to a chosen point in its long-lost past, then using a combination of what he could save, what he could substitute, and what he could shoehorn into the picture that could aesthetically, if not genuinely, represent what he wanted.

Winslow knew he was playing a difficult game. He did not yet know that he would end up losing it.

⸎ ⸎

Winslow's drawings for the house were nearly all finished by September 1949. Only a few areas remained to be designed. One of them turned into the renovation's first dispute.

Truman had long been dissatisfied with the White House's staircase, an enclosed W of Joliet stone that lifted from a gated portal on the east end of the Cross Hall, then branched at a landing into a pair of narrower steps that ran the rest of the way upstairs. While the staircase was lovely to behold—a kind of miniature Scala Regia, Bernini's famous stairs at the Vatican—it was wildly impractical. During the state dinners' procession of the Marine Corps Color Guard, the split staircase bottlenecked the VIPs upstairs and then, downstairs, dumped them off at the hall's far end, where none of the guests in the foyer could see them.

Winslow himself had long thought of reconfiguring the W layout into an S, creating a single run of stairs that could round two half turns and slip effortlessly into the foyer through an opening he would cut in the staircase's western wall. Unfortunately, Winslow could never realize this plan because a brick support pier stood in the way. But now that the renovated White House would have a steel frame, his hands were free.

At his drafting table, the architect conjured his new staircase on paper. When Winslow finished, he looked at his work and loved it. He showed it to Truman, who also loved it. Then on September 7, Winslow motored up to New York to show his drawing to Delano, who hated it.[11] A Cerberus of the mansion's original layout, the seventy-five-year-old Delano believed that altering the stairs changed things too much. He was equally alarmed that Winslow had taken the liberty of erasing the double pair of columns that had delineated the mansion's entrance foyer from the hall. As the renovation's consulting architect and elder statesman, Delano could not be crossed.[12] The issue might have ended there had Delano not been foolish enough to fight Harry Truman.

First, Delano fired off a condescending memo to the president that excoriated Winslow's stair plans as "neither reasonable nor good architectural design," while praising his own judgment by suggesting that Thomas Jefferson would have agreed with him.[13] Truman already possessed a visceral dislike of arrogant men, and soon Delano had a letter back from him. "I don't agree with a single argument that you make," Truman said.[14]

The matter dragged on nearly two more weeks while Winslow tweaked his design. To placate Delano, Winslow agreed to keep the stairs' original portal in place, turning it into a balcony overlooking the Cross Hall. He also put the pair of columns back.[15] But Truman would get his new staircase.

⊷ ⊶

When Lorenzo Winslow had driven into New York City on Wednesday, September 7, 1949, to show his staircase drawing to Delano, he was not alone. With him in the car was a woman—identified in his diary only as "J." J did not happen to be the first letter of the name of either Winslow's wife or daughter.[16] The other thing that Winslow's colleagues did not know about this particular trip to Manhattan was that Winslow had set up an appointment to speak to another man after he was finished with Delano—and that second man happened to be dead.

The architect was never particularly verbose in his pocket diary. It held quick, economical notations of what he'd done during the day, and rarely did Winslow's compact handwriting reach the bottom of a page. But taken in the aggregate, across the weeks and months, a picture emerges of a man with a second life.

Winslow conducted numerous dalliances. His diary pages are replete with half-decipherable but sufficiently clear signs of a man struggling to force his various deceptions to coexist: "Everything made clear for Joan to come to my office." And: "Saw M. Not good at all. Met J. at 2."[17] Lorenzo Winslow would certainly not be the first man with an office in the White House to run around with various women, but his other companions were entirely unique. They were ghosts.

Starting in 1949, Winslow began to make cryptic references to various "wonderful messages" and "fine messages" he had received, though by what channel he failed to reveal.[18] Then, suddenly, the story burst from the shadows. On September 7, after the 9:30 A.M. meeting with Delano, Winslow returned to his hotel. Sometime around sunset, he and J. went out. "To Stead Memorial Séance at 8:00 PM," Winslow later wrote. "Most wonderful word from the master. J thrilled at the 2 hours. Wish so much could go again."[19]

Séances had reached a cultural high point in the late nineteenth century, but by the postwar period they had largely devolved into "spook shows"—rigged spectacles that theaters held, usually at midnight, to scare up extra revenue. A true séance was a relative rarity in 1949. And who was Stead? Why was he a "master"? Seeing as Winslow also subsequently mentioned visiting the Stead Memorial—a forsaken bronze plaque that to this day remains embedded in Central Park's eastern perimeter wall at Ninety-first Street—it's all but certain that Winslow was referring to William Thomas Stead, the famous British journalist and outspoken proponent of spiritualism. Between 1893 and 1897, Stead published a quarterly called *Borderland*, a "review and index of psychic phenomena." As a medium, Stead claimed proficiency at "automatic writing"—in a trance, he scribed messages relayed to him from beyond the grave.

Lorenzo Winslow was a man with a security clearance that enabled him to stroll into the West Wing and speak to the president pretty much at will. That he believed a white-bearded Englishman who'd been dead for thirty-seven years was sending him messages is, perhaps, a bit disquieting. But this, one might say, was just the tip of the iceberg. William T. Stead had been booked into stateroom C-89 on the shelter deck of the *Titanic*, bound for New York when she struck an iceberg on the night of April 14, 1912. The story goes that W. T. Stead retired to the first-class smoking lounge with a book as the liner's bow slipped beneath the sea.[20] His body was never recovered.

If Mr. Stead had specific things he wished to say to Winslow from the eternal beyond, he was apparently not finished. The White House architect would return to New York City again on November 9, checking into the Hotel Piccadilly on West Forty-fifth Street, just off Times Square. The séance was "very good," noted Winslow. The following day, he paid a call on Delano to show him drawings of the East Room, then slipped over to the Park Central Hotel at Fifty-fifth Street and Seventh Avenue for a prearranged rendezvous with "J.," who'd taken the train up from Washington to meet him.[21]

Several years hence, a reporter from the *Washington Post* would observe that Lorenzo Winslow was "a quiet, unassuming man" who didn't much like to talk about himself.[22] And little wonder why.

◦╍═╍ ═╍╍◦

On September 26, 1949, the commission released its terms for the White House renovation contract. The document enumerated a job of dizzying proportions: interior demolition; removal and storage of historic decorative elements; shoring, bracing, and underpinning; excavation, ironwork and concrete; plumbing, electrical, and on it went. The contractor was to stock all raw materials, furnish all equipment, and supply the skilled labor—and do it all within the confines of an 85-by-165-foot shell of fragile historic sandstone. Here was a long, complicated, nerve-racking job. Few construction companies in the nation were fit to even try for it.

Buildings commissioner Reynolds made clear that inexperienced or undercapitalized contractors need not apply: "The national and historical importance of this project demands that all materials and workmanship be of the highest grade and that the work be executed by individuals, firms or corporations . . . [with the] most skillful talents in the field of their work."[23] As a filter, Reynolds required all interested firms to complete a questionnaire. Only the contractors that met his definition of having "special qualifications and experience" would be invited to submit a bid, and even they would have to do it in person. At 1:00 P.M. on October 28, 1949, Reynolds opened the doors of the General Services Administration Building's auditorium, where he waited.[24]

Because of the risks and uncertainties of the White House renovation, the commission invited bids on a cost-plus-fixed-fee basis. This structure provided that the government would reimburse the contractor for all materials and labor necessary to get the job done (the cost), while establishing a set profit (the fixed fee.) The arrangement afforded a measure of protection to the contractor on a dicey job by guaranteeing his margin.[25] Even so, on a job this complex and dangerous, bidding was high-stakes poker.

In the end, only fifteen contractors had the nerve to play. The George A. Fuller Company, builders of New York's Flatiron Building, dropped off a bid for $242,500. From Chicago, Bates & Rogers came in at $950,000. Most of the contractors had tossed their hats in around the quarter-million-dollar range, and it looked like one of them would snag the job. At least, it did until PBA administrator Fay Slater rose at day's end and read the lowest bid aloud to the room. A "murmur of surprise," as the *New York Times* termed it, rose from the audience.[26]

The winner was John McShain, Inc., of Philadelphia, which agreed to take the job for $100,000. It was madness. No firm could make a profit on a fee that low. But once the reporters finally located John McShain, he was entirely composed. "I figured nobody would go as low as that," remarked the builder, "so I bid it."[27]

Eight days later, a letter from the Public Buildings Administration arrived at McShain's office at Seventeenth and Spring Garden streets. "Your proposal dated October 28, 1949, for the renovation and modernization of the Executive Mansion, Washington, D.C., is hereby accepted," it said.[28] The White House renovation now belonged to him.

A trim man of fifty whose speech still carried a trace of Irish inflection, John McShain was the sort of man who did not leave the house without a pocket square in his double-breasted suit. His freshly blocked fedoras parted the air like the prow of a ship. The streaks of silver that had begun to appear in McShain's trimmed mustache and neatly oiled hair only added to the air of success about the man.

It had not always been this way. The death of McShain's father in 1919 had forced him to drop out of Georgetown to take over the family's small construction company, and for years he made only a modest living building churches and schools for Philadelphia's Catholic parishes. Then, in 1927, a misunderstanding over a minor contractual clause found him blacklisted from bidding on further diocesan work.[29] With his prospects in Philly dried up, McShain looked toward the District of Columbia and decided to try his hand at building for Uncle Sam.

His timing could not have been better. With the onset of the Depression, FDR's New Deal programs had supercharged the engine of government building, and McShain started snapping up contracts one after the other. Between 1935 and his White House bid of 1949, the McShain firm would build no fewer than twenty-three structures in the capital city: civic leviathans like the Jefferson Memorial, the Bureau of Engraving and Printing, and the 6.6-million-square-foot Pentagon. In the decade following 1942, McShain's building contracts with the federal government swelled to one billion dollars. *Nation's Business* magazine quipped that the company signs McShain pitched at each building site popped up "with the speed and unpredictability of freckles rising on a schoolboy's face."[30]

Around D.C., McShain was a bona fide celebrity. Tour guides complained that their standard spiels about George Washington weren't enough anymore. "Now they want to hear about this guy McShain," said one.[31] There was even a spoof song penned at the Women's Press Club about "a guy like John McShain" who sends you "diamonds on a chain" because every contract "bears his name."[32] By now, McShain had acquired the sobriquet that would stay with him for life: "the man who built Washington."

There were plenty of big dogs in the construction business in those days, but none of them could match McShain's head for numbers. John McShain coaxed his margins not from high bids, but low costs. According to his daughter, Pauline, her father could estimate a job "to the last nail."[33] McShain, said the *Washington Post*, had made cost estimation into "a fine art."[34] Everyone in the trade knew better than to compete with the man. "You're lost once John starts beating away on prices," bricklayer John B. Kelly said. Matthew McCloskey, a fellow builder from Philadelphia, attested, "I really believe that today John McShain can figure a job tighter than most men alive."[35]

Even so, nobody could see how John McShain was going to squeeze a profit from the pittance he'd be paid for the White House job—including McShain himself. "Look," he admitted, "we'll be lucky if we come out even on it . . . but I wouldn't give up that job for any money you could name."[36]

No, he wouldn't, and the reason why lay rooted in a part of McShain's character that fewer people knew. McShain had already made a sizable fortune and had reached that magical point in his life where he sought some jobs not for profit, but prestige. As McShain himself put it, "I would rather break even on a memorial than make a million dollars on a warehouse."[37]

In 1943, McShain had taken a 5 percent hit just to snare the Jefferson Memorial job. When he finished, he took out a magazine ad thanking Thomas Jefferson "for this mighty nation you helped create."[38] After he'd completed Franklin Roosevelt's presidential library in Hyde Park, McShain built a magnificent fieldstone gatehouse for it, for which he invoiced the president exactly one dollar. "Dear John," FDR wrote back, "You are not only a grand fellow but you are a real friend in time of need!"[39]

As he saw a chance to become part of history, there was simply no way McShain wasn't going to snare the White House gig. *That* was the reason for his measly $100,000 bid. "He knew he'd lose money on it, but he couldn't have cared less," Pauline McShain said. "It meant so much to him to have the privilege of building the White House. He was absolutely thrilled."[40]

Back in the East Wing at 1600 Pennsylvania Avenue, Winslow was not thrilled. His plan to return the mansion to its Federal-period roots had run into problems almost immediately. With the exception of the classically-influenced woodwork carved in 1902, little of the interior would have made Thomas Jefferson feel at home. Draperies, wallpaper, carpets—all of it was a mishmash of styles from more recent administrations. And since none of the design drawings had survived from the early days, Winslow would end up going to New York's City Hall (completed in 1812) to copy its period interiors.[41] Mantels were another headache. The oldest ones dated to 1818, and there had once been twenty-four of them. But "we have only three of the original marble mantels left," Winslow bemoaned in a letter to a colleague.[42] Chester A. Arthur was to blame for that situation. It was he who, in 1882, deemed much of the White House unfit for occupancy. Arthur had filled twenty-four wagonloads with White House "junk," clopped it over to Duncanson Bros. Auctioneers, and had it all sold off.[43]

When the *Washington Post* caught wind of Winslow's predicament, the editors reasoned that some of the original White House mantels might still be floating around the city, and the paper ran a story about it. Phones at the city desk began to ring immediately. Unfortunately, most of the callers did not understand that "original" for Winslow meant the early 1800s. The White House had actually discarded some one hundred mantels over the years, but most hailed from later periods. Soon, Winslow found himself roped into inspecting each one that turned up. "Mantel details in Wash. Post brought deluge of telephone calls," he wrote in his diary on October 20. The following day, he grumbled, "Mantel troubles. Pestered all day with telephone calls."[44]

Annoyed though he was, even the slightest chance that an 1818 mantel might turn up kept Winslow running down the leads. Some of them revealed the epic journey it was possible for a chunk of fireplace to make. For example, after President Arthur dumped one particular mantel at Duncanson Bros., a scrap dealer snapped it up and resold it to a Unitarian minister, who installed it in a house that was later demolished. Sold twice more, the white marble mantel had finally ended up stashed under a porch at 208 8th Street S.W. Winslow went over to have a look. Sure enough, the mantel was from the White House, but Winslow dated it to 1840. That made it more Victorian than Georgian—but too recent in any case. "Very interesting," Winslow told the house's owner. "If you find any more, I'd be glad to look at them."[45] However, Winslow had already decided to have reproduction mantels made and just be done with it.

On a rainy Tuesday, December 13, 1949, four workmen lumbered across the dormant grass and stopped at the house's western corner, near the hedge that delineated the upper fringes of the flower garden.[46] Here, the ground lay lower than on the north side of the house, exposing enough of the basement floor to permit four barred, nearly square windows to overlook the slope. The mansion's weathered but resplendent face loomed above, some fifty-four feet up to the roof balustrade.

The men from Spencer, White & Prentis fanned out along the wall of the house on a bare patch of earth where the shrubs had been pulled up. As the rain would be cold and continuous this day, they wore overalls and thick flannel shirts. One had on what appeared to be an army-surplus cap. At least one of the laborers was a black man. Another seemed to be holding some kind of plans in his hand. The whole thing might have happened a few days sooner, except that McShain hadn't finished disconnecting the utilities yet. There had been talk of a kick-off ceremony, too, but the commission decided to just get on with it.[47] Nevertheless, this was an important moment.

Abbie Rowe was ready for it. He was a slender man, his face craggy but handsome, with horn-rimmed glasses and a thatch of unruly hair atop his head. He lingered nearby in the wet grass with his Speed Graphic camera and a four-by-five-inch magazine of unexposed sheet film loaded into the back.

Franklin Roosevelt had hired the forty-six-year-old Rowe as the White House's official photographer in 1941. It was the culmination of an incredible combination of luck and nerve. One day during 1938, when a Depression-felled Rowe was working on a shovel gang for the Bureau of Public Roads—no mean feat for a disabled man who wore a leg brace—none other than Eleanor Roosevelt clip-clopped past on horseback. Rowe grabbed his camera and snapped the First Lady's picture. Later, taking a chance, he sent Mrs. Roosevelt a copy of it. The First Lady was impressed. Before long, Rowe found himself working as the White House's photographer.

All too aware of his luck, Rowe had since committed himself to documenting every facet of presidential life. That he left out anything that might have shown Roosevelt in his wheelchair was an act of respect as well as solidarity: Rowe understood what life was like when your legs did not work, and he himself walked with both difficulty and pain. And yet, when word had reached him that the White House was going to be rebuilt, Rowe decided he would thoroughly document the entire project.

Presently, out in the yard below the mansion, one of the workmen took a shovel in his hands and rested his boot atop the blade. Rains had swept through the city the previous day, as they did today, and the moist earth yielded easily. The first shovel sank in; the others followed suit. Camera shutters clicked quietly from the lawn. Within a few minutes, the men had excavated a knee-deep trench along the foundation stones.

The renovation of the White House had begun.

Early on the morning of Monday, December 19, Truman crossed Pennsylvania Avenue from Blair House to start his workday in the West Wing. As he passed the high iron fence of the north lawn, he noticed something that hadn't been there the Friday before. Over the weekend, workmen had raised a gargantuan sign by sinking a fifteen-foot post in the earth. Swinging from a crossbar, a three-foot placard, topped by a Colonial pediment, proclaimed JOHN MCSHAIN, INC., BUILDERS.[48] Truman passed usher Crim on his way in. "Take that thing down right now," he barked, and kept walking.[49]

THIRTEEN

WRECK IT GENTLY

Remove not the ancient landmark, which thy fathers have set.
—Proverbs 22:28

*T*he place looked like the scene of an invasion. Stacked lumber rose in huge piles everywhere, while the sound of hammers cracked above the rumble of the dump trucks, growling through the east gate with loads of clay-sodden earth. Derricks did slow pirouettes above the South Lawn, sharing the sky with poles raised to carry the Oval Office's Western Union cable across the grounds. The site crawled with carpenters, laborers, plumbers, electricians, painters, steamfitters, and demolition men. The Otis Company had sent over men to take apart the elevator. The Agriculture Department sent over an expert on termites. Glassless windows flapped with covers of chicken wire and plastic.

General Edgerton had moved into an "office" on the site—a clapboard shed with a tar-paper roof, much like the electrical, paint, and carpentry shops nearby. It wasn't the Ritz, but it was the perfect spot for the general to keep an eye on everything—and that was precisely his job. Edgerton had begun a typewritten log of each day's progress, hammering out entries in his precise, emotionless prose. Sometimes, that task fell to Col. George William Gillette, Edgerton's assistant, who occupied the other desk in the shack. At six feet tall and two hundred pounds, the sixty-two-year-old Gillette had the bearing of an amphibious landing craft. Together, Edgerton and Gillette would run the renovation like a military campaign.

Skill saws screamed and crowbars wrenched; a hydrocrane's engine coughed as it hoisted loads of topsoil. Sometimes, the clangor from the house was so loud that the State Department, located across the street, ordered the site shut down just so its employees could hear themselves think for a while.[1] Now and then, a worker would whirl around in surprise at a question barked at him—only to find that the interrogator was not General Edgerton, but President Truman, who'd acquired this funny way of just dropping by. But, as the *New York Times* would point out, "he used to live in the house until it threatened to collapse on him," and the man had a right to ask how things were going.[2]

It was January 1950, and in point of fact, things were going very well indeed.

It had taken weeks of preparation just to get this far. Each and every one of McShain's workmen, plus those of his subcontractors, had been fingerprinted and screened by Secret Service chief James Rowley. "We checked them back in their hometown[s], and ran them down," Rowley would recall many years later, still cagey about his methods. Combing the local police files? Check. Running the names by the FBI? Check. Interviewing old neighbors? Yes, even that.[3]

Still unhappy at the prospect of up to three hundred laborers working just steps from the West Wing, Rowley had made McShain enclose the entire construction zone in an eight-foot fence topped with barbed wire. The one-hundred-foot stretch that ran past the Oval Office was ten feet high and made of plank timber, so nobody could watch the president working.[4]

Viewed from overhead, the fence assumed the shape of an enormous gourd, some nineteen hundred feet in circumference. Its stem bent toward East Executive Avenue—the sole means of entry and egress for the men, materials, and debris. A security shed stood at the gate, where each worker would present his identification badge at 7:30 each morning, then pick it up again on his way out at 4:00 each afternoon.[5] White House police searched every single dump truck on its way in.

McShain was used to security like this—and he was even used to
Harry Truman. Back during the Pentagon job, whispers of "irregulari-
ties" had reached the Capitol. Smelling possible graft, Congress dispatched its resident pit bull, Senator Truman, who spent three days on
the site and scrutinized everything. McShain was clean.[6]

Not surprisingly, Truman decided early on to inspect the White
House site, too. McShain had put his men to work a few days before
Christmas. Truman slated his inspection for December 31, a Saturday,
when the work site would be deserted. At 10:30 A.M., with Winslow
and usher Crim in tow, Truman emerged from his office in a tweed
overcoat and a brown felt fedora. He exchanged a few words of greeting with McShain, who'd come with J. Paul Hauck—"my head man in
Washington," as John McShain termed him.[7] With the Secret Service
tailing, the group set off for the White House.

The president was cordial but all business. The first thing he said
was that he "did not want the job to draw out like other government
jobs and be going on for six years."[8] Truman pretty much barked like
that for the entire tour. McShain's crew had been on the site less than
two weeks, but they'd already reduced the house to shambles. Bare
bulbs hung from dangling wires where the chandeliers had been. Floor
slabs had been pried up and carted off. Dismembered bookcases and
window frames slumped against the walls. Truman seemed satisfied
with the progress, but it did not stop him from delivering a litany of
demands for the "best workmanship" in the "fastest time."

At length, John McShain spoke up. "You know," he reminded the
president, "we completed the Pentagon in fourteen months." "Yes, I
know you built the Pentagon," Truman snapped back. "I was watching
you." The relationship was not destined to be an easy one.

As 1950 dawned, McShain was determined to move the job ahead as
quickly as possible. His men would be working in tandem with Spencer, White & Prentis, which had snared the underpinning subcontract
back in November. In this first stage of the work, Spencer had begun
excavating outside the foundation walls, starting on the way down to
the gravel layer twenty feet below the base of the footings. Meanwhile,
McShain's crew trooped into the empty mansion to dismantle the
rooms.

On a normal demolition job, the men would be hauling old doors
and window frames off to the dump, but not on this one. The wood-

workers Charles Follen McKim had hired back in 1902 had produced stunning neoclassical panels and pilasters, and all of it squared with Winslow's goal of restoring the house to its Federal roots. Why create new interiors when the old ones were already so beautiful? Winslow had made a long list of what he wanted set aside, which was nearly everything: wainscoting, paneling and trim, shutters, doors and door frames, stone floors, and marble fireplaces. Once the new house was finished, Winslow planned to put it all back in.[9]

The actual disassembly work fell to McShain's carpentry foreman, Murray ("Murph") Bonham, who was slightly less than thrilled with his assignment. "The boys were all accustomed to using TNT," Bonham said. "But there was no blasting on this job, and we tried to save everything."[10]

Try they did. But as Bonham would soon discover, men who swung sledgehammers for a living lacked what you might call finesse. Much of the woodwork split and cracked as the workers coaxed it loose. Murph tried to get the guys to ease up. Sometimes he'd end up yelling, "We aren't wrecking a tenement." The idea, he explained to his giants, "was to wreck the White House gently."[11] Some of them simply couldn't do it. If a workman broke too much, Murph stuck him on wheelbarrow duty instead.[12]

For those who could be gentle, tasks of otherworldly tedium awaited. Men taking apart the stone fireplaces found themselves numbering each and every stone.[13] All the wooden panels received numbers, too. As General Services Administration head Jess Larson recalled, "It was necessary to completely dismantle, and I mean *completely* dismantle, everything from the White House except the four walls."[14] Winslow and his draftsmen had created detailed drawings of every inch of the White House's interior. As the wood panels came off, Winslow gave each of them a number (in brass, stapled to the back) that corresponded to a number he marked on his drawings, assuring that everything could be returned to its original spot.[15]

But there was just *so much* of the stuff—thousands of items and pieces of items, all of which had to be cataloged and crated, tagged and stored. The long open shed on the South Lawn could hold some of this salvage, but the commission would end up procuring space in a warehouse down at Seventh and D streets S.W. to hold all of Winslow's treasures.[16]

Sometimes, the enormity of the task distressed him. "Dismantling proceeding. Much in a mess," Winslow noted in his pocket diary for January 16. While Winslow did not say so in his journal, he fell under enormous pressure to finish the salvage quickly so that the "real" work could begin. Winslow was truly the only one who seemed to care about the old interiors still left inside the house. Perhaps for solace, he'd found a local spirit medium around this time. As 1950 progressed, Winslow would spend his evenings attending séances at a place he referred to as "Mr. Burroughs's Church."[17]

Abbie Rowe set up his floodlights to capture the house's interior as it quickly disappeared. In the East Room, the walls were already down to the bare stone and a huge hole had opened up over the ground floor below. Most of the second floor had been stripped down to the 1817 timber, while workmen elsewhere were busy sawing away what remained of the ornamental plaster ceilings. "The innards of the old mansion are pretty well spread out now," the *New York Times* noted on January 16. "There are piles of stuff all over the place, although the work was started only two months ago."[18]

A few days before, two marble setters had been lifting up the enormous floor slab in the foyer. Laid to commemorate the White House's previous renovation, the stone bore the bronze dates 1792–1902. The men discovered a fourteen-inch-square wooden box buried below the slab. Its musty insides contained a scattering of coins, some newspapers, and an electrical-wiring diagram from the Harry Alexander Co. There was also an empty bottle of Hunter's Baltimore rye, which the marble layers of forty-eight years before had apparently consumed and then stuffed with a piece of paper on which they'd signed their names. The makeshift time capsule found its way to the Oval Office, where Truman examined all of its contents, fascinated, before ordering the chest reburied—but only after that day's newspapers could be added to it.[19]

Reporters had taken to playfully chiding the president for playing "sidewalk superintendent," but Truman really did pay a visit to the site most every morning and, often, other times of the day, as well.[20] "Never a day passed while construction was in progress," a Masonic publication reported, "that an inspection by the President was not made."[21] Everyone had expected Truman to watch the work closely, but the man literally popped up everywhere.

One afternoon, commission chairman McKellar decided to have a walk around the dying White House, just to take a last look at the place. Up on the third floor, McKellar was growing impatient waiting for the rickety old elevator to climb up the shaft when suddenly the car appeared—with Truman working the button panel. "Mac, I heard you were over here," the president said. "There is one part of the building I want you to see before they begin to tear it down." McKellar hopped into the cab and Truman whisked them down to the ground floor, where he showed McKellar a prominent bulge in one of the walls. "The wall was more than a foot out of place and it did look dangerous," McKellar said. But what he found truly surprising was not the crumbling wall, but that the president of the United States had found the time to go poking around a construction site.[22]

McKellar wasn't specific about which wall Truman had found the bulge in, but that February some of the workmen noticed that one of the walls on the eastern end of the house appeared to be listing even more off vertical than the other ones. A little pick and shovel work revealed why: The wall had been built directly on top of an old well that Thomas Jefferson had ordered dug some 150 years before. Three feet of water still remained in it.[23]

By March 25, 1950, Murph Bonham's men had carried the last of the historic material out of the mansion. The demolition phase could now begin in earnest—even though, in many parts of the house, it already had. For McShain's men, the clock was always running. The contract stipulated that the job had to be wrapped in 660 days, and patience had quickly worn thin with this man Winslow and all the old junk he wanted to save. Winslow had been rushed to the point of distraction. One day, he discovered that a souvenir hunter had pried off the bronze accent pieces of the Blue Room's fireplace. The architect flew into a rage. Didn't anyone respect this house? The commission ignored him.[24]

The house gave up secrets as it came apart. As the men laid into the place with picks and prying bars, they found evidence of the 1814 inferno everywhere: Blackened joists and studs showed their sooty blisters to the daylight. One day, Truman pulled J. B. West over to a spot near the landing of the grand staircase, where the dismantling work had exposed some charred beams. "See?" Truman said, "That happened during the war of 1812 when the British set us on fire."[25] On another occasion, as Winslow wandered amid the debris, he stooped to pick up another relic from the Federal period: a brick with a dog's paw imprinted on it.[26]

Before the wreckers got down to the floor joists, Edgerton sent a

memo to the PBA project manager William Kelley: "When the dismantling has reached the beams in Room 16 (Miss Margaret Truman's
Room) which was reinforced by the cantilever angle irons, it is requested
that you have the entire assembly kept together and retained intact."[27]
President Truman wanted the beam that had failed beneath his daughter's piano kept as a personal souvenir.

Margaret Truman might have been amused to know that the beam
below her piano would be saved, but she could not bring herself to
watch what was happening to the mansion. "Although I knew it was
necessary," she wrote, "the thought of the White House being 'gutted'
stirred distress in the pit of my stomach."[28]

It was better that she didn't look. By now, the mansion was a trans-
fixing ruin. A jagged, cavernous hole in the East Room floor opened
clear into the ground floor below, where the brick walls stood gnawed
down to waist level. The Cross Hall was gone. Stray pieces of its ornamental plaster dangled over a chasm two stories deep. Upstairs, empty
rooms sat in varieties of disembowelment, some stripped down to the
house's outer stone walls, some bearing their lath like skeletal ribs, the
floors hidden beneath moonscapes of fractured plaster. The telltale
scents of mold and rotting wood—a *pourriture noble* of old houses—hung
in the air. Standing like gravestones in the shadows, many of the old
brick walls still had pieces of faded wallpaper stuck to them, florals
and flabelliforms once the height of taste, now dirty and rotting from a
century of entombment.

Workmen lumbered back and forth with wheelbarrows piled high
with chunks of cement, brick, and plaster, which they dumped into a
long plywood chute cantilevered out of a window on the second floor.
Avalanches of detritus rolled down the trough and into the backs of
dump trucks pulled up below. McShain's men worked like piranha,
scraping the place clean, until only the interior brick walls were left—
and they only left *those* alone because crumbling masonry was all that
was holding up the roof.

Some of the mansion's floor beams—too thick and long to be sent
down the chute into the trucks—found their way to the storage shed
on the South Lawn. The task of hauling them there fell to a young
black foreman named Clifton Nelson. When Nelson learned that a
particular cluster of beams his men carried had come from room number 223, Abraham Lincoln's old office, he took it upon himself to wrap
them in a tarpaulin and set them aside. "We wanted to keep this material in a special place," Nelson explained later. President Lincoln, he
added, "used to pace up and down on these boards."[29]

But those beams were lucky. Most of the house's innards ended up in the trucks, whose mission was a sticky little matter the commission was not eager to discuss. The gutting of the White House generated tons of building material, some of it dating to the founding days of the republic itself. Winslow's advocacy had routed the more important pieces of the mansion's interior into storage. But the commissioners designated everything else—beams, bricks, nails, and lath—as "surplus material."[30] The trucks hauled all of it over to Fort Myer, an old army base on the Virginia side of the river, and dumped it on the ground.[31]

Edgerton had been surprised by the hundreds of letters he'd already received from everyday Americans who wanted a piece of the debris—anything, even a bent nail or chip of brick—as a souvenir. At one point, the general would quip, "We could have demolished the old building just by inviting the souvenir hunters to come and help themselves."[32] He was only half joking.

The commission was working on a plan that would make the souvenir hunters happy, but it wouldn't go public with this until the following year. For now, the guts of the White House sat in great piles on the western border of Arlington National Cemetery.

At the same time the demolition men broke up the house, shovel teams for Spencer, White & Prentis broke a sweat deep below. Douglas Orr referred to them as "the moles."[33] These were the men who would burrow beneath the mansion's outer stone walls to create a new foundation—nineteen feet deeper on the mansion's east side and twenty-two on the west. It was a job few men would want.

Once the diggers wiggled themselves beneath a stretch of the old stone outer wall, they hand-shoveled a four-by-four-foot pit straight down to the gravel layer below. After cribbing the pit with plywood, the moles would fill the shaft with concrete nearly to the top. Once the concrete hardened, the remaining space could be "dry-packed" with a second layer of cement, creating a supporting column that fused to the White House's original stone and formed a single integral mass. Spencer, White & Prentis sank the pits at twelve-foot intervals, which meant that the men would make several loops around the house before all 126 of them united to form a thick new wall for the White House to rest on. The entire job would take six months.

That the contractor trusted in the stability of a layer of gravel just twenty-two feet below the lawn—rather than the solid rock that lay at seventy-eight feet—was testament to the expertise of one man. He was Donald Burmister, a Columbia University professor who probably knew more about the behavior of dirt than anyone alive. A decade earlier, when the organizers of the 1939 New York World's Fair decided to locate their exposition atop a former ash dump in Queens, it was Burmister's soil analysis that permitted the ten-thousand-ton Trylon and Perisphere to rise.[34]

White House consulting engineer Emil Praeger was no stranger to soil mechanics, but even though he already had two studies of the underground strata to use, he called Burmister anyway. Praeger's caution was warranted. The renovation project would do more than undergird the troubled White House; it would transform it from a wall-bearing structure to a steel-frame one, redistributing its weight and exerting complex demands on the earth below. As Burmister himself later attested, "this was not an ordinary foundation problem."[35] Using the results of Spencer's 1948 soil borings and the caisson test pits sunk in the summer of 1949, Burmister ran his calculations and gave his blessing: The gravel layer was up to the job.[36]

Praeger's vigilance about the foundation's depth mirrored his colleagues' vigilance about everything else. Nobody wanted the blame if the White House collapsed during the digging. The commission had even stipulated that no more than four feet of the outer walls could be left unsupported at any given time. For his part, Robert White, son of Spencer, White & Prentis partner Lazarus White, felt that everyone was being a little too cautious. The White House "was a fairly routine job," he said. "We had to build a whole new foundation and brace up the walls at the same time."[37]

But White's nonchalance glossed over the true danger of the work. One day, a 150-year-old foundation stone tumbled into one of the pits and struck a digger in the head.[38] Nothing seemed to calm the nerves of the PBA engineers, who were nearly sick with worry as the moles burrowed beneath the historic walls. "People got excited," White conceded. "One engineer went around saying we were collapsing the building. We were pretty glad when it was over."[39]

Shoveling their way downward along the dank inner lip of the mansion's original footings, some of the men brushed the dirt away from curious markings chiseled into the backs of the stones. Odd configura-

tions of triangles, X marks, and hooks, they resembled hieroglyphs—
except that they were at least three thousand years too recent, and on
the wrong continent, to be that. But Truman recognized the symbols
immediately. They were "mason's marks," cut into the unfinished side
of the stones by the master carvers who'd started the work in 1792.
Masons had used this practice since the medieval period, largely on
cathedrals, as a way of both "signing" their work and claiming wages
for the stones they'd cut. For the president, himself a master Mason
since 1909, the connection was irresistible. He ordered the marked
stones not integral to the structure set aside. Before long, he had so
many of them that Winslow incorporated them in a new hearth for the
mansion's kitchen. Truman ordered the rest crated and shipped off to
Masonic Grand Lodges across the country.[40]

As McShain's men gutted the house and Spencer's moles sank the underpinning pits, the third major component of the 1950 schedule, the
shoring operation, had already begun. It called for the raising of three
temporary towers inside the house to hold up the roof until the mansion's new steel framework could take over the load. Simple enough in
theory, the scheme was monstrously difficult. Even Richard Dougherty—
the man who'd run a railroad through the bellies of Manhattan
skyscrapers—called it a "whacking engineering problem."[41]

The towers were rectangular steel frames that would rise from
footings down on the gravel layer and reach seventy feet up to the
lower chords of the mansion's roof trusses. The trusses enclosed the
third floor that Delano had put in for Coolidge in 1927. Once the towers reached those frames, they could shoulder the 360,000 pounds of
steel and concrete that the house's crumbling brick interior walls were
still carrying—if barely.

The engineers were understandably eager to get the towers to the
top of the house as quickly as the ironworkers could bolt them together. Even as Winslow was removing the mansion's decorative interiors, McShain's men had torn open three twelve-by-twenty-five-foot
holes in the floors of the State Dining Room, the East Room, and the
Blue Room to make way for the skeletal behemoths.[42] Once the towers
were in place, they would not only transfer the dead load off the old
brick walls (which McShain's men would then demolish); they would
also brace the house laterally. Ironworkers threaded long, spindly
beams through the towers horizontally until the ends touched the

White House's original outer walls, where they attached to vertical struts drilled into the crumbling sandstone.

Any of the White House operations taken by itself—demolition, underpinning, and shoring—was a major job. The fact that they all ground along simultaneously made for a mind-boggling spectacle. Even a seasoned architect like Douglas Orr looked on in awe. "It is difficult to describe the intricacies of these operations," he reflected later.[43]

By the beginning of May, the White House sat atop of new foundation walls anchored deep in the subterranean gravel. Building the mansion's new steel framework could not begin until all of the soil within those walls was removed. There were ten thousand cubic yards of it. Excavating that much earth would require bulldozers—a delicate assignment that taxed the confidence of even seasoned operators like Jimmy Brown. "Up here in the driver's seat," Brown told a visiting reporter, "a guy's got a sense of power. A bulldozer man don't take nothing from nobody." But Jimmy Brown did not care for driving around inside the White House. He'd already brought his scooper too close to the outer walls several times, lifting up historic stones meant to be left in place. The foreman had yelled at him over the din: "That ain't junk, Jimmy!" Now Brown was dispirited. "This is no place for a bulldozer," he said.[44]

FOURTEEN

"WE ARE NO LONGER AHEAD"

Difficulty is the excuse history never accepts.
——Edward R. Murrow

*A*s the midpoint* of 1950 approached, a palpable feeling of confidence settled over the Commission on the Renovation of the Executive Mansion. If the group's office space was less than desirable—the men had found "permanent" quarters in a curtained-off end of a corridor in the East Wing—progress on the mansion was excellent. "White House Work Ahead of Schedule," proclaimed the *New York Times* on May 14, and indeed it was: forty-two days ahead. When the commission convened on May 24, project manager Kelley had nothing but good news: 80 percent of the shoring done, 97 percent of the underpinning. Barring a catastrophe, the outer walls—ones it had taken the government so long to decide that it wanted to save—would not fall now. Even commissioner Rabaut, the man who'd pushed for building a new White House, found himself congratulating Kelley on "the excellent report."[1]

At the work site, the great cacophony of machinery and the thunder of rubble into the backs of the dump trucks had largely abated. Inside the house's shell, a lonely pneumatic drill gnawed at a stubborn section of brick wall, while a lone bulldozer nuzzled a pile of debris near the south wall. "As the bulldozer digs and dumps," a visiting reporter noted, "it has to dodge the temporary steel framework which holds up the third story and roof."[2] The trucks and tractors had compacted the dirt into a serpentine road that wound its way around the three shoring towers like a country lane.

That season's flock of tourists to the capital, frustrated by the fact that few vantage points from the street gave them a view of the White House construction they'd read about in the papers, discovered an excellent vantage point at the top of the Washington Monument.[3] But even from that perch they could not see inside the mansion. They had come too late anyway: By June 20, 1950, nearly all of the White House's interior had been hammered to pieces, rolled down the dumping chutes, and carted away.

The space left was an envelope of humid air laced with the scent of soil and stone. I-beams slashed across the cavernous space at every angle, as though the house were part of the old sword-and-basket trick of a traveling magician. Here and there—usually high up beneath the trusses, construction lights swung from electrical cable the men had looped and draped around the temporary steelwork. Daylight spilling into the box of stone from window openings high above gave the place the feeling of a ruined cathedral. It was a shadow realm—"a maze of shoring and bracing," Orr called it.[4] Inexplicable things lay within, sinister sights for the uninitiated visitor: hoisting chains dangling from high places, shoring towers that resembled gallows, and deep gouges scarring the inside of the mansion's old walls. Some of those furrows hewn from the stone were the flues left from old fireplaces; others were abandoned conduits for long-vanished heating ducts and gas pipes.

For the contractors' men, none of these sights were new, but President Truman found them—found the entire shell of the mansion, in fact—thoroughly engrossing. Like a rigger in a theater, the president picked his way unafraid along the catwalks high above, his nearsighted eyes blinking at the face of the cold stone.[5] Secret Service agent Rex Scouten didn't like Truman's habit of taking his high aerial excursions, especially because "his eyesight wasn't very good."[6] But Truman wouldn't have missed these trips for the world. Later, he would express his feeling of amazement in his diary: "They took all the insides out, put in steel and concrete like you've never seen in the Empire State Building, Pentagon or anywhere else."[7]

Were a spectator to have spotted the president moving about in the shadows and hazarded a guess about what he was thinking, it could well have been a sense of silent wonder in what he had wrought here. Though future historians might judge the effort critically—question whether such a thorough gutting had been necessary—there could be no doubt that President Truman had made his mark. In fact, so violent were the changes imposed on the structure that the entire mansion had actually *moved* in a vaguely counterclockwise direction—by .0216 of an inch—during the course of the work.[8] None of the presidents who had work done on the house had clawed so deeply into its soul as had Truman. And with the whole of the interior ripped out, there was no turning back now.

Newspapers trumpeted the work's progress. "If construction continues at the present pace," one story proclaimed, "President Truman and his family will be carving their 1951 Thanksgiving turkey beneath this roof."[9] For his part, General Edgerton took pains to toss a wet blanket over such talk. "On a job as big as this it's too early yet to preen ourselves," he cautioned. Instead, said the general, "we just say, better a month ahead than a month behind."[10]

Edgerton uttered those words to a clutch of reporters and photographers assembled outside the White House on July 11, 1950. Nearby, a steam-powered crane grumbled as it lifted a steel beam toward an open window. Grimy men in hard hats lumbered past, some of them pausing to pull the grip on their pneumatic drills, whose skull-cracking staccato tore into the heavy summer air. The broken earth that lay about the house oozed with a vaguely unsettling red color—the clay in the soil, the very mushy stuff that had caused the house to sink.

Though some journalists had been lucky enough to get a peek at the site since the work had started, this was the first large press event since January. As one of them later said, the reporters "were hardly prepared for what they saw."[11] The cavernous room of stone stretched 168 feet from east to west, 82 feet across, nearly 80 feet up, and was, in total, well over one million cubic feet of open space. Discounting the 150 tons' worth of steel beams crisscrossing the expanse, it was enough room in which to stack five Douglas DC-3s atop one another, or lay the Statue of Liberty down on her back—still leaving seventeen feet to spare above the torch.

Reaching for adequate language to convey the scene, the reporters resorted to metaphors. "The White House looks like a vast barn slowly being filled with steel cobwebs," said one.[12] Others called it "one cavernous room"[13] and "a shell at its emptiest."[14] Standing on mud-caked planks over a pit prowled by a bulldozer, *Christian Science Monitor* reporter Emilie Tavel contemplated the vertical row of soot-blackened niches that crept up the walls—fireplaces that had once kept thirty-two presidents warm. Staring overhead, she envisioned the old second-floor guest rooms and then, down where the State Floor had been, the landing of the now-vanished grand staircase. "Is it possible," she wondered, "that this barren, pitiful shell could have been the scene of so many brilliant occasions, so many history-shaping decisions, the home of so many great and near great?"[15]

On July 20, the president sat down to write to his cousin Ethel Noland back in Missouri. "The old building is nothing but a shell," he told her. "There is not a thing in it from cellar to garret."[16]

Bethlehem Steel's blast furnaces had so diligently hopped to the order for 800 tons of structural steel that by late July 429 tons of it were stacked up and waiting on the property.[17] Spencer, White & Prentis had already excavated the footings for the house's permanent steel columns back in February, and some of the permanent pieces of steel were already in place. But the commission needed a separate firm to build what engineer Richard Dougherty called the "box within a box"—the steel framework that would fill up the empty space left inside the old stone walls.[18]

Both structurally and symbolically, the steel frame was everything. It would fill the house, carry the house, *become* the house. It would support the old outer walls themselves, which would eventually be tied to the framework via light bent anchor bars and hence allow the mansion—inner steel and outer stone—to stand as an integral whole. *Everything* depended on getting that steel inside and welded together. And here was, just as Edgerton had feared, exactly where the job's progress began to falter.

The commission had awarded the subcontract for raising the mansion's steel framework to the McCormick Construction Company, whose low bid of $61,700 hinged on its ability to use its "special crane" to erect the beams—a crane that could not maneuver inside the building with so much of Spencer, White & Prentis's cross-bracing in place. The commission tossed Spencer an extra six thousand dollars to remove whatever braces were in the way. That solved one problem; there would be others, however.

The work was painfully slow. The shoring towers had been like a boy's Erector set compared to the structural steel's thickness and weight. One of Abbie Rowe's photographs shows an ironworker standing beside an I-beam that, even lying on its side, rises to the height of the man's belt buckle. Its rivets are the size of doorknobs. This was probably one of the house's twenty-two-foot-long supporting girders; each of them was three feet thick. As Gen. Jess Larson recalled, putting steel that could support a skyscraper into a three-story house had been Truman's idea: "He said that this was going to be the last time that the White House was to be rebuilt."[19] No kidding.

Yet even with nearly forty ironworkers on the job at a given time, the task of getting a single beam inside the house's shell was a formidable challenge. Performing a kind of industrial ballet, the crane operator would toggle his boom and hook block as the suspended beam floated toward the mansion. It took at least seven men to thread the steel though a window opening, usually with no more than nine inches to spare on either side.[20] John McShain, his daughter, Pauline, recalled, took out a "huge" insurance policy to cover his firm in case a beam took a bite out of the historic facade.[21]

McCormick held the steel subcontract, but it was ultimately the McShain firm that bore responsibility for the work. J. Paul Hauck kept fastidious track of how much steel was going into the house.[22] The foreman measured by weight—forty tons in place by the end of June, for example—and reported these figures to the commission. Initially, the numbers looked good. But they did not reflect how close McCormick was cutting it.

As the summer progressed, the handful of pioneering floor beams multiplied into a cubical grid. The Bethlehem steel soared, reached, and connected in flawless perpendicular formations. Any perch within the house gave the feeling of being inside an Escher drawing. Aware that these thrilling vistas of planes and convergence points would never be seen again, photographer Abbie Rowe ventured out to capture them.

Two decades earlier, Lewis Hine had wrangled himself onto terrifying perches to photograph the ironworkers raising the Empire State Building, creating perhaps the most important and poetic photographs of a construction job ever taken. Rowe now replicated that mission within the million cubic feet of space inside the White House. Dragging his braced leg and heavy camera out onto the open beams, Rowe must have stood just inches from a fall that would have killed him. He chose his angles with excruciating care, harnessing the light to bring clarity and detail to his images, yet permitting an ominous gloom to encroach, too. Rowe coaxed beauty from piles of broken stone and, like Hine, he was careful to include the workmen in his shots, understanding his responsibility to show that great buildings required men of great bravery and skill to raise them—and that those men often risked their lives to do it.[23]

Rowe was not the only one who couldn't keep away from the shadowy interior of the great house as the steel rose within it. "Every once in a while," the *Washington Post* noted, "the cheerful sound of pounding and riveting brings President Truman out of his office in the West Wing to inspect the progress, just like any other proud owner waiting for his new house to be finished."[24]

But the cheerful sounds had been misleading. By the time of the commission's August thirtieth meeting, work on the mansion had officially fallen behind schedule. The steel frame was supposed to be finished by October 15, yet here it was nearly September and McCormick had only half the beams in place—and many of them still had not been riveted. Project manager Kelley had run into trouble hiring men for the riveting gangs. "We need several," he admitted, "but they are very difficult to get."[25]

There were other problems, too. McShain was to have begun new masonry construction, but he lacked even the bricks to start it with. Still another delay had arisen over the awarding of subcontracts. McShain would need forty-eight of them to install everything from heating ducts to light switches. Yet many of the contractors had either not started work or not been selected at all.[26]

The unhappy duty of disclosing these facts fell to Kelley, who would discover at the commission's meeting of August 30 that the fatherly dispositions of Douglas Orr and Richard Dougherty could turn into withering cross-examinations when a construction job strayed off the calendar:

MR. DOUGHERTY: Up to now on structural steel, are we ahead?

MR. KELLEY: Yes.

MR. DOUGHERTY: How about generally?

MR. KELLEY: On the borderline.

MR. ORR: We were ahead on excavation and underpinning, and now where are we?

MR. KELLEY: We are on the minor side, I'd say.

MR. DOUGHERTY: What put you there?

MR. KELLEY: The fact that we can't have the drawings.[27]

Drawings were another problem. Before he could so much as rivet a beam in place or slap mortar atop a brick, a government contractor had to have all of his paperwork in order—exact specifications for the materials, plus the customary architectural, structural, and mechanical drawings to show him what to do. On the White House job, generating this paperwork was the shared responsibility of Lorenzo Winslow and PBA chief Reynolds. There lay the bottleneck. The men—Winslow in particular—seemed unable to produce the documents fast enough to keep the contractors on schedule. John McShain himself had seen this problem coming. "For at least three months," he'd fumed at the commission in August, "we have been begging for plans."[28]

Hailing from the more improvisational world of the private sector, Orr and Dougherty were unable to get their heads around the fact that McShain required a signed government form to do anything short of visiting the rest room. And since John McShain was not in the room, the commissioners took their frustrations out on Hauck. "You should have had prices by now," Dougherty scolded him. "You should have had the material by now," Orr added. "McShain Company was given mechanical and architectural plans 95% complete on June 16."

Poor Hauck. It was not his fault that there were no bricks on the property; he lacked both the specs to order them and the drawings for what to do with them. What plans he'd been given were just preliminary, and he couldn't move on those. Hauck tried to defend himself. "I have heard that we have had drawings since June 16," he said. "We did *not* have drawings. I think it is ridiculous that we still don't." He continued: "I seem to be criticized throughout for not doing certain things. Could *you* work without drawings?" Rabaut spoke up: "No, I think you are right." But the other commissioners gave no quarter. Orr pressed Hauck on why he couldn't just proceed with the estimates and worry about the paperwork later. "Mr. Orr," an exasperated Hauck said. "You don't quite understand the Government procedure. We have to have documents to proceed with."

And on it went. Hauck had few friends in the room. Breaking along the fault line that separates management from labor, the commission preferred to protect Winslow and lay the blame at the feet of the builder from Philadelphia. It was a practice that would continue.

McShain kept the work at full throttle. Most of the steelwork was up by the end of October, and soon his men were pushing rubber-wheeled gondolas in and out of the house in endless rotations, dumping wet concrete onto the wood and wire forms packed around the steel beams. But the problems with the delayed drawings persisted. Worse, Mc-Shain and Hauck began to notice something strange about the drawings and specifications they did get: The government was revising them, demanding that cheaper materials be used, and that some be left out altogether.[29]

A major cause for the substitutions was Lorenzo Winslow's expensive tastes. To cite just one example, Winslow had decided to order that the columns, pilasters, and wainscoting of the foyer, Cross Hall, and main stairway be hewn from marble—and not just any marble. "It is my opinion," Winslow stated, "that only Westland Cream Light Cloud Vermont Marble is architecturally acceptable." There was only one quarry in the entire country that could fill this kind of order. In the summer of 1950, that quarry happened to be flooded, so the commission would have to pay to drain it before procuring the stone. The total bill would come to $19,530—four times the annual income of the average American family that year.[30]

Winslow got his marble, but the price forced the commission to cut corners elsewhere, and a domino effect began. McShain now had to wait even longer for the revised specifications and drawings. While he waited, he was unable to subcontract the remaining work, and so the job lagged even further behind.[31]

When Edgerton led another group of reporters around the construction site that fall of 1950 he explained how "the threading of the permanent steel in through the windows and around the temporary bracing was more tedious than anyone had foreseen. Last Spring we were way ahead of schedule. We are not behind now, but we are no longer ahead."[32] But Edgerton was equivocating. The job had hit serious setbacks now—including one so big and so grave that the general was forbidden from mentioning it at all.

The truth of the matter was that the paperwork and diagram problems were not the only reasons the renovation had run into trouble midway through 1950. Two significant events had taken place on the global stage—one the previous year, one that very summer—that had led to a decision to alter the plans for the White House dramatically. It was a decision that would affect all parties involved in the renovation, and generate setbacks and confusion all on its own. In August, right around the time the commission had begun to argue with McShain about the construction delays, Douglas Orr had received a secret memorandum from Adm. Robert L. Dennison, naval aide to the president, informing him that the two new subbasement levels of the White House were about to undergo radical design changes.

The White House was getting a bomb shelter.

FIFTEEN

THE HIDDEN
WHITE HOUSE

Besides protecting you from blast and heat, basements also provide shielding from explosive radiation. Because, the lower you
get, the more barriers against radiation there are likely to be
between you and the bursting bomb.
—*Survival Under Atomic Attack*, Civil Defense booklet, 1950

The chain of events that would eventually lead to Admiral Dennison's August 1, 1950, memorandum to the commission vice
chairman, Douglas Orr, reached back to September 3, 1949,
when a war-worn B-29 descended from the clouds and touched down
on the frozen runway of Eielson Air Force Base in Fairbanks, Alaska.

Atomic Energy Commissioner Lewis Strauss's idea of using old
B-29s to fly secret atomic reconnaissance missions over the Arctic
Circle—a strategy he'd been pushing through the corridors of power
since 1947—had finally become an official air force project when two
daily missions flown by the 375th Squadron began lifting off from Eiel-

son in April 1949. Just beneath the tail assembly of the aircraft (known as WB-29s, war-surplus Superfortresses converted into weather planes) was a pair of traps, each fitted with a nine-by-twenty-two-inch paper filter.

A far-seeing and sophisticated administrator, Strauss understood that if the Soviet Union somehow did manage to detonate an atomic weapon, it wouldn't be necessary for the Americans to see it in order to prove its existence. The radioactive isotopes released by an explosion were known to drift hundreds of miles from the point of detonation, which meant that the 375th Squadron's sorties over the Arctic—disguised as ordinary weather-observation flights—ought to be able to pick them up.

Not that many people thought the planes would be picking up anything anytime soon. Sir Henry Tizard, Churchill's scientific advisor and chairman of the British Defense Research Policy Committee, was confident that the Soviets would not master the physics of the bomb until at least 1957. Gen. Leslie Groves, who'd masterminded the atomic bombings of Japan, believed it would take them decades. Truman had been even more confident than that. In the heady days after the war, he'd had a blustery exchange with the Manhattan Project director, J. Robert Oppenheimer:

"When will the Russians be able to build the bomb?" the president asked. Oppenheimer replied that he did not know.

"I know," Truman said.

"When?"

"Never."[1]

Less confident and better informed, the president's Air Policy Commission had finally settled on the year of 1952 or 1953 as the soonest the United States could expect Stalin's physicists to catch up with them. Nobody in the American intelligence community yet knew that British physicist Klaus Fuchs, a "fellow traveler" who'd worked deep within the Manhattan Project at Los Alamos, had been passing detailed plans for the bomb to the Soviets since 1945.

The September 3, 1949, weather-plane mission out of Eielson A.F.B. had taken its samples at eighteen thousand feet, just east of the Kamchatka Peninsula. That landmass protruded from the Pacific side of the Soviet Union but still lay well within the wind patterns blowing eastward from Semipalatinsk. When technicians at Tracerlab in Berkeley, California, unpacked the filters sent down from Alaska, they blinked hard. The scientists found the paper infested with isotopes of cerium, lead, barium, and molybdenum—and at readings so high that no natural geological event, such as a volcanic explosion, could account for them. The Tracerlab men checked their work for two weeks to make sure they were correct, but their conclusion did not change: A nuclear device had been detonated somewhere inside the Soviet Union.[2]

On September 19, when Truman received the news about Vermont—the code name quickly coined for the Soviet explosion—he was incredulous. "Are you sure? Are you *sure?*" he kept asking, shaking his head.[3] The Oval Office's sage-colored curtains were tied back on the trio of windows behind the president's big desk. In his diary, the Atomic Energy Commission's chairman, David Lilienthal, later recalled seeing "bright sunlight in the garden outside"—so effectively had McShain's high-plank fence prevented the White House construction site from being a distraction to the president.[4]

Truman could not bring himself to believe that the Soviets had built an atomic bomb on their own.[5] But the consensus of the nuclear scientists in Washington simply could not be ignored. Running calculations based on the radioactive decay rate, they had estimated that the explosion had taken place sometime between August 26 and 29. When the weight of the news settled on the president, he sighed gravely. "This means we have no time left," he said.[6]

The president's announcement tore across the front pages of the national papers on September 24, 1949. Beforehand, fearing panic in the streets, the White House begged editors not to overplay the story. Truman's brief statement deliberately omitted the word *bomb*, saying only that the government had obtained "evidence" of an "atomic explosion" in the Soviet Union. Truman also reminded the public that as early as 1945 it had been the government's assumption that "no single nation could, in fact, have a monopoly on atomic weapons."[7]

The most tangible result of "Joe 1" (the military's popular nickname for the first Soviet nuke) was Truman's decision in January 1950 to proceed with Campbell, the code name for research on the super-bomb, the thermonuclear warhead—what Americans would later know as the hydrogen bomb.[8] Still, for the single atomic weapon that the Soviets had blown up, the U.S. atomic stockpile stood at 235 "Fat Man" bombs. These were the plutonium-implosion devices of the sort that had leveled Nagasaki. In this, the very start of the arms race, the United States at least knew that it had a significant head start.

Still, even that margin offered few comforts. The way the military brass saw it, even one atomic bomb in Soviet hands was one bomb too many. On November 8, 1949, Secretary of Defense Louis A. Johnson had a top secret memo on his desk from the air force. "After almost two months of careful consideration of the significance of the Russian atomic explosion," the document stated, "we must conclude that the question of the survival of the United States may be involved."[9]

The renovation work on the White House proceeded as usual, and it might never have suffered any change of course had it not been for another big noise from the Communists—this one the sound of North Korean boots marching across the 38th parallel.

The United States had already occupied South Korea for five years when the Soviet-supported government of Kim Il-Sung launched an invasion. Secretary of State Dean Acheson called Truman with the news at 9:20 P.M. on June 24, 1950, reaching him at the family home on North Delaware Street in Independence. "Mr. President," he said, "I have very serious news."[10]

From the beginning, the significance of the event was one that went well beyond Asia (where Mao Tse-tung's Communist forces had seized power in China the previous October). Not only was the USSR already a nuclear power; it was now clear that the Soviets—who had, among other things, supplied the North Koreans with their T-34 and T-70 tanks—were willing to engage the United States in armed conflict. "The attack upon Korea makes it plain beyond all doubt," Truman's statement of June 27 read, "that Communism has passed beyond the use of subversion to conquer independent nations and will now use armed invasion and war."[11] More telling, however, was what Margaret Truman recalled her father saying just before he rushed to the airport to fly back to Washington. "My father made it clear, from the moment he heard the news," she said, "that he feared this was the opening round in World War III."[12]

On August 1, 1950, one day before American boots hit the ground in Pusan, Truman's naval aide, Robert L. Dennison, sat down to compose his message to Douglas Orr at the Commission on the Renovation of the Executive Mansion:

> *The President has authorized certain protective measures which include alterations at basement level in and adjacent to the wings of the White House. Plans for this work are now being developed by the Architect of the White House and the Public Buildings Service.*
>
> *In addition, and in order for these protective measures to be effective, certain minor modifications of the plans adopted by your*

Commission on Renovation of the Executive Mansion will be re-
quired. These modifications are confined to improvement of protective
characteristics in the basement of the Executive Mansion.[13]

Dennison closed by saying that "the cooperation of the commission to
this end is solicited." But the message was not really a request; it was a
directive.

As his memo had indicated, Dennison had already approached Lorenzo
Winslow (and almost certainly W. E. Reynolds at the Public Buildings
Administration) with the order to draw up plans for the "protective
measures" in the basement.[14] Though Winslow made no mention of any
such conversation on August 1, the date of Dennison's letter, three days
later he did—and there is no mistaking what was afoot. "At noon," Winslow penciled in his pocket diary, "I took the new shelter sketches in to
Adm. Dennison and he approved the work to go ahead without delay."[15]
Let the admiral speak about "certain protective measures" all he wanted,
but there was going to be an atomic-bomb shelter somewhere below the
White House.

Winslow had known about the secret project since at least the
middle of July, when he mentioned various conferences with Dennison
about it in his journal.[16] In a meeting on July 26 that included the admiral, Truman's assistant David Stowe, and budget director Frederick
J. Lawton, Winslow was ordered to begin drawing up the plans. The
group brought Edgerton in on the secret at this point. Clearly, the
project was now urgent: Winslow sketched late into the night, pushing
himself to the point of exhaustion.[17] The structure in the offing was
going to be substantial. The following day, Winslow requested three
more draftsmen for his department.

The commission's next scheduled meeting was for August 16. It's
probable that after receiving Dennison's memo Orr made a few phone
calls. Not only were he and Dougherty down in Washington a full day
before the commission's meeting; so was William Delano, who seldom
left his gilded perch in Manhattan. Together, the three men met with
Winslow, who noted in his diary that he began his "final plan for the
shelter" that very day.[18]

When all of the commissioners gathered around the big wooden table the following morning, it was the twenty-sixth time they had convened. But never in fourteen months of meetings had they faced a piece of business like the one before them now. Edgerton read Admiral Dennison's memo in full, then briefed those present on what it would mean. While the construction of the shelter itself would be a separate project, "it affects the renovation work substantially in the basement area,"[19] the minutes read. Winslow's plans to use the two subterranean levels to house various machine and storage rooms would remain mostly unchanged, but Dennison wanted the lower-level basement massively fortified.

Walls and ceilings in the northeast quadrant—which would serve as the shelter's primary means of access from both inside and outside the mansion—would all be muscled up with two feet of steel-reinforced concrete.[20] Several weeks earlier, Spencer, White & Prentis's steam shovels had scooped out five thousand cubic yards of earth near the northeast corner of the house. Edgerton's original plan had been to build two large chambers down there—"utility rooms," the press had called them.[21] But in the wake of Dennison's memo, Winslow appropriated this underground space for a far more important purpose: "Part of the area," the meeting minutes explained, "would be used in connection with the protective project."[22] For this reason, Edgerton had already halted all work on the mansion's north side until further notice.[23]

In his letter to Orr, Admiral Dennison had referred to his planned changes as "minor," but that was nothing but bureaucratic lowballing. "This is a large project," Winslow noted in his pocket diary, "with much work involved."[24]

The commissioners knew it, too. In their stuffy meeting room, they began to debate what effect the bomb shelter would have on a renovation that was already running behind schedule. A quarter of the footings for the house's new supporting columns were still not finished. The deteriorating "international situation" (the Korean War) was applying a steady chokehold on the supply of men, equipment, and steel. And now this?

By the time the commission gathered again two weeks later, tensions had reached a breaking point. When Orr started picking on McShain's foreman, demanding to know if his men had started the brickwork down in the basement, Hauck simply unraveled. "I do not know *what* to start in the basement now," he said, "with [all the] changes being made."[25] Tired of the indecision, Rabaut cut in: "This is getting to be like a bunch of lawyers—just talk." The usually taciturn Senator Martin was rankled now, too. To him, the shelter was just another delay—and for a purpose that seemed of questionable value to start with. "The Commission should resolve that there are not going to be any more changes in this thing," Martin fumed. "We have been changing too much—practically every meeting there have been changes made. The idea of security in the White House is good, [but] we can't have complete security anyway." Smoothing feathers, Dougherty said, "These changes by Admiral Dennison were beyond our control. Mr. Orr and I looked over [the] plans and it is quite a job."

The shelter *was* quite a job. It was also an inevitable one. Though the nuclear age had dawned a mere five years before, atomic security protocols were already not new for the White House. Back in October of 1945—a mere two months after Hiroshima and Nagasaki—the Secret Service closed the streets surrounding the executive mansion off to traffic. "We are living in the atomic age," said Secret Service chief Frank Wilson. "We can't take a chance."[26]

Wilson was being ridiculous. Not only did no foreign nation possess an atomic weapon in 1945; each Mark III bomb in the U.S. arsenal was ten feet long, five feet in diameter, and weighed five tons—not exactly the sort of device that a saboteur could hide in a Studebaker.

Still, Agent Wilson was scared. Everybody was scared. In 1946, a survey by the Social Science Research Council revealed that two-thirds of Americans fully expected another world war.[27] In April 1948, the Daughters of the American Revolution asked Maj. Gen. W. H. Arnold to address one of its meetings on the topic of what would happen if a nuclear bomb exploded over Washington. And in 1949, during the debate over what to do with the recently condemned White House, Senator John J. Sparkman of Alabama stepped forward and demanded an interior restoration that could withstand an atomic blast, even though such a construction was, in a practical sense, impossible.

Nor was Truman any stranger to the fear that a nuclear conflict might ignite at any time. In the early days of the Berlin Airlift, the operation that thwarted the Soviet blockade of the city by landing food and supplies in its western sector, Truman had ordered three support squadrons of B-29s into England—squadrons that, according to one official, carried atomic bombs. "We put B-29 bombers in England and took our weapons with us. We hauled those old weapons called 'Fatman,'" Col. Anthony Perna said.[28] The United States had already created a top secret plan called Charioteer, which laid down an attack pattern of seventy Soviet cities with 133 nuclear warheads. On

September 13, 1948, eighty-two days into the airlift, Truman wrote in his diary, "I have a terrible feeling . . . that we are very close to war."[29]

Then, on April 14, 1950, just two months before the Korean conflict started, the National Security Council sent Truman a top secret report known as NSC-68, the foundational document of the Cold War. Its exaggerated but horrifying contents assured the president that "the cold war is in fact a real war in which the survival of the free world is at stake," and that "the risk of war with the U.S.S.R. is sufficient to warrant, in common prudence, timely and adequate preparation by the United States."[30]

It was no wonder that the brass wanted a bomb shelter below the White House.

If the Truman bomb shelter would add to the White House's physical space, it would add even more to its mythology. Local legend was already rich with tales of things that supposedly existed beneath the city of Washington. In fact, stories about the White House's subterranean chambers and tunnels had floated around since the War of 1812, when Dolley Madison was believed to have escaped to the Octagon House through a fifteen-hundred-foot underground passageway. Many years later, another popular story held that President Harding used a tunnel to reach 1625 K Street N.W., a secret house filled with card games and painted ladies. Still other stories told of an underground tunnel connecting the White House to the Capitol (a distance of nearly two miles), a passage wide enough to drive a limousine through.[31] All of it was bosh.

The first time any sort of basement appeared below the White House's ground floor was 1902, when architect Charles Follen McKim sank a pit for Teddy Roosevelt's new boiler. Nothing happened for another thirty-four years, until, in 1935, FDR undertook a subterranean expansion plan that resulted in a complex of storage and workrooms below the North Portico. The White House grounds were left alone for another five years, until the Japanese attack on Pearl Harbor bred a new horror of death from the skies. Soon after, the Secret Service issued a memo warning that the White House would collapse if a kamikaze struck it. Another communication from the War and Navy Departments ventured that, should enemy planes appear over Washington, the president would be the "number one target."[32] These findings resulted in the creation of the White House's first underground defense installation, the FDR bomb shelter.

Work on it started a few weeks after December 7, 1941. Working directly below the East Wing, men wielded their shovels in three shifts around the clock to build the $65,000 bunker. The place was "relatively small . . . about the equivalent of two rooms," recalled David Stowe, who had served as chief examiner of the Bureau of the Budget during FDR's final years.[33] Still, the accommodations were state-of-the-art for the time. The forty-by-forty-foot enclosure boasted seven-foot-thick walls and a nine-foot ceiling slab of poured concrete. Two stairways led down to the shelter—one in the East Wing, the other in the garden. Inside, one hundred people could survive for days, perhaps even weeks, given that the bunker had its own food and water supply, medical room, and diesel-driven power and communication plants. FDR "could be moved from his office in the White House [to the shelter] in about 3 or 4 minutes," Lorenzo Winslow recalled. He also called the structure "about as permanent as anything in the country."[34]

But the elaborate bunker wasn't even the whole story. Even before work on the FDR shelter began, workmen commenced digging a tunnel seven feet high and ten feet wide below Fifteenth Street to connect the East Wing with the Treasury Building. Unlike the White House, the Treasury boasted tremendous foundations of granite. Bank vaults nested within the stone, and at least one of them was appropriated to create a subterranean apartment for FDR.[35] Once the president was wheeled through the tunnel and safely on the other side of a heavy steel door, he'd find himself in eleven hundred square feet of comfortable quarters. This shelter, two stories below the cash room in the Treasury's North Wing, boasted ten rooms. Surviving photos show a fully stocked kitchen and a bedroom with plush carpeting and a leather easy chair. The place was every bit as nice as a room at the Mayflower Hotel—except, of course, there were no windows.

When it came to whipping up plans for an atomic bunker on the double-quick, Lorenzo Winslow was good man to have around. His years of government service had given him a taste for survival architecture. Not only had he designed the FDR bomb shelter to take a direct hit from a five-hundred-pound piece of ordnance; he had also "work[ed] with Admiral Dennison in cooperation with other defense services," the commission noted obliquely.[36] Winslow had studied the effects of the Luftwaffe's blitz on London to develop the specs for Roosevelt's bomb shelter; no doubt he multiplied them for Truman's.

Even though the bomb shelter was technically a separate undertaking from the White House renovation, the two projects shared so much in common—timing, location, and Winslow as the architect—that the two jobs came to be seen as one. Clearly, the president viewed things that way. Stowe would later relate that when Truman made his regular inspection trips of the White House, he happily worked the shelter into his circuit. "I went over on many of these trips with him," Stowe said, "because one of the things I wanted to see each time was how they were doing with the shelter."[37]

Construction of the underground fortification progressed quickly. It would take just ninety-five days to pour its 660 cubic yards of concrete and to waterproof the rooms. Before the White House reopened, the shelter's location—backfilled with earth and topped with a toupee of sod—would be undetectable.[38] But no such smooth progress would be made on the White House basement. By mid-November, three months after the shelter had been announced to the commission, Hauck was still reporting "considerable delay."[39] The new drawings and specifications were more complicated than the old ones, and Hauck scrambled to mitigate the two.

For example, the entrance to the shelter would be through a door of four-inch steel with a retracting slit at eye level. Plans also called for a series of heavy-duty doors to line "the Tunnel"—the nickname for the corridor that ran the entire length of the basement, not only connecting its various storage rooms but serving as an artery between the East and West Wings belowground. According to Winslow's revised drawings, those doors had to be anchored in place before McShain's men could pour the Tunnel's extra-thick concrete. But since the doors had not been delivered, Hauck had no choice but to wait; McShain's foreman was, in the commission's words, "holding up much of the work that is part of the original contract until it can be tied in with the added work."[40]

That J. Paul Hauck was versed in such security details points to still another interesting wrinkle in the story: the degree to which John McShain, Inc., was involved with building the shelter itself. Nestled in McShain's surviving papers is not only an estimate sheet for the Tunnel but one attached to it titled "Shelter." On it, in McShain's characteristically tiny handwriting, is a detailed job estimate that enumerates 150 tons of gravel, 1,000 tons of steel, and 3,030 cubic yards of concrete.[41] Save for this single page, any other reference to the underground bunker is mysteriously missing from the McShain papers, but a logical conclusion can be drawn: John McShain's men built not only the reinforcements to the White House basement but very likely its contiguous bomb shelter, too.

"My father never mentioned it," Pauline McShain said, though she speculated he did build the shelter, then kept quiet about it, as any man in his position would have had to. "I'm sure he was sworn to secrecy," she added. "He never said a word about it."[42]

Back out in the everyday world beyond the White House gates, the public knew nothing of the bomb-shelter project, either, and the commission worked very hard to keep it that way. Members of the commission refused to acknowledge it publicly. When a reporter asked Orr if there were any plans to fit the White House with a bunker to shield the president, Orr was adamant: "There is nothing we can do about building such a shelter in the White House," he said.[43]

Really? Well, Americans were certainly trying it with their own basements. Ever since the news that the Soviets had gotten the bomb, millions of Americans had begun to regard that space under the stairs differently. "People have got to become underground-conscious," an army colonel told *The New Yorker* in 1947.[44] In no time, that's exactly what they did. Soon, Civil Defense offices in most every city started passing out handy booklets with titles like *Survival Under Atomic Attack* and a page-turner called *The Family Fallout Shelter*, which came complete with detailed plans for cinder-block refuges that could be built right downstairs next to the water softener. Americans stocked up on canned goods and dry cereal. Some stores even stocked items like fallout protection suits. Before the decade was out, one public-opinion poll would reveal that 40 percent of Americans were giving serious thought to building a shelter of their own.[45]

So it was only natural that the public began to wonder about the potential of the deep new basements below the White House. A few months after Orr denied that anything was going on underground, another reporter tried asking General Edgerton if a White House shelter was in the offing. "I don't have that word in my vocabulary," Edgerton replied.[46] The renovation's executive director was more or less telling the truth. An apparent code name—Project 9—usually appeared in the commission's papers anytime it was necessary to make reference to work going on below the east side of the mansion. Edgerton appears to have slipped up only once. A 1951 entry in his construction log reads "OCE Engrs. Inspect Project No. 9. Steel in Shelter OK."[47]

Try as it might, however, the commission could keep no secrets from *Washington Post* reporter Drew Pearson, whose syndicated "Washington Merry-Go-Round" column was among the most widely read in the United States. Pearson knew that the capital city had more leaks than an old inner tube. On September 24, 1950, Pearson whispered a rumor into the ears of his millions of readers: "Eventually, these two basement floors will have a bombproof underground shelter."[48]

In the end, the American public would officially learn about the secret project not from a muckraker, but an accountant. In a closed-door hearing before the House Appropriations Committee, Frederick J. Lawton, director of the Budget Bureau, revealed that Truman had dipped into the presidential Special Fund to pay for a bomb shelter below the mansion. Most of Lawton's testimony stayed secret, but the parts that leaked out were enough. "Truman Digs into Special Fund for $881,000 A-Bomb Shelter," announced the *Washington Post* on April 18, 1951, reporting that the White House shelter "will protect the President against an A-bomb blast and against radioactive particles."[49]

Even though the documents are well over sixty years old as of this writing, Winslow's drawings of the mansion's subbasements and shelter complex are restricted from public view. The Truman Library's copy of Winslow's basement plans was withheld from the author, and a Freedom of Information Act request to the Public Buildings Service yielded only a letter maintaining that no archival records of the shelter's construction could be found.[50] These outcomes are not surprising, given the present-day concerns over domestic terrorism and the fact that the Secret Service still regards the subbasement tunnel and its connection to the Treasury Building as a viable escape route from the White House.[51] Nevertheless, using the available body of documents from the period, it is still possible to piece together a fairly detailed picture of what the facility looked like when it was new.[52]

Truman's atomic shelter most likely included part or all of the five thousand square yards excavated below the east bend of the front driveway, along with the rooms of FDR's old bomb shelter, which sat just below the East Terrace, the slender corridor that connected the mansion to the East Wing. The grouping would have created a fairly sizable complex contiguous to the northeast corner of the mansion— some beneath its East Terrace, some immediately to the north.[53] What might have happened in a doomsday scenario? Electrician Traphes

Bryant said that "the president could be whisked underground in seconds."[54] In her memoirs, Lillian Parks made reference to various "escape hatches."[55] In view of Winslow's having added heavy-duty rebar and concrete reinforcements not only to the tunnel running below the house but to the walls and floors of the basement's northeast corner as well, it seems likely that Admiral Dennison was allowing for multiple escape routes from the West Wing and from the White House itself. Most captivating is an elevator shaft constructed just outside the foundation wall of the mansion's northeast corner. The elevator would have permitted quick access from the grounds outside down to the deepest level of the house. Did Winslow put it there simply to allow easier access to his basement storage areas—or was the elevator meant to lead to something far more important?[56]

The single known description of the shelter's interior comes from the private diary of Roger Wellington Tubby, who served as Truman's assistant press secretary from 1952 until 1953.[57] Tubby's memoirs state that the shelter's entranceway lay off a passage in the mansion's northeast corner. Beyond a heavy steel door lay a shower room (to be used if shedding atomic fallout became necessary), followed by a large chamber equipped with some seventy U.S. Army–issue cots. The beds were, presumably, intended for whatever White House officials and staff were fortunate enough to make it underground in time.

Branching off the shelter's main room were several smaller chambers, including a communications center with direct telephone lines to the Pentagon—which, of course, had its own shelter. Another room in the underground warren contained water and food rations. "The president and his advisors could stay [in the shelter] for days or even weeks, if necessary," the *Washington Post* would later report.[58] Winslow had also designed an eight-by-ten-foot room for the private use of the Trumans. It contained four bunk beds, a chemical toilet, and, as a nice finishing touch, a supply of books.

Exactly how or why Truman would care for leisure-reading materials while the city above him vanished in a fireball is hard to say. Then again, perhaps it isn't. As Admiral Dennison himself knew, the president would never be reading those books because he had no intention of ever using his bomb shelter. "Of course, you've got to go ahead with all of this planning and all of these arrangements," Truman had told the admiral. "But I want to tell you one thing. If a situation ever develops . . . I don't intend to leave the White House. I am going to be right here." Dennison absorbed this piece of information, and replied, "Well, I expected that, knowing you."[59]

Truman's assistant David Stowe had been put in charge of developing plans to evacuate Congress and other departments—exhaustively detailed plans, as Admiral Dennison would reveal many years later. "We had places all over the countryside for various parts of our government to go," the admiral said. "We had railway trains on either side of the river and plenty of automobiles. We had a number of different options for evacuation."[60] At this time, early in the Cold War, those facilities included Camp David (then known as "Shangri-La") and the presidential yacht *Williamsburg*, which doubled as a floating command center. Six miles north of Camp David, construction had already begun on the top secret "Site R" (also known as Raven Rock Mountain), an underground city of three five-story buildings hewn out of the Blue Ridge Summit granite some two thousand feet beneath the ridge.[61]

But Truman himself—captain of a ship of state—would not be leaving his post. The shelter was for everyone else in the White House, not him. From Dennison, Truman merely sought assurances that if the Soviet bombers were to take off for the United States, the president would be able to make a broadcast to the American populace and "assure them that I am here, not up in the hills some place."[62]

The building of the Truman bomb shelter raises one final question. Did anyone truly believe that a cluster of rooms some thirty feet belowground would be strong enough to withstand a nuclear blast? The plutonium-implosion weapon that the Soviets had tested the year before had yielded an explosive force of twenty-two kilotons. But even as construction of the shelter was under way, the Soviets were preparing to test a bomb of *double* that yield. The American quest for thermonuclear weapons had already begun, too. It would move atomic weaponry from the kiloton to the megaton range, and the Defense Department understood it was only a matter of time before the Soviet Union possessed these weapons, as well. Would this underground bunker, strong as Winslow had made it, really be of any use once it was finished? The answer was no, and everyone knew it. "No structure could be built to withstand a near hit," General Larson revealed years later. But, he added, the planners went "as far as [they] could."[63] In the spooky, bewildering logic of the Cold War, something was always better than nothing.

SIXTEEN

TWENTY-SEVEN ROUNDS

> The Secret Service wasn't happy about the security situation [at] Blair House. The Secret Service people proved to be entirely right.
>
> —Harry Truman

*A*s the planning and preparation for the bomb shelter pushed ahead in the final weeks of 1950, the Trumans prepared to mark their second anniversary living across the street from the White House. To make the contiguous Blair and Lee houses into a single dwelling, Truman had ordered passages cut through the brick wall that had separated them. Now, Blair House became shorthand for both dwellings. The place was still tiny as a dollhouse, but the Trumans had grown comfortable there. And since J. B. West had brought over enough of the furniture, Blair House even looked a little like the White House. Certainly, it was just as chaotic.

Butler Alonzo Fields would never forget June 25, a Sunday he'd been enjoying at home until the telephone rang. It was usher Charles Claunch, ordering him to Blair House on the double. With the situation in Korea deteriorating by the hour, Truman had decided to fly back to Washington from Missouri for an emergency meeting with his senior staff. Fields shaved and jumped into a cab, planning out the entire dinner menu on the way. By the time the president walked in from the airport, Fields was serving cocktails in his white tie and tails. Blair House or the White House—Fields knew it didn't matter. "They can't do much here without us," he used to tell the other servants. "They've got to eat, you know."[1]

The presidential routine at Blair House was also much the same as it had been over at the White House. The immensity of Truman's schedule never ceased to astonish those around him. "He put in a 16- to 18-hour day," said press secretary Charlie Ross, "—and was fresher at the end than I was at the beginning."[2] The president still rose at 5:30 A.M. and read five newspapers before setting off on his morning walk. He'd head due south to the Ellipse, turn left, and skirt the Mall all the way to the Capitol. "A man in my position has a public duty to keep himself in good condition," Truman told J. B. West. "You can't be mentally fit unless you're physically fit."[3] Four years shy of his seventieth birthday, Truman marched two miles a day in those wingtip shoes. The District of Columbia's Traffic Advisory Board had recently honored Truman with its "Pedestrian of the Week" award for "his firm decision to wait faithfully for a green light."[4]

Truman seemed nearly as proud of being a pedestrian as he was of being a president, and living at Blair House had given him even more chances to clomp around than the White House had. Truman loved to walk the block and a half to the West Wing in the morning, then walk back to Blair House for lunch. At some point, a local tour operator began selling tickets to tourists who wanted to watch him walking between the two buildings.[5]

Journalists had learned that the chance to interview the president often meant tailing him while he walked "at a pace normally reserved for track stars," complained UPI reporter Merriman Smith.[6] Even the First Daughter would not escape the forced march. When a bout of bronchitis laid her low midway through a 1949 concert tour, Margaret found herself locked up in Blair House until the malady cleared. Once it did, her father decided that a 6:00 A.M. outing was just the thing. He'd left her in the dust after one block. "Come on, Margie. What's holding you up?" Truman yelled behind him. "Where's the fire?" she shot back. "Why don't you buy some sensible shoes?" he replied.[7]

⇥ ⇤

If Margaret didn't much care for her father's sidewalk escapades, the Secret Service liked them even less. "If there was one trait of Harry

Truman's that had been a thorn for the Secret Service, it was the morning stroll," recalled agent Rufus Youngblood.[8] Still fresh was the shame of that morning in 1945 when oblivious agents had allowed Truman to simply walk out to Pennsylvania Avenue unguarded.

The big bad world had grown no safer since then. In 1947, a packet of gelignite-packed letter bombs addressed to Truman had arrived at the White House, as had an Ohio man who insisted he had an invitation to see Truman—but had two ice picks on him instead.[9] The last two presidents who'd been assassinated, Garfield and McKinley, had both been walking out in public at the fatal moment. Secret Service chief U. E. Baughman dreaded the hour of Truman's morning stroll. "Walking along the street . . . made Mr. Truman a slow-moving target," Baughman said, "the delight of a sharpshooter."[10]

The Secret Service knew it would never dissuade Truman from hitting the sidewalk, though the agents had done everything they could think of to reduce the risks. At one point, they'd gotten municipal authorities to synchronize the traffic lights ahead of Truman's path, assuring a green light at every corner. The boss caught on pretty fast, though, and told them to cut it out.[11]

Back in 1933, an out-of-work bricklayer had emptied six rounds into the back of Franklin D. Roosevelt's limousine, mortally wounding Chicago mayor Anton Cermak. The brush with death had made a deep impression on FDR, who slept with a revolver under his pillow.[12] But Truman had no such fears. He'd made it through the bloody trenches of the Meuse-Argonne during World War I, and nothing that skulked on the streets of Washington was likely to scare him. Truman's genuine affection for common folk also left him unable to grasp why anyone would do him harm. "Who'd want to shoot me?" he asked.[13]

Much as his agents disapproved of Truman's public strolling, they took an even dimmer view of his living quarters. Blair House might be a comfortable stand-in for the White House in Truman's view, but the Secret Service saw the place as a security nightmare. Sure, they'd set up guard booths near both corners of the house. In theory, sentries posted there could stop a man trying to ascend the front steps of number 1651 or number 1653, Blair House's two doors on Pennsylvania Avenue.

But everyone on the force knew that the place was wide open. At the White House, MPs could walk the roof with machine guns and survey acres of lawn protected by the high fence. At Blair House, though, the fence was low and ornamental. It didn't close off the front steps, either. Worst of all, Blair House's "lawn" was nothing more than a five-foot strip of grass. Little wonder that Lillian Parks had felt a tug of anxiety during the move two years before. "Blair House was so close to the street," she had thought, "that I could see it right out the window."[14]

It was easily the biggest irony of the entire renovation project: The very process of making the White House safe for the president quartered him in a house that was, in a different way, just as dangerous. "Theoretically," Secret Service agent Andrew Tully wrote, "a man can stand in the middle of Pennsylvania Avenue and send bullets whistling into Blair House's windows."[15]

On the night of Tuesday, October 31, 1950, the Pennsylvania Railroad's "Afternoon Congressional" swept down the New York Avenue approach and slipped in between the skinny fingers of Union Station's platforms. The 227-mile trip from New York had taken four and a half hours from the train's 3:00 P.M. boarding time at Pennsylvania Station in New York, and so the sun had already set when Griselio Torresola and Oscar Collazo stepped from one of the coaches.

The conductor had taken their tickets somewhere on the way down. Though both men lived in New York City and knew nobody in Washington, they'd purchased one-way fares. That had been a sensible decision. Both the thirty-six-year-old Collazo and his young companion of twenty-five understood that, come the next day, they would almost certainly be dead. No use paying for a train you would never take.

The men crossed under the track gates and into the station's vast passenger concourse, a cavern of marble with a coffered ceiling. Their footfalls would have made a pleasing tap on the polished floor. Collazo and Torresola were wearing new dress shoes and new suits, too—gray and navy chalk-stripe ones. Dandy dress was one of many things these men shared in common. Here were the others: Both men were radically dedicated members of the Nationalist Party of Puerto Rico; both were armed with World War II–era, German-made semi-automatic pistols; and both had come to Washington together to kill Harry S. Truman.

The logic of their plan still confuses, all these decades later. Torresola and Collazo believed that murdering the president would somehow reflect favorably on the cause of the tiny island's independence. The assassination was supposed to give rise to a revolution in the United States, during which Puerto Rico could declare its sovereignty.

According to the FBI files on the men, the U.S. government had been watching the Nationalist Party of Puerto Rico since the mid-1930s, when its tactics had turned violent. But the NPPR's best days were long behind it. In fact, a majority of Puerto Ricans were satisfied with the island's commonwealth status and didn't want independence at all. By 1950, the group's membership had shrunk to an anemic 995 people. Nevertheless, the alliance boasted a charismatic leader by the name of Pedro Albizu Campos, and as Griselio Torresola walked across Union Station's concourse, he carried on his person a letter from this very man. It charged Torresola with undertaking "the supreme needs of the cause" and expressed Albizu Campos's wish that the "mission may be a triumph."[16]

On Massachusetts Avenue, not far from the train station, the pair found a threadbare hotel called the Harris. Lodgings were $3.50 a night. In Torresola's room, the men found a map of the city in the pages of the telephone directory and, after scanning the confusing grid of streets, managed to locate the White House.

The only trait that matched Collazo's and Torresola's daring was their stupidity. Not only had they come to Washington with no idea of where the White House was; they were also unaware that Truman was not living in it. This latter bit of news came to the pair on the following morning when, during the drive over to the White House, the cabbie told the men that the mansion was empty. Hadn't they heard? The old place had been torn up for two years now. See? Just look. Then the helpful man at the wheel pointed to the pale yellow houses across Pennsylvania Avenue. There, he told them, was where President Truman lived.

The pair from New York cased the block quickly, then left to lay out their strategy. The murder was to work like this: The assassins would approach Blair House from opposite directions along Pennsylvania Avenue—Torresola from the west and Collazo from the Lafayette Park side. First they would shoot the guards in the security booths. Then Torresola would cover Collazo as he sprinted up the front steps, entered the house, and fired a round into President Truman.

Among the many naïve assumptions that the men would make that day, one of them turned out to be correct: Truman was actually home. Though the president would normally be at the Oval Office on a weekday afternoon like this, Truman had been invited to unveil a statue at Arlington and was grabbing a quick nap before the ceremony. His bedroom window was just above Blair House's front door.

Fate improbably favored Collazo and Torresola in another way that afternoon: A freakish heat wave had descended on Washington, pushing the mercury to eighty-five degrees. It meant that the president—asleep atop his bed and wearing only his underwear—had opened his window. It also meant that Blair House's heavy front door had been left open. "There was only a screen door with an ordinary little latch between them and the inside of the house, where Mrs. Truman and I were in our bedrooms," Truman later recalled.[17]

When Torresola and Collazo paid their return visit to Blair House at 2:19 P.M. on that All Saints' Day of 1950, there were five lawmen out in front.[18] White House police officers Joseph Davidson and Leslie Coffelt sat in the east and west guard booths, respectively, some 130 feet apart. Just minutes before, the guards had completed their rotation—"the push," they called it—which posted Donald Birdzell at the bottom of the front steps. Joseph Downs, just relieved of his post, was heading into the security office in the basement. Secret Service agent Floyd Boring was standing outside, too, bantering with Davidson in the east booth.

Boring was a big-framed man who, like the president, sometimes wore bow ties. He'd wandered outside to escape the heat in the house and had begun to tease Officer Davidson about his new glasses, accusing him of wearing them just to get a better look at the girls passing by.[19] At that moment, Oscar Collazo breezed past the east guard booth, produced a Walther P-38 from his waistband, and aimed at Birdzell on the steps.

Collazo pulled the trigger, but the hammer fell with a harmless click. Never having fired a semiautomatic before, Collazo had engaged the safety by mistake.[20] As Birdzell drew his gun to return fire, Collazo smacked the Walther with his free hand and the gun went off, driving a bullet deep into Birdzell's right knee. Blinded with pain and immediately spouting blood, Birdzell nonetheless did exactly the right thing: He stumbled out into Pennsylvania Avenue to draw Collazo's attention away from the house. Sure enough, Collazo turned and kept firing—and missing.

Bess Truman heard the shots as she was coming down the main stairs. "What's happening?" she asked J. B. West, who'd looked out the front door and seen just enough to yell, "Close the door!"[21] Bess ran back up the stairs and burst into Truman's bedroom. "Harry," she cried, "someone's shooting our policemen!" Truman bounded up and, without thinking, poked his head out the window. From the street came a voice (nobody was sure whose) that yelled, "Get back! Get back!" Truman did. Then he walked over to his bedroom door and opened it slightly— enough to see Special Agent Stewart Stout in the corridor, crouching behind a machine gun, its nuzzle aimed down the stairs.

While Collazo shot at the wounded Birdzell on Pennsylvania Avenue, Torresola—a mercilessly accurate marksman—had produced a sleek Luger service revolver, aimed it into the west booth, and pumped three bullets into Private Leslie Coffelt's chest. As the officer's body slumped through the booth's open door, Torresola took aim at Officer Downs, bringing him to the ground with another three shots.

Lillian Parks was up on the third floor with Rose Booker, a maid who'd just been hired. The heat had led Parks to open her window, too. She'd set her sewing machine on the wide sill when the sound of gunfire erupted from the street below. Booker ran to see what was going on. "Rose—take your head in!" Parks yelled.[22]

As Torresola looked east and saw Collazo reloading on Blair House's front steps, he took his own shot at the wounded Birdzell, striking him in the other knee. It was the last act that Torresola would perform on this earth. Mortally wounded and lying on the street outside the west booth, Officer Coffelt propped himself up, steadied his aim, and blew a hole through the back of Torresola's skull.

Alonzo Fields was in the kitchen, planning menus, when one of the assistant housekeepers rushed in to say that Officer Downs lay wounded in the basement. The butler ran down the stairs. Downs was on the couch, bleeding from holes in his chest and neck. Fields remembered cutting the blood-soaked tie off of Downs's neck.[23]

Now Collazo was alone. Before he could turn for the Blair House door, a fusillade of bullets erupted from the street, striking him in the face and chest. He folded like a rag doll and fell.

The revolution had failed. It had all taken less than forty seconds. Twenty-seven rounds lay scattered on the pavement or buried in flesh.

Agent Floyd Boring ran upstairs to check on the president, finding him in his bedroom.

"What the hell is going on down there?" Truman blurted.[24]

Unharmed and on his feet, Truman saw no reason not to attend the unveiling ceremony at Arlington, and so he did, taking his deeply shaken wife along. At the last minute, Mrs. Truman dashed back into the house to telephone Margaret, who was scheduled to sing that evening in Portland, Maine. Bess was afraid that Margaret would hear the news of the shooting over the radio. But while she sought to reassure her daughter, Bess Truman didn't want to give her the news and risk it destroying her composure for the concert. The call was a tricky one. "I just want you to know everyone's all right," the First Lady said. "Why *shouldn't* everyone be all right?" Margaret replied.[25]

Officer Leslie Coffelt died on the hospital operating table. Margaret went on with her scheduled tour.[26] Oscar Collazo survived his wounds, and he would later be sentenced to death in the electric chair—a sentence that Harry Truman later commuted to life in prison.[27]

Those who expected a profound change in Harry Truman following the assassination attempt would wait in vain. "A president has to expect those things" was all he said.[28] But life changed dramatically at Blair House. Glaziers arrived to install bulletproof windows. City officials banned traffic from Pennsylvania Avenue. The streetcar stop disappeared. Now even veteran staffers would have to show identification to get into the house.

After an exhaustive investigation, the Secret Service issued an official report on the incident. The biggest share of the blame fell on the house itself: "Having President Truman reside in the Blair House while renovations were being completed at the White House had in fact actually amplified the security risk to the President," the document stated. "The Blair House offered, by its architectural design and placement, a limited-security environment."[29]

At first, the Secret Service used the shootings to halt Truman's morning constitutional. "They won't let me go walking or even cross the street on foot," Truman complained to his cousin Ethel in a letter of November 17. Eventually, the president had his way—but with a few concessions. On his morning stroll, one agent marched beside him, while three brought up the rear. (All of them were "good men, athletes, and *good shots*," Truman said.[30]) An undercover agent watched the block directly ahead of the president's path, while six agents rode in a car half a block behind.

◦⊨⇒ ⇐⊨◦

Thanksgiving Day arrived at Blair House twenty-two days after the shooting. To the president's delight, Bess stayed in town and Margaret came down from New York. The family shared a thirty-five-pound Pennsylvania turkey at the Blair House dinner table with exactly the number of guests that Bess liked: zero. Sometime after dinner, as the lingering late-day light sparkled on the Potomac, Truman slipped across Pennsylvania Avenue with his family in tow and passed through the gates of the silent construction site.[31]

The timber scaffolding with its exterior stairs clutched the White House like an enormous mantis. To the east of the North Portico, the ground had been torn up, exposing a warren of subterranean spaces—most probably the "utility rooms" destined, in all likelihood, to become part of the president's atomic-bomb shelter.[32]

Inside the foyer of the mansion, the Trumans stood amid all the recently poured concrete floors and could see the perfect flat planes reaching clear to the opposite end of the house. The stunning vistas of open steelwork filling up the shell of the old building—the sights of the house's great stone shell that had so captivated reporters the summer before—were already gone. Now ductwork had begun to snake its way around the gray cement floor slabs like fat silver earthworms. Both the mechanical and electric work had recently gotten under way. McShain's men had begun to raise the partitions, too, conjuring the shapes of actual rooms for the first time. Cables lay across the floor, skirting past the random ladder and puddle of hose water. Above, bare bulbs glowed from the temporary wiring strung across the expanse.

Did Truman see progress in the cold, damp concrete, or just a job running behind schedule? He never said. But as the family looked around, a clutch of tourists began to gather outside the gates. Word had spread quickly: The president of the United States was, if only for these few minutes, back inside the White House.

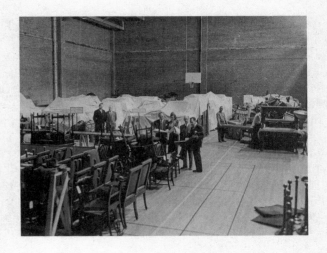

Seventeen

FURNITURE, RUGS, AND DRAPERIES

"Won't you come in?"—that's the note in every Altman decorated room. This is a nice assembly of antique furniture and fine
reproductions—harmonious colors against warm pine paneling,
with a bow to the popular white contrast in today's color schemes.
Let Altman decorators help you with furniture groupings for
single rooms, entire homes, yachts or planes.

—B. Altman & Co., advertisement for the Decorating Shop

On *September 21*, 1950, John S. Burke, Sr., a studious, silver-
haired man with rimless spectacles, sat in his office on Fifth
Avenue in Manhattan and composed a letter. Burke was the
president of B. Altman & Co., the legendary department store in the
shadow of the Empire State Building. Even in a city filled with fine
stores, B. Altman's had a reputation that dated all the way back to
the Gilded Age. The *New York Evening Sun* once called it "one of the
greatest department stores in the world," and even now, in the postwar era, the moniker still rang true.[1] From steamer trunks to French

perfume, gentlemen's suits to Waterford crystal, there was little the cosmopolitan New Yorker might want that B. Altman did not stock inside its Renaissance palazzo of French limestone in midtown. Burke had taken his first job at the store fresh out of Yale. Now, at age sixty, he ran the place. He was a gifted executive, a generous philanthropist, and a brilliant marketer.[2] The letter Burke was writing to the Commission on the Renovation of the Executive Mansion was evidence of all three.

Burke was aware that the commission would soon have to select a decorator for the White House—a mansion with twenty-five bedrooms to furnish, 147 windows to treat, and formal state rooms demanding the skills of fine-art hangers and wall upholsterers. What decorator was capable of managing a job so large and prestigious? Burke informed the commission that B. Altman & Co. not only stood at the ready but would render its services for free.

Of course, the country counted many fine department stores equipped with skilled decorating teams, but none of them boasted the connection that John S. Burke did. On B. Altman's seventh floor was a wood-paneled department stuffed with antiques and oil paintings. It was called the Decorating Shop, and its supervisor was a talented young designer everyone knew as Chuck. Chuck was none other than Charles T. Haight, the decorator who'd swooped in to help a desperate usher Crim evacuate the furnishings from the collapsing White House back in 1948. It had been the sort of gesture impossible to forget, and Crim had not. When John Burke sat down to write his proposal to the commission, it was Howell Crim who'd encouraged him to send it.[3]

The envelope found its way to Edgerton's desk. The general opened it and read "Gentlemen: In connection with the re-furnishing of The White House, we wish to submit to the Commission the following proposal for consideration. If called upon to furnish furniture, rugs, draperies, accessories or any other furnishings for The White House, the firm of B. Altman & Co. will be happy to supply these goods at absolute cost."[4]

Edgerton must have blinked. "Absolute cost" meant that the department store would invoice the government for only the wholesale price of the decorative pieces. All other expenses would be borne by the store. Not least of these were the talents of Haight himself, who'd written a separate cover letter detailing the services he could offer—

selection of fine rugs and period antiques, restoration of all existing furniture, presentation of fabric and carpet swatches, the sewing of all panels, valences, swags, jabots, cascades, and tiebacks, plus full water-color renderings of every room before work began.[5]

The offer sounded too good to be true, a fact that Burke himself must have sensed. He closed his letter with the assurances that his store had no ulterior motives of "publicity or profit in any form." Burke was, he said, offering his services in "a spirit of helpfulness."[6]

No doubt that was true. Nevertheless, the publicity value of land-ing the White House decorating contract could not have been lost on an executive of his standing. "I am sure he felt that [offering the store's labor] would be an important contribution to the U.S. and that the White House should be spectacular and represent the best of Amer-ica," says Jane B. O'Connell, president of the Altman Foundation, and also Burke's daughter. As for the standing rule that contractors en-gaged to work on the White House were prohibited from advertising that fact for commercial gain, Burke would have known that public relations can do the heavy lifting when advertising cannot. "[He] was a master marketer," O'Connell says. "He knew perfectly well that the word would get out and that B. Altman & Co. would get plenty of credit for its generosity."[7]

The task of hiring a firm to redecorate the mansion had already come up several times during commission meetings, but the men had always put it off. Delano had started to warn them that their procrastination was going to cost them if they kept it up. Crim added that the decorat-ing budget was looking a little thin as things stood.[8] So when Burke's letter arrived—the wonder of coincidental timing that it was—the com-missioners took the hint. They slated the decorating issue for the next meeting, and Haight packed a valise for Washington.

On November 29, 1950, the commissioners assembled in their make-shift conference room in the East Wing. Their chairman, Senator McKellar, had found the group these quarters exactly one year before to the day.[9] The space did not rise to the dignity of its business, but the commissioners made the best of it. Clad in their woolen suits, the men wedged themselves around two library tables piled high with binders, leather books, and ashtrays. Pleated curtains encircled the space in a feeble attempt to afford privacy. The old leather chairs sat so close to-gether, their upholstery nails rubbed.[10]

Orr opened the proceedings. Since B. Altman & Co. was already storing so many of the mansion's furnishings in its warehouse, he said, it only made sense just to let the store handle all of the decorating. In view of the store's offering its decorating services free of charge, the commission noted that Senator Martin "did not think the commission could do better" than the offer before them.[11] Edgerton had made copies of Burke's offer and handed them around the table, though he really needn't have bothered. What part of "free" did these businessmen not understand? Orr invited Haight to step into the meeting.

The tall, debonair decorator took his seat. After the pleasantries, the commissioners began to question him. Could Altman's complete such a big job in only eight months? Yes, it could, Haight assured them.[12] Had the department store decorated any other houses comparable in aesthetic or historical importance? Well, Haight replied with his easy charm, there was no home *quite* like the White House. But yes, he continued, Altman's had decorated the Argentinean and Egyptian embassies in Washington, and also restored the interiors of the late Franklin D. Roosevelt's cottage in Warm Springs, Georgia. Haight also reminded the commissioners that he'd worked in the White House before, too, sprucing up the Green Room, the Oval Office, and the Cabinet Room during Truman's first term. Though he'd studied at Parsons and apprenticed in Paris, the Minnesota-born Haight still had his humility and good midwestern manners. Even President Truman liked Haight—no small plus. The bird was in hand.

Then the issue of money came up. Haight presumed that the government had set aside a generous purse to purchase the needed furnishings. After all, was the White House not the most important residence in the United States? So when Douglas Orr informed Haight that there was only $210,000 left in the budget for decorating, he might as well have spilled a glass of ice water into the decorator's lap. "My God," Haight blurted, "do you know how many rooms you have? You could spend your $210,000 in the blinking of an eye—on one or two rooms."[13]

Was the commission embarrassed at having so little money to offer? It should have been. According to the final accounting, the commissioners had spent $232,000 just to build the temporary construction shacks on the South Lawn.[14] Now, here they were offering $22,000 *less* than that, and expecting to decorate 66 rooms with it.

When he'd walked into the meeting just a few minutes earlier, Haight had entertained visions of scouting out the finest period pieces for the White House, of filling it with the treasures it deserved. In an instant, his grand plans were shattered. "I can spend your $210,000 the best it could be spent and Altman's will not make a penny," Haight said, still reeling. "But it is not enough."[15]

No, it wasn't. And that made this moment a defining one for the White House's aesthetic and cultural legacy. Could the commissioners— men of considerable power and influence—truly have found *no* means of obtaining period furnishings for the executive mansion? If wringing more money out of Congress was a long shot (and, admittedly, it was), there was always the option of asking wealthy private collectors to donate the needed pieces to the mansion—the very course of action that Jacqueline Kennedy would deploy a decade later, with stunning results.

But the commission did neither of these things. In fact, when several offers to donate fine furnishings did begin to trickle in, the commission turned them away with the mystifying explanation that it wanted no "relics" piling up at the house.[16]

In the space of a few minutes, Haight's entire calculus had changed. Rather than embark on the commission of a lifetime, he'd be stretching every dollar. Haight had little choice but to make the best of the situation: Burke's offer was already on the table and the commissioners were eager to accept it and move on with other business.[17] Leapfrogging the customary requirement for competitive bidding, the commission evoked the convenient loophole in Public Law 119 by declaring that accepting B. Altman & Co.'s offer was "in the interest of the United States."[18]

And that was that. Two weeks before Christmas of 1950, Charles Haight became the interior decorator of the White House.

Haight might have consoled himself with the thought that he could at least work with all of the rare, antique furnishings that he and Crim had carefully taken out of the White House back in 1948, were it not for an unpleasant truth: Most of the pieces were neither rare nor antique.

While the man on the street might easily presume that the White House was bursting with artifacts dating to the earliest days of the republic, it just wasn't true. Even on the State Floor, showplace of the house, nothing remained from the first one hundred years of the mansion's existence except for a set of candlesticks, two clocks, and a couple of paintings.[19] True, the house did have some beautiful furnishings, in particular the gilded banquettes by L. Marcotte and the Davenport chairs from Boston. Yet even these pieces, purchased in 1902, were barely half a century old. And it would take more than a few chairs and benches to furnish a mansion.

Crim had learned just how historically bankrupt the White House furniture collection was back in 1946, when he'd asked curators from the National Park Service to determine the provenance of everything in the public rooms. Haight had learned it as he'd eyeballed all of the pieces being trundled out of the house in 1948. Eventually, Truman learned the truth, too, and it made him angry. "I hate to think of all the valuable relics that have been thrown out of the White House, or sold away, just because there wasn't room for them," he said. "It would be nice if we could get some of those things back again."[20]

It certainly would have been. But everything was long gone by now. As Winslow had lamented during his fruitless hunt for the house's original mantelpieces, Chester Arthur's notorious 1882 purge had sent twenty-four wagonloads of items clattering off to the auction house, never to return. But Arthur wasn't the first president enamored of furniture sales. James Madison had auctioned off White House furnishings as early as 1810. Andrew Johnson and James Buchanan had cleaned house, too, as had the widowed Mary Lincoln.[21] For more than a century, auction houses all over Washington did a brisk trade in selling off discarded White House furniture, much of which found its way to inns and taverns. After Ulysses S. Grant redecorated the White House in 1873, several pieces from the East Room sold to businessman John T. Ford, who had discovered that used-furniture auctions were an economical way to furnish the theaters he owned.[22] And when Theodore Roosevelt ordered the famous wall of Tiffany stained glass removed from the foyer in 1902, a real-estate developer snapped it up for $275.[23]

When an old piece of furniture wasn't tagged for auction, it found its way upstairs to the servants' rooms on the third floor.[24] It was there, in 1923, that a progressively minded Grace Coolidge decided to rummage around in hopes of finding some piece of furniture that had belonged to any of the twenty-nine presidents who had preceded her husband. When an unusual-looking chair slathered in paint caught her eye, she ordered it stripped and refinished. Later, historians determined that the piece was none other than Abraham Lincoln's office chair. It was a small triumph, but Mrs. Coolidge knew she'd simply lucked into a rare survivor. "I think every new mistress of the President's house is disappointed to find so little of the original furniture there," she reflected later. "I know of no piece which has been there from the beginning."[25]

Grace Coolidge finally pressed Congress into passing a law protecting the White House's historic furnishings, but the legislation came too late to bring the oldest and rarest pieces back. In 1927, the Coolidges' housekeeper, Elizabeth Jaffray, scandalously admitted that "there are hundreds of homes in America that are better furnished than the White House."[26]

Now, in 1950, Charles Haight could say the same thing.

Three weeks after taking on the White House job, Haight, Crim, Winslow, and Edgerton slipped into the cool, echoing hallways of the National Gallery of Art.[27] Passing the potted ferns in the East Garden Court, the men passed through a doorway and into an enormous chamber with bare brick walls. The room had been designed as gallery space but had never been completed. For a time, the museum's security guards had used the space as a basketball court. They'd even put up a backboard and painted foul lines on the floor.[28] But the room had been given over to storage since then. Concealed below peaks and valleys of undulating white cotton tarp lay hundreds of pieces of furniture from the White House.

If he'd had his druthers, Haight would probably have chosen none of these pieces to go back into the house. Now that the commission's paltry budget forced his hand, however, he at least wanted to take stock of what he had to work with. Haight tugged the sheets off the pile and began the laborious process of examining every chair, writing desk, pier cabinet, and drum table. The room was so jammed that Haight had no space to spread the pieces out, but he did his best. The decorator chose what looked plausibly Colonial or Federal enough and could be fixed up in a hurry.[29] Already, he was rushing. Winslow had supplied him with the documents left from the 1902 renovation so that he could reproduce McKim's upholstery patterns and work in the color palettes of the early 1800s. Haight promised watercolor renderings and fabric swatches by February. Then he filled two of B. Altman's moving vans with pieces and set off for New York.

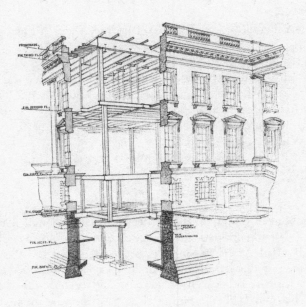

EIGHTEEN

THE TOUR

From time to time, President Truman, like an anxious home-owner whose place was being done over, would take a close look at the repairs being made within the central, residential part of the White House. One Saturday morning, he took me along.

—John Hersey

The same week that the commission hired Charles Haight as interior decorator, another man who'd come down from New York City was contemplating the White House's hulking, empty rooms. For weeks, *The New Yorker* magazine had been trying to finagle enough face time for reporter John Hersey to write a lengthy, intimate profile of Truman. Dismissive at first, the White House Press Office had finally let Hersey sit in on a cabinet meeting, attend a press briefing, and even go along for one of the president's famous morning walks. But the invitation that came for the morning of December 16, 1950, was just the sort of break Hersey had been waiting for: He would get a private tour of the unfinished White House—and President Truman would be his tour guide.[1]

It had been two years since Hersey had listened to the president stumping from the railing of a campaign train, and four years since *The New Yorker* had published Hersey's best-known magazine piece, "A Noiseless Flash," recounting the atomic obliteration of Hiroshima. At 31,000 words, the story was so long—yet so impossible to cut down—that the magazine had given over its entire August 31, 1946, issue to it. The response had been monumental. Within hours, the entire press run sold out.[2] Albert Einstein tried, unsuccessfully, to order one thousand copies. Arthur M. Squires, a chemical engineer who'd worked on the Manhattan Project, read the article and wept. "Every American who has permitted himself to make jokes about atom bombs," editorialized the *New York Times*, "ought to read Mr. Hersey."[3]

Truman mentioned none of this as he greeted the writer on that December morning, but it's impossible he was unaware of the kind of audience Hersey's writing could command. Up until now, it was General Edgerton who'd escorted journalists into the house—leading them in herds, permitting only a quick peek. For this tour, Truman would take Hersey to every floor, and spend nearly two hours doing it.[4]

The customary newspaper spiel likening the president to a sidewalk superintendent swinging his cane while he made his "inspections" of the house typified a widespread assumption that Truman's involvement with the renovation was just an act he put on for the photographers. Didn't the man have a country to run? Communists to fight? What president gives a damn about closet space? As Hersey was to learn, this one did.

Though the commission was officially in charge of the renovation, Truman was the man who ultimately ran the show—a fact that had made itself apparent as early as January of 1949, when Winslow furtively sought the president's approval on his early drawings. As General Services Administration chief Jess Larson recalled, the commissioners tended to disagree over "almost every detail" of the work. Truman, he said, "solved this problem by making the decisions himself. He literally made decisions about where a partition would go here or there, where an outlet would be, what veneer taken from the White House would be preserved and put back, and what wouldn't."[5] During Truman's early-morning visits to the site, Larson followed behind, noting each complaint and preference, which would be passed onto the commission later. "It has never been generally known and recognized just how much Harry Truman . . . put into the rebuilding of the White House," Larson said.[6]

A self-described "architectural nut," Truman saw his involvement with the work as duty, not meddling.[7] "Since I am the only President in fifty years who has had any interest whatever in the rehabilitation of the White House," he told Delano, "I am going to see that it is done properly and correctly."[8] But it was also true that some of Truman's delight with the house was simple, and necessary, escapism. By the end of 1950, Truman found himself languishing at the lowest point of his presidency. Assassins had come close to killing him. China had launched a devastating attack on MacArthur in Korea. Senator Joseph McCarthy—who'd charged that Truman's party was "the bedfellow of international communism"—had whipped the country into a virtual panic.[9] Then, early in December, Truman's press secretary and lifelong friend Charlie Ross slumped over at his desk, dead of a coronary occlusion. Ross's passing, Margaret Truman said, "seemed at the time like the last possible thing that could go wrong."[10] When Truman attempted to read a tribute to Ross before a clutch of reporters, he broke down in tears and walked away.

The White House had always been a point of historical fascination for Truman. But now, as he looked up from the chaos and isolation of the presidency, he felt the old pile assume a new significance. It was a respite, his sanctuary.[11] On a chilly December morning in 1950, Truman welcomed John Hersey inside.

⌁⇌ ⇌⌁

Truman met Hersey at the Oval Office at 11:00 A.M. sharp and then led him into the White House's ground floor via the West Colonnade. General Edgerton, straight-backed and compact, hovered close behind, as he always did when reporters were around.[12] Edgerton had answers for every technical question. He was also ready to put a good spin on a job that was now running late and over budget. But Truman would require no such hand-holding on this day. When the group reached the wall of high timber planks, Edgerton fished out his key ring and unlocked a small door in the fence. The men stepped through.

Truman's choice of a Saturday had apparently been deliberate: The cavernous house was deserted. At this point in the renovation, most every visible surface wore a mottled gray suit of concrete. Shortly after signing the general contract, John McShain had placed an order with the Allentown Portland Cement Company for $763,225 worth of its namesake commodity, to which he'd added gravel and reinforced with steel mesh. The president and his guest were standing on some of the 212,247 cubic feet of the concrete that McShain's bucket brigades had poured. The thick slabs had taken shape in quick succession—the ground floor in September, the first in October, the second in November, and the third just a few days before this tour. Now, with sixty tons of cement drying, the very air smelled of lime, water, and clay. And with no interior finishing begun yet, the ground floor resembled a subway tunnel. Edgerton and Truman were accustomed to the sense of desolation, but the effect chilled Hersey. "We found ourselves in an eerie space," he wrote, standing "on a raw concrete floor." Over their heads loomed another floor of concrete, supported by columns made of concrete, too. "It was," Hersey said, "as if someone had decided to set up a modern office inside a deserted castle."

Truman's oxfords shuffled across the gritty floor as he pointed out rooms that had existed in the past and would exist once again, but for now they were just empty expanses of gray: the housekeeper's and doctor's offices, the kitchen and butler's pantry, and the diplomatic reception room, distinguished from the rest only because it was shaped like an oval. "I don't like these oval rooms," Truman said, his voice echoing in the chilly expanse. Hersey asked the president why not. "My office in the West Wing is oval," he replied. "I like a square office."

Edgerton guided the group cautiously to an open well in the floor where stairs were to go, although they had not yet been installed. Hersey peered down into the shadowy realm beneath, making out not one but two enormous levels below the floor on which they stood. Without knowing it, the journalist whose work had brought to millions of readers the horrors of the atomic bomb was staring into a space that would soon lead into a shelter designed to protect the president from that very weapon—one that was now in the possession of the Soviet Union, as well. Truman told his guest that "there'll be room to store things" down there. He breathed not a word about the shelter.

Nearby stood an elevator shaft without its passenger car, which had been removed and sent over to the Smithsonian. "I wanted to get that old bird cage back in here," Truman complained, "but they told me you couldn't get modern elevator works in with it." McShain's men had used the shaft as a makeshift stairwell, hammering together a tightly coiled wooden staircase inside of it. The group climbed the plank treads up to the State Floor.

Up here, the ceiling was much higher, but the rest looked the same as downstairs. "What we saw was dull and drab," Hersey wrote, as though he'd expected something more interesting to have arisen from 367 days of construction. "We were standing, once again, on a crude concrete slab among bare concrete columns."

But the president saw more than concrete—much more. Indeed, he began to lead Hersey around as though they were touring the gilded chambers of Versailles. Here and there, right side and left, Truman pointed out the various "big state rooms," even though carved mahogany doors, chandeliers, and brocaded walls were nowhere to be seen. Truman was showing his guest only the contents of his imagination, a White House to-be. "His constant use of the present tense as he described the features of the White House made the tour seem a kind of fantasy," Hersey wrote.

But it wasn't a fantasy for Truman, who regarded the bare expanse with the confidence of a bridge builder regarding the opposite shore. The president had warmed up; he was in his element, now. For the rest of the tour, he announced his aesthetic views as though they were great public decrees. Showing Hersey his controversial balcony, Truman insisted that he'd brought an aesthetic balance to the South Portico that Thomas Jefferson could not.[13] Looking out a window at the alignment of Pierre L'Enfant's Mall and Ellipse, Truman proclaimed that "that old Frenchman did a pretty good job." And in the family dining room, the president grimaced at the crooked fireplace flue. "That's no way to build a chimney," he scoffed. "You're right, Mr. President," Edgerton intoned, never failing to back up the boss's viewpoint.

A moment of pity, please, for Edgerton: He was one of the army's most distinguished civil engineers, a commander of men, and he did not care for being a tour guide.[14] Worse for him, Truman began showing off for Hersey at Edgerton's expense. He'd been barking mock orders: "You're going to manage this incline here without stairs, General?" and "Are you going to get me a new roof, General?" Yes, sir. Yes, sir.

Finally, perhaps sensing that he'd jabbed a bit too much, Truman looked at Edgerton and told him he thought that the North Portico lacked proportion as much as the south one had. "Get a bulldozer and knock off the front two pillars," Truman ordered him. After realizing that the president was kidding, Edgerton finally laughed. Without quite realizing it, Truman had conjured himself out of his own gloom. Or perhaps the White House had done it.

Hersey's time was nearly up, but now Edgerton had a question for Truman: Had he ever shown him his photograph of James Hoban's ghost? "No, you didn't," Truman replied, aware that now Edgerton was pulling *his* chain. Still, it was an intriguing question. Nobody really knew what the Irish-born architect who'd designed the White House 158 years earlier had looked like.[15] The president's schedule was tight: He was nearly late for a scheduled lunch with Chief Justice Vinson. But even that wasn't about to keep Truman from seeing Hoban's ghost. "Well, what are we waiting for," Truman told Edgerton. "Let's go!"

The group circled westward around the house to the South Lawn, where the little village of construction shacks that McShain had built stood nestled together in the cold. Edgerton's humble quarters bore a sign that read OFFICE—COMMISSION ON RENOVATION OF THE EXECUTIVE MANSION, a grandiose pronouncement for a ordinary clapboard building.

Inside, the general's athenaeum consisted of a space just big enough for two desks heaped with mountains of paperwork. A gray light slipped inside from between the slats of the window blinds. An outhouse in the Ozarks had more comforts. "You've got a nice place here," Truman deadpanned. The general rummaged around while Truman smiled, waiting patiently. "Here it is!" Edgerton declared, producing the photo.

The print was almost certainly one of Abbie Rowe's. It had been taken earlier that summer, when the bulldozers had burrowed their way deep into the earth inside the house's shell, propped up with its skeleton of steelwork. The lack of light inside had forced Rowe to hold his shutter open on a long exposure. One of the workers standing in the frame had moved, blurring his shape into a phantomlike smudge.

"It's Hoban," Edgerton said, "come back to see what we were doing to his building." "It's Hoban, all right," Truman agreed. Then the commander in chief within him took over in a mixture of authority and jest. "Has he given you any trouble?" he asked. "None at all," General Edgerton replied.

NINETEEN

SOMETHING TO
REMEMBER YOU BY

Looking for a souvenir from the White House? Maybe an old nail, or a sliver of wood, or a partly charred timber, or some antique hardware? You'll have to take it up with the commission.
—*Washington Post*, March 31, 1949

W hen Truman had finished his laugh over General Edgerton's photograph of Hoban's ghost, another thought occurred to him. "Say, General," he began, "do you have some of the things they took out of the White House down here? I'd like to see some of that again." Edgerton said, "Sure enough," and pushed open a door that led to a chamber behind the wall. Hersey likened what he saw to "a cross between a museum and a junk shop."[1] Here, tucked away among the South Lawn's construction shacks, was the general's cabinet of curiosities—objects removed from (or found hidden inside) the house that would not be put back but were too interesting to be tossed out. There were old work boots that had been entombed behind a wall, a saber discovered below the North Portico, and the brick imprinted with the dog's paw that Lorenzo Winslow had fished from the rubble underfoot.

Then something on the room's far wall caught Hersey's attention. It was an array of unusual objects hanging from hooks screwed into a board. There were pieces of old wood, whole bricks, and paperweights fashioned from ornamental trim. There was even a walking stick whose color and grain were a perfect match to the yellow poplar and white oak of the White House's old floor beams. Hersey had become the first member of the public to get a peek at one of the most unusual government projects ever: the White House renovation's official souvenir program.

From the commission's earliest meetings, the most aggravating item on the agenda had been deciding what to do with all of the demolition debris. The material in question did not include the finely crafted decorative interior pieces that Winslow had removed and set aside. It was the guts of the house that needed to be dealt with: floor joists and wall studs, chips of fractured plaster and hammer-broken stone. As Edgerton admitted to a reporter, "We've got a quarter of a million bricks, about 30,000 hand-hewn laths and more handmade nails than we like to think about."[2] Where was all of it supposed to go?

Had the debris come from any other building in the country, that answer would've been obvious: It would top off the nearest landfill and that would be that. But these were pieces from the president's house; a kinder, gentler version of the scrap heap would have to be found. It wasn't sentimentalism that drove the commission to think this way so much as the fear of complications: If the White House's insides were carelessly tossed out, someone would find them and sell them. After all, it had happened before.

Winslow was old enough to remember how, during the installation of Coolidge's new roof, workmen went home each night with bulging pocketsful of old White House nails. The men sold them for fifty cents each—a fine markup for 1927. Surplus wood had found its way off the property, too. Superintendent W. F. Lusk cut up the old roof timbers, and before long, pieces of long-leaf pine began turning up at public auctions. The National Lumber Manufacturers Association bought up some of the wood to use as promotional giveaways.[3] One local man even paneled an entire room in his home with wood that had once held up the White House's roof.[4]

This time around, Winslow cautioned, they had better police the debris more carefully. "There are 1,000,000 old bricks there that would bring $1 apiece," the White House architect warned. Winslow even proposed installing X-ray machines at the East Gate to make sure no workmen were smuggling home nails or pieces of plumbing.[5]

Souvenir hunters had already made the White House the most picked-over property in the country, even when the place *wasn't* under renovation. Guests at Abraham and Mary Lincoln's parties sometimes cut away squares of the carpeting to spirit home. Birchard Hayes, son of President Rutherford B. Hayes, remembered how the butlers kept baskets of spare chandelier crystals to replace the ones guests picked off like fruit. Even FDR's little Scottie dog, Fala, had once been subjected to an unwanted haircut by navy men seeking the dog's fur as a presidential souvenir.[6] For his part, Harry Truman tried to keep sticky-fingered guests in check by having matchbooks, pens, and pencils embossed with "The White House" and giving them away to guests.[7]

While no scheme would stop the public's craving for pieces of the executive mansion, the renovation vaulted an old problem to an entirely new level.[8] With the house's interior broken up and carted off, there would be *millions* of souvenirs ripe for the picking. Just before work on the house began, a reporter from *Time* magazine had asked John McShain if he had any worries about the job. "Dodging the souvenir hunters," the builder said.[9]

When Congress created the Commission on the Renovation of the Executive Mansion, it had specifically outlawed the "commercial exploitation" of the house's debris.[10] In other words: Nothing could be sold for profit. That provision effectively shooed away the professional buzzards, including the salvage company that had offered a flat one million dollars to buy the rubble pile. But it failed to give the commissioners a workable alternative.[11] Most members of the public advocated selling the detritus and donating the proceeds to charities—a touching, if prohibited, solution. A Miami man named Reynold Burt penned a letter to Margaret Truman, entreating her to have her father render the debris into an array of devotional bric-a-brac, including having the faces of past presidents carved—Mount Rushmore–style—into chunks of plaster.[12] There's no evidence that Margaret brought the idea up with her father.

By January 6, 1950, the commission had finally agreed on a course of action.[13] Everything removed during the interior demolition would be declared U.S. government surplus, then given away. Since not all debris was created equal, the distribution would follow a four-tiered classification system.[14] Class I debris—items with "intrinsic as well as historical value," such as mantels and large pieces of decorative plaster ceiling—would be donated to museums and cultural institutions.[15] Class II material consisted of building material, such as bricks, beams, and piping, which, because it still had some service life left, would go to agencies in the federal government to use as they saw fit. The very bottom of the heap—Class IV debris—included excavated earth and pulverized rubble. These remains were so insignificant that the commission felt comfortable burying it all at Fort Myer—yet still "in a hole where speculators cannot possibly get at it," noted the *New York Times*.[16]

That left Class III debris, the hulking mounds of house wreckage that included bits of molded plaster, chunks of marble, sections of wood, and flat iron nails. Though these quirky, pocketable pieces were "of principal value [only] on account of their association with the White House," was that *not* the very definition of a souvenir? And it was souvenirs that this material would become.

By the time McShain's wrecking crews finished gutting the mansion in the summer of 1950, the pulverized innards of the White House were sitting in three different locations in or around Washington. The most valuable material (Winslow's preserved interiors, along with the Class I marble mantelpieces) reposed in the General Services Administration's warehouse down at Seventh and D streets. Other objects that the commission thought "may be desirable to re-use" piled up inside the long, open storage shed on the White House's south lawn. Everything else—including the mountains of Class III debris—had been trucked over to Fort Myer.[17]

Because the commission couldn't just throw open an army base's gates and let the mobs take what they wanted, it would have to cook up some means of orderly distribution, and that would take time.[18] The public was not really in the mood to wait. Newspapers had been steadily stroking everyone's desire for a piece of the mansion for more than a year already. Back in March 1949, the *Washington Post* had teased readers with the headline WANT A WHITE HOUSE SOUVENIR? COMMISSION MAY HAVE 'EM.[19] Now, sixteen months later, editors continued to get good copy out of the topic. "It is still too soon to start polishing up your corner cupboard or mantel to receive a White House souvenir," reported the *Christian Science Monitor* on July 28, 1950, but "there will be tons of material available," the paper promised.[20] Even Douglas Orr had inadvertently gotten the public salivating when he mentioned—as a joke—that there was sure to be plenty of interest in President Grant's bathtub. "A few days later," Edgerton recalled, "we started getting letters asking us to please send the bathtub, express collect."[21]

Indeed, the commission—and sometimes President Truman himself—had been getting letters for months now, begging for everything from White House doorknobs to wooden pegs. Secretaries kept a record of each and every letter, including one from nine-year-old Jimmy Brown of Hayward, California: "Desires two nails from the White House to add to his collection of nails."[22] Some of the petitioners were rather picky. Duke Baker of Dayton, Ohio, wanted a piece of wood—"preferably a piece of burned wood."[23] Margaret Bennett of Maywood, New Jersey, wrote to say she'd accept any chunk of debris—just so long as Abraham Lincoln had touched it.[24] Pleas had come in from institutions, too: The Valley Forge Military Academy desired a limestone block to serve as a cornerstone for a new campus building. From New York City, the Cooper Union design school asked if it wouldn't be too much trouble to send a scrap of old White House wallpaper.

The requests—by turns charming, presumptuous, and infuriating—bloated the mailbags. In time, there would be twenty thousand of them. The commission realized that it would have to not only create a special office dedicated to handling the volume but also standardize the offerings. It was here that Colonel Gillette, Edgerton's assistant, saved the day.

Gillette started by collecting and arranging various pieces of debris, until he had twelve different souvenir "kits" that could be ordered by number. Then, one night, the colonel took home some chips of stone and a few old nails. Cutting an empty beer can in half, Gillette put three artifacts inside and then filled the container up with shellac. When it hardened, Gillette popped the form out and—voilà—he had one more souvenir for his list: an official White House debris paperweight.[25]

The official announcement kicking off the program appeared in the papers on January 13, 1951. For history buffs and collectors who'd been waiting for months, the news seemed too good to be true. "Anyone can get a 'historical memento' of the White House for as little as 25 cents," proclaimed the *New York Times*.[26] "Wood, stones, wire and old handmade nails originally used in building the President's mansion will go on sale next month," promised the *Washington Post*.[27] To claim your piece of the White House, all you had to do was request an order form by writing to: "Souvenirs, Fort Myer, Virginia."

Inside the army base's grounds, the commission had spent seven thousand dollars to build a 313,800-square-foot corrugated-steel shed in front of Wainwright Hall, bachelor officers' quarters.[28] Day after day, dump trucks from the White House had disgorged the detritus, which eventually filled the shed up to its rafters. Men in uniform guarded the debris pile around the clock, though it was all but certain that plenty of McShain's wrecking crew had gone home with nails in their pockets anyway.[29]

Next to the warehouse was the office of Capt. James V. Little, whose staff of four would be responsible for operating the souvenir program. It was they who'd assemble the kits, process the payments (the only fees charged were for postage and handling), and ship the orders. Gillette had stocked the place with plenty of wrapping paper, twine, boxes, and address labels. He'd also commissioned ten thousand tiny metal authentication plates. ORIGINAL WHITE HOUSE MATERIAL—REMOVED IN 1950, each one read. Little's staff would glue the plates onto every single piece ordered. The unusual little enterprise opened for business on January 2, 1951.

Those who'd written in for an order sheet (technically "Form 2—Application for a Memento of the White House") received a mouthwatering list of available items. There was something for every price range. A kid with only a quarter to spend could buy himself Kit No. 8, a piece of wooden lath about a foot long. A dollar was enough for the seven-pound. Kit No. 10: "One brick, as nearly whole as practicable." For the more ambitious buyer, there was Kit No. 12: "Enough stone for a fireplace (1,600 lbs.)." There were gavels and walking canes hewn from White House beams, wood for picture frames, and chunks of ornamental plaster that could be used as "desk ornaments."

Near the top of the list was Kit No. 4, the clear acrylic paperweight. Like Gillette's prototype, the five-ounce souvenir still contained two chips of stone and an iron nail. But the half a beer can had been replaced by a professionally cast mold, a clear acrylic trapezium in which the relics floated in place. At fifty cents, it was a steal.[30]

The public response to the program was immediate and overwhelming. "Each week hundreds of Americans write to ask for a piece of the White House—a brick, a stone, a handmade nail," said *Collier's* magazine. "For a nation of souvenir hunters, the dismantled mansion is a treasure trove."[31] By May 1951, four months into the program, Captain Little's office had already received sixteen thousand orders—an average of 126 per day.

Seldom had an act of Congress created something as tacky yet undeniably exciting as this. "Demand for the small souvenirs exceeded the expectations," the commission later reported.[32] Little's staff of four ran a month behind in filling orders until the commission enlarged it to six full-time workers, then eight, and finally eleven. After extending the deadline for applications—twice—the commission finally closed up shop on October 31, 1951, after nine months and seventeen days in business.

In the end, Little's workers shipped thirty thousand kits all over the United States. Even the most expensive and unwieldy lots found takers. Fifty-six Americans had purchased enough stone to build themselves a fireplace. The commission sold 1,139 lengths of timber for walking canes, 2,967 pieces of lath, and 2,208 pairs of rectangular blocks— pieces of the White House's grayish-white sandstone and the rarest material on the list, it would serve as bookends.[33] But it was Colonel Gillette's kitschy little paperweight that stole the show: Americans ordered 5,919 of them.[34]

Originally designed only to pay for itself, the souvenir program did so well that it turned a profit of exactly $10,034.70, money that the commission deposited into the U.S. Treasury.

While ordinary Americans filled out their forms and waited patiently for their White House mementos to arrive in the mail, other relics changed hands under the table. In Washington's political economy of favors and gestures, it didn't take long for fragments of the old White House to develop into a kind of insider currency.[35]

Those higher on the totem pole fared best. For example, the lovely little mantel that had once stood in Margaret Truman's sitting room wound up in the public library of Bonham, Texas, after Speaker of the House Sam Rayburn, a close friend of Truman, put in a request for it.[36] Secretary of State Dean Acheson bought up so much White House wood that he was eventually able to make a dining table out of it, which he placed in his estate in Maryland.[37]

Fragments from the old White House also became small but potent ways of keeping the right people happy. Truman's assistant Donald Dawson sent a piece of wood to Eleonore Dmitrieff, the secretary for U.S. Army Band leader Capt. Hugh Curry, which she used to have a baton made for him.[38] Colonel Gillette gave the president the gift of one of his paperweights. It was a one-of-a-kind casting by the Vernon-Benshoff Company of Pittsburgh. Inside the clear plastic form was the brick with the dog's paw print on it.[39]

Meanwhile, elected officials without top connections scrambled for pieces of the mansion in order to stay in favor with the constituents back home. Senator Hubert Humphrey wrote personally to Truman's secretary, Matthew Connelly, asking for "a small piece of stone" for a group of businessmen in his district. The men wanted a White House relic to mortar into the fireplace of their clubhouse. "Surely a tiny morsel can be salvaged to satisfy this patriotic group," Humphrey wrote.[40]

Some of the legislators sounded surprisingly desperate to acquire a fragment of the gutted mansion. Desiring "a couple of nails [and] a board" for one of his valued constituents, Nevada congressman Walter S. Baring pleaded with Connelly: "As a good Democrat and Administration supporter, I am calling on you for help."[41]

Connelly (who by his own account received "hundreds" of supplications like this from Capitol Hill) passed many of them on to Lorenzo Winslow, who knew how to deal with them. Generally speaking, if the beneficiary was a top dog, Winslow sent the goods. The architect drew from his own personal stash of White House fragments, including pieces of wood from the 1927 Coolidge renovations and even chunks of the mansion's original 1792 stonework. Winslow had come to understand the political value of such tokens. In fact, he admitted, "for a considerable number of years, I have followed the procedure of furnishing small mementos of old White House material when requested by a member of the Congress."[42]

Then there was the case of Truman's chief military aide, Gen. Harry H. Vaughan, a pear-shaped crony whose gold-braided uniform and ubiquitous cigar lent him the air of an equatorial potentate. The president had installed his old World War I buddy in an East Wing office, often summoned him for a much-needed laugh, and looked the other way more than once when Vaughan's slippery ways did no favors for Truman's public image.

Vaughan had been a link in the chain of what became known as the "Five Percenter" scandal, which had dragged the Truman administration over the coals during the summer of 1949. A young man named Paul Grindle, owner of a woodworking company, had tried to get his small shop a piece of the cabinetry work for the White House renovation. Connections had led him to one Col. James V. Hunt, who'd promised Grindle that it would be "no problem" to get him in on the White House job—all he had to do was fork over 5 percent of the value of the contract in advance, plus a one-thousand-dollar up-front "fee." In exchange, Hunt promised, he'd fix it all up through his friend Gen. Harry Vaughan. "General Vaughan is Harry Truman's closest friend," Hunt explained to the woodworker, "and I am one of Vaughan's closest friends."[43]

Grindle didn't take the bait. Instead, he took his story to the *New York Herald Tribune.* In June 1949, the paper blew the story across its pages and eventually dragged Vaughan in front of a Senate subcommittee investigating government influence peddling. The committee got nothing out of the general. Vaughan had technically broken no laws, even though he had, to quote one witness, used "his general's stars, his White House telephone and his place in Harry Truman's affections" to run what amounted to a favor machine.[44]

So it was no surprise that some of Vaughan's little favors included pieces of the gutted mansion. In the summer of 1951, Vaughan received a request from Congressman Clare Magee for some pieces of White House wood he intended to have made into a gavel for the Missouri Federation of Women's Democratic Clubs. The deadline for souvenir requests had long passed, but that was no trouble for General Vaughan, who procured the wood, had the gavel made, and delivered it "with my kindest regards and good wishes."[45]

Where did Truman himself fit into the souvenir grabbing? On the record, the president seemed uneasy as he watched pieces of the old house being trundled off in the backs of the trucks. "I just hate to see these things scattered around carelessly," he'd told Hersey. "There's so much history in that old place."[46] Yet privately, his attitude was more relaxed. When Truman found himself in need of staff Christmas presents one year, he did his shopping on the debris pile. "He gave all of us a little something," recalled aide Robert Landry, who received "a plaque . . . with a piece of the rock foundation, a nail, [and] a piece of wood."[47]

And, in the end, it was Harry Truman who wound up taking the biggest White House souvenir of them all. The story is not flattering to the president, especially since he claimed to have no interest in keepsakes. But here's how it went. During his visit to Edgerton's office with John Hersey, Truman had noticed a bulletin board tacked with photographs of the White House fireplaces. "Aren't they going to put those back in?" Truman had asked. The general told him no. A few hearths and mantels would be returned to the house, but the rest would be replaced. "And you're going to unload those on the public?" the president inquired. "That's the present plan, sir," Edgerton told him. "How about giving me one for Christmas?" Truman asked. Truman was only joking, but the general made it clear that the president was free to take anything he wanted that had been removed from the house. "Oh, pshaw!" Truman said. "I was just teasing. I don't want anything for myself."[48]

Didn't he, though? A few months earlier, in May of 1950, Truman had asked Edgerton to save the floor beam that had cracked beneath Margaret's piano—a beam ultimately destined for Truman's presidential library in Missouri. Then, a little more than a year after the tour with Hersey, Truman asked Winslow for a little something else: the carved stone fireplace from the State Dining Room.[49]

This was none other than the famous "Buffalo Mantel," a lavishly carved showpiece that Theodore Roosevelt had installed in 1902. The mantel was a thematic complement to the big-game heads the president had proudly mounted around the room. Alonzo Fields would always chuckle at the story Eleanor Roosevelt had told him about her childhood horror of dining with "Uncle Ted" and "suddenly look[ing] up to find the eye of a stuffed moose or some other animal staring down at you."[50] Nevertheless, bison were important to TR. That's why he'd had them carved onto his fireplace. But Winslow, hell-bent on returning the White House's interiors to their American-Georgian ancestry, condemned the mantel as "Italian in character" and "out of keeping."[51] He had it torn from the wall and carted off. Truman was welcome to it.

Nobody missed it, either—at least until 1962, when First Lady Jacqueline Kennedy decided that the White House's overall heritage was far more important than Winslow's unyielding notions of Federal-era purity. So Mrs. Kennedy wrote to the retired president in Missouri and politely asked if he would return the mantel. He refused.

"Mr. Truman would not part with it," reported the *Kansas City Times*, and when his recalcitrance forced Mrs. Kennedy to have a replica made for the State Dining Room instead, Truman went on the defensive.[52] "During the renovation that mantel . . . was thrown out on the junk pile by the Renovation Commission," he said. "I rescued it and kept it until my Library here in Independence was built and had it brought here and that is where I intend to keep it."[53]

In point of fact, the president did *not* rescue the mantel from a junk pile. A commission memo from 1951 makes clear it had already been placed in storage.[54] Regardless, the biggest souvenir ever carried out of the White House belonged to the president of the United States. It remains on display in Truman's presidential museum in Missouri to this day.

The Buffalo Mantel was not the only piece of fine artisanship to be weeded out in the course of Winslow's purging; nineteen other mantels would be banished from the house, too. In fact, of the twenty-six mantels inside the White House when the renovation began, only six of them (including the rare trio of white Carrara mantels carved after the 1814 fire) would be welcomed back into the renovated house. Together with sections of ornamental plaster sawed from the old ceilings, the mantels slated for expulsion formed the core of the Class I debris—the rarest and most valuable artifacts on the roster. The commission figured that museums would jump at the chance to own these artifacts.

One of them did. When the United Daughters of the Confederacy of Mansfield, Louisiana, learned that they could have a White House mantel simply by asking for one (and agreeing to pay the shipping costs), they inquired immediately. Edgerton was happy to hear from the Confederate daughters and wrote back without delay. He even offered the southern belles a choice of a small wooden mantel from the ground floor or one of the six-foot marble Goliaths hoisted out of the East Room. "The East Room [mantel] is very heavy, large, and ornate," Edgerton cautioned, "and would be extremely costly to ship."[55] The ladies didn't care; they took the big one.

But the general soon learned that finding homes for the remaining eighteen mantels would not be this easy. After three months passed without a single letter of interest arriving on his desk, Edgerton had no choice but to go looking. Using a list of worthy cultural institutions suggested by members of Congress, the general began writing their curators one by one.[56]

He was wasting his time, and he knew it. The director of the Philadelphia Museum of Art had already assured Edgerton that no serious art museum in the country would touch his mantels.[57] The man was right: Of the thirty museums Edgerton wrote to, eighteen of the most prestigious (including New York's Metropolitan Museum of Art and

Boston's Museum of Fine Arts) turned him down flat. Interest in the pieces of ornamental plaster was scarcer still.[58]

Nine cultural establishments did accept one mantel each, but these tended to be local institutions lacking world-class museum status: Boston College, the Morris House of Germantown, Pennsylvania, and the Buffalo Historical Society. After months of effort, Edgerton still had nine mantels left over and no one left to call. Finally, the Smithsonian agreed to take the rest off his hands.[59]

Why did the art establishment think so little of the executive mansion's relics? Simple: Curators applied a standard stricter than sentiment. Just because a mantel had spent time in the White House did not necessarily make it an important work of art.[60] What's more, looks could be deceiving. One of the mantels from the housekeeper's room, for example, appeared to be a confection of carved marble from the sixteenth century. It was, in fact, a wooden piece with a marble liner bought locally in 1937: The mantel was just 14 years old.[61] Harry Truman had bow ties in his closet that were more "antique" than this.

In the end, though the souvenir program had been a smash and Edgerton successfully disposed of all of the mantels, only a small scoop had been taken out of the mountain of White House debris. The 4,520 souvenir bricks that Captain Little's team boxed up and mailed away, for example, accounted for a mere 2 percent of all the bricks that had tumbled out of the gutted house.[62] Much of the remaining material fell into the Class II category—tangled piles of plumbing pipe, acres of worn-down flooring, I-beams dragged from beneath the East Room. Valued only in terms of its potential for reuse, the stuff was unloved and unlovely. It didn't make for good newspaper copy. And as it slowly disappeared, few people noticed.

Shangri-La, the presidential retreat in Maryland (later renamed Camp David), received a shipment of old White House steam radiators, pipes, and fittings. The commission sent 95,000 bricks up to Mount Vernon, George Washington's estate, to help with the restoration of some of the walls and buildings. The Capital Parks Department made the gift list, too. The commission gave it four truckloads of stone—both the gray-white Aquia stone from the White House's exterior as well as Joliet stone from the Cross Hall. The department used the former to rebuild some collapsed sections of the old Chesapeake and Potomac Canal near Georgetown. Masons recut the amber-colored Joliet stone to make an entrance gate for the Rock Creek Park amphitheater.[63]

Back in 1951, the commission was adamant that "no publicity will be given to the source of the stone," which is probably why, today, Rock Creek Park's Cultural Resources program manager, Simone Monteleone, was unaware that the amphitheater gate had been hewn from the White House's central corridor. But four truckloads is a great deal of stone, she pointed out, and it's quite possible that the National Park Service did not use all of it. In an undisclosed location in the park, there is a "boneyard" of mossy stone blocks that, according to the old-timers, arrived back in the 1950s. "There are carved pieces from the Capitol," Monteleone said, "but there are other stones that are not carved, and we've always wondered where they might be from."[64] This pile is, very possibly, what remains of the 1951 shipment from the White House.

Inmates, too, benefited from a little White House charity. The District of Columbia prison at Lorton, Virginia, received two truckloads of steel beams, piping, plumbing fixtures, and exactly one refrigerator.[65] But the commission was most generous to the United States Army, whose two nearby bases—Forts Myer and Belvoir—were able to do lots of sprucing up thanks to the White House's castoffs. The bases divvied up ten thousand bricks and sixteen thousand square feet of old flooring. Fort Myer already had a lively Enlisted Men's Club, but thanks to the bricks, it soon boasted an outdoor terrace for dancing.

One day, probably in 1950, Pauline McShain received a visit from her parents. The only child of contractor John McShain and his wife, Mary, Pauline had become a nun in 1946, joining the Sisters of the Holy Child Jesus. The order had recently sent her to teach second graders at the Oak Knoll School in Summit, New Jersey. Visits from family were permitted only once a month, and so the young sister always looked forward to her parents making the seventy-mile drive up from Philadelphia. This time, they'd loaded up the car with a surprise— quite a few surprises, in fact.

"I have a distinct memory of their bringing with them bricks from the White House," a now-retired Sister McShain recalled on a recent winter afternoon in the living room of her residence in Bryn Mawr, Pennsylvania.

And what did her parents do with all the White House bricks they'd loaded into their sedan? "They gave them out as souvenirs," she said.[66]

TWENTY

"EVERY DOLLAR MUST BE SAVED"

I have always understood that funds were ample for the work of reconstruction and furnishing but it now appears that . . . we must make savings in many ways.

—William Adams Delano

O n New Year's Day of 1951, Philadelphia's Municipal Stadium opened its turnstiles for the Army-Navy game. The annual gridiron battle between West Point's cadets and the midshipmen from the Naval Academy at Annapolis seldom failed to pack the old horseshoe arena with 100,000 fans or more. In that sea of fedoras, an attendee wasn't likely to bump into someone he knew. But that's exactly what happened when Harry Truman spotted his general contractor, John McShain.

A successful man in his home city, McShain was in a good mood that day—optimistic and confident, and perhaps overly so. No other reason could explain why, after a few minutes of banter, McShain told Truman that he saw no reason why he couldn't move back into the

White House in five months—the summer of 1951.[1] It's anyone's guess why McShain made a promise so brazen, especially when, not five weeks earlier, he had written to Reynolds at the Public Buildings Administration to declare that "it is practically an impossibility to complete this project by October of 1951."[2]

It was a hell of a football game. By a score of 42–7, the army got clobbered. A week later, so did John McShain.

Though the builder would later insist that his remark had been made "in a joking manner," Truman (being Truman) had taken McShain at his word, and he proceeded to inform the commissioners about the contractor's pledge. It left them red-faced. It also added to the anxiety that had soured the commission meetings since Hauck reported the first delays during the summer of 1950. The glossy coat of confidence the commission enjoyed during its early days had cracked and fallen away, revealing an inner sense of doubt and urgency that would only worsen as 1951 progressed.

It had been two months since the attempt on President Truman's life, a near catastrophe the Secret Service blamed on Truman's having to live in Blair House. The implication was obvious: Had Truman been at the White House on that warm November day that the killers came to call, no bullets would have come near him. In fact, the official report of the attempted assassination unequivocally stated that the moment Truman could move back into the White House, all threats to his security would "recede."[3] It only added to the pressure to get the renovation done quickly.

Yet the work inside the house had only just begun. Even though Truman had been pleased by the vistas of fresh concrete he'd shown to John Hersey, the White House was no more habitable than a parking garage. Making his rounds of the chilly house that January, Edgerton knew that the renovation was really just 40 percent finished—and running 10 percent behind. Yet this man McShain need had the nerve to tell President Truman he could move back in by the summer? Edgerton could sooner have made the White House levitate.

As it turned out, the president had his own reason for wanting to move back so badly, and it had nothing to do with the lack of security at Blair House. Truman had already made up his mind not to seek another term. His final year in office would be 1952, and he was determined to spend it living back inside the mansion he'd had the courage and foresight to rebuild. It was only fair. "If Teddy or Coolidge had done the job we now have done," Truman wrote in his diary, "the President of this day could have stayed in the President's House."[4]

The commission tried to appease him. It kept October 1, 1951, as the target completion date, and doled out the remaining subcontracts— hardware, cabinetry, tile, stonework—at breakneck speed. But everyone must have sensed that wrapping up the job in 1951, even by Christmas, was a fantasy. The gremlins that had appeared the previous year had not gone away: inflation, the labor shortage, shop drawings that moldered around while awaiting approval.[5] By March, McShain's foreman, Hauck, told the commission that the only hope of finishing by October was to pay the workmen $300,000 worth of overtime. Everyone knew that the United States government, with boots on the ground in Korea, was not about to write that kind of check. And so the renovation moved along, but the clock moved faster.

On February 28, 1951, Charles Haight reappeared in the East Wing, armed with the promised sketches for the White House's interiors. The designer had brought his tall and elegant assistant, Marguerite ("Peggy") Watts, with him, and between Haight's tuxedo and Watts's white gloves and broad-brimmed hat, the pair looked like a couple taking an after-dinner stroll on the *Queen Mary*.

Haight pulled away the chairs on one side of the long conference table and pinned his watercolors up, arranging his upholstery swatches and rug squares nearby.[6] Each twenty-by-thirty-inch watercolor blushed with pastels—aquamarine carpeting in the president's Oval Study and pale pink armchairs in Margaret Truman's drawing room. The renderings even included flowers bobbing from cut-glass vases.

With a wary eye on its cash reserves, the commission had decided to spend most of its money on the furnishings for the State Floor rooms— the spaces that visitors would see. The commissioners also decided, as Dougherty recalled, "to follow, as closely as might be reasonable, the previous decorations, particularly in the main public rooms on the first floor."[7] In other words, when it came to the main floor, the orders were to make everything look exactly like it had before. There would be a few exceptions, of course, and the biggest was the dining room.

Ever since the 1902 renovation, the oaken wall paneling in the State Dining Room had worn a coat of dark brown varnish. The room looked either dignified or funereal, depending on whom you asked. But Haight saw an opportunity to rescue the space from what butler Alonzo Fields called its "dark and somber" atmosphere.[8] The designer had his water-colorist render two views of the room: one with the paneling in its usual dark stain, the second showing the walls wearing a luminous coat of celadon green. This was shocking stuff. It was also, Haight argued, historically accurate to Winslow's desired period. More surprising still, Harry and Bess loved the color.[9]

That should have settled the matter. It didn't. At the very moment that the commission might have concentrated on getting the job back on schedule, it instead threw itself into a protracted debate over whether to paint a single room. Dougherty liked the paint but didn't like its seven-thousand-dollar cost. Winslow *should* have liked the paint, but he worried it would draw visitors' eyes to the carvers' tooling marks on the oak. The commission held off its decision until Winslow drove up to the Baltimore factory of Knipp & Co., the woodworking subcontractor, and returned with two panels—one with paint and one without. The props only deepened the disagreement. Seeing the way the paint brought out the wood's chisel scars and natural crotch marks, Dougherty changed his mind: no paint. But Orr and Delano were charmed by the rustic look: yes paint. At some point, usher Crim spoke up and reminded all present that the Trumans had liked the paint all along. Even so, the commissioners refused to vote until Crim dashed across Pennsylvania Avenue to show the panels to the president and his wife. A few minutes later, the phone rang. It was the Trumans—and they still liked the paint. Motion made, seconded, and adopted: The walls of the State Dining Room would be painted. It had taken two months to reach this decision.[10]

For the first several weeks of 1951, as Abbie Rowe had peered into the viewfinder of his Speed Graphic camera, all that had looked back were slabs of concrete. Gradually, though, the workmen's progress gave him more to shoot. Interior walls of terra-cotta hollow block began to climb, sectioning the floors into rooms, with bucks left for the doorways. Shiny metal air ducts swept across the open spaces, forking and branching to destinations deep in the shadows. The commission had doled out eighteen thousand dollars on a temporary heating system to keep out the winter cold; it allowed the masons to put the fireplaces in. Then, by the middle of March, Edgerton's diary noted the first undeniable return of civility to the White House rooms. Men began to cover the masonry walls with a layer of smooth white plaster.

Few parts of the mansion's interior would prove as aesthetically crucial, and ultimately frustrating, as the plaster. The contract itself went to Novinger's and the James A. Kane Company, two small firms that had joined forces to bid on the job. They managed to beat out the venerable McNulty Brothers, whose claim to plastering fame was doing Chicago's Merchandise Mart, the largest commercial building on earth. It was said that Jim Novinger could figure his costs nearly as tightly as John McShain could figure his. In fact, Novinger had worked under McShain before, when he'd run the plaster for the veterans' hospital at Mount Alto, near Georgetown.

Jim Novinger still recalled the bruising his ego had taken on that job. When he first offered the services of his tiny firm to the mighty Philadelphia contractor, McShain had laughed him off as "just a little old house plasterer." Insulted, Novinger rose to walk out the door, but McShain stopped him, smoothed his feathers, and offered to give him a shot. Not only did Jim Novinger run plaster smooth as milk; "I brought the job way in under the minimum," he recalled, "which McShain and I shared. We did a lot of jobs together after that." Now the two contractors were working the most famous job in the country.[11]

Yet as good as Jim Novinger was, he could only help Lorenzo Winslow with part of the house's plastering needs—and not the harder part, either.

Winslow was determined to rescue all of the mansion's ornamental plasterwork, the intricate bracket scrolls and medallions that graced the ceilings high overhead. During demolition, some of Murph Bonham's men had even discovered some of the mansion's 1817 ceilings entombed above the ones McKim had put up in 1902.[12] Winslow had measured, drawn, and made rubbings of every inch of it. He had to. He knew that the cracking and fracturing that would result from taking the ceilings down would make them impossible to put back. The only way to "preserve" the old plaster was to make new castings.

And there lay the trouble. Novinger and Kane's companies—union shops that covered lathwork for a living—did not do artisanal work. Worse still, as J. B. West would recall, Winslow "couldn't find a single craftsman in America" who could.[13] "The casting of plaster ornaments seems to be becoming a lost art," Orr lamented.[14]

But Winslow kept looking, and his diligence paid off. Eventually, he located Quirino Fioravanti and Harry Nagle, two graybeards who still knew the old-world craft (and, incredibly, lived within commuting distance). Fioravanti's brother Arnolfo joined the job, and together the men became the rare birds of the renovation effort. Winslow set them up in their own casting shop on the grounds, where they worked their messy magic.

Fortunately, the 1902 plasterwork had been cast with backings of cheesecloth, which permitted McShain's men to remove large chunks without all of it falling apart. The Fioravantis made shellac and gelatin molds from the salvaged pieces, into which they poured fresh plaster for the new castings.[15] The resulting ornaments—some mere inches long, some taller than the men—were stunning: fleurettes, medallions, and arabesques, each delicate as a French pastry. Winslow dried all the pieces on wooden racks outside the shop, where he would make an elaborate show of inspecting them, especially when the newspaper photographers were around.[16]

The American public in general—and its housewives in particular—hungered for news about what the interiors of the new White House would look like. That spring, reporter Ruth Gmeiner of the *New York World-Telegram and Sun* managed to coax an entire story out of the rumor that Truman's shower tiles would be blue-green. It wasn't Gmeiner's fault that her copy was thin on details. "The commission," she wrote, "is not ready to talk about the decorating."[17]

The reason may have been because the commission had found another trivial matter to waste its time with. On the heels of its long debate over whether or not to paint the dining room, the commissioners were gearing up for their next fight—over wallpaper.

On June 19, 1951, Haight presented two samples of upholstery fabric for the Blue Room's walls. The first, copied from McKim's 1902 renovation, was a motif of flower baskets and snowflakes. The second featured a pattern of rosettes and stars with a frieze of eagles. Truman had already expressed his preference for the baskets, and the matter would have ended there had it not been for David Finley of the Fine Arts Commission.

The president's relationship with the chairman of the Fine Arts Commission was civil but strained: Truman had not forgotten how "high hats" like Finley had tried to foil his balcony plan four years earlier. The frail, soft-spoken Finley never officially possessed more than advisory power as he sat in on the commission's discussions about the house's interior design, but that didn't stop him from trying to flex far more muscle than his bony little arms had.

Frowning over Haight's fabric samples, Finley declared baskets inappropriate, dismissed both designs, and somehow managed to convince Haight to create a wholly new design, one that swapped out the baskets for eagles and the stars for snowflakes. Haight had the new pattern created (at great expense) by F. Schumacher & Co. The tight schedule forced General Edgerton to travel up to New York to fetch the sample and bring it back to Washington. Inspecting the new design at their meeting table, the commissioners still couldn't agree. Delano considered it sufficiently "Federal," but Orr derided the pattern as "Napoleonic." Finley complained that he was still "not completely satisfied."

After ten days of wasted time, the only solution was to go back to the original basket pattern.[18]

The subcontractors pushed the work forward all through the spring and early summer. At this stage of the job, tradesmen from nearly every field necessary to finish a house were all packed into the mansion's sprawling interior. On some days, the workforce swelled to three hundred. Whole offensives took place simultaneously. Plastering teams from Kane and Novinger's had decided to attack the house story by story, starting on the ground floor. A team of lathers would nail the long thin strips of wood onto the wall studs, ceding their place to the plastering teams following on their heels with bucks, hawks, and floats.

Elsewhere in the house, architectural details sprouted like spring flowers. On the ground floor, stone setters built the kitchen's new hearth out of the recovered foundation stones, the mason's marks showing outward. In the corridor outside, the churchlike groined arches had reappeared, trimmed by wall marble the color of coffee with cream. Upstairs, carpenters roughed in the new grand staircase. The whole house breathed with the sounds of hammers, saws, and scraping trowels, its air a perfume of spackle, concrete, and sweat.

Taking shape within the old sandstone shell were 132 new rooms, above ground and below. If 200,000 old bricks had tumbled out of this space in 1950, then 279,000 new ones would go back in 1951, as would 120 tons of wall plaster, half a million feet of electrical wiring, 2,700 pounds of sheet-metal duct, 33,000 feet of piping, and exactly 92 radiators. Just a few months earlier, as the president had led John

Hersey around the echoing floors, little of this interior work had even begun. But by May 1951, the masons had built nearly all of the interior walls, stairwells, elevator shafts, and chimneys. The plumbers and electricians were half finished, down to the panel boxes and chilled-water pumps. Door frames awaited the arrival of doors (there would be 412 of them), and Armstrong Cork Co. had blanketed the place in $25,900 worth of thermal insulation.

On the afternoon of June 20, 1951, a group of one hundred Illinois schoolkids arrived at the West Wing on a class trip. After the children had clambered off the buses, Truman gathered them on the lawn and lectured them about the renovation of the White House. But the students of the heartland were more impressed by simply seeing the president than by listening to his lecture. When he finished, Truman asked if there were any questions. Silence ensued. Then one small hand rose like a periscope over the sea of heads. It was a little girl clutching a box camera. "Grin, will ya?" she asked. Truman grinned and the girl snapped his picture.[19]

Only a handful of men would have known that there was a new strain hiding behind the president's smile that day. A week before the children's visit, Truman had received a letter from Douglas Orr, and even the Yale-bred architect's courtly prose could not take the sting out of its news: The commission was broke. Without an emergency infusion of cash, the renovation would stop dead. "The over-run is principally attributable to effects of the Korean war," Orr explained in his June 13 letter. "Costs have risen rapidly during the past year and if the original estimate were to be revised to reflect prices now current, it would be raised from $5,400,000 to $6,000,000."

Orr wasn't even telling the worst of it. Materials costs had soared so high that subcontractors were now too scared to bid on the government's price-restricted contracts. The commission had hired whom it could and paid what it had to. Now the well was dry. To keep the job going, the commission needed another $250,000.[20]

Orr's missive had inadvertently pointed out the elephant in the room: The White House was a very expensive thing. Few other dwellings in the country called for the sort of materials that the executive mansion required, many by the truckload, and the adding machine spat out frightening figures: $50,000 for wrought iron and a whopping $380,000 for the fine woodwork that carvers were creating from oak.

Some of the exorbitant bills simply could not be helped, but many of them were the result of Winslow's insistence on the finest materials. The architect's idea of replacing plaster with marble for the foyer columns and wainscoting had helped push the White House's interior stone bill up to $224,000.[21] Winslow wanted Fontaine marble, too, though less expensive varieties would have performed just as well. Up on the roof, ordinary slate had sheathed the recessed walls of the third floor for the preceding quarter century, but Winslow insisted that it be replaced with limestone. President Truman didn't care about toilet handles (so long as they flushed), but Winslow mandated that they be made of white bronze.

The architect made no apologies for his Park Avenue tastes. "After all," he'd told a reporter in 1950, "this isn't a private home, it's an institution."[22] And so the invoices for exotic accessories rolled in one after the next: the Mosler wall safes hidden behind hinged panels ($6,000), custom grilles for the fire-alarm boxes ($21,000), and the automatic can washer for the kitchen ($3,000.)[23] These figures seem lofty even today, but to the average American of the postwar years, they were utterly prodigal. When the Long Island, New York, suburb of Levittown opened in 1947, a single-family home could be had for $6,990; the commission would spend nearly half that amount just on the White House's bug screens.[24]

There had been no skimping thus far. Indeed, before the renovation had even begun, Winslow had made it clear that "it is the President's desire" that the White House work be finished to the highest standards, inside and out, so as to last "for many generations to come."[25] But now, in late June 1951, a new directive came down from the Public Buildings Administration to everyone on the renovation job: "Effective immediately, every dollar that can be saved must be saved."[26]

The commission had already begun cutting costs by "practical substitution of materials and simplification of work," as Orr would later phrase it.[27] What did that mean? Woodworking contractors Knipp & Co. would be among the first to find out. To begin, Edgerton persuaded them to drop their fee from $29,700 to $25,000. Then the commission informed Knipp—which had already turned out exquisite pieces, including the richly carved entablature over the East Room door—that using "compo" (a mix of sawdust and glue pressed into various decorative shapes) would be acceptable in lieu of actual decorative carving. When Congressman Rabaut questioned whether such a cheap material would be appropriate for the White House, he was told that so long as it was painted, the ersatz panels "will look just like the carved wood."[28]

For his part, consulting architect William Delano had already presented the commission with his own ideas for cost cutting back in January. Delano was worried—with justification—that there would be little money left to actually furnish the White House once its interiors were complete, so he proposed taking the items too worn out for the State Floor and sticking them downstairs, where fewer people would see them: "On the Ground Floor, we should be able to use historic pieces even if they be ugly," Delano wrote, "and we could probably have curtains made from stuff no longer fitting for the Main Floor."[29]

And so it went. After a year of soaring pride in the house's high standards, the commissioners now pushed the yoke into a nauseating dive, jettisoning items left and right in a desperate attempt to offload $250,000 worth of expenses from the books. So long as the cutback would not constitute an "intolerable detriment" to the White House, everything was fair game.[30] Commissioners Orr and Dougherty had already pondered whether to use limestone instead of granite, and if they really needed that aluminum catwalk on the roof. Crim reluctantly gave up the eleven-hundred-dollar potato peeler he'd wanted in the kitchen (though he stood his ground when it came to the ice-cream maker).[31] Winslow agreed to forgo the purchase of a $1,027 light fixture for the Blue Room and reuse one from the Red Room instead—"no alterations, rewiring, or refinishing necessary," noted the commission with evident satisfaction. "New cost: $0."[32]

Several days after getting Orr's request for additional funding, Truman wrote "Approved" at the bottom and signed his name. You can almost hear him sigh, just looking at the thing. The extra money would not be easy to get.

There was one salve: Truman could still hope that McShain might have him back in the White House by year's end. Yet even that hope lasted a mere nine days. It fell to Crim to deliver the bad news, very possibly because others lacked the courage to face Truman with it. On July 17, Crim approached the chief and—"reluctantly," he remembered later—told him what the commission had decided that morning: There was no way the house would be finished by Christmas. Perhaps by March 1952? Nobody could say.

The renovation was now eating into Truman's final year in office.

TWENTY-ONE

THE GENERAL'S BURDENS

Father was Executive Director of the Commission on Renovation of the Executive Mansion. "Renovation" may not be the precisely correct word, for there was a lot more to it than painting and plastering.

—Bruce Edgerton

Despite all visible evidence to the contrary, Truman really *had* believed he would get back into the White House before 1951 was up. Had he not thought so, he never would have let his daughter invite Princess Elizabeth over to the house. Earlier that spring, Margaret Truman had embarked on a six-week tour of Europe. In England, she'd lunched at Chartwell with Winston Churchill, then paid a visit to Buckingham Palace. There, Margaret asked the twenty-five-year-old princess to visit Washington in November. Certainly, the White House would be finished by then.

That had been in May, two months before Crim's disastrous news that the mansion would, in fact, be a disemboweled mess until some-time in 1952. The Trumans were horrified: They had just asked the future queen of England to pay a state visit to a construction zone. "The Trumans were more than a little set back," said J. B. West, who recalled how he and the rest of the staff would need to, ahem, "scurry" to make other arrangements.[1]

West's ushers weren't the only ones scurrying around Pennsylvania Avenue that summer. In August, as mercury crept up into the nineties and a noose of humidity tightened around the city, workmen at the White House noticed that they had company—rats. Though vermin had cursed the mansion with their presence since the nineteenth century it was long the custom to deny it publicly. "There are no rats," Winslow had told reporters back in 1948. "We haven't had any for a long time."[2] But it was a lie. Maintenance man Traphes Bryant knew better than anyone. "The rats never had it better" than they did at the White House, he said.[3] And now, with the garbage from the construction site's cafeteria to keep them fat and happy, the rats had multiplied into an occupying force. White House police inspector Hobart Francis was so sick of watching the beady-eyed creatures scampering among the lumber piles and beneath the sheds that he sent a memo to usher Crim. The rats were "becoming a menace," Francis wrote.

The situation forced General Edgerton to convene a special rat summit in his office. It was not the sort of thing that the commission's executive director really had the time for. "The general reluctantly ad-mitted that the subject has been discussed many times," Crim later recalled, "but that actually nothing had been done about it."[4]

And nothing would be, either. The second half of 1951 was shaping up to be tough—tough on McShain, on his foreman, Hauck, but espe-cially tough on General Edgerton.

⁂

The plasterers had been making noise about wanting a raise for weeks. James Kane and Jim Novinger had agreed to give them one in the new year, but the plasterers wanted their pay hike by November. Tensions mounted. On August 2, 1951, the men put in a full day on the scaf-folds, covering the walls and trimming off the astragal moldings in the foyer. Late in the afternoon, they all put down their trowels and walked out of the house. The strike was on.

Edgerton made a brief note of the incident in his log—"Plasterers complete Lobby plaster and go on strike at 4 PM"—but his usual dispassionate tone belied the trouble he was now in. Even though most of the plastering was completed as an absolute percentage of the work, only a handful of the rooms had been fully coated. Without finished plaster, painting could not begin; without painted walls, there could be no woodwork or parquet; without that, no draperies or furniture, and so on. Simply put, the plasterers had the job by the tail.

They knew it, too. The men were so confident their terms would be met that most of them skipped town. "Many of the plasterers are working in other cities while waiting for the strike in Washington to be settled," the commission noted during its meeting of August 17, 1951. Dougherty had the idea of summoning American Federation of Labor brass to the East Wing for a talking-to by the commission. Hauck told him it wouldn't do any good.[5]

The strike's timing could not have been worse. The day before the plasterers walked, Hauck had submitted a document stamped "Confidential" to the commission. It was a revised completion schedule for the whole job—one that proved that McShain still clutched a thread of hope that the work could be wrapped by December 15. But even if the contractors had followed McShain's gulaglike work schedule, the plasterers had destroyed any chance that the deadline would be met. By the time men returned to the house, they'd stalled the job by nearly a month.

Unable to ignore the commission's looming insolvency any longer, on August 17, 1951, the president informed Congress that the renovation required a bailout. In fact, in the eight weeks since Orr's letter, the renovation had staggered deeper into debt. The $250,000 they were asking for was now $321,000.[6]

It would take a miracle to pry that kind of dough from the 82nd Congress's hands. The Hill had been smoldering at Truman since his dismissal of the recalcitrant Gen. Douglas MacArthur in April—a move that had driven Truman's public approval rating down to 26 percent.[7] The only way this plan would fly was to assure the legislators that the taxpayers' money was going to essential work. "Once again," J. B. West said, "a president had to assure Congress that the White House would not be a royal palace."[8]

Actually, the president wouldn't have to do that; Edgerton would. In a closed-door meeting with the Senate Appropriations Committee on October 8, the renovation's executive director did his best to justify why Congress's original $5.4 million in funding wasn't enough. Though Edgerton explained how the war in Korea had driven up the prices for labor and materials, some senators charged that the real problem was that they were building a presidential castle down there. "There is no royal elegance in the building," Edgerton replied. The White House, he assured the committee, contained nothing that "many a private home throughout the country" did not have.[9]

The good general was shoveling it now. How many homes throughout the country boasted three elevators, marble-columned foyers, and walls swathed in silk damask with gold thread? In any case, Edgerton stuck to the script, and it worked. The committee agreed to fork over another $261,000, and sent him home. The money was sixty thousand dollars short of what Truman had requested, but Edgerton—crew-cut, stiff-lipped, reliable as gravity—had come through once again.

Few leaders in the army (or anywhere else) possessed the wholly unflappable, can-do spirit of Maj. Gen. Glen Edgar Edgerton. When he'd served as chief engineer of the Alaska Road Commission in 1910, Edgerton had found an abandoned boxcar in Valdez and made it into a home for himself and his new bride.[10] Hacking his way through the malarial jungles of Panama, Edgerton still managed to take his dinner on white linen each evening.[11] On the White House job, when snow had brought a halt to the outdoor work, Edgerton searched for ways to melt the snow mechanically.[12] He'd brought order and discipline to what the *Architectural Record* called "an expensive, uncertain job," and all the while served as a lightning rod for a tempestuous president.[13] "My father," Bruce Edgerton would later say, "knew all about Give 'Em Hell Harry quite some time before the play was written."[14]

But the general was *not* a magician, and he could see that the commission's desperate measures to save time and money were now hurting the job more than helping it. McShain's men were being driven hard, and some were making costly mistakes. A few weeks earlier, Edgerton had noticed that the brick masons had faced two fireplaces in the wrong direction and the piston caisson for elevator number 3 had been installed a foot off center.[15] Then there were the last-minute change orders. These had already caused Edgerton no shortage of headaches. "Two electricians (4 hrs.) changing outlets in Library due to architect's change in thickness of jambs," grumbles one of his diary entries, and there were quite a few like it.[16] Paring down some of the luxuries might have been fiscally prudent, but each deviation from the original plans required new paperwork and revised drawings, which slowed the renovation at the very moment that everything needed to move faster.

⁂

By early September, John McShain finally realized that his December 15, 1951, completion date had been a figment, and he humbly requested an extension on his contract. The injury to his pride must have been enormous. With egg still on his face from his assurances that the Trumans would be back in the house by the summer, McShain wasn't even going to speculate on a new finish date. Instead, he asked only that "a sufficient number of days" be granted him, with "the number of days to be determined at a later date."[17]

McShain was clearly worried now. Two blocks north of the White House stood the Hay-Adams Hotel, where the contractor kept a suite when he had to spend the occasional night in the capital. As fall approached, he'd be spending more nights there, laying a head full of troubles on a starchy, unfamiliar pillow.[18]

Until now, J. Paul Hauck had been McShain's eyes and ears on the site. But as 1951 drew to a close, the workers saw more and more of the boss in the flesh. John McShain was not difficult to spot: He was the one stalking through the house, pointing and yelling, while a troupe of worried-looking underlings trailed behind. McShain "literally ran through the rooms," one reporter recalled, "not one of them escaping his inspection or comment." Anything missing, incomplete, or off-spec resulted in a "beating" for J. Paul Hauck.[19]

There was a lot to take a beating for. A photo of the State Floor from this period shows the sort of unfinished work that would have pulled John McShain's trigger: pilasters missing their bases and capitals, wood trim untouched by a paintbrush, gaping holes where wall sconces should now have been, and slabs of marble stacked like enormous playing cards. Most glaring of all were the floors: Instead of a sumptuous expanse of amber parquet, there was only ugly gray cement.[20]

Pauline McShain reflected on how desperate those days must have been. "They had an impossible challenge," she said. "Doing [the renovation] during wartime was tough, and my father was struggling to do the best job he could." Of course, so was his foreman. "Daddy had total trust in Hauck's competence and his ability and his trustworthiness," Pauline McShain added. "Yet Daddy took out his frustrations on Hauck, and I think Hauck just took it."[21]

McShain also showed up in person for the commission's September twenty-first meeting, where he cut to the quick. Two major problems now stood in the way of the house's completion, he said, the marble and the flooring. The house could function without the first but certainly not without the second.

For months now, the mansion's demand for marble had been nearly insatiable. Winslow's fetishistic love of the stone knew no limits. His specs required 4,655 feet of the metamorphic rock in twenty-three varieties for 250 different locations throughout the house. Before it was all over, the government's marble bill would total fifty thousand dollars—more than the cost of the steel beams that held the whole place up.[22] The Vermont Marble Company was hoisting stone out of two separate quarries at this point, but it was no longer making deadlines. "Lack of marble holding up job," Edgerton hammered into his diary for September 20.

It did not help that Winslow had a habit of rejecting whole marble shipments if the color didn't precisely match the samples he'd preselected. The tweedy architect had recently sent back a batch because its shade was "distinctly green" instead of the "light cloud" his heart was set on. The rejected pieces would now take a month to replace, and an exasperated Hauck told the commissioners that there was no time left to be fussy about this sort of thing.[23]

So far as the flooring went, the situation was even worse. The parquet contract had gone to the John Hasbrouck Co. But not only was the parquet missing; so was Mr. Hasbrouck. McShain had been trying to reach the man since late August, but the subcontractor "has not yet appeared," the commission noted.[24] McShain suspected that Hasbrouck was in over his head. His $74,500 bid for the work was so low, it had easily won the flooring contract, but Hasbrouck had never sent more than four or five men to the White House since he'd begun laying the base flooring that summer. The contract called for 18,892 square feet of parquetry in four different patterns. At this rate it would take years to finish the house. Desperate, McShain had even offered money out of his own pocket for Hasbrouck to hire more men. He'd received no reply.[25]

The prerenovation Blue Room of 1947. The mighty Pendeloque, five and a half feet of gilded bronze and Bohemian crystal, hangs in the center. *(Abbie Rowe, National Park Service, courtesy of Harry S. Truman Library)*

The family floor's center hallway, facing east, shown in 1948. This was the passage from which Truman heard the "ghosts" walking while he sat in his office. *(Abbie Rowe, National Park Service, courtesy of Harry S. Truman Library)*

White House architect Lorenzo Winslow's disastrous 1946 West Wing addition—one that Congress refused to fund. *(Author's collection)*

The South Portico balcony, which Truman funded on his own. *(Abbie Rowe, National Park Service, courtesy of Harry S. Truman Library)*

The East Room as it appeared on April 7, 1949, with scaffolding in place to hold up the collapsing ceiling. Standing near the door, dwarfed by the bracing, are structural engineer Charles W. Barber (his face obscured) and Lorenzo Winslow. *(Reprinted with permission of the D.C. Public Library, Star Collection, © Washington Post)*

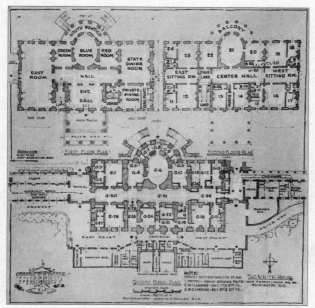

Winslow's 1949 plan for the renovation—one that depended on retaining the mansion's original outer walls. Though the architect retained the basic layout of the house, everything built within would be new. *(Abbie Rowe, National Park Service, courtesy of Harry S. Truman Library)*

Weeks into the interior demolition, stripped plaster and lath on the second floor reveal 135-year-old timber. This framework dated from the house's first rebuilding, following the British fire of 1814. *(Abbie Rowe, National Park Service, courtesy of Harry S. Truman Library)*

Contractor John McShain's demolition teams often became inadvertent archeologists. In the Cross Hall, they discovered this 1817 ceiling hidden just inches above the one installed in 1902. *(Abbie Rowe, National Park Service, courtesy of Harry S. Truman Library)*

A March 1950 view of what remained of Truman's Oval Study (top) and the Blue Room (below). Dry and riddled with cracks, these wooden beams had caused the floor to shake when butler Alonzo Fields walked across it. *(Abbie Rowe, National Park Service, courtesy of Harry S. Truman Library)*

Members of the Commission on the Renovation of the Executive Mansion inspect the site. This open shed was used to store large, decorative items removed from the house's interior. *(Abbie Rowe, National Park Service, courtesy of Harry S. Truman Library)*

Proud of his latest plum contract, legendary Philadelphia builder John McShain (fifth from right) poses with his men on the South Lawn in the spring of 1950. J. P. Hauck, McShain's favored superintendent, stands to his left. *(Hagley Museum and Library)*

By the summer of 1950, shoring steel holds up the roof and stabilizes the outer sandstone walls while a bulldozer begins excavation of the new basements. The house, Truman wrote, "is nothing but a shell." *(Abbie Rowe, National Park Service, courtesy of Harry S. Truman Library)*

Demolition workers remove what little remains of Room G-17, the old kitchen pantry in the northwest corner of the ground floor. The old mansion would surrender some half a million bricks in total. *(Abbie Rowe, National Park Service, courtesy of Harry S. Truman Library)*

The renovation expanded the White House's existing suite of maintenance rooms below the North Portico, as shown in this view from July 26, 1950. When the bomb-shelter directive materialized, General Edgerton gave two of the new concrete rooms over to the "protective project." *(Abbie Rowe, National Park Service, courtesy of Harry S. Truman Library)*

The temporary steel shoring towers and heavy-duty structural steel both went into the mansion simultaneously. "It is difficult to describe the intricacies of these operations," architect Douglas Orr later said. *(Abbie Rowe, National Park Service, courtesy of Harry S. Truman Library)*

One of the mansion's new twenty-two-foot girders dwarfs the two men asked to pose with it. In all, 800 tons of structural steel would be used in the renovation. Truman vowed that this would be the final time the mansion would be rebuilt. *(Abbie Rowe, National Park Service, courtesy of Harry S. Truman Library)*

During World War II, the government hastily built a bomb shelter inside the vaults below the Treasury Building's East Wing, connecting it to the White House with a tunnel below the street. Shown here is FDR's bedroom. *(Department of the Treasury)*

On September 3, 1949, a B-29 weather plane similar to the one above touched down at Alaska's Eielson Air Force Base. Radioactive particles trapped in its filters confirmed that an atomic explosion had taken place within the Soviet Union. *(National Museum of the US Air Force®)*

A rare photograph of "the Tunnel," the steel-and-concrete artery that ran through the White House's lower basement level. The Tunnel connected the West and East Wings and also furnished a secure means of access to the atomic shelter. *(Abbie Rowe, National Park Service, courtesy of Harry S. Truman Library)*

Construction under way in February 1951 below the East Terrace, the narrow corridor that connected the mansion to its East Wing. Lorenzo Winslow's diary makes clear that Truman's new atomic shelter complex would be in this area. *(Abbie Rowe, National Park Service, courtesy of Harry S. Truman Library)*

Flanked by assistant Peggy Watts, a tuxedo-clad Charles Haight presents watercolor renderings of the new White House interiors to the commissioners. Haight wears a smile, but he was appalled by the beggarly budget given to him. *(Abbie Rowe, National Park Service, courtesy of New Haven Museum & Historical Society)*

The B. Altman rendering for Room 220—the presidential bedroom. A press release hailed the White House's new interiors as "an American interpretation of the Georgian epoch," but Eleanor Roosevelt later said they reminded her of a Sheraton hotel. *(Author's collection)*

May 1951: Historic wood ripped from the mansion sits in a storage shed at Fort Myer, Virginia, where it will be chopped up into souvenirs of the old White House. *(Abbie Rowe, National Park Service, courtesy of Harry S. Truman Library)*

July 1951: Using virgin timber, a carver from Baltimore's Knipp & Co. works on reproduction trim soon to fill the new White House. *(Abbie Rowe, National Park Service, courtesy of Harry S. Truman Library)*

Shown here in November 1951, the State Dining Room was one of the few to have its exquisite 1902 oak paneling returned to its walls. Other rooms were not as lucky. The fluted pilaster on the left has just received its first coat of celadon paint. *(Abbie Rowe, National Park Service, courtesy of Harry S. Truman Library)*

The same room two months later—perilously close to Truman's deadline and nowhere near finished. Parquet contractor John Hasbrouck, chronically short on men, supplies, and cash, delayed the mansion's completion by weeks. *(Abbie Rowe, National Park Service, courtesy of Harry S. Truman Library)*

Charles Haight and Peggy Watts take stock of furnishings in the presidential bedroom. With most of the decorating budget diverted to the main floor, the duo economized by using inexpensive reproduction pieces upstairs. *(Abbie Rowe, National Park Service, courtesy of Harry S. Truman Library)*

The foyer as it appeared just days before the house's reopening. Refinished and wrapped, the mansion's handful of valuable pieces await a return to the state rooms as a guard keeps watch. *(Abbie Rowe, National Park Service, courtesy of Harry S. Truman Library)*

In the East Room, electricians send the current through one of the restored 1902 Caldwell chandeliers. Even though the enormous fixtures had been shortened, Truman still called them "monstrosities." *(Abbie Rowe, National Park Service, courtesy of Harry S. Truman Library)*

Dusk on March 27, 1952: Holding up his new gold key to the front door, Truman officially reopens the White House. J. B. West stands behind, just to the right of Bess Truman. *(Abbie Rowe, National Park Service, courtesy of Harry S. Truman Library)*

The White House's official photographer from 1941 to 1967, Abbie Rowe documented everything from state dinners to legislation signings. But his thorough, precise, and hauntingly beautiful images of the renovation became his greatest legacy. *(Fred Bell, National Park Service, courtesy of Harry S. Truman Library)*

The last formal photograph of the commission, taken nearly three years after the first. Though the group wasted months fighting over trivialities and dumped truckloads of historical artifacts into a landfill, it did save the White House from the wrecking ball. *(Abbie Rowe, National Park Service, courtesy of Harry S. Truman Library)*

As the delays in the work made their way into the news, it was Edgerton who answered for it. News accounts on October 3, 1951, should have carried the announcement of a resumed entertainment schedule. Instead, the *New York Times* reported that the social season had been canceled once again due to "the still-unfinished state of the remodeled mansion." When reporters collared Edgerton to ask him when the house would be finished, he told them "shortly after the first of the year"—but said not to hold him to it.[26] This wouldn't be the last time the general would take the heat over a bunch of canceled cocktail parties. A few weeks later, when a reporter asked social secretary Edith Helm if she knew when the White House would be fit for entertaining, she replied, "White House entertaining is in the laps of the gods, General Edgerton and the workers."[27]

At least Edgerton had brought closure to one part of the job. At the end of October, as the stonemasons laid the diagonal checkerboard of pink-and-gray Tennessee marble across the foyer, Edgerton reburied the time capsule that the men had discovered nearly two years before. The old wooden box had held a special significance for the electricians, because the Harry Alexander Company was the only contractor to work on both the 1902 renovation and the current one. Many of the signatures on the wiring diagram stuffed into the bottle had been those of Alexander's men.[28]

And by now, Edgerton certainly knew why that whiskey bottle had been found empty.

Even though the commission had known about the plans for the interior design for several months, it made no public announcement of the B. Altman designs. Charles Haight and Peggy Watts needed time back in New York to obtain the silks, rugs, and furniture for all the rooms. They needed nerve, too: The commission's paltry budget for the job forced them to nickel-and-dime their best suppliers.[29] Finally, more than eight months after inking the deal with the store, the commission went public with the decorating plans on October 20, 1951. Perhaps because the commission was so desperate to announce some good news for a change, its press release ran to five whole pages.

Haight called his designs "an American interpretation of the Georgian epoch," but it was hyperbole.[30] Anyone who made it past the commission's regal talk of Brussels carpets, Louis XVI prints, and Hepplewhite chairs would have noticed the frequent use of words like *copied, reproduction*, and *of the style of the original period*. The fact of the matter was that, with the exception of the handful of historic furnishings on the State Floor, most of what would go into the executive mansion were Colonial-reproduction pieces by Drexel Heritage, Kaplan, and Kittinger—the sort of inexpensive furniture commonly found in hotel rooms. (A decade hence, when Jacqueline Kennedy joked that the true historic period of the White House was "early Statler," she truly nailed it.[31]) The ersatz furniture and the matching drapes and rugs may have looked, to quote the press release, "characteristic of many used in the 18th century," but they had no more historical validity than the props on a Hollywood back lot.

Writing for the *Washington Post*, Marie McNair tried to put a polite spin on the fact that the commission had to salvage most of the usable furniture in the house. In the State Dining Room, it refinished fifty chairs and even reused the old curtains in an effort to save every penny. "The U.S. Government, like a thrifty housewife," she wrote, "has made things 'do.'"[32]

Haight never did get to buy the antiques he'd dreamed of buying, and rather than using his considerable talent to stretch Aubusson rugs across the White House's grand open spaces, he stretched dollars across those spaces instead. Indeed, when the rug from the State Dining Room proved too tatty to go back into service, it was Haight's idea to cut it up and make four smaller rugs from it for the rooms upstairs.[33] The mansion would stand as a testament to Haight's improvisational abilities, but a "Georgian epoch" it was not.

Reproduction furniture wasn't the only dubious touch. Many of the rooms in those watercolors simply didn't *look* Georgian. Thomas Chippendale had *not* created Bridgewater sofas. The sherbet hues were questionable, too. Though Haight had claimed that his color schemes were all drawn from the eighteenth century, they bore a curious resemblance to the vibrant postwar pigments turning up on Hudson Hornets and Hotpoint electric ranges. If the press noticed this astonishing coincidence, it was too polite to say so. The *New York Times* remarked on "the introduction of gayer colors," while the *Washington Post* chimed in that "a cheerful informal air is achieved by use of colorful chintzes and toiles."[34]

What Haight had done was the midcentury equivalent of kicking it up a notch, lighting his palettes until they reflected the atomic-era glow from the horizons of suburbia. Those pastel hues had not come from Haight's memories of Versailles—they came from Bess Truman. Officially, the Trumans had been given the "last word" only on the decor for the residential floors.[35] But as Gen. Jess Larson recalled, Bess Truman's sway extended downstairs, too. The state rooms, said the General Services Administration chief, "were carefully reconstructed as they had been traditionally, with some lightening up of color schemes which were Mrs. Truman's ideas."[36]

⊶⊷ ⊷⊶

On November 2, with the Duke of Edinburgh in tow, Princess Elizabeth stood on the dais that had been set up before the TV cameras and newspaper photographers in the Rose Garden, where she presented King George VI's contribution to the White House renovation effort, a late-seventeenth-century English overmantel mirror surmounted by a floral still-life painting. It was a stunning piece, one that would look lovely in the Blue Room—once the Blue Room was finished, of course. Fortunately, Edgerton had had the foresight to have the White House's first floor swept the previous day, which allowed the Trumans to give the princess a hard-hat tour.

That King George's gift had also included a pair of gilded bronze candelabra turned out to be fortuitous: With the commission pinching every penny until it screamed, some of the items it could not afford would turn out to be the lights.

The category known as "Special Lighting Fixtures" represented a major financial hardship for the commission. Because many of the mansion's most distinguishing features happened to be its chandeliers, the men had no choice but to have them cleaned and rewired. Fortunately, Caldwell & Co.—which had made the glistening monsters back in 1902—was still in business in New York. Unfortunately, its invoice would come to $74,000. Though the commission was duty-bound to pay whatever it cost to restore the signature pieces (the tent-and-bowl chandeliers of the East Room were "a critical item," the record would note), other filaments would have their plugs pulled. On November 16, General Edgerton ordered that the new lantern planned for the foyer should be stricken from the installation roster. "The Commission," he wrote, "will not have sufficient funds to purchase one."[37]

⊶⊷ ⊷⊶

Christmas of 1951 would fall on a Tuesday, and the president planned to gas up *The Independence* and fly home to Missouri. On Saturday, the twenty-second, he gave his staff their Christmas presents. One by one, the maids and butlers filed through Truman's first-floor office, just off the vestibule of Blair House's door at No. 1653. The First Lady was not there; she'd left a few days before, and so Truman would play Santa by himself. A president can't do very much store shopping, so it was understandable that everyone would be receiving the same gift. It was a lovely blown-up photograph, mounted on eleven-by-fourteen-inch heavy stock matte and perfect for framing. The picture was of Blair House—the place in which President Truman and each of the men and women who faithfully served him were, for now and the fore-seeable future, stuck.[38]

TWENTY-TWO

MISSING PIECES

*Whatever is goode in its kinde ought to be preserv'd in respect
for antiquity, as well as our present advantage, for destruction
can be profitable to none but such as live by it.*
                                        —Nicholas Hawksmoor, 1662–1736

*T*wo blocks south of the Mall, a warehouse of wheat-colored stone
took up the entire D Street block from Seventh to Ninth Streets,
the approach tracks to Union Station trimming its northern corners at the Virginia Avenue bend. The General Services Administration had built the place back in 1932, and built it big. Behind the tall
rows of casement windows was 845,178 square feet of storage space.
Because the General Services Administration's job was to funnel supplies to every office in the federal government, there was no telling
what castoffs might turn up in here. Publicity photos taken of the storage rooms during the postwar years show them stuffed with electric
fans, office chairs, and typewriters—and even baseball mitts and one-
hundred-pound bags of iodized salt.[1]

After 1950, a visitor to this warehouse (if he knew where to look)
could have navigated the dank maze of corridors and located the most

unusual trove in the whole place: the ornamental interiors of the White House's state rooms that Murph Bonham's men had disassembled, removed, and hauled down here. Each relic bore a tag. Some sat within crates. All waited beneath the nimbus of the bare ceiling bulbs for the promised day of their return.[2]

To Lorenzo Winslow, this was sacred salvage. The commission could quibble over the Blue Room's new wallpaper all it wanted, but the integrity of these beautiful interiors installed back in 1902—the richly carved wall panels, the chair rail, and the glossy mahogany doors—was beyond debate.[3] Not only did their neoclassical lines fit comfortably within the envelope of Winslow's Federal aesthetic; the interior pieces had been part of the mansion's physical fabric for half a century, a period inclusive of two world wars and eight presidents. They deserved to be put back.

From the earliest days of the project, the White House architect had made it clear that he intended to do exactly that. In June 1949, six months before the renovation even broke ground, Winslow had briefed the commission about an issue of "vital importance." This was "the careful dismantling, removal and storage of all interior . . . finish materials." These, said the White House architect, must "be reinstalled in the reconstructed building."[4]

Truman agreed. "We are saving all the doors, mantels, mirrors and things of that sort so that they will go back just as they were," the president had written back in May 1949.[5] The renovation's key officials lined up behind him. A few months later, Public Buildings Administrator Reynolds assured the *New York Times* that "as much as possible of the old will be put back."[6] Douglas Orr described the "material to be saved for reuse" in at least one speech.[7] And in a letter dated July 3, 1950, chairman McKellar informed Congress that the commission's plan was "to re-use in the White House as much of the material of historical importance as practicable."[8] With so many officials on the record, it was no surprise that the press also consistently informed the public that the historic interiors of the mansion would be returned to the house. Typical was this AP dispatch from the summer of 1950: "the old rooms, taken apart and stored, will be put back together, just as they were."[9]

Even Katie Louchheim, the Democratic National Committee envoy and Georgetown hostess, whose grapevine curled itself deep into the corridors of power, assured her preservation-minded social set that the White House's old interiors, thanks to Mr. Winslow, were in good hands: "The authentic solid mahogany doors, the heavy handmade mahogany window sashes and hand carved window panes," she wrote, "all of these precious fittings would be put back into place."[10]

That the president and the commissioners had pledged themselves to the painstaking work of preserving the house's fine interiors was a popular and inspirational story. But a year into the renovation work, it began its descent into a factual and circumstantial muck from which it never fully emerged. Only two things are clear. First, the high-minded assurances given in 1949 and 1950 that the mansion's interiors would be put back were clearly in trouble by 1951, when the time to put them back actually arrived. Second, though some of the mansion's hard-carved oaken panels, window frames, and trim would indeed return to their former places within the mansion, most of them would never see the White House again.[11]

Like varying amounts of cloud cover, Truman's desire for the renovation's prompt completion had always loomed over the job, shadowing all involved with a task that was, at its core, a contradiction. Truman expected the men to do their finest, most conscientious work—and he expected them to work like hell. From the very first inspection tour of the house, the president had hammered on the "necessity for speed," and he followed up the demand with his constant visits. "President Truman was right there on the job every day," General Larson recalled.[12] As Pauline McShain characterized it, the renovation was "a kind of tug-of-war: Get it done perfectly, but get it done fast. It was a huge amount of pressure on my father."[13]

The commission had learned that Truman's occasional elbow in the ribs was tolerable so long as the work stayed on schedule and under budget. But by 1951, the work was neither, and Truman decided to do something about it. That summer, J. B. West recalled that the president told him, "I've been using a curry comb on the contractors to try to speed up reconstruction."[14] A curry comb is a coarse-bristled brush used to loosen dirt and dead hair from a horse's coat. It is not a gentle instrument, but it gets a messy, necessary job done. Truman, who'd no doubt used a real curry comb during his farming days, chose his metaphor well. Later, he would look back on this period and admit that he'd run out of patience: "I found it necessary," he said, "to apply pressure to rush completion."[15]

The chronology is important here. If Truman's impatience and pressure began to manifest themselves in earnest during the summer of 1951, the timing turns out to be most unfortunate: That was the same period during which Winslow's historic interiors were to be put back into the house.[16]

· ⊷ ⟶ ⟵ ⊷ ·

At first, the plans to restore and reinstall the house's delicate interior woodwork proceeded smoothly. Toward the end of January 1951, the renowned woodworking firm of Knipp & Co. took possession of a large quantity of the mansion's old doors, windows, paneling, and trim.[17] Sending a company truck down from Baltimore, Knipp fetched 3,800 board feet of old pine flooring. On another run, it picked up the State Dining Room's paneled English oak walls and a quantity of original mahogany doors. The truck apparently made several trips like this, returning to the family's two-story factory in Curtis Bay.[18]

Knipp's contract included both the restoration of the house's old interior architecture as well as the milling of new pieces. The two parts of the contract were, at first, not at odds: Some of Winslow's renovation plans called for breakfront bookcases and tall, sculptural chimneypieces that simply hadn't existed before, so Knipp had to make them. Winslow had also wanted Knipp to take the old one-and-a-half-inch straight-grain pine flooring and make it into molding and bookcases for the ground-floor library. Excellent carvers and joiners, Knipp's men were as skilled at restoration as they were at creating new pieces.[19] By February, much of the old pine floor had been transformed into beautiful paneling for the library. The restoration work was slower going, but by March 15, the commission noted that Knipp was "re-working woodwork as required."[20]

But here the picture begins to cloud. Though Knipp's men were refinishing some of the old paneling and trim, concentrating on the state rooms for the main floor, it's clear much of the restoration work was harder and more time-consuming than expected. The old wood was fragile and thus a challenge to handle. Knipp's men were spending a great deal of time and effort on the windows in particular, removing the panes and scraping out the old putty, then repairing and refinishing the sashes.[21] Come July, Edgerton made a telling note in his diary: In addition to restoring the old window sashes, Knipp's men had started to make replacement ones, too.[22]

That July, Abbie Rowe devoted a day to documenting Knipp & Co.'s handiwork. But while a handful of his photographs show restoration of Winslow's salvaged interiors, the vast majority of them portray carpenters creating new pieces.[23] In one image, an artisan named Klapka, loose overalls hanging off his bony frame, applies a chisel to a molding of acanthus leaves hewn from what, almost certainly, is virgin timber. The work in these images is exquisite, but it begged an enormous question: If Lorenzo Winslow had *already saved* all of the mansion's sumptuous oak and mahogany interiors from 1902, why were Knipp's men carving new ones?

That is a question that, even today, the record does a fine job of obfuscating. Here is what is certain: J. B. West recalled that when the renovation began, the workmen salvaged "every door, every window, every length of woodwork, mantelpiece, piece of molding [and] wood paneling" from forty-eight rooms.[24] When the renovation ended, the number of rooms that had received their original interiors back was—in total—four.

What had happened? In a word, time. Not only did Knipp have only a few months in which to restore a mansion's worth of old paneling and millwork; the job was clearly more than anyone had bargained for. The 1902 woodwork was brittle, some of it damaged, much of it buried under decades of paint. Many of the pieces of paneling would also need to be recut to fit snugly around the corners and nooks of the White House's new interior walls, whose configurations now differed from the old ones that had been ripped out.[25] In the brief time allotted to them, Knipp's craftsmen did accomplish some beautiful restoration work, in particular the oak of the Red Room, the Green Room, and the State Dining Room. In theory, they could have kept going. But with Edgerton harping on the need "to speed up the work" and Truman applying his curry comb, the commission concluded that milling new pieces to replace the original wood was simply easier and faster.[26] As White House curator Rex Scouten would confirm in 1991, the mansion's beautiful historic interior may have been "carefully removed, but it was not put back in."[27]

The machination of the historic interior's disappearance was both methodical and official. The commissioners began to reject as unfit one lot of the old wood after another (eventually, they'd condemn all the paneling from the East Room), steadily clearing the way for Knipp to use new lumber for the accent pieces. Who was going to object?

Certainly not McShain or Knipp; both of their crews preferred to work with virgin timber anyway.[28] Indeed, those delicate old pieces of 1902 oak had only one champion, and that was Lorenzo Winslow. As the historian William P. O'Brien has written, the White House architect "watched helplessly in horror" as his treasured interiors were discarded.[29] In fact, it would turn out even worse than that. During the commission's meeting of September 21, 1951, Winslow actually gave his personal consent to surrender all of the old woodwork that Knipp & Co. had not yet restored. It was a huge trove of artifacts, including everything in the South Lawn storage shed, all of the old window jambs, blinds, and panels, and all the "old mahogany sash rejected for replacement in the building." The commission gave no reason why the mahogany had been "rejected," or why Winslow, turning his back on all that was precious to him, suddenly decided to relinquish his artifacts "for future use and disposition"—a bureaucratic euphemism whose true meaning is anyone's guess.[30] But according to the minutes, Winslow agreed to give up the old fittings following a "discussion" with usher Crim. The conversation was never recorded. But it's quite likely that Crim—ever the reliable bearer of bad news—made it clear to Winslow that time had run out on his dream of seeing the old White House put back inside the new one.

What happened to all of it—those countless pieces of hand-carved oak and mahogany that had graced the White House's rooms since the days of Theodore Roosevelt? Many of the interiors were simply thrown out, tossed into the backs of trucks bound for Fort Myer. It's probable that the historic wood was mixed in with other debris to make it all look like junk.[31] Eminent White House historian William Seale has written that, as the pressures mounted to speed the work along, "greater quantities" of interior woodwork such as doors and paneling found a place in the convoy heading over the Potomac. The decision of what to do with the precious interiors had long "haunted" the commission, which understood how easily the matter could become "a political hot potato."[32] In the end, the commissioners decided to toss that potato all the way to Virginia.

The saddest fact was that throwing the White House into the garbage was perfectly legal. Public Law 377 of the 81st Congress gave the commission full authority to decide the "appropriate disposition of all the materials removed from the Executive Mansion."[33] During the optimistic days of 1950, the old interiors enjoyed the lofty status as "articles and material which it is expected to re-use in the reconstruction."[34] But as time dragged on and pressures mounted, the commission simply reclassified the relics to make them easier to get rid of.[35] By 1952, most of Winslow's salvaged interiors had been demoted to Class II "usable building material," which allowed it to be given away to various federal agencies. Trash and treasure mingled in this batch: Along with the bricks, pipes, and steel beams in the backs of the trucks heading off for Forts Myer and Belvoir were also the White House's old wooden shelving, twelve doors, and so much flooring that Fort Belvoir's superintendent made a roller rink from it. Lorton Prison would receive a bounty of artifacts that were supposed to have gone back into the White House, too, including ventilation grilles and firebacks, three crates of door frames, twelve crates of window trim, and twenty-two crates of the mansion's stately panel doors.[36]

Yet these were the fortunate pieces. Some of the old woodwork wound up in the souvenir program.[37] The rest, designated as Class IV debris, became landfill.[38] The debris pit at Fort Myer was located just inside the Hatfield Gate. Open since 1939, it already held the construction debris from the Pentagon. According to the base's historian, Kim Holien, pieces from the White House went in alongside the older refuse. "They intermingled the debris and then just covered it up with earthen fill," he said. Today, some open stretches of lawn and a softball field sit atop the site. Is Fort Myer worried that souvenir seekers might come and dig up the property? "They *couldn't*," Holien said. "They'd have to dig down through thirty feet of dirt." Asked if any curiosity seekers have ever inquired as to the White House's interment the historian said no. "In my eighteen years here, you're only the third person who's asked. There is no institutional knowledge of this event whatsoever."[39]

The dismemberment and dumping of the White House's elegant interiors was obviously not the image that the commission wanted Americans to see, so ultimately it was a story that was not told. When the commission published a beautiful hardcover account of the renovation for the public, its text suggested that every splinter of the old wood was lovingly restored and returned to the house. Heroic prose trumpets dedicated workers "who eased valued shapes from their places and after many months, carefully eased them back into their former locations"— accomplishing an "accurate restoration" that "gave no indication that [the original interiors] had ever been absent."[40]

It is a lovely, stirring passage. The problem is that, with the exception of a handful of rooms, it does not happen to be true.

The loss of the White House interiors marked not only the destruction of a significant piece of the mansion's heritage but also the symbolic destruction of Lorenzo Winslow, the only man on the commission who'd really cared about the old interiors to start with.

He was a flawed messiah. Even as the devoted architect logged long hours at his drafting table, his diary entries show how he permitted his personal life to encroach on his responsibilities. Frequent were his lunches with his paramour "J.," as were entire weekday afternoons he took off to be with her.[41] At one point, an "inspection" of the marble quarries in Rutland, Vermont, somehow turned into a six-day trip, which the couple spent hiking and taking long drives along the Atlantic coast.[42] Eventually, even Truman himself noticed and grew angry over Winslow's willingness to let his private life compromise his responsibilities to the White House.[43]

Still more perplexing was Winslow's devotion to the spirit realm. His diary entries just for the first half of 1950 mention his attending seventeen séances, some of which took up entire evenings. Apart from Mr. Burroughs and his euphemistic "church," other mediums—a Mrs. Fabian and a Mrs. Candler—entered the picture, as did spirit photography and the Ouija board.[44] In two incredible sessions, the callers from beyond included Presidents Andrew Jackson and Franklin Roosevelt ("F.D.R. appeared and presented a rose to me," Winslow wrote in his diary). Still another ghost appeared and informed Winslow that James Hoban had *not* designed the White House after all.[45]

Nevertheless, whatever his personal failings, Winslow cared deeply for the house. He had worked in it, studied it, drawn it, and repaired it for the preceding eighteen years—in addition to having masterminded the very renovation plans that the contractors were now following. Because Winslow stopped keeping his daily diary in the fall of 1950, we cannot know for certain how the loss of the original interiors affected him, but it does not stretch credulity to imagine his heart broken by what took place. Not long after the completion of the White House, Lorenzo Winslow would retire.

In 1973, a year after Harry Truman's death, White House curator Clement Conger prompted more than a few jaws to drop when he went public about how much of the mansion's interiors had been tossed out. Americans had already heard some criticism of the Truman renovation once the Kennedys moved in, but that had been focused largely on the cheap furniture. But Conger, speaking to the *Baltimore Sun*, disclosed the travesty that had been perpetrated on the building itself. The curator called the Truman renovation "one of the greatest disasters in White House history" and revealed how much of the old woodwork had been chopped up to make souvenirs. "It should have been saved," Conger said. "No attempt was made to restore the building to what it had been."[46]

One of the readers who chanced upon Conger's quotes in the *Sun*'s Sunday magazine section that November was none other than Franklin Knipp, whose craftsmen—whose own hands—had been involved in the work on the mansion twenty-two years before. A few days later, the newspaper's editors received a chestnut of a letter from Mr. Knipp. "I question [Conger's] knowledge of the reconstruction which took place," Knipp wrote, then proceeded to give his version of the fate of the mansion's old interiors.[47]

The woodworker maintained that his men had taken every piece of the paneling and trim of the Green, Red, and Blue rooms, refurbished them, and put them back. The same was true for the window frames and sashes in those rooms, he said, adding that some had simply been left in place. Most significantly, Knipp was adamant that his woodworkers had restored and reinstalled all the intricate paneling of the State Dining Room. "In fact," he said, "we had to re-carve the frieze around this room in several places where President Theodore Roosevelt had smoothed them down to receive his moose heads."

It was a compelling piece of testimony, and there is no reason to doubt it. Nevertheless, Knipp's version of events had accounted for only four of the mansion's rooms. Knipp said nothing about the rest of the State Floor, much less the rooms upstairs. What fate befell the chair rails and cornices of the family dining room? What happened to the carved bookcases in Truman's upstairs study? And what had become of all of the treasures from the East Room—the Corinthian pilasters carved in New York by Herter Brothers, the ornate gilded mirrors that stood atop the fireplaces, the twelve panels of scenes from Aesop's Fables rendered by the famous Piccirilli brothers? Knipp's letter did not say. As the years have worn on, it's become increasingly evident that nobody can. As Fort Myer's maintenance chief told an inquiring newspaper reporter back in 1994, "I'm afraid the only people who could tell you about this now are in the cemetery."[48]

Occasionally, the White House ghosts have reappeared. In 1989, one of the mantelpieces that had stood in the Diplomatic Reception Room turned up in a government warehouse outside of Suitland, Maryland.[49] Sometime around 1985, a twelve-foot-long piece of paneling that had once stood over one of the East Room's doors arrived at the White House curator's office. Its owner had found it in his garage.[50]

The commission hid its sins well, but one of the last documents it generated, which can be found at the Truman Library, has survived as testimony to what took place. A single-page memo titled "White House Storage Material," it is a damning piece of paper.

A little more than a month after the White House renovation was complete, Congressman Rabaut and General Edgerton went down to inspect the General Services Administration warehouse down at Seventh and D streets. A Public Buildings Administration architect named Frank A. Galante went along to generate the official report. Making their way through the old warehouse's rooms, the men discovered the gilded mirror frames that had once stood atop the East Room mantels. They also found the carved frames that had once held portraits of George and Martha Washington. Nearby were four more gilded mirrors, including the ones that had been removed from the bedrooms of Bess and Margaret Truman on the second floor. Inside the warehouse lay fourteen mahogany doors, too, along with pieces of marble and sections of wood paneling, window shutters, and carved ornamental corner blocks. Then the party spotted a huge transom window, its half-moon so large that it could only be the one that had stood over the White House's front door. Galante's notes were meticulous. He had marked only two items as either "damaged" or "broken." The rest of the pieces were perfect.[51]

TWENTY-THREE

"A RACE AGAINST TIME"

Old houses mended,
Cost little less than new before they're ended.
—Colley Cibber, 1671–1757

*T*he West Wing's Cabinet Room lay just steps away from the Oval Office. It was a spacious room with a fireplace on its northern wall and four tall windows looking out on the Rose Garden. Taking up most of the carpet space was a long octagonal table buffed to a mirror shine and encircled by twelve heavy leather chairs. At 4:00 P.M. on January 25, 1952, Truman sat in one of those chairs. Occupying the rest was every man with a supervisory role in the White House renovation. Truman had ordered his assistant Matthew Connelly to summon them all, regardless of where they happened to be. Douglas Orr had come down from Connecticut, General Edgerton had walked in from the South Lawn, and John McShain—forced to put an early end to a trip—had traveled all the way from South America.

As the late-afternoon shadows lengthened across the dormant rose-bushes in the garden, the light from the wall sconces glinted in the lenses of the president's Marshwood glasses. The eyes behind them were angry.

Earlier in the day, the Commission on the Renovation of the Executive Mansion had held its fifty-ninth meeting. The business discussed had sounded depressingly like that of the fifty-eighth, fifty-seventh, and fifty-sixth meetings: delays and more delays. There was the ongoing drama of John Hasbrouck, for instance. The elusive parquet contractor had finally appeared at the White House, but Edgerton had caught Hasbrouck's men laying down green lumber and had forced them to rip it all back up and dry it. The wait would set the job back by a month.[1] Edgerton fumed over the shoddy workmanship, but even Hasbrouck didn't deserve all of the blame. Running weeks behind, Vermont Marble was still carving mantelpieces. Up in New York, the chandeliers' electrical guts still sprawled across the workbenches of Caldwell & Co. And while Hauck had put eighteen full-time painters on the payroll, many of the rooms wore only primer coats. Stone treaders had not arrived. Medicine cabinets were missing. The White House still had no heat, no electricity, and no running water. It did not, in many places, even have faucets.

The executive mansion had now been under construction for 774 days. The original deadline was four months in the dust. Blair House, meant as temporary lodging, had now been President Truman's home for more than three years, and by now the place thoroughly exasperated him. Since the assassination attempt, the Secret Service had insisted on driving the president to work—a distance of five hundred feet—in a bombproof limousine, tailgated by a convertible packed with machine gun–toting agents. Truman's detail had gone so batty about his security that Peggy Watts had once seen them squeezing the president through a window, apparently to avoid using the front door.[2] "It is a hell of a way to live," the president complained in his diary.[3]

By now, Truman wanted back into the White House so badly, he could taste it. When Elizabeth Taylor had visited the Oval Office in October 1951 along with a group of Hollywood heavies, Truman motioned toward the uncompleted mansion outside the windows and told her, "I'd sure like to get in by Christmas, but I don't think I will."[4]

He hadn't. Nor had he gotten in for New Year's. And with the 1952 social season on hold indefinitely, there was no telling when he ever would get in. Edgerton was now telling him May 1952, but that was only assuming the latest estimates held. None of the previous ones had.

As the president glared at his renovation team on this late Friday afternoon, the only thing missing was smoke from his ears. It is a pity that his colorful speech went unrecorded. John McShain would later characterize it as "most inspiring."[5] Whatever his choice of words, Truman gave the men hell as only he could. He demanded "every day possible" slashed from the construction schedule.[6] Unable to stomach another blown deadline, Truman now issued his own: April 2, 1952. The White House, Truman informed the room, would be finished by then. Indeed, it would *have* to be: Queen Juliana of the Netherlands had already accepted Truman's strategically timed invitation to visit Washington and stay as his guest. If there was no pillow for her royal head, whose fault would that be? The president was playing hardball now.

The men pushed back as much as they dared. Truman's deadline was only sixty-eight days away. Not counting weekends, only forty-eight days. McShain told the president that it was physically impossible to finish construction by April 2—and for once, the commissioners got behind him.[7] As McShain later recalled, even General Edgerton "went on the record saying that such a feat was impossible"—and this was a man who'd diverted the courses of the Tigris and Euphrates rivers.[8]

But Truman would not budge. Not again. The meeting was over.

Two days later, the president received a personal letter from John McShain. In the privacy of his Philadelphia office, McShain had apparently given the matter more thought. "In spite of the fact that I informed you that it was almost a physical impossibility to complete the White House in time for April 2nd," McShain said, "I am still going to make every human effort possible to have your desire realized."[9]

Truman's terse reply of January 30 simply lashed McShain tight to his word: "I sincerely hope that you can accomplish the finish of the White House by the date you referred to," he wrote.[10] But if the president knew what was about to happen next, he might have taken a kindlier tone with his general contractor. John McShain's definition of "every human effort possible" was a personal one: He had decided to bring this job in by himself.

Edgerton was a supremely competent administrator and, of course, there would be no replacing him. But McShain was still the immediate boss of the subcontractors—and they were at the root of the trouble.

On a normal McShain job, a subcontractor blew a deadline at his peril, but the White House operation had been slippery from the start. Even Hauck had complained that "on this project it has been almost impossible to set a definite schedule and adhere to it."[11] This, McShain was determined to fix.

The dapper Irishman sat down and hammered out an entirely new construction schedule. Then, with Hauck at his elbow, McShain spent the next two days collaring his subcontractors one at a time. He showed each man his new deadline and explained that no time existed beyond it. If a work gang needed overtime to hit the date, McShain would pay—but there would be no more excuses.[12] The Philadelphia builder even applied to the commissioners for permission to supervise the B. Altman decorating team so that, he said, "this particular contractor will not fall down on his part of the project."[13]

Amid his probable feelings of regret and relief, Hauck must have also sensed déjà vu: His boss had seized the helm like this before. Back in 1942, when the pressure of the Pentagon job had driven Hauck to the verge of a nervous breakdown, McShain had relieved him and run the job personally for the next two weeks. The men under his command would never forget it. In a single day, McShain drove them to pour 2,875 cubic yards of concrete—a new record.[14] Watching the imperious contractor in action, a *Washington Post* reporter had called McShain "a dynamo of construction energy."[15] *Nation's Business* was more sober in its characterization: John McShain, it said, "drives his men unmercifully."[16]

McShain sent a letter outlining his new schedule to Edgerton in time for the commission's February fifth meeting. If the general disagreed with anything the general contractor had planned, the record does not reflect it.[17]

⊶⊷ ⊷⊶

During the first week of February, Truman led a group of reporters on an impromptu tour of the White House. By this point, twelve days after delivering his ultimatum, the president would have received McShain's personal pledge to wrap the job quickly. Truman should have left the matter there. But he couldn't—or, at any rate, didn't.

Merriman Smith, veteran correspondent for the Associated Press, could tell right away that "Pepperpot Truman" (as the press corps called him when he was mad) was "irritated" that his house was not finished. The president held it together for a while, but then his temper flared like a blowtorch. As the subsequent news stories told it, Truman said he was "getting pretty tired of delays" and that he could have built five new White Houses for the money it had cost to rebuild this old one. Truman also boasted how "he applied a curry comb to officials in charge of the project" to get them to move faster.[18] Truman knew he was on the record, yet even that didn't stop him from claiming that he'd "had to keep a shotgun after the builders all the time."[19]

That last comment had clearly been directed at McShain, and it was evidence of an anger that would smolder for years. During a 1961 television interview with David Susskind, Truman told a nationwide audience that if he hadn't threatened to move a house cat into the mansion, the workmen would never have finished up and left. His allegations were so inflammatory that McShain wrote to the former president, informing him that "your remarks have been a source of great embarrassment to me among my business associates as well as my friends." Only then did Truman relent.[20]

Truman and McShain may never have been chummy, but the president had no right to make a whipping boy of the man. Whether Truman realized it or not, the renovation would have been doomed without John McShain. It was he who'd bankrolled all the overtime, and he who'd offered thirty thousand dollars out of his own pocket to spare the commission the embarrassment of begging Congress for money.[21] When the two-thousand-dollar bill for the renovation's commemorative plaque arrived, the commission was flat broke, and it was McShain who'd pocketed the invoice.[22] Later, the builder would estimate that his company had performed *double* the amount of work stipulated in the original contract, and lost $200,000 doing it.[23]

And that was just money—something McShain had always expected to lose on this sinkhole of a job. Where McShain paid the dearer price was with his time. For years, he had found a way to run one of the country's ten most powerful construction firms and still have time for his family, assembling a trusted coterie of superintendents to manage the company's daily affairs. Even in 1950, when his government contracts totaled fifty million dollars, the Man Who Built Washington came to Washington just once a week. And no matter the business to be done, he'd always made it home to Philadelphia in time for dinner with his wife, working his job estimates on a pad of paper to the gentle sway of a northbound Pennsylvania Railroad coach. Often, he'd set his work aside and write to his daughter instead. "Most of the letters he wrote to me—and he wrote to me almost every day—he wrote from the train," Pauline McShain recalled.[24]

But as problems at the White House had multiplied, McShain's once-weekly trip to Washington had turned to two and then three. Instead of greeting his wife, Mary, each night, McShain trudged into an empty room at the Hay-Adams instead.[25] By the time he made his pledge to Truman to finish the work by April, McShain had all but put the rest of his life on hold, setting up a temporary office down in the old White House kitchens so he could direct his men. McShain would later admit that no building he'd ever built would tax him, reduce him, like this one. "In the past thirty-two years," he confessed, "I have never given so much of my time to any project as I did to the White House."[26]

John McShain had just turned fifty-three years old. He did not know it yet, but his days of vigorous health would come to an end soon after the White House was finished. In this, the final weeks of the titanic project, the already-trim construction man would lose eight pounds.

Inside the mansion, McShain's new schedule took immediate effect. Now it was "a race against time," said the *Washington Post*.[27] On February 12, General Edgerton left himself a note: "Get up punch list"—the final roster of undone work that signals the final, frantic days of a job. Knipp & Co.'s men fanned out through the house, hanging doors and handle sets. The stone setters cemented the missing marble bases in the Red Room. As Abbie Rowe crept around the family quarters he snapped a photo of a workman wrestling a big electric floor sander across the oak. The herringbone parquet tiles were supposed to be hand-sanded, but there was no time for that now. Outside, as workmen patched and painted the house's exterior stone, masons from McLeod & Romberg laid the pavers for the walkways and eased curbstones into the cold earth. Nearby, grading tractors from the Capital Parks Department covered the bomb shelter with a toupée of sod. From this point forward, few visitors to the house would know the secret that lay beneath the lawn.

The first B. Altman & Co. truck from New York had pulled up to the house on February 8, and Edgerton immediately gave the decorators exclusive use of elevator number 2 to begin their work on the top floor. By some miracle, John Hasbrouck had finished the second-floor parquetry on time, so the family rooms were ready when Haight's decorators moved down a floor. Pleased that the work was finally in lockstep, McShain wrote a letter to Truman on the fifteenth. "If you have an opportunity, over the week-end, to visit the building I am sure you will be very much encouraged," he said.[28] Truman did exactly that, though the tone of his reply evinced only a slight thaw: "I spent yesterday afternoon going through the house and it does look to me as if you will attain the objective," the president wrote. He closed with a thorny "I sincerely hope so."[29]

Toward the end of February, parks workers began tearing apart the temporary outbuildings on the South Lawn, first reducing the sheds to skeletons of two-by-eights and finally trucking all the lumber away. The demolition evicted not only the rats but also General Edgerton, who dumped his papers in a shack near the southwest gate. On the north facade of the house, the last of the scaffolding came down, revealing a sight unseen for two years: a luminous White House standing wholly on its own. Soon the broken earth and stray bits of lumber strewn about its base would vanish below sod rolls of Merion bluegrass and creeping red fescue. The landscapers unfurled it all like carpeting, then trimmed it with tea roses and boxwood. The Agriculture Department's experimental farm in Beltsville, Maryland, outdid itself for the occasion: The botanists had sent over no fewer than twenty-seven varieties of azaleas.

Two days later, social secretary Edith Helm called a press conference and announced the resumption of the White House entertaining schedule. "Now don't ask me when the White House will be finished," Helm snapped. "I don't know—and you can spell that in capital letters."[30] The reporters suspected that Helm *did* know, but they got nothing from her. Still, Queen Juliana's visit was approaching on April 2. Would Truman have bothered to invite the monarch if he didn't expect to have a new White House to show off?[31]

As the final months of the Truman administration ticked past, the president decided to make one more trip to his retreat down in Key West. Nothing could relax him more effectively than a few days camped out at the old submarine base, wearing straw hats and playing marathon games of poker—"my favorite form of paperwork," Truman called it.[32] He'd managed ten trips down there so far. This one would be his last. And since Bess would be staying behind, it would also be his final chance to drink all the bourbon he wanted and wear his horrendous red pants without threatening the stability of his marriage. Truman announced he'd be leaving on March 7, 1952, and staying away for three weeks.

Lest the men on the White House job interpret his vacation as a chance to relax a little themselves, Truman ordered usher Crim to turn the thumbscrews. A few days before Truman's departure, Edgerton wrote in his diary, "Mr. Crim advises that the President is going away in March and expects to go direct to White House on his return."[33] Truman's return date was March 27, a full six days before the April second completion date he'd imposed earlier. The Missouri Mule had dug in once again, moving the deadline up by a week.

Two days after the president left town, the *Washington Post* decided to send a reporter to the White House to see how things were going. It seems that the editors presumed the house was all but complete, because they dispatched Dorothy McCardle—the society reporter. It was an unfortunate mistake.

"There is a lot of debris still kicking around under foot as you enter the ground floor," wrote McCardle, "and workmen with paint cans and blueprints elbow you out of their way." The poor dear. McCardle's beat was tea and gossip, not paint and plaster. She leaned her head of curly hair into the kitchens ("full of electric cables and wiring at the moment") and then marched up to the State Floor, where she seemed to expect the dinner candles to be lit. Instead, she found only more rude, sweaty men. "I must report," McCardle huffed, "that the famous reception rooms are not nearly that far along. There is still much to be done."[34]

That McCardle had obviously set out to write a frilly piece probably explains why she did not trouble herself to quote anyone, and why her March ninth story ultimately missed the point. Stray wires and wet paint aside, the big old house was actually almost finished. One week after her visit, the commission declared the house's interior—flooring, marble, woodwork, kitchens—complete.

The exception, of course, was what McCardle had come to inspect: the interior decoration. As the other subcontractors wrapped up their work, Charles Haight and the B. Altman decorators fell increasingly under the gun.[35] On the family floor alone, Haight had nearly twenty rooms and four sitting areas to dress up. For these, he would unroll 13 rugs, hang 114 curtains, and position 225 pieces of furniture. Adding to the pressure was the hovering presence of Bess Truman, who'd decided to "supervise the final preparations for the reopening," as Margaret put it.[36]

Not that there was much she could do. Haight wasn't exactly about to ask the First Lady to help lift a sofa. Besides, she had already made her aesthetic contributions to the house—at least the ones Haight could afford to buy. As Margaret later wrote, "the lawmakers declined to put up any serious money to decorate the place."[37] And since the lion's share of the budget went for the state rooms, the only true decorating Mrs. Truman had gotten to do upstairs was limited to picking out fabrics and maybe some rugs. And even then, Haight could have easily guessed her selections. The White House had not changed Bess Truman. Much as she had in 1945, the First Lady simply opted for the bright colors and floral chintzes she'd always loved. "I'm only going to be around for a year," she told J. B. West. "It would be unfair to the next First Lady to impose too many of my ideas upon the house."[38]

Armed with the decorating budget's "principle sums of money," as the commission generously described it, Haight at least got to conjure a little opulence down on the State Floor.[39] Gliding around in his dark suit, he must have taken some pleasure in hanging the creamy silk draperies and rolling a plush red chenille rug down the Cross Hall. Several of B. Altman's artisans still knew the dying craft of wall upholstering, and Haight had indulged them with yard after yard of luscious damask in crimson, green, and blue. Tucked in the backs of the twenty-seven trucks that had driven down from New York were the State Floor's precious historic pieces: the L. Marcotte & Co. banquettes of French walnut, the 1903 Davenport dining chairs from Boston, the 1817 Hannibal clock by Deniére et Matelin. Haight's artisans had restored each piece, then wrapped and tagged it. The movers lined everything up in the foyer, where each item waited for Haight's eye to discern the perfect spot for it.

Bess Truman had been prudent not to overinvest her energy in the decoration of the family quarters. As J. B. West later told it, the first morning after President Eisenhower's inauguration, Mamie sat up in bed, lit a cigarette, and announced, "I'd like to make some changes right away."[40] But there was one thing Bess Truman created that was so wonderful nobody would dare touch it. When Harry Truman had moved Mary Lincoln's rosewood bedroom set down the hall in 1945, he'd put some of the Lincoln furniture into a room, but it would take Bess Truman to truly create the Lincoln Bedroom.

During the sixteen administrations that came between Abraham

Lincoln and Harry Truman, the surviving pieces of Lincoln furniture had been strewn far and wide. Charles McKim had actually wanted to toss the bedroom set out during the 1902 renovation, but Edith Roosevelt had stopped him. Grace Coolidge had happened upon Lincoln's desk chair moldering up on the third floor, and Truman himself had discovered four mice-gnawed chairs up in the attic of the Treasury Department that turned out to be the ones Lincoln had used for his cabinet meetings. He ordered the chairs restored at once.

As the various pieces of surviving Lincoln furniture came together, Lillian Parks recalled, the First Lady saw the sense of putting them all in the same place. "Mrs. Truman worked diligently to restore the Lincoln [Bed]room . . . with all the Lincoln furniture, which had been spread all over the house," the seamstress wrote. "She brought back the Lincoln bed to its rightful place, as well as Lincoln's old dresser and tables. She also found a couple of Lincoln chairs around the White House to complete the restoration."[41] Margaret Truman would later apportion the credit by saying that while her father had first assembled the Lincoln Bedroom, he'd been "aided and abetted by his wife, Bess."[42]

Herman Perlman had a secret. Sometime on or about March 13, as the workmen laid in the marble in the bathrooms, Perlman climbed the White House stairs to install some plate glass in B-220, the president's bathroom. Perlman surveyed the bright expanse with its tiled floor and gleaming hardware. Then he spotted a long, thick slab of marble propped nearby. An eagle had been etched onto the marble's polished side, and Perlman knew that the stone layers would soon be fitting the piece onto the front of the bathtub to make it flush with the wall. He knew this because he'd already recruited the two marble setters as his accomplices.

Perlman never said if he composed his lines beforehand or on the spot, but he quickly got to work etching a verse onto the stone's unfinished side. His cohorts took a rubbing for proof, then sealed the slab into place. The secret would keep for another two years. Only when Perlman found himself on the TV game show *I've Got a Secret* did he confess what he had written: "In this tub bathes the man whose heart is always clean and serves his people truthfully."[43]

Down in the foyer, workmen hurried across the checkerboard floor on their way to screw in switch plates, check the phone lines, and finish installing the stair rail. Amid the frenzy, General Edgerton paused to watch a painter dabbing gold on a mirror frame.

Eleven days left.

The polished amber stone between the lobby columns now bore the years 1792, 1817, 1902, and 1952 in bronze numerals. The first was the year that workmen had started the White House; the others marked the years they had rebuilt it.

Nine days left.

The picture hangers returned George P. A. Healy's 1869 portrait of Abraham Lincoln to its perch of honor over the State Dining Room's fireplace. Painted in black tie and leaning forward in his chair, the president looked like he might reach down to the table himself.

Five days left.

In the East Room, electricians from O. R. Evans & Bro. hoisted the first of the twelve-foot Caldwell chandeliers to its plaster medallion high over the floor. When the juice flew through the circuit, six thousand prisms of Bohemian crystal hurled rainbow light through the air.

TWENTY-FOUR

OPEN HOUSE

He is the happiest, be he king or peasant, who finds peace in his home.

—Goethe

*P*ilot Francis W. Williams got a visual of Washington National Airport as he reduced his airspeed and dropped his gear and flaps. He laid the forty-six-ton *Independence* down the centerline as if putting a baby into its crib. At 5:56 P.M., the silver plane rolled to a stop at the Military Air Transport Terminal. Williams cut the props, the hatch dropped open, and Truman clomped down the steps to the tarmac. He'd changed into a suit on the way up, but his deep tan betrayed weeks of beach bumming. It was Thursday, March 27, 1952. Harry S. Truman was back in town, right on schedule.

Bess waited at the bottom of the rolling steps. Margaret would have come, too, but she'd lucked into a booking on *The Jimmy Durante Show*. The broadcast wasn't slated until April 4, but Margaret had gone out to L.A. early to rehearse with "the Schnoz." They had some vaudeville thing planned—top hats, canes, the whole bit—and she wanted to get it right.

A clutch of officials had motored out to the airport with Bess to wait for the president's plane. A welcoming party for any executive touchdown was customary, but this one had some high-ranking attendees. F. Joseph Donahue, commissioner of the District of Columbia, had come. So had John Farr Simmons, the State Department's chief of protocol. Standing close by was Secretary of State Dean Acheson, a dandy who often tucked a boutonnière into the lapels of his Farnsworth-Reed suits. The assembly of these men was a signal that some history was in the offing that night. For the first time in nearly three and a half years, the presidential motorcade would be returning to the White House.

Thanks to traffic, the drive from the airport took nineteen minutes. The sun had already ducked behind the magnolias and forsythia bushes as the black Lincoln leaned into the circular drive, following its gentle bend to the east. The big car floated past the West Wing, past the place where the chain-link construction fence had bisected the property. Then chauffeur Harry Charnley threaded the car's bulbous nose between the portico columns, heeling the brake until the three-ton car lurched to a halt.

There were people everywhere, come to witness the president's triumphal return to the mansion that had nearly collapsed on him back in 1948. The Secret Service kept nearly all the spectators outside the portico, leaving them to crane their necks for a glimpse inside the floodlit enclosure of white stone. Aside from the reporters and photographers, only a handful of officials made it past the cordon. The Commission on the Renovation of the Executive Mansion numbered among them, but even these men kept themselves behind the cameras. This was the president's moment, not theirs. His exile had lasted three years, three months, and sixteen days.

One of the photographers had set up a portable spotlight just inside the portico's northwest corner. Its beam bounced off every inch of the shiny black limousine with the D.C. "1" license plate. With the cameras fluttering and police holding back the onlookers, the whole thing felt more like Oscar night than a trip home from the airport. Just then, the Lincoln's rear door swung open on its heavy hinge, giving the crowd a glimpse of the car's cream-and-green leather upholstery. A pair of sensible black shoes appeared, then the hem of a black dress with a black coat over that. And there she was: Bess Truman, facing the beautiful white mansion, and proving once again that you can't go wrong in black. The president shimmied out of the car behind his wife, then stood to her left at the curb. This was the moment. The forty press photographers popped off their bulbs like a fireworks show. The couple began their ascent up the White House's front steps.

At the top were familiar faces—ushers Crim and West, head doorman John Mays, and, cutting a striking figure in his white tie and tails, Alonzo Fields. Their smiles shone with pride and also relief. As Fields later said, "It had been a tough job putting the old place back into shape."[1] But Fields wrestled with an emotion that the others did not have, which was regret.

He knew he would be putting in an official request to leave his post as soon as he could find a comparable government job in Boston, where he could be closer to his wife, Edna. She lay dying, slowly, at the Lahey Clinic. Fields knew that no job would ever compare to the one he had inside the mansion behind him. He also knew that he'd have to bid farewell to the Trumans first, and he didn't relish the task. The White House could be cruel like that. It was a lesson the butler had learned long before. "In the morning you serve breakfast to a family with whom you have spent years," he said. "At noon that family is gone out of your life."[2]

When the president reached the top, he shook hands with everyone. He even slipped his coat off and handed it to Mays, as he always did. Standing to the right were a trio from the General Services Administration, project manager William H. Kelley, commissioner W. E. Reynolds, and administrator Gen. Jess Larson. In his hand, Larson cupped a leather box that had arrived a few days earlier from the Yale lock company. Inside was a gold key for the front door.[3] When the president greeted Larson, the general pressed the box into his palm. ("Mr. Larson gave me a gold key to the House," Truman recollected soon afterward, "which Mr. Crim assured me would *not* open any door on the place."[4])

The timing could not have been more dramatic. It was now 6:20—sunset—and the president stepped toward a cluster of chrome microphones, smiling and lofting the box in the air like a kid who'd won a trophy. He kept his remarks brief, as he always did: "I am very happy to move back into the President's House," Truman said. "The beautiful part of it is that I didn't have to do any of the work of moving in."[5]

Laughter, applause, more flashbulbs. Then Truman turned, took his wife in arm, and disappeared into the White House.

Truman had been right: He *hadn't* had to do any of the work of moving in. He would never know what he had put everyone through by tightening that deadline and then flying down to Key West to eat corn on the cob and wiggle his toes in the sand. Perhaps it was the president's prerogative to expect the impossible, but that made it no easier to deliver.

Throughout Truman's sojourn in Key West, the White House Press Office had insisted that it knew neither when the president would return nor the date the White House would be finished. It was a flimsy story, but it would hold until the press could prove otherwise. On March 13, it could. When trucks from Allied Van Lines pulled up beneath the North Portico and began unloading the Trumans' effects from Blair House, it was clear that the renovation was winding up in a hurry. The White House flacks refused to talk, but the moving men were happy to. "The word among workmen moving scores of items into the White House," said the *Washington Post*, was that Truman would head straight for the mansion after touching down from Key West.[6]

The bureau boys from the *New York Times* had noticed the vans, too, and reported that men were hefting furniture in through the White House's front doors "at the double quick."[7] The movers were only beginning. In fact, they would work until the very last minute, unloading the president's clothing just hours before his limousine pulled in. Crim pitched in to help, ordering his staff to carry the linens and clothing back across Pennsylvania Avenue not unlike the way they'd moved it all over to Blair House years before. Seamstress Lillian Parks did not end up leaving White House service as she'd feared. Did she remember how Mr. Reynolds of the Public Buildings Service had reassured her? "Lillian," he'd said, "you are going to be the first person to come into the new house." And, in fact, she was.[8]

By March 18, social secretary Edith Helm dropped the act and admitted that the mansion would indeed be ready in time for Queen Juliana's visit. Come the weekend, VIP tours were already moving through the house, mingling with the laborers in the same space. One of the groups getting an advance peek at the family quarters was the Women's Press Corps, and its guide was none other than the First Lady. "Mrs. Truman broke her own rule of silence to the press," J. B. West said, as surprised as everyone else.[9]

The female reporters paid polite attention to the furniture and draperies, but what they really wanted to know was whether Bess's husband had decided to run for another term.[10]

"That is a question," Bess replied, "to which you are not going to get a yes or no out of me. But I'll admit it was a fair enough question." The reporter tried again: "But could you stand it if you had to?" "Well," said the First Lady, drier than an old-fashioned, "I stood it for seven years."[11] And, God, had she.

The commissioners toured the house later that same day. When they finished, Rabaut cabled Truman down in Key West: "REPORT THAT THE TOUR OF THE WHITE HOUSE TODAY BY THE MEMBERS OF CONGRESS BROUGHT NAUGHT BUT WORDS OF PRAISE. I AM PLEASED TO MAKE THIS FACT KNOWN TO YOU."[12]

Rabaut had omitted the fact that the mansion wasn't actually finished that Sunday, and it wouldn't be on the day of Truman's return, either. Favoring General Edgerton with every possible spare moment, the commissioners waited until just hours before the *Independence* touched down on March 27 to conduct their final inspection. As they did, workmen were still scurrying to and fro with brushes, touching up the mansion's paint and trim. The commissioners had declared the house "substantially" complete. They'd hedged it with an adverb. Close was close enough.[13]

For the record, the last piece of the renovation work took place in the East Room. Electricians from O. R. Evans were assembling the massive Caldwell standards when they discovered that one of the candelabra arms was too close to a silk curtain. Fearing a fire, the men decided to leave the bulb out. And that was that: Eight hundred and thirty-six days of the most ambitious rebuilding effort in Washington's history came to an end with a empty light socket.

With the spotlights, cameras, and reporters behind them outside, the Trumans were suddenly alone in the sanctum of the foyer. Below their feet, the pink-and-gray checkerboard stretched all the way to the Cross Hall, where potted palms gently brushed their fronds across the columns of white Vermont marble. High over the crimson carpet, Waterford chandeliers glistened like clusters of icicles. The walls and ceilings were whiter than notebook paper. The bronze torchieres had been polished down to their claw feet. Not since its rebuilding after the War of 1812 had the house felt so new—and maybe not even then, either. The Trumans began to walk.

Off to the left was the portal for the new grand staircase, the one to which the president had fought with Delano to add two extra turns so that its steps could spill into the foyer. The couple passed below the stony gaze of Herbert Hoover, ensconced in his frame high on the wall, and turned left. They found the East Room waiting in a magisterial silence, its silken curtains pooled on the Fontainebleau parquet, its three immense chandeliers glowing like jewels in candlelight. Most everything in sight was entirely new, yet somehow the fact did not diminish the weight of history here—"a gentle hush," as Edwin Bateman Morris would write, "reminiscent of so many great things."[14] This was the space where Lincoln had greeted guests, where Alice Roosevelt had been married, where (Truman remembered himself) FDR's flag-draped casket had lain beside his empty wheelchair.

The Trumans slipped into the Green Room, sinking their heels in the plush Savonnerie rug. The mantel of white Carrera marble, a rare survivor of the twenty-four carved in Italy after the 1814 fire, looked soft and beautiful as cake icing. A quiet ticking sound emanated from the gold clock on its top, guarded by a miniature Hannibal standing beside his Roman helmet. In the Blue Room, Haight had left the herringbone parquet unobstructed, returning the Marcotte armchairs and footstools to their former places along white enamel wainscoting and giving the chamber a feeling of extravagant openness. Up on the walls was the flower-basket pattern that the commission had debated so long and hard over, its faint gold threads shimmering in an ocean of blue. Where the ovular wall pushed out beneath the portico, a trio of windows looked onto the South Lawn. The last of the sun's honey-colored rays nested in their silk gauze curtains.

The president and his wife crossed the Red Room, with its plush chenille carpet and the 1850 Rococo sofa that Haight's furniture restorers had rescued with new upholstery. Passing through another paneled passageway, they found themselves on the west side of the mansion. Even though the Trumans had personally approved the painting of the State Dining Room's wall paneling, nothing could have prepared them for the effect of a room so large sporting a coat of celadon. His impulses creatively suffocated on the other floors, Haight had clearly enjoyed himself in here. Celadon—the color of lake water, of lichen, of pickled green tomatoes—is an aloof pigment. But Haight had fearlessly woven it into the chenille for the Geneva rug and into the damask of the Queen Anne high-back chairs. The startling color had chased off the dining room's baronial moodiness. "Once you saw the change," Fields said, "it surprised you how much [the color] added to the room."[15] The Trumans were pleased. And just in case subsequent families might not be, the commission had discreetly ordered the painters to slap on some clear coat first, so the celadon paint could be easily stripped off.[16]

Having cycled clockwise through the state rooms, the Trumans concluded their tour. There would be time enough during the coming days to explore the rooms upstairs, time to blink at all the new appurtenances that Winslow had dreamed up to take the already insulated and pampered life of a president and insulate and pamper it that much more. The dozen new closets were desperately needed. Less certain was the indispensability of in-room loudspeakers, the central vacuuming system, and ice water on tap. A future president would not even need to trouble himself to escape to a place like Key West; he could just zip up to Winslow's rooftop Solarium, complete with its bamboo furniture (to "give the place a tropical atmosphere," said the *Washington Post*[17]). And if he wanted to pick flowers, Winslow had stuck a greenhouse up there, too.

For now, however, the president had seen enough. As Alonzo Fields later summed it up, "Though there were many fine improvements, the house looked the same."[18] Yes, it did. This was what the public would expect, and Truman could take some comfort in knowing he could show it to them. Truman's latest public-approval rating had slid to 22 percent. Possibly, he reasoned that unveiling a beautifully renovated White House might help him leave office to fewer jeers.[19] "Bess and I looked over the East Room, Green Room, Blue Room, Red Room and State Dining room," Truman wrote in his diary later that night. "They are lovely."[20]

Bess had RSVP'd for a Salvation Army dinner at the Shoreham Hotel. When the car came around, she departed. With Margaret out in Los Angeles, Truman was left to eat dinner alone. Fields served him in the family dining room. When he laid down his napkin, the president rose from the table and devoted the rest of his night to roaming. Even if he'd wanted to, Truman probably wouldn't have seen the entire mansion that first night. The place was too big. The domain the ushers served had grown to 66 rooms, but, factoring in the new subterranean levels, the total number of rooms in the house had swelled to 132.[21] Winslow had turned Room G3 (the White House kitchens until 1850 or so) into a "futuristic" TV broadcast center.[22] Directly below the State Dining Room, Winslow had built Truman's physician, Dr. Graham, his own operating room (one he would never use). The lower levels even boasted a dentist's office and a barbershop.

"We really have done a job on the old White House," Truman soon would marvel in a letter to Douglas Orr, joshing that "McKim, Mead and White would probably turn over in their graves."[23] But on this first night, as the president walked the plush, silent corridors alone, a grave question shadowed him: With three years and $5.8 million gone, had all the time and money been spent wisely?[24] Writing about this fateful night many years later, Margaret—who was 2,300 miles away on the evening of her parents' return—was certain her father had had no regrets. "One might wonder if regaining this now really palatial mansion might have given Harry Truman second thoughts about his decision," she wrote. "But raising that question would only prove you did not know Harry Truman very well."[25]

Would it, though? This time, Truman's only child had him wrong. The president *did* have second thoughts, quite a few of them.

After he'd poked his head into enough of the rooms, Truman sat down to make his nightly entry in his diary. "I spent the evening going over the house," he wrote. Then he delivered his verdict on the renovation: "With all the trouble and worry it is worth it—but not 5½ million dollars! If I could have had charge of the construction it would have been done for half the money and in half the time!"[26]

That was just Pepperpot Truman talking again; there was no way that the White House could have been renovated faster or more cheaply than McShain had done it. Truman kept his discontent to himself. When he wrote to commission chairman McKellar the following day, he imparted nothing but praise and gratitude. "I stayed in the White House last night for the first time since November 11, 1948," he wrote. "It is beautiful inside and out."[27] Truman wrote to Richard Dougherty with equal effusiveness: "The more I look at it, and examine the fundamental basis on which you worked, the more pleased I am with the finished job."[28]

But he wasn't pleased, not really, and the renovation's high cost and slow progress were not his only complaints. Truman began to notice problems with the house—minor at first, but still evidence of a carelessness that angered him. On the presidential seal in the Cross Hall, the eagle's head had been cast in the wrong direction.[29] The house had gone from having no storage space to having so much of it that Truman couldn't find his own clothes.[30] And Crim turned out to be right about the gold key being useless. "It opened all of [the doors] tonight but the I wanted to get into!" Truman wrote in his diary.[31]

As time went on, the list of annoyances grew. Everyone seemed to appreciate the mansion's new $617,000 air-conditioning system—at least until the night it broke down and plunged fifteen hundred formally attired guests into the sweatiest dinner of their lives. Noise was an issue, too. Winslow's penchant for sheathing everything in marble had turned the house into an infuriating echo chamber. "It's dreadful," future curator Clement Conger would complain. "Very bad because of the noise."[32]

Then there were the fireplaces. Aware of the chimneys' notorious habit of belching smoke into the rooms, Edgerton had fussed over the flues and even hired a special fireplace consultant.[33] But the backdrafts had returned with a vengeance. "When the wind was in the northwest," Margaret recalled, "it came whistling down the fireplace in the corner of my bedroom."[34] Even when there was no fire in the grate, the drafts made some rooms uninhabitable. Late one night, the currents were so bad, Margaret decided to lean a card table against her fireplace to keep the cold air off her bed. No sooner had she fallen asleep than a gust knocked the table flat on the floor. Awakened in terror, Margaret flew across the corridor to cower in her mother's room just as Bess burst through the door into her husband's. "Did you hear that awful noise?" the First Lady screamed. The president put on his bathrobe and ventured across the hall to investigate. Had the White House ghosts returned? "Mother and I were scared silly," Margaret confessed. Then the president discovered the card table on the floor and told everyone to go back to bed.

In time, Bess Truman grew just as annoyed as her husband. The new White House "was shot full of errors," Lillian Parks recalled. The pantry sinks were too small for the dinner dishes, the cabinets were too high for anyone to reach, and the Solarium—a glass-walled room that baked in the southern sun—lacked a single duct for air-conditioning. What had Lorenzo Winslow been thinking when he'd failed to give the sewing room any electrical outlets? Or when he'd put the valets' presses two stories below the room where the president actually got dressed? "Mrs. 'T' was furious," Parks said. "She spoke bitterly of all the errors."[35]

Most of these ills could be fixed by a plumber or carpenter. Sadly, nobody could help with what turned out to be the new White House's biggest problem: It simply wasn't the White House anymore. Some of the old hands thought that in gutting the mansion, the commission had substituted its warm and stately personality with a generic lookalike, an imposter. Lillian Parks felt the difference the first time she walked in. "It was a sad inspection," she wrote later. "I felt a deadness as I walked up the stairs and through the rooms." Parks tried to be diplomatic, but in the end she believed there was just one word for the new White House: "institutional."[36]

She wasn't alone. The renovated mansion, J. B. West later said, had "an impersonal, store-decorated look."[37] (And little wonder, since a store *had* decorated it.) Margaret Truman couldn't understand how a house could be so "painted and papered and decorated down to the most minute details" and still come out feeling "more hotel-like than ever."[38] The most damning appraisal would come from Eleanor Roosevelt. Though the visiting former First Lady assured Truman that his new house was "lovely,"[39] her true feelings would emerge later on. "Mr. Truman showed me around the White House," Mrs. Roosevelt said, ". . . which looked to me exactly like a Sheraton Hotel!"[40]

It was telling that so many people who had known the old house believed that there was something missing from this polished, pristine new one. And they were right; something was: the actual White House. This feeling might have been different—lessened, certainly—had the commissioners just allowed Winslow the extra time to reinstall all of the old interior finishing he had so meticulously removed and warehoused. But they had not. Under pressure, they had scraped the old house of its innards and stuffed it with a replica of itself. In doing so, these wise men of architecture and politics had ignored the inevitable by-product of such work: that a gut renovation alters not just appearance but soul. The new White House might *look* just like the old house, but even the finest craftsmanship could never make it *be* the old house, alive with its familiar musks and creaks. Having pledged to save the White House, the commission had actually lost it—or most of it.

It was true that a radical rebuilding had been necessary to prevent the house from collapsing,[41] and that the White House's aging infrastructure was no longer adequate to house and protect a modern, postwar president.[42] It was also true that none of the work departed from the wisdom of the era—that "saving" a building's shell was as good as saving the whole place, or that to be "authentic," architecture and interior treatments needed principally to *look* authentic.[43]

Yet it was difficult not to feel that someone in power should have known better. Had Haight been given the funds to buy true antiques, had Truman not rushed the work so mercilessly, had the commission not regarded everything tumbling into the dump trucks as little more than "souvenirs," might the results have improved? Most probably.

For his part, Winslow had erred in failing to see that nearly everything inside the White House had *some* value simply for having been there, be it a smoke-damaged brick or a Victorian mantelpiece not in keeping with his visions of Federal purity. He'd failed to understand that old houses safeguard the aggregations of time; they are not places in which time freezes. In forcing the house to conform to a preselected aesthetic—"restoring it back," as the parlance still goes, to 1810—Winslow had not only negated the value of all the components that had come after that time; he had also ignored the organic process of history in favor of a selective, myopic, and hopelessly idealistic vision of what the White House "should" look like. His had been a contorted, unnatural exercise, and once it had been paired with the commission's far more egregious decision to discard most of the old interiors that Winslow had salvaged, the White House renovation turned down the road of no return, one that ended with a clone dwelling, a familiar face that belonged to a stranger.

It is easy to point fingers from the vantage of hindsight. It's also appropriate to credit one figure who recognized the errors at the time, and had the courage to call them out. In July of 1952, Alice Winchester, editor of *The Magazine Antiques*, warned her readers that "enthusiasm for saving significant old buildings has increased remarkably in recent years, but enthusiasm without knowledge is a dangerous thing, and well-meaning but ill-informed 'restoration' has ruined many a fine old building. Often important architectural elements have been lost forever by enthusiastic ripping out or scraping off, replacing or repainting."[44] Winchester wasn't just tossing theory around; she was referring to the White House.

EPILOGUE

Only an earthquake or an atomic bomb . . . could wreck the old building now.

—Harry Truman

Two days after moving back to 1600 Pennsylvania Avenue, Truman ascended the dais below the smoke-filled rafters of the D.C. Armory to deliver his Jefferson Day speech. He whooped the one-hundred-dollar-a-plate crowd, as expected, but only his final lines would make the news. "I shall not be a candidate for reelection," he told the audience. "I have served my country long, and I think efficiently and honestly. . . . I do not feel that it is my duty to spend another four years in the White House."[1] With those words, Harry S. Truman put an end to the political career that had begun in 1922. The only smile in the room belonged to Bess Truman.

As Truman's presidency entered its twilight, the mansion he'd rebuilt was starting its new life. On April 2, the DC-6 "Flying Dutchman" touched down at Washington National and, as the *New York Times* said, "opened a new chapter of social history in the White House."[2] Queen Juliana, the rebuilt mansion's first official visitor, had arrived.

Looking a decade younger than her forty-two years, Juliana popped out of the hatch in a raspberry organza dress with a shoulder cape of fox. Her husband, Prince Bernhard, followed in his military uniform. It rained on the royal parade, but the queen smiled and waved regardless. An official offered the queen an umbrella, but Juliana seemed fine with getting wet. She even noticed all the tulips that had been hastily stuck in the earth before her arrival.

Truman put Juliana and Bernhard up in the White House's master guest rooms. That night at dinner, the queen raised her glass and thanked Truman for inviting her and her husband. "We wanted to come and you wanted us to come," Juliana intoned, then added, ". . . and you even wanted us to see the White House in its new state."[3] Unfortunately, the house's new state didn't include an operative kitchen, which was why Juliana was giving her toast in the ballroom of the Carlton Hotel.

But soon enough, the kitchens were ready, and Truman immediately pressed them to their limits. The number of luncheons he'd hold over the next two months would break all previous records. Frantic to accommodate the swelling guest lists, Crim juggled the seating charts until he figured out how to squeeze 140 place settings—up from Edith Roosevelt's 107—into the State Dining Room.

On April 9, Truman made good on an old promise and threw a thank-you lunch for all the men who'd worked on the White House renovation. Once again, Douglas Orr would make the trek down from New Haven, and Dougherty from New York. Truman also invited John McShain and the long-suffering J. P. Hauck. Tottering around the State Floor in his double-breasted suit, Senator McKellar, the commission's eighty-three-year-old chairman, glanced approvingly at everything. "I have not seen all of the homes of the rulers of foreign countries," he would later write, "but in my judgment no ruler of any country has as beautiful a home as the White House now completed."[4] Shortly after 1:00 P.M., Truman marshaled his commissioners out through the main doors and into the shade of the North Portico. There, at the bottom of the front steps, Abbie Rowe waited with his camera.

It had been exactly two years, nine months, and twenty-one days since the first time Truman had posed for a portrait with his newly formed Commission on the Renovation of the Executive Mansion. On that distant June morning, the men had chosen the South Lawn for the photo, and the fate of the stone house looming over their shoulders had yet to be determined. Now they were back before the camera again. Fortunately, so was the house. Rowe released his shutter.

The commission met eight more times following its luncheon on that Wednesday afternoon (the group would continue to exist on paper until October 31, 1952), disposing of remaining business. There were piles of invoices to pay, letters of appreciation to wealthy benefactors to be written, papers to be organized for deposit in the National Archives. Some 150 pieces of broken White House furniture were still sitting in the storage room over at the National Gallery, and the museum's management had made it clear they wanted their room back. Tying up all these loose ends was colorless, obligatory work—except for one last order of business that actually mattered a great deal.

The commissioners had decided that, for the sake of posterity, an official account of the renovation should be published. For obvious reasons, the work would have to go to press before Truman's term expired. The commission also wanted to create a book that the public might actually want to read, which ruled out all of them as possible authors. Edgerton hired the famous playwright Edwin Bateman Morris for the job, which turned out to be perversely fitting: Before it was all over, Bateman's book—*The Report of the Commission on the Renovation of the Executive Mansion*—would produce a drama all its own.

Packed with photographs, the book imposed only fifty-two pages of text on its readers, each of whom paid $2.50 for the hardbound edition. From a press run of 12,500 copies, 10,000 went on public sale, and Americans bought every last one of them. The balance landed on the desks of officials, the press, and men involved directly with the work on site. One of those men was John McShain, who discovered, to his horror, that his name had been omitted from the copy.[5]

There was little doubt that McShain had been deliberately slighted. Certainly, he felt that way. Had the commission somehow forgotten who he was? The book included the names of nearly everyone else who'd played a role in the renovation (right down to the stenographers), but not him. When it came to the parts of the story that would logically have called for mentioning McShain's name, the prose conveniently shifted to the passive voice: The old walls "were removed," a steel frame "was installed," and so on.[6]

Calling the omission "a direct affront" and a "grave injustice,"[7] McShain fired off phone calls and letters, one after another—to Senator McKellar and Congressman Rabaut, to Douglas Orr and Richard Dougherty, to General Edgerton, and finally to President Truman himself. "I literally sacrificed two and one-half years of my life in the reconstruction of this building," the exasperated contractor told Truman's secretary Matthew Connelly, "and I would be embarrassed to confess the amount of money that actually it cost me to do this rebuilding."[8] To McKellar, he said simply, "I am crushed to think that I was so completely ignored."[9]

The only sympathetic ear belonged to Rabaut, who suggested that a fly sheet bearing the contractor's name be inserted into the books. It never happened.[10] A deeply wounded John McShain had the box of fifty complimentary copies of the report sent back unopened.[11]

Asked if she recalls her father's pride having been injured by this and other slights from the commission, Pauline McShain answered without hesitation: "Yes, I do. He was angered that he wasn't given more recognition for the challenge that this had been." Both her father and the commission, she said, shared the same goal of building a strong and beautiful house. "But the officials didn't understand the problems" a contractor faced, and blamed McShain again and again for circumstances beyond his control. It wasn't fair. Nothing in Washington was. "Nonetheless," Pauline McShain added, her father "continued to the day he died to be proud of the White House. He never stopped bragging— and he bragged about it a lot."[12]

At some point in the ensuing years, McShain would have a large rendering of the mansion added to the lower left-hand corner of his office letterhead. The caption read THE WHITE HOUSE, just in case the letter's recipient didn't recognize the place.

Just as John McShain's name made no appearance in the public account of the White House renovation, neither did the bomb shelter tucked below its foundations. No sooner had the *Washington Post* sniffed it out just eight months into its construction, than the shelter became a nonstory. Perhaps it was because Americans were turning their attentions closer to home, worrying about their own chances of survival. Still, Lorenzo Winslow's two new floors below the house, and the lure of atomic sanctuary that lay just beyond their doorways and passages, created a mystique that remains to this day.[13]

The shelter had cost nearly one million dollars, and had tortured Edgerton until the very last days of the renovation. (As the general related in his diary, army inspectors fussed over every inch of the place, decrying faults like "cheap . . . shower curtain rods."[14]) And now that the shelter was all finished, was the White House truly the better for it?

Well, yes, in theory. The shelter's existential dilemma was that its value stood in reverse proportion to that of the house above it. So long as life remained normal, the shelter crouched uselessly in the darkness. Only if Washington faced nuclear attack would the shelter become a structure of value and purpose—yet at the price of the city itself. One value would inexorably be traded for the other, and for this reason the shelter probably demanded more in anxiety than it gave in reassurance. For some in Truman's circle, perhaps, the underground bunker offered a weak comfort in its promise of preparedness. For everyone else, though, it served as mute witness to the coming of a future that nobody wanted to contemplate. And it was coming, good citizens, it was coming. As early as July 1950, the *Washington Post* told its readers that "it is a military certainty that no enemy can be stopped from dropping at least one bomb on Washington."[15]

But in the two years that had elapsed since Truman learned about the shelter, he had not changed his mind about it: He wasn't going to use it. Should a Soviet attack come, he would not flee the White House, certainly not to crawl into some dank hole beneath it. Truman had made his intentions clear to both Robert Dennison and the Secret Service. "In his mind," the admiral would later say, "the primary requirement was for the people of this country to realize that he was not going to run anyplace."[16] The Secret Service apparently had a more succinct understanding: The president wished to remain aboveground for "morale reasons."[17] It was a captain-of-sinking-ship scenario, expanded to kiloton proportions.

Did Truman mean it? Indeed he did—and he proved it.

Though the details of what took place remain scant, here is what the record says. At some point after Truman's move back into the White House, a radar operator monitoring the airspace over Washington gazed into his luminescent green scope and beheld a horrifying sight: a squadron of aircraft—none of them belonging to the United States Air Force—inbound for Washington. The operator counted twenty-five planes. It could mean only one thing.

Word was passed to the White House, probably by phone, certainly right away. In the ensuing minutes, the White House staff dashed belowground. They made it down to the lowest level and, presumably, through the blast doors. But the president was not with them. Harry S. Truman was still upstairs in the house, where he'd said he would be.[18]

The minutes passed. Nothing happened. The story never made it to the newspapers. Those who had fled presumably crept back upstairs. The "attack," which the radar had dangerously misread, had been a single small plane that had lost its way.[19]

The Trumans enjoyed precisely twenty-six days of privacy in the refurbished White House before the mansion reopened to visitors. On April 22, 1952, the first of them appeared at the East Wing entrance at 6:00 A.M., untroubled by the prospect of a four-hour wait before being allowed to enter. By the time the guards swung the gates open, those in line stood two and three abreast, snaking down Pennsylvania Avenue all the way to Seventeenth Street. Visitors wore their Sunday best, even though it was a Tuesday. People came to wait even though they knew that the gates would close again at noon, and there was no guarantee they would get in. But 5,544 of them did.

A stringer for the *Washington Post* loitered in the driveway outside the North Portico to ask the visitors what they thought of the spruce-up that had taken so many years and cost so many millions. But if the reporter was looking for grumbles, he heard none; everyone loved the place. "Beautiful," said Mrs. H. P. Thomas, visiting from Kansas City. "Money well spent," declared twenty-one-year-old Marshall Thompson, a local salesman. A farmer named F. B. Kitterman had come down from Cedar Grove, Maryland, to have a look at the house and was happy that he had. "I think the President did exactly right," Kitterman said, "even though I'm a Republican."[20] Only one visitor the reporter could find felt indifferent about the house. This was Ronald Melvin Miller, a six-month-old baby who'd been asleep in his mother's arms the entire time.

B. Altman & Co.'s final bill came in at $213,500. We will never know how much the store swallowed in labor and other costs; its records from this period are long gone. But a surviving letter from John S. Burke evinces no regrets. "If we have had a share in enhancing [the White House's] beauty and usefulness," Burke wrote to his Manhattan neighbor William Adams Delano, "the knowledge that we have fulfilled the responsibility given us is ample reward in itself."[21] Within days of the Trumans' return to 1600 Pennsylvania Avenue, B. Altman & Co. put bolts of the curtain and upholstery fabric on display in its Fifth Avenue windows, arranged with Charles Haight's watercolors. Staying just within the official ban on advertising, the store posted a placard that read, simply, THE WHITE HOUSE IS OPEN AGAIN, RESTORED AND REDECORATED.[22] New Yorkers came, saw, and got the hint.

Margaret Truman had no shortage of complaints about the family quarters, yet she would at least concede that "Altman's did amazingly well on a limited budget."[23] But the White House's budget-hotel look continued to irritate the president, until finally he couldn't stand it anymore. Late in June of 1952, he sent usher Crim up to Capitol Hill to ask the House Appropriations Committee for another fifty thousand dollars to do more decorating—as a "courtesy" to the next president. Committee chair Albert Thomas cut Crim off before he'd even finished his pitch. "You tell the president," Thomas said, ". . . that when the new President comes in, he can do the job to suit his own taste." With that, the committee sent Crim home. "It was nice of you to come see us," the usher heard as he skulked from the chamber.[24]

Truman never got over the slight. "Dad left Washington grumbling that the exterior had been improved," Margaret wrote years later, "but the interior looked worse than ever."[25]

The White House renovation would turn out to be the last genuinely popular thing that Truman would do while in office. The mounting casualties in Korea, the incessant pummeling from Senator Joseph "Low-Blow Joe" McCarthy, a weak-kneed domestic economy—all proved to be more than even the old Missouri Mule could stand up to. By June 1952, 58 percent of Americans disapproved of Harry S. Truman.[26] He had just turned sixty-eight years old. The head of steam that had powered Truman's presidential turbines through years of eighteen-hour days began to weaken. The staff looked with alarm on a president who now shuffled, pale and exhausted, through his days. Truman began to put off signing documents—not because he couldn't make up his mind, but because his hands shook too much to hold the pen. Margaret would later remember that "dad was close to burnout," but she was wrong: He was well *past* burnout now.[27]

Truman agonized that too few Americans understood just how big a threat the Soviet Union was quickly becoming on the global stage (the ensuing years would prove him right). He could have kept his head low through his last months in office, but instead he threw what little strength he had left into the Adlai Stevenson campaign. Truman's last duty to Cold War America, as he saw it, was to "keep the isolationists out of the White House."[28] But Stevenson, the bookish former governor of Illinois, was a reluctant candidate and surely no match for Dwight David Eisenhower, the five-star general who'd driven the Nazis to their knees. Americans admired Adlai, but they liked Ike—and swept him into office by a margin of 6.6 million popular votes.

On January 20, 1953, the yardmen coupled FDR's Pullman car "Ferdinand Magellan," the old warhorse Truman had used on his whistlestop tours of 1948, to the end of the Baltimore & Ohio train that would take the Trumans the nine hundred miles home to Independence. After the inauguration ceremony, Margaret sat on the jump seat of the presidential limousine as it made its way to Union Station. She stared thoughtfully into the deeply lined face of her father, the man whom kings, diplomats, and schoolchildren had for more than seven years referred to as President Truman. "Hello, *Mr.* Truman," she said to him. Her father smiled.[29]

Harry S. Truman did more than hand over the presidency to Dwight D. Eisenhower on that cold Tuesday afternoon; he handed over the White House, too—a place he'd regarded mainly as just the digs that came with the job, yet one that had nonetheless become a political and cultural masterstroke of his administration.[30] As such, the transfer should have been a cordial and ceremonious affair, but an ugly 1952 campaign had made enemies of the two men, and so it was not.

Seated in the back of the idling limousine, Eisenhower snubbed Truman's invitation to come inside the White House for tea before the swearing-in ceremony. Furious, Truman stomped out of the mansion alone. Adhering to tradition, he wore a tall silk top hat—one that looked archaic beside the svelte new homburg that Ike was sporting (some said to purposely humiliate Truman). The mile ride to the Capitol grandstand passed in stony silence. "I was glad I wasn't in that car," J. B. West said.[31] Later, a heartbroken Lillian Parks would watch Eisenhower order Truman's portrait removed from the White House, along with every other trace of him—his office globe, his grand piano, and even the Secret Service men known to have liked him.[32]

Yet, for as unfortunate as Truman's relinquishment of the mansion turned out to be on inauguration day, the event was of little consequence in the end. The reason was simple: Truman had *already* handed over his White House—not to a successor, but back to the American people. Were they not the house's owners anyway? The occasion was unofficial, but made history nevertheless. It had lasted for forty-eight remarkable minutes on May 3, 1952, and it began at the moment that all midafternoon programming across the United States paused in unison in order to bring you, ladies and gentlemen, the first-ever televised tour of the White House.

And here comes our host now.

The Big Three networks had already hauled trucks full of television equipment down to the mansion, snaking cables through the hallways and setting up their enormous TK-30 image orthicon cameras at strategic points. One of the CBS cameras stood in the center hall of the ground floor, its lens turret aimed at the stairs. At 4:00 P.M., eastern standard time, the camera's tally light flicked on. A crewman gave the signal, and Truman started down the marble steps, trotting right into the camera's vision field. The show was on. One-fifth of the American populace was watching.

Later estimates said that thirty million people stopped what they were doing to stare at the newly renovated mansion through the blue glow of a cathode-ray tube. There were so many people watching that even Truman seemed a little nervous. This was live television—no rehearsals, no scripts, no retakes. Margaret had been on TV before, but this audience was so big that even she kept herself safely behind the camera. Bess was so terrified that she hid across the street.

"I'm glad to have this opportunity to show the people just what the revamped White House looks like," Truman said. Then, as though to reassure everyone, he added, "Those familiar with it will see very little change."[33]

A dark-haired young CBS newsman named Walter Cronkite would pick up the lead segment. But it was apparent right away that Truman didn't need the escort. While Cronkite dragged the heavy microphone cable behind him, Truman showed off the new Diplomatic Reception Room. The elliptical chamber had been stripped of its paintings of the dour past presidents in favor of those of their wives. "I think [the room] looks much better with these good looking ladies," said Truman, smiling at Cronkite, who smiled back. The president was already getting a little spicy.

Truman walked Cronkite across the hall to show off the new Broadcast Room that Lorenzo Winslow had fashioned out of the mansion's original kitchen. He pointed out the rebuilt hearth and their stones bearing the marks that the masons of 1792 had chiseled into them. "You find those marks in all the great cathedrals of Europe," Truman pointed out, reaching into his trove of historic facts. When the pair came to the wood-paneled China Room, Truman pointed out that the paneling had been milled from the mansion's 1817 floor beams. Cronkite was impressed that the tiny square nail holes were still visible. "Yes," Truman said, "it adds that much."

Then Truman noticed the nearby portrait of Grace Coolidge and her white collie, Rob Roy. Unable to resist a good yarn, Truman recounted a story that Senator Morris Sheppard had told him about the afternoon he'd lunched with President Coolidge. The dog had scampered into the room and barked at Sheppard. "Senator," Coolidge calmly told him, "he wants your sausage." Sheppard surrendered the sausage to the dog, but Coolidge was too stingy to have the butler bring his guest a replacement. Now Truman delivered the story's punch line to Cronkite, mimicking the voice of his long-dead senate friend: "I gave him my sausage and I didn't get another one!"

Bess Truman was watching all this on the TV in Blair House, and she began to think the same thing that millions of Americans were no doubt also thinking by now: Harry Truman was a natural on camera.[34] *Time* magazine would later say the president's on-screen performance was "outstanding."[35] "As the star of a Nation-wide television show," the *Washington Post* reported, "he put on a terrific 48-minute act."

Of course, Truman had put on terrific acts before, many times, like during all of those whistle-stop speeches of the 1948 campaign. But this time there was a key difference: Truman wasn't proving himself worthy of an office he sought, but as the master of one he'd already held—and one whose powers he had deployed to rescue, rebuild, and preserve a landmark that, without him, might very well have disappeared. Yes, the White House he'd returned to them was flawed, with pieces missing and corners cut. But the place had survived, and now Truman's tour channeled its personality and reconsecrated its dignity.

With so many other rooms to see and two other networks to split the time with, Cronkite handed Truman over to ABC's Bryson Rash, who covered the State Floor segment as far as the Red Room. Then, as the engineers slipped a prerecorded tour of the family quarters into the broadcast, the two slumped down on the couch to rest. When the tiny on-air light clicked on again, Truman passed into the care of his third and final anchorman.

At thirty-two years old, NBC's Frank Bourgholtzer still had college-boy looks and the swept-over haircut to match. The White House had been Bourgholtzer's beat since 1947, and he and the president already enjoyed an easy rapport. The cameras began rolling again as the pair walked down the hall and disappeared into the Blue Room.[36]

"It's a beautiful room, this room is," Truman said. Then he stepped to the very center of the parquet floor so he could show Bourgholtzer where he and the First Lady had stood for the diplomatic receiving lines. The president used his usual trick, looking up to find the pendant on the chandelier, then positioning himself below it. On the grainy archival copy that survives of this episode, the president's eyes dart up for an instant. Yet in that instant, Truman closed a loop that had begun more than four years before, when the five-and-a-half-foot-tall Pendeloque had menaced the guests below, swiping its razor-sharp crystals just over their heads. Did the president remember that day? If so, he didn't let on. "Just the other evening," Truman continued, "we stood here and shook hands with 15,039 people by count. It was a diplomatic reception."

Truman did not seem aware that the chandelier hanging above him now was a different fixture. The old Caldwell & Co. monster was gone—crated up, trucked off, and sitting in storage, where it remains to this day. In its place hung a delicate puff of crystal and white tapers—much smaller, and certainly lighter, too—crafted in London around 1870. Someone (a good bet it was Winslow or Crim) probably had made sure that the old Pendeloque would cause no more problems.

"The clock here on the mantle," Truman continued, turning to his left and pointing, "was brought back here by James Monroe when Jefferson was president."[37] From atop the pearly white mantelpiece, Minerva lay across her gilded bronze clock, contemplating the TV reporter and the president with the same half-interested glance she'd directed at the Daughters of the American Revolution on that chilly afternoon in 1948 when Truman had nearly come crashing down through the ceiling in his bathtub.

The pair turned to leave. Before they reached the door to the Cross

Hall, Bourgholtzer stopped. A thought had just occurred to him. "Mr. President," he said, motioning upward, "wasn't it this ceiling that first began to tremble when you decided the White House needed to be renovated?" Truman didn't hesitate. "Yes," he told the newsman. "My study's right over this." Then the president related the story of the time Fields had brought him his lunch on a tray and the floor had bounced up and down like a trampoline. "I had an engineer and architect come in," Truman finished the story, "and they moved me out." "And that was the beginning of the renovation?" Bourgholtzer asked. "Of the *disintegration*," Truman replied, correcting him and laughing.

As the president and his guest left the room, one of the TV cameras trained its lens up at the ceiling, framing a shot of the lacy, glimmering chandelier for the audience at home. It held the shot silently for one, two, three seconds. Then the screen faded to black.

ACKNOWLEDGMENTS

Recounting the near collapse and improbable resurrection of the White House is a project that has taken me nearly three years. In a sense, however, the process began four decades ago—and with an entirely different house.

On the occasion of one of my single-digit birthdays, my mother and father (practitioners of cultural-heritage tourism before there was a name for it) took me to visit the sixty-five-room Beaux Arts mansion of the industrialist Ogden Mills. Built in 1896 but long since turned over to the state parks authority by heirs born to the age of income taxes, the plush and dusty old place sprawled on a weedy stretch of cliff overlooking New York's Hudson River Valley. That October morning was stiff with wind and rain, as I remember, and no other visitors turned up. When the ranger learned that her morning tour group would consist solely of the birthday boy and his parents, she decided to toss in a little something special. Pausing midway up one of the house's sweeping staircases, she pushed on a wall panel, which swung gently open. I stared, saucer-eyed, at a hidden passage of steps that led up into the shadows of the attic.

That was the day I learned that houses, like people, are the keepers of secrets.

There cannot be a house in this country that harbors more secrets than the one at 1600 Pennsylvania Avenue. It was a fact brought home to me as folders (then boxes, then steamer trunks) of photocopied documents engulfed my apartment, and also by the news that—coincidental to the start of this project—the renovation I was writing about was in fact in the process of repeating itself.

In the summer of 2010, the General Services Administration commenced a $376 million rehabilitation of the White House that the public buildings commissioner called "the biggest upgrade since the complete renovation of the executive mansion in the Truman era." Now, as then, the work was controversial, not only for its scope and price tag, but for its bureaucratic murk. It's still not clear what took place behind a tall fence that encircled a pit dug several stories deep below the West Wing—a pit that, as I write these words, has only recently been landscaped over. The GSA claims it merely replaced aging water, steam, and sewer lines. Suspicious observers contend that the convoy of trucks delivering untold tons of steel and concrete were building far more than that. Meanwhile, the four-year project appears behind schedule and spokespersons are no longer commenting. All of this feels terribly familiar.

It will be up to a future writer—one possessed of the hindsight, contacts, and forbearance that I lack—to write *that* White House renovation story. So far as this one (the Truman one) goes, it seems no small miracle that it happened at all—both in physical fact and, for me, now, in the form of a book with my name on its cover. But just like an architectural undertaking, a book cannot get done without the assistance and expertise of many talented people. Were I to gather all of the ones who made this one possible, I could easily fill the Blue Room for tea. Regrettably, that same fact also makes it impossible for me to thank everyone who helped me by name, but I would like to single out a few.

My cardinal gratitude goes to my agent, Gary Heidt, who liked this idea from the moment I showed him a photograph of the gutted White House while we sat in a West Village bistro in the summer of 2010. I am also greatly indebted to Peter Wolverton of Thomas Dunne Books, who granted me the time and resources to write this book, served as its enormously capable editor, and never failed to support my decisions and my work. To associate editor Anne Brewer, I am impressed by your talent, grateful for your diplomacy, and mystified by your patience with me. I also wish to thank Jay Barksdale of the New York Public Library, who assured me that I always had a desk and bookshelf at the Frederick Lewis Allen Memorial Room, where parts of this book were written.

Personal thanks go to my parents, who supported my efforts even when my talk of the White House's secrets—albeit sixty-year-old ones—made them nervous, and to my sister, Maria, who always made time to meet up and supply me with equal quantities of coffee and encouragement. To David, my mate of several years now, who endured my unstable moods, passing paranoias, and innumerable Harry Truman stories, I cannot repay you for the emotional security you've brought to my life.

In the course of my research, I received help from a number of gifted archivists and historians. Among them were William G. Allman, curator of the White House, who graciously furnished me with copies of Lorenzo Winslow's diary. Archivist Randy Sowell served as an unwavering guide through the labyrinthine holdings of the Harry S. Truman Library in Independence, Missouri. James W. Campbell of the New Haven Museum and Historical Society unearthed wondrous documents salvaged from the architectural office of Douglas Orr. Historian Michael J. Brodhead of the U.S. Army Corps of Engineers shared his encyclopedic knowledge of the corps with me, and also sent me General Glen E. Edgerton's complete White House reconstruction diary, without which this book's chronology would not have been possible.

My heartfelt thanks also go to Lucas Clawson and Jon Williams of the Hagley Museum and Library, Jennifer Cohlman of the Cooper-Hewitt National Design Library, Brett Stolle of the United States Air Force's National Museum, Maygene Daniels of the National Gallery of Art, and Simone Monteleone of the National Park Service. To Jane B. O'Connell, president of the Altman Foundation, thank you for telling me about the grand department store that your father ran; to Kim Bernard Holien, historian of U.S. Army Joint Base Myer-Henderson Hall, thank you for showing me where the insides of the White House lay buried.

I save a particular gratitude to Sister Pauline McShain, SHCJ, daughter of the late John McShain, who responded to my request for a phone interview by inviting me down to her home for an entire day. Her rich and lucid observations, her stories of her father's relationships with FDR and Harry Truman, and her driving tour of the Philadelphia main-line suburbs (punctuated by her pointing to one astonishing stone building after another and calmly saying, "Daddy built that") constituted the finest day of this entire project. When I asked her why her father chose to involve himself with the White House renovation despite the certainty of its being long, costly, and exasperating, Pauline McShain replied that some jobs are simply worth doing for their own sake. I believe that, now, I have a sense of what that means.

Robert Klara
New York, New York
April 28, 2013

ENDNOTES

PROLOGUE

1. New parquet for the Blue Room had last been laid down in 1902 by G. W. Koch & Son, New York. The draperies had been replaced in 1942, and FDR halted the social calendar after the 1941 attack on Pearl Harbor. See Stanley E. McClure, "A Preliminary Handbook of Historical Information Concerning the White House and Its Furnishings," February 9, 1950, 5, box 1, Peggy Watts Papers, Harry S. Truman Library and Museum, Independence, Missouri; Betty C. Monkman, *The White House: Its Historic Furnishings and First Families* (New York: Abbeville Press, 2000); J. B. West, with Mary Lynn Kotz, *Upstairs at the White House: My Life with the First Ladies* (New York: Coward, McCann & Geoghegan, 1973), 36.

2. While written accounts of the fateful tea given for the Daughters of the American Revolution appear in several sources, not one of them gives an actual date for it. The White House's Social Office lists no teas for the DAR around the time period, though its files were less than comprehensive when it came to events as frequent and informal as teas. The DAR itself also has no record of this tea, but the organization only keeps records that pertain to "the official activities of DAR's national officers and business at our headquarters," according to archivist Rebecca Baird (e-mail to author, March 29, 2011). The

author is relying on two sources that place the DAR tea early in the winter of 1948—most likely early January, given that the results of the initial second-floor inspection from the Department of Public Buildings would come at the end of that month (January 29), which would have brought an end to mysterious events like the one that took place during this tea. See West, *Upstairs at the White House*, 98; "Remodeling Job at 1600 Pennsylvania Avenue," uncited clipping in the Peggy Watts Papers, Harry S. Truman Library and Museum.

3. Charles Moore, "The Restoration of the White House," *Century*, April 1903, 807.

4. Monkman, *The White House*, 62, 188–92.

5. Original drawing of the Blue Room chandelier from the papers of Edward F. Caldwell & Co, collection of the Cooper-Hewitt National Design Museum Library, New York; letter to author from White House curator William G. Allman, September 14, 2010.

6. This is the estimated current weight of the East Room chandeliers, which were shortened during the Truman renovation. The fixtures would have weighed *more* than twelve hundred pounds at the time of this story. See "The East Room Chandelier," The White House Historical Association, at www.whitehousehistory.org.

7. John Whitcomb, *Real Life at the White House: Two Hundred Years of Daily Life at America's Most Famous Residence* (New York: Routledge, 2000), 321.

8. Bess Truman's loathing of White House functions is well documented—both in the memoirs of former White House staffers and by her own daughter, who recounted how when one journalist asked the First Lady in 1946 whether she, given a free choice, would have gone to live at the White House, she responded, "Most definitely would *not* have." See Margaret Truman, *Bess W. Truman* (New York: Macmillan, 1986), 297–98.

9. Margaret Truman, *Bess W. Truman*, 297.

10. Lillian Rogers Parks, with Frances Spatz Leighton, *My Thirty Years Backstairs at the White House* (New York: Fleet Publishing Co., 1961), 79–80.

11. Ibid.

12. Margaret Truman, *Bess W. Truman*, photo insert following p. 274.

13. Whitcomb, *Real Life at the White House*, 332.

14. West, *Upstairs at the White House*, 59.

15. Alonzo Fields, *My 21 Years in the White House* (New York: Coward-McCann, 1960), 121.

16. Presidential tour of the White House, May 2, 1952, NBC archival footage, at http://video/msnbc.com.

17. West, *Upstairs at the White House*, 98.

18. Ibid.

19. The quotes and details regarding this scene are all drawn from ibid., 98–99.

20. Alfred Steinberg, *The Man from Missouri: The Life and Times of Harry S. Truman* (New York: G. P. Putnam's Sons, 1962), 335.

21. West, *Upstairs at the White House*, 99.

22. Debs Myers, "The New White House," *Holiday*, November 1952, 121.

23. West, *Upstairs at the White House*, 99.

24. "Remodeling Job at 1600 Pennsylvania Avenue."

25. Fields, *My 21 Years in the White House*, 146.

26. Edmund Purves, "A Few Recollections of the White House," Harry S. Truman Papers, Post-Presidential File, Harry S. Truman Library and Museum.

27. Milton Lehman, "The White House Shudders," *Collier's*, November 13, 1948, 13.

28. West, *Upstairs at the White House*, 99.

1. MOVING DAY

1. John Whitcomb, *Real Life at the White House: Two Hundred Years of Daily Life at America's Most Famous Residence* (New York: Routledge, 2000), xxi.

2. David McCullough, *Truman* (New York: Simon & Schuster, 1992), 384.

3. Carl Sferrazza Anthony, *America's First Families: An Inside View of 200 Years of Private Life in the White House* (New York: Simon & Schuster, 2000), 131.

4. Margaret Truman, *Bess W. Truman* (New York: Macmillan, 1986), 134.

5. This is an after-tax figure. Truman's salary as an ordinary senator had been

ten thousand dollars a year. See Robert P. Watson, ed., *The Presidential Companion: Readings on the First Ladies* (Columbia: University of South Carolina Press, 2003), 131. With the promotion to vice president, his salary had risen to fifteen thousand dollars. The take-home figure for February—his last full month of pay before becoming president—appears in the *Report of the Secretary of the Senate*, 79th Cong., 2d sess., July 1, 1944–January 29, 1945, S. Doc. 184, 453.

6. McCullough, *Truman*, 255. In point of fact, even a year and a half into his presidency, Truman wrote to Bess telling her he was in favor of a presidential living allowance—one he planned on using to move back to 4701 Connecticut Avenue. See Harry S. Truman, *Dear Bess: The Letters from Harry to Bess Truman, 1910–1959*, ed. Robert H. Ferrell (New York: W. W. Norton, 1983), 534–35.

7. Jim Bishop, *FDR's Last Year* (New York: William Morrow, 1974), 601.

8. Margaret Truman, *Harry S. Truman* (New York: William Morrow, 1973), 210.

9. Margaret Truman, *Bess W. Truman*, 249.

10. Whitcomb, *Real Life at the White House*, 320–21.

11. Cormac O'Brien, *Secret Lives of the First Ladies* (Philadelphia: Quirk Books, 2005), 204.

12. J. B. West, with Mary Lynn Kotz, *Upstairs at the White House: My Life with the First Ladies* (New York: Coward, McCann & Geoghegan, 1973), 57.

13. Whitcomb, *Real Life at the White House*, 318.

14. Elliott Roosevelt and James Brough, *Mother R.: Eleanor Roosevelt's Untold Story* (New York: G. P. Putnam's Sons, 1977), 39.

15. Roosevelt and Brough, *Mother R.*, 40; Henrietta Nesbitt, *White House Diary* (Garden City, NY: Doubleday, 1948), 312.

16. Margaret Truman, *Harry S. Truman*, 220.

17. Ibid., 223.

18. Margaret Truman, *Bess W. Truman*, 253.

19. West, *Upstairs at the White House*, 57–58.

20. Ibid.

21. Margaret Truman, *Bess W. Truman*, 259.

22. The quote here is Margaret Truman's, though she appeared to be quoting the former First Lady, too. See ibid., 260.

23. FDR believed that forgoing the White House painting was an important sign that the president was doing the same kind of belt tightening that ordinary Americans had been asked to do during the war. See Bess Furman, *White House Profile* (Indianapolis: Bobbs-Merrill, 1951), 328.

24. Margaret Truman, *Bess W. Truman*, 260.

25. Margaret Truman, *Harry S. Truman*, 241.

26. West, *Upstairs at the White House*, 58.

27. Margaret Truman, *Harry S. Truman*, 241.

28. West, *Upstairs at the White House*, 58.

29. Margaret Truman, *Bess W. Truman*, 260.

30. Harry S. Truman, *Where the Buck Stops: The Personal and Private Writings of Harry S. Truman*, ed. Margaret Truman (New York: Warner Books, 1989), 94n.

31. Steve Neal, ed., *Eleanor and Harry: The Correspondence of Eleanor Roosevelt and Harry S. Truman* (New York: Citadel, 2002), 24–25.

32. Margaret Truman, *Harry S. Truman*, 241.

33. West, *Upstairs at the White House*, 59.

34. Margaret Truman, *Bess W. Truman*, 260.

35. Margaret Truman, *Harry S. Truman*, 241.

36. Alfred Steinberg, *The Man from Missouri: The Life and Times of Harry S. Truman* (New York: G. P. Putnam's Sons, 1962), 215.

37. McCullough, *Truman*, 314.

38. Jonathan Daniels, *The Man of Independence* (Philadelphia: J. P. Lippincott, 1950), 258.

39. William D. Leahy, *I Was There* (New York: Whittlesey House, 1950), 348–49.

40. Daniels, *The Man of Independence*, 262.

41. West, *Upstairs at the White House*, 60.

42. Ibid.

43. Ibid.

44. Ibid., 59.

45. Margaret Truman, *The President's House* (New York: Ballantine Books, 2003), 212.

46. West, *Upstairs at the White House*, 61–62.

47. John Hersey, *Aspects of the Presidency* (New Haven, CT: Ticknor & Fields, 1980), 88.

48. Whitcomb, *Real Life at the White House*, 330–31.

49. Harry S. Truman, *The Wit and Wisdom of Harry S. Truman*, ed. Alex Ayers (New York: Meridian, 1998), 130.

50. West, *Upstairs at the White House*, 61–62.

51. Betty C. Monkman, *The White House: Its Historic Furnishings and First Families* (New York: Abbeville Press, 2000), 218.

52. West, *Upstairs at the White House*, 62.

53. Margaret Truman, *Harry S. Truman*, 241; West, *Upstairs at the White House*, 62.

54. The Gulbransen migrated to various rooms on the second floor. Electrician Traphes Bryant recalled that "if [Margaret] wanted a piano moved to another room you had better move it that instant." Traphes Bryant, with Frances Spatz Leighton, *Dog Days at the White House: The Outrageous Memoirs of the Presidential Kennel Keeper* (New York: Macmillan, 1975), 42. According to a letter in the Truman Library Vertical File on pianos, the second-floor corridor housed a Gulbransen upright—the only one likely to have been moved into Margaret's room (letter from Betty C. Monkman, White House Office of the Curator, to one Mr. Johnson, December 18, 1978). J. B. West recalled that the Gulbransen had been purchased originally for entertaining down on the first floor during the Roosevelt years, but the instrument had obviously been moved upstairs since then. See West, *Upstairs at the White House*, 87.

55. Harry S. Truman, *The Wit and Wisdom of Harry S. Truman*, 111.

56. The Steinway company archives do not have a surviving record of any pianos sold to the Truman family, though the Steinway name is clearly visible in photographs of Margaret's baby grand in her White House room. See photo no. 82–157, Harry S. Truman Library and Museum. Weight taken from the Bluebook of Pianos, at www.bluebookofpianos.com.

57. Author's estimate based on photographs of the Oval Study taken by Abbie Rowe in 1948 (photo nos. 82-54-50, 82-54-51, and 82-54-52, Truman Library). The piano appears to have been a Steinway A or B, factory weights of 695 pounds and 760 pounds, respectively. See www.bluebookofpianos.com.

58. Margaret Truman, *First Ladies* (New York: Fawcett Books, 1995), 3–4.

59. Margaret Truman, *Harry S. Truman*, 242.

2. THE GREAT WHITE JAIL

1. Margaret Truman, *Bess W. Truman* (New York: Macmillan, 1986), 258.

2. Ibid.

3. J. B. West, with Mary Lynn Kotz, *Upstairs at the White House: My Life with the First Ladies* (New York: Coward, McCann & Geohegan, 1973), 59.

4. Clark M. Clifford, *Counsel to the President: A Memoir* (New York: Random House, 1991), 53.

5. West, *Upstairs at the White House*, 63.

6. Henrietta Nesbitt did not last very long in the Truman White House. Her bland cooking and imperious manner was not to Bess Truman's liking from the start, but when Nesbitt had the audacity to scold the First Lady for taking a stick of White House butter to a potluck lunch, the latter made it clear that "I think it's time to find a new housekeeper." See West's *Upstairs at the White House*, 82–83. Nesbitt's quote in this passage is taken from Henrietta Nesbitt, *White House Diary* (Garden City, NY: Doubleday, 1948), 313.

7. Lillian Rogers Parks, with Frances Spatz Leighton, *My Thirty Years Backstairs at the White House* (New York: Fleet Publishing Co., 1961), 21–22.

8. Carl Sferrazza Anthony, *America's First Families: An Inside View of 200 Years of Private Life in the White House* (New York: Simon & Schuster, 2000), 338.

9. This was the number of ties counted at the Truman home immediately following Truman's death, which is the only known count. See *Harry S. Truman National Historic Site: Home to a People's President* (Washington, D.C.: National Park Service, n.d.), 16; Parks, *Backstairs at the White House*, 45.

10. Other figures have been given for Truman's pace, but all agreed that the president was very difficult to keep up with. See Margaret Truman, *Harry S. Truman* (New York: William Morrow, 1973), 441.

11. Rufus W. Youngblood, *20 Years in the Secret Service: My Life with Five Presidents* (New York: Simon & Schuster, 1973), 33–34.

12. West, *Upstairs at the White House*, 73.

13. Ibid., 76.

14. Parks, *My Thirty Years Backstairs at the White House*, 47.

15. Ibid., 281.

16. Lilian Rixey, "Bess Truman and Her Town," *Life*, July 11, 1949, 92.

17. Clifford, *Counsel to the President*, 81.

18. West, *Upstairs at the White House*, 77, 127.

19. Margaret Truman, *Bess W. Truman*, 271.

20. John Whitcomb, *Real Life at the White House: Two Hundred Years of Daily Life at America's Most Famous Residence* (New York: Routledge, 2000), 321.

21. Robert H. Ferrell, *Truman: A Centenary Remembrance* (New York: Viking, 1984), 182.

22. Bonnie Angelo, *First Families: The Impact of the White House on Their Lives* (Waterville, ME: Thorndike Press, 2006), 50. See also West, *Upstairs at the White House*, 79–80.

23. Cabell Phillips, "President or Goldfish? An Issue Reopened," *New York Times*, February 20, 1949.

24. Margaret Truman, *Bess W. Truman*, 263.

25. Ibid., 271–72.

26. Parks, *My Thirty Years Backstairs at the White House*, 22.

27. Harry S. Truman, *Dear Bess: The Letters from Harry to Bess Truman, 1910–1959*, ed. Robert H. Ferrell (New York: W. W. Norton, 1983), 515.

28. Robert H. Ferrell, ed., *Off the Record: The Private Papers of Harry S. Truman* (New York: Harper & Row, 1980), 145.

29. David Halberstam, *The Fifties* (New York: Villard, 1993), 21; Phillips, "President or Goldfish?"; McCullough, *Truman*, 875.

30. Harry S. Truman, *Dear Bess*, 516.

31. Ibid., 515–16.

32. Ibid., 516.

33. Rogers was the mother of Lillian Parks. Mother's and daughter's years of service in the White House would even briefly overlap. See Parks, *My Thirty Years Backstairs at the White House*, 70.

34. Parks, *My Thirty Years Backstairs at the White House*, 68.

35. Leslie Lieber, untitled magazine clip from Truman Library Vertical File, *This Week*, April 24, 1954.

36. Ferrell, *Truman*, 148.

37. Ibid.

38. Margaret Truman, *Harry S. Truman*, 327.

39. Milton Lehman, "The White House Shudders," *Collier's*, November 13, 1948, 13.

40. Ibid. The president granted him that point: "Why they'd want to come back here I could never understand," he said. See Margaret Truman, *Harry S. Truman*, 327.

41. These characterizations of Winslow are based largely on Benjamin Briggs's exhaustive biographical research into the architect, some of which appears in the entry "Lorenzo S. Winslow (1892–1976)," in *North Carolina Architects & Builders: A Biographic Dictionary*, at http://ncarchitects.lib.ncsu.edu. See also Matt McDade, "Retiring White House Architect Separates Fiction from Fact," *Washington Post*, May 31, 1953; William J. Moyer, "The Man Behind the White House Remodeling," *Washington Star Sunday Pictoral Magazine*, December 16, 1951, 14–15.

42. Briggs, "Lorenzo S. Winslow (1892–1976)."

43. Margaret Truman, *The President's House* (New York: Ballantine Books, 2003), 39.

44. Ibid.

3. THE PORCH

1. J. B. West, with Mary Lynn Kotz, *Upstairs at the White House: My Life with the First Ladies* (New York: Coward, McCann & Geoghegan, 1973), 96.

2. Ibid., 97.

3. The original 1782 sketch for the White House by architect James Hoban showed neither a North nor a South Portico. Both materialized as part of the improvements drawn by Benjamin Henry Latrobe, under Jefferson's influence. After the South Portico's construction, Hoban would claim that both additions had been part of his scheme all along. The North Portico, Hoban said, was "part of the original plan of the President's House, according to my design, approved by General Washington. That to the south front has since been constructed, and the one intended for the north is the only part of the entire design remaining unexecuted." See untitled architectural history of the White House by architect Douglas Orr, Douglas W. Orr Papers, MSS. 128, box 2, folder J, New Haven Museum & Historical Society Library, 3; William Seale, *The President's House: A History*, vol. 1 (Washington, D.C.: White House Historical Association, 1986), first set of plates, 3; Randle Bond Truett, *The White House: Home of the Presidents* (New York: Hastings House, 1949), 13; C. Ford Peatross, ed., *Capital Drawings: Architectural Designs for Washington, D.C. from the Library of Congress* (Baltimore: Johns Hopkins University Press, 2005), 98.

4. Letter from President Truman to George Rothwell Brown, January 20, 1948, Harry S. Truman Papers, President's Secretary's File, Harry S. Truman Library and Museum, Independence, Missouri.

5. Margaret Truman, *Bess W. Truman* (New York: Macmillan, 1986), 287.

6. Ibid., 314.

7. It isn't an exaggeration to characterize the balcony as an instrument of warfare between the president and the Congress. West later wrote that the balcony idea was the president's "counterattack" against a Congress that had not "reckoned wth Harry Truman." See West, *Upstairs at the White House*, 96. Margaret Truman would later characterize the balcony incident not as an issue of architecture, but as "a pitched battle with Congress." See Margaret Truman, *Bess W. Truman*, 314.

8. "Memorandum on a Proposed Addition to the Executive (West) Wing of

the White House, 1946," December 17, 1952, Harry S. Truman Papers, President's Secretary's Files, Harry S. Truman Library and Museum.

9. Ibid.

10. Felix Belair, Jr., "White House Funds Held Up by House," *New York Times*, January 25, 1946.

11. White House press release, January 11, 1946, appended to end of the "Independent Offices Appropriation Bill, 1947," U.S. Senate Subcommittee of the Committee on Appropriations, transcript of the hearing, Tuesday, February 5, 1946, 209.

12. "Repairs at 1600 Pennsylvania Avenue," *Newsweek*, February 11, 1946, 25.

13. "The Proposed Extension to the Executive Office, the White House," architectural drawings by Lorenzo S. Winslow, White House architect, 1946, Harry S. Truman Library and Museum.

14. "White House Mutilation," *Washington Post*, January 26, 1946.

15. "Let It Alone," *Washington Post*, January 19, 1946.

16. Only the *New York Times* made an attempt to clarify this point, stating that "the exterior of the 'President's House' will not be changed." See Felix Belair, Jr., "To Spend $1,650,000 on White House," *New York Times*, January 12, 1946.

17. Belair, "White House Funds Held Up by House."

18. The salt in the wound had come from Appropriations Committee chair Kenneth Douglas McKellar, who, though an old-line southern Democrat and the product of the same sort of political machine that had minted Harry S. Truman, never wavered in his opposition of the president's plans. See Bess Furman, *White House Profile* (Indianapolis: Bobbs-Merrill, 1951), 332; "Truman Reconstruction, 1948–1952," at www.whitehousemuseum.org.

19. David McCullough, *Truman* (New York: Simon & Schuster, 1992), 496.

20. William A. Degregorio, *The Complete Book of U.S. Presidents* (New York: Wings Books, 1993), 507.

21. George Allen, *Presidents Who Have Known Me* (New York: Simon & Schuster, 1960), 181.

22. Truman would eventually advance yet another vaguely plausible reason for his addition: that a balcony had actually been part of Thomas Jefferson's origi-

nal vision for the White House as drawn by James Hoban. But the president's secretary, Matthew Connelly, quietly dispatched on a research mission to determine if the claim was true, had broken the bad news to his boss that Hoban's original drawings contained not a trace of a balcony. Letter from John W. McCormack to Matthew J. Connelly, March 22, 1948, Harry S. Truman Papers, White House Central Files, "White House Balcony," Harry S. Truman Library and Museum.

23. West, *Upstairs at the White House*, 96–97.

24. William Seale, *The President's House: A History*, vol. 2 (Washington, D.C.: White House Historical Association, 1986), 1012.

25. West, *Upstairs at the White House*, 97.

26. Ibid.

27. Harry S. Truman, *Dear Bess: The Letters from Harry to Bess Truman, 1910–1959*, ed. Robert H. Ferrell (New York: W. W. Norton, 1983), 544.

28. Margaret Truman, *Harry S. Truman* (New York: William Morrow, 1973), 368.

29. Letter from Matthew J. Connelley to William A. Delano, August 1, 1947, Harry S. Truman Papers, White House Central Files, "White House Balcony," Harry S. Truman Library and Museum.

30. U.S. Commission of Fine Arts, at www.cfa.gov.

31. Margaret Truman, *Bess W. Truman*, 314.

32. Letter from William Adams Delano to H. G. Crim, chief usher of the White House, September 24, 1947, Harry S. Truman Papers, White House Central Files, "White House Balcony," Harry S. Truman Library and Museum.

33. Letter from William Adams Delano to President Truman, November 6, 1947, Harry S. Truman Papers, White House Permanent Files, "White House Balcony," Harry S. Truman Library and Museum.

34. Matt McDade, "Retiring White House Architect Separates Fiction from Fact," *Washington Post*, May 31, 1953.

35. The exact materials and construction method of the balcony—like so many other aspects of the Truman White House—are difficult to fix with precision because the National Archives and Records Administration considers the mansion's architectural drawings to be "Documents of Concern" and, hence,

unavailable to researchers for reasons of national security. The *Washington Post* of January 3, 1948, described the balcony as being "built of iron and tile on concrete slabs"—a confusing image at best. The *New York Times* of the same day furnished a clearer picture by mentioning cast concrete, though it said nothing about steel beams. Those, however, are clearly visible in a picture shot by a photographer from *Life* magazine as the construction neared completion early in 1948. See "Truman Balcony," at www.whitehousemuseum.org.

36. Height refers to the distance from the lawn to the underside of the balcony. "The White House," blueprint, sheet 33 (south elevation), Historic American Buildings Survey, DC-37, National Park Service, United States Department of the Interior, 1988–1992; letter from William Adams Delano to Lorenzo Winslow, November 6, 1947, Harry S. Truman Papers, White House Permanent Files, "White House Balcony," Harry S. Truman Library and Museum.

37. Letter from William Adams Delano to President Truman, September 29, 1947, White House Permanent Files, Harry S. Truman Library and Museum.

38. William Adams Delano, "A Letter to My Grandson," privately printed by Josephine B. Manning, 1942, William Adams Delano Papers, Avery Architectural & Fine Arts Library, Columbia University, New York.

39. Milton Lehman, "The White House Shudders," *Collier's*, November 13, 1948, 66.

40. West, *Upstairs at the White House*, 98.

41. One political cartoon of this period portrayed Truman standing atop his creation, proclaiming, "Love me . . . Love My Balcony!" while holding a scroll that read "Four Fine Arts Commissioners Who Opposed Balcony Have Been Replaced." See Robert H. Ferrell, *Truman: A Centenary Remembrance* (New York: Viking, 1984), 157.

42. West, *Upstairs at the White House*, 98.

43. "Architect," *The New Yorker*, April 5, 1958, 23.

44. "Truman Decides to Have a Porch at White House to Cost $15,000," *New York Times*, January 3, 1948; Robert Bruskin, "White House Plans Balcony," *Washington Post*, January 3, 1948.

45. Letter to William Adams Delano from President Truman, November 8, 1947, Harry S. Truman Papers, White House Permanent Files, "White House Balcony," Harry S. Truman Library and Museum.

46. "White House Porch," *New York Times*, January 6, 1948.

47. D. M. Giangreco and Kathryn Moore, *Dear Harry . . . : Truman's Mailroom, 1945–1953* (Mechanicsburg, PA: Stackpole Books, 1999), 119.

48. Edward T. Folliard, "Why Mr. Truman Built the Balcony," *Washington Post*, May 25, 1965.

49. Ferrell, *Truman*, 187.

50. Letters received at the White House about the balcony are from Harry S. Truman Papers, Official File, Harry S. Truman Library and Museum.

51. William P. O'Brien, "Reality and Illusion: The White House and Harry S. Truman," *The White House History Journal* 5 (Spring 1999): 5.

52. Clark M. Clifford, *Counsel to the President: A Memoir* (New York: Random House, 1991), 363. Much of the public's fury centered on the severe postwar problems of inflation and a shortage of housing—problems that made most Americans certain that Truman stood no chance against Thomas Dewey in the upcoming 1948 elections. Many people weren't upset so much that Truman wanted a porch; it was that they could hardly afford a roof.

53. McCullough, *Truman*, 594.

54. Letter from President Truman to William Adams Delano, November 22, 1947, Harry S. Truman Papers, White House Permanent Files, "White House Balcony," Harry S. Truman Library and Museum.

55. The Truman balcony made its appearance with the Series 1934C bills. E-mails between the United States Treasury Department and the author, June 9, 2010.

56. West, *Upstairs at the White House*, 98.

57. Letter from President Truman to Ethel Noland, January 30, 1948, Harry S. Truman Papers, President's Secretary's Files, Harry S. Truman Library and Museum.

4. "LIKE A SHIP AT SEA"

1. Letter from President Truman to Ethel Noland, January 30, 1948. Harry S. Truman Papers, President's Secretary's Files, Harry S. Truman Library and Museum.

2. "Major Renovations" in "Truman Reconstruction: 1948–1952," the White House Museum, at www.whitehousemuseum.org.

3. Bess Furman, *White House Profile* (Indianapolis: Bobbs-Merrill, 1951), 328.

The figure of three hundred gallons is a present-day statistic from "White House Facts," The White House Historical Association, at www.whitehousehistory .org. "Off-White" joke is from Samuel A. Tower, "The White House: A Plumber's History," *New York Times*, November 24, 1946.

4. Matt McDade, "Retiring White House Architect Separates Fiction from Fact," *Washington Post*, May 31, 1953.

5. William Seale, *The President's House: A History*, vol. 2 (Washington, D.C.: White House Historical Association, 1986), 1024.

6. Milton Lehman, "The White House Shudders," *Collier's*, November 13, 1948, 13.

7. Furman, *White House Profile*, 324.

8. Oral History Interview with General Jess Larson, conducted by Jerry N. Hess, May 26, 1967, §15, Harry S. Truman Library and Museum.

9. William Seale, "The White House: Plans Realized and Unrealized," in *Our Changing White House*, ed. Wendell Garrett (Boston: Northeastern University Press, 1995), 22.

10. E. John Long, "Repairs Come to the Rescue—Just in the Nick of Time," *Christian Science Monitor*, July 28, 1950.

11. "Sagging White House," *New York Times*, November 14, 1948.

12. Furman, *White House Profile*, 323–24.

13. Lillian Rogers Parks, with Frances Spatz Leighton, *My Thirty Years Backstairs at the White House* (New York: Fleet Publishing Co., 1961), 287.

14. Ibid.

15. Furman, *White House Profile*, 332; "Independent Offices Appropriation Bill, 1947," U. S. Senate Subcommittee of the Committee on Appropriations, transcript of the hearing, Tuesday, February 5, 1946, 194, 200.

16. "Press Release on Addition to Executive Offices," "Independent Offices Appropriation Bill, 1947," U.S. Senate Subcommittee of the Committee on Appropriations, transcript of the hearing, Tuesday, February 5, 1946, 209; James. E. Chinn, "White House Is in Sorry Shape (This Refers to Decorations)," *Washington Post*, February 9, 1946.

17. "Favor White House Repair," *New York Times*, March 20, 1946.

18. Chinn, "White House Is in Sorry Shape."

19. Ibid.

20. D. M. Giangreco and Kathryn Moore, *Dear Harry . . . : Truman's Mailroom, 1945–1953*. (Mechanicsburg, PA: Stackpole Books, 1999), 106–7.

21. Margaret Truman, *Harry S. Truman* (New York: William Morrow, 1973), 328.

22. Robert H. Ferrell, ed., *Off the Record: The Private Papers of Harry S. Truman* (New York: Harper & Row, 1980), 242.

23. Six dinners had been slated for that season. The exact date of the state dinner in this episode has managed to go unrecorded, but it was most likely the one held on January 14, 1947 (the other possibilities are January 28 and February 4). That date would have permitted the elapsing of "several weeks," according to Margaret Truman's accounts, before Crim reported the initial finding of structural defects to Truman on February 11.

24. Margaret Truman, *The President's House* (New York: Ballantine Books, 2003), 39.

25. Harry S. Truman, *Where the Buck Stops: The Personal and Private Writings of Harry S. Truman*, ed. Margaret Truman (New York: Warner Books, 1989), 94n.

26. Margaret Truman, *Harry S. Truman* (New York: William Morrow, 1973), 397.

27. The East Room chandeliers were shortened not long after they were first installed in 1902, and the Truman renovation would see them shortened a second time. The current curatorial dimensions of each chandelier are 68 inches wide and 129 inches tall. At the time of the 1947 dinner, they would have been slightly taller. See Betty C. Monkman, *The White House: Its Historic Furnishings and First Families* (New York: Abbeville Press, 2000), 297–98.

28. "Music: Court Pianist," *Time*, April 22, 1946, 51.

29. Margaret Truman, *Harry S. Truman*, 398.

30. The president employed this delicious bit of understatement in a letter he wrote to his mother two days after the near disaster. See ibid.

31. Margaret Truman, *Harry S. Truman*, 398.

32. Harry S. Truman, *The Wit and Wisdom of Harry S. Truman*, ed. Alex Ayers (New York: Meridian, 1998), 32.

33. Margaret Truman, *The President's House*, 39.

34. Margaret Truman, *Harry S. Truman*, 398.

35. Margaret Truman, *The President's House*, 39.

36. "Table of US Nuclear Warheads, 1945–75," Archive of Nuclear Data, the National Resources Defense Council, at www.nrdc.org.

37. L. Douglas Keeney, *15 Minutes: General Curtis LeMay and the Countdown to Nuclear Annihilation* (New York: St. Martin's Press, 2011), 36, 39.

38. Stephen M. Younger, *The Bomb: A New History* (New York: HarperCollins, 2009), 35.

39. T. A. Heppenheimer, "How to Detect an Atomic Bomb," *American Heritage of Invention & Technology* 21, no. 4 (Spring 2006).

40. Ferrell, ed., *Off the Record*, 107.

41. John Hersey, *Aspects of the Presidency* (New Haven, CT: Ticknor & Fields, 1980), 89.

42. Alfred Steinberg, *The Man from Missouri* (New York: G. P. Putnam's Sons, 1962), 335.

43. Margaret Truman, *The President's House*, 39.

44. This quote is taken from Truman's diary entry of March 2, 1952, but is a look back at events that took place five years earlier. The shaking-floor event with Fields appears in numerous sources as having taken place sometime in the latter half of 1947. Ferrell, ed., *Off the Record*, 242–43.

45. Steinberg, *The Man from Missouri*, 335. In her own memoirs, Lillian Parks recalled a shaking floor, too, but she set the scene (mistakenly) in the Family Dining Room, where the steel placed beneath the floor in 1902 would have made shaking highly unlikely. Nevertheless, the seamstress recalled that the president looked up and said, "The dining room seems to be shaking." See Parks, *My Thirty Years Backstairs at the White House*, 287.

46. William Manchester, *The Glory and the Dream: A Narrative History of America, 1932–1972* (Boston: Little, Brown, 1974), 579.

47. The floor thickness is the author's estimation based on enlarged photos of the balcony and known measurements of nearby architectural components, checked against the elevation drawn for "The White House," blueprint, sheet

33 (south elevation), Historic American Building Survey, DC-37, National Park Service, United States Department of the Interior, 1988–92. The tonnage of the balcony is an estimated calculation based on the measurements determined (in some cases approximated) from White House second-floor drawings or blueprints taken from the final report of the Commission on the Renovation of the Executive Mansion, the White House drawings of the Parks Department's Historic American Buildings Survey, and *The Building Estimator's Reference Book* (which furnishes the average weight of a cubic foot of poured concrete). The author is not taking into account the weight of the steel supporting beams, which would, of course, have added many hundreds of additional pounds to this figure.

48. Furman, *White House Profile*, 334.

49. Testimony of Charles W. Barber, "Second Deficiency Appropriation Bill for 1949, Additional Hearings Before the Subcommittee of the Committee on Appropriations, House of Representatives, Renovation and Modernization of the Executive Mansion," 81st Cong., 1st sess., 1949, H. Doc., 91773.

50. Memorandum from Commissioner Reynolds to President Truman, January 29, 1948. Harry S. Truman Papers, President's Secretary's Files, Harry S. Truman Library and Museum.

51. Lehman, "The White House Shudders," 14.

52. Margaret Truman, *The President's House*, 41.

53. Letter from President Truman to Ethel Noland, January 30, 1948, Harry S. Truman Papers, President's Secretary's Files, Harry S. Truman Library and Museum.

54. William P. O'Brien, "Reality and Illusion: The White House and Harry S. Truman," *The White House History Journal* 5 (Spring 1999): 3.

5. THE INSPECTION

1. William A. Widersheim, "Douglas Orr's New Haven," *The Journal of the New Haven Colony Historical Society* 26, no. 3 (Summer 1979): 7.

2. Though the AIA's offices, which Orr was then heading, were in Washington, it was and remains the practice of the AIA to allow its presidents to conduct all business from their own offices (letter to the author from Nancy Hadley, manager of archives and records, American Institute of Architects, April 5, 2011). While the Truman Library is missing the actual letter sent to Orr, there is a specific reference to it in Cross Reference Sheet, February 3, 1948, filed under Dougherty, Hon. W. E./Public Buildings Administration,

General File, Harry S. Truman Library and Museum, Independence, Missouri.

3. "R. E. Dougherty, Rail Officer, Dies," *New York Times*, October 1, 1961; John Walker Harrington, "A Railroad on Cushions," *Popular Science Monthly*, September 1928, 21. This incredible structure, which New Yorkers called the "West Side Freight Line" throughout its half century of service, is today a popular city park called the High Line. Benches and flower beds have replaced the rails, but one can still follow the viaduct straight through the bellies of buildings along the route.

4. Richard E. Dougherty, "The White House Made Safe," originally published in *Civil Engineering* magazine and reprinted in the *Report of the Commission on the Renovation of the Executive Mansion* (Washington, D.C.: U.S. Government Printing Office, 1952), 97.

5. Ibid.

6. Margaret Truman, *Harry S. Truman* (New York: William Morrow, 1973), 324.

7. Lillian Rogers Parks, with Frances Spatz Leighton, *My Thirty Years Backstairs at the White House* (New York: Fleet Publishing Co., 1961), 46.

8. Robert Dallek, *Harry S. Truman* (New York: Henry Holt, 2008), 70.

9. Zachary Karabell, *The Last Campaign: How Harry Truman Won the 1948 Election* (New York: Vintage Books, 2000), 43.

10. Winston Churchill had first warned of an "Iron Curtain" descending across Europe during a commencement address he delivered at Westminster College in Fulton, Missouri, on March 5, 1946. Truman was standing just behind him as he spoke. FDR's old adviser Bernard Baruch had introduced the term "Cold War" the previous April. See Alfred Steinberg, *The Man from Missouri: The Life and Times of Harry S. Truman* (New York: G. P. Putnam's Sons, 1962), 281; *Chronicle of America*, (Mount Kisco, NY: Chronicle Publications, 1988), 737.

11. Robert H. Ferrell, ed., *Off the Record: The Private Papers of Harry S. Truman* (New York: Harper & Row, 1980), 118.

12. Margaret Truman, *First Ladies* (New York: Fawcett Books, 1995), 84.

13. Dougherty, "The White House Made Safe," 97.

14. Douglas Orr, "The Reconstruction of the White House," *The National League for Woman's Service Magazine*, August 1950, 10.

15. Dougherty, "The White House Made Safe," 97.

16. Ibid.

17. Orr, "The Reconstruction of the White House," 10–11.

18. Dougherty, "The White House Made Safe," 97.

19. Eben A. Ayers Papers, diary entry for March 6, 1948, Harry S. Truman Library and Museum.

20. "Report to the President on Structural Survey, Second Floor, White House," February 25, 1948, appendix 1, *Report of the Commission on the Renovation of the Executive Mansion*, 90.

21. The wording in the memo is paraphrased here. See Cross Reference Sheet, February 3, 1948, filed under Reynolds, Hon. W. E., Commissioner, Public Buildings Administration, General Files, Harry S. Truman Library and Museum.

22. Orr, "The Reconstruction of the White House," 11.

23. J. B. West, with Mary Lynn Kotz, *Upstairs at the White House: My Life with the First Ladies* (New York: Coward, McCann & Geoghegan, 1973), 99.

24. Edmund R. Purves, "A Few Recollections of the White House," Harry S. Truman Papers, Post-Presidential Files, Harry S. Truman Library and Museum, 9–10.

25. Dougherty, "The White House Made Safe," 97.

26. Doris Kearns Goodwin, *No Ordinary Time* (New York: Simon & Schuster, 1994), 16.

27. "Report to the President on Structural Survey," February 25, 1948, in *Report of the Commission on the Renovation of the Executive Mansion*, 90.

28. West, *Upstairs at the White House*, 100.

29. Bess Furman, *White House Profile* (Indianapolis: Bobbs-Merrill, 1951), 334.

30. West, *Upstairs at the White House*, 100.

31. Edith Iglauer, "The Biggest Foundation," *The New Yorker*, November 4, 1972, 130.

32. "Skyscrapers: Builders and Their Tools," *Fortune*, October 1930, 85.

33. Meyer Berger, *Meyer Berger's New York* (New York: Fordham University Press, 2004), 93.

34. Untitled paper by Douglas Orr recounting the stages of the structural investigation, Douglas W. Orr Papers, MSS. 128, box 2, folder J, New Haven Museum & Historical Society Library, 8.

35. Later in 1948, when the need for work on the house became public, Winslow would look back at this period during the investigation and make this comment about its difficulties to UPI. See "Repairs Ordered on White House May Keep Next Incumbent from Occupancy for Year," *New York Times*, September 30, 1948.

36. Karabell, *The Last Campaign*, 40.

37. "The Man Nobody Wanted," *Time*, January 3, 1949, 11.

38. Paul F. Boller, Jr., *Presidential Campaigns*, rev. ed. (New York: Oxford University Press, 1996), 268.

39. West, *Upstairs at the White House*, 100.

40. Dougherty's article on the renovation suggests that he and Orr may well not have been on-site at the White House again until the second official meeting of the committee on September 8, 1948, though of course they were nominally in charge. In any case, Winslow and Reynolds were men of equal force and influence. The other men to join in the effort included Charles W. Barber and C. K. Yingling, Jr., of the Public Buildings Service. See Dougherty, "The White House Made Safe," 97.

41. West, *Upstairs at the White House*, 103.

42. *Report of the Commission on the Renovation of the Executive Mansion*, photo, 36.

43. "Fire Trap," *Time*, November 22, 1948, 24.

44. *Report of the Commission on the Renovation of the Executive Mansion*, 35.

45. Purves, "A Few Recollections of the White House," 10.

46. E. John Long, "Repairs Come to the Rescue—Just in the Nick of Time," *Christian Science Monitor*, July 28, 1950. During the 1902 renovation, McKim's men had also noticed wiring that lacked insulation, but while it's clear

that some of it was replaced, it's not certain that the electricians ever got to all of it, especially in a mere six months' project time. See Ethel Lewis, *The White House* (New York: Dodd, Mead, 1937), 262.

47. Testimony of L. C. Martin, assistant to the director of the Bureau of the Budget, hearing on H.R. 3856, "To provide for a commission on the renovation of the Executive Mansion," Committee on Public Works, House of Representatives, 81st Cong., 1st sess., March 30, 1949, 5.

48. Ibid.

49. Purves, "A Few Recollections of the White House," 12.

50. West, *Upstairs at the White House*, 87.

51. Only an estimate is available here, but using the weight of a Steinway Model S baby grand (540 pounds), and the weight of a studio upright (about 500 pounds), one arrives at a total weight of 1,040 pounds—a significant burden that does not even take into account the weight of Margaret, her friend, and the furniture in the room. It's no surprise that the split beam below started to bounce; the wonder—as Purves said—is that it did not "precipitate the President's daughter, her friend and the two pianos, twenty feet to the room below." See West, *Upstairs at the White House*, 87; Purves, "A Few Recollections of the White House," 11, "Studio Upright Model 1098," Dimensions/Net Weight, at www.steinway.com.

52. It was Edmund Purves who recalled this anecdote, but he did so many years after the White House renovation and thus furnished no date for it. It would have to have preceded the incident of the falling piano, of course, because Margaret and her friend would not have played duets in her room after that. See Purves, "A Few Recollections of the White House," 10–11.

53. While Margaret's plunging piano has been written about widely, the actual date that the piano fell failed to appear in any of the accounts uncovered by the author. Chronologically, both J. B. West and Margaret Truman place the incident during the summer, and immediately before Truman was sent packing down to the Lincoln Bedroom (which was sometime during late July or early August). In placing this incident in June, the author is relying on usher West's memory: "While the Trumans had been living in a railroad car . . . one leg of Margaret's piano nearly went through the floor." (See *Upstairs at the White House*, 102.) This was a clear reference to the president's first whistle-stop trip of June 3–18, 1948.

54. Matt McDade, "Retiring White House Architect Separates Fiction from Fact," *Washington Post*, May 31, 1953.

55. There remains some confusion over which of the pianos actually fell. In

two of her books about her father's presidency, Margaret Truman said it was the upright, though given that grand pianos triangulate their weight distribution among three spindly legs, the baby grand was the more likely victim from a physics point of view. See Margaret Truman, *Harry S. Truman*, 398–99; Harry S. Truman, *Where the Buck Stops: The Personal and Private Writings of Harry S. Truman*, ed. Margaret Truman (New York: Warner Books, 1989), 94.

56. During the televised tour of the White House that he would give in 1952, Truman himself claimed that the piano leg had punched clear through the ceiling. See transcript of tour of May 3, 1952, Harry S. Truman Papers, President's Secretary's Files, Harry S. Truman Library and Museum.

57. According to Margaret: "One of the two pianos in my sitting room—a spinet—broke through the floor one day." See Margaret Truman, *Harry S. Truman*, 398. She confirmed this fact a second time in a later book, *Where the Buck Stops*, in which she wrote, "But the coup de grace occurred when a little spinet, one of the two pianos in my sitting room, suddenly broke through the floor" (94n).

58. The story is very possibly apocryphal. Steinway recalled that the piano was "falling through the floor" of the East Room, which never happened. See "Theodore E. Steinway Is Dead; Chairman of Piano Company, 73," *New York Times*, April 9, 1957.

6. THE EVICTION

1. Memo from J. P. Hauck to John McShain detailing inspection tour of the White House, January 13, 1950, John McShain Papers, box 159, folder 6, Hagley Museum and Library, Wilmington, Delaware.

2. Oral History Interview with Robert B. Landry, conducted by Hugh A. Ahmann, March 1–2, 1983, §272, Harry S. Truman Library and Museum, Independence, Missouri.

3. Margaret Truman, *The President's House*, (New York: Ballantine Books, 2003), 41.

4. *Backstairs at the White House*, Ed Friendly Productions, NBC miniseries broadcast in 1979 (Acorn Media, DVD, 2005, disc 4, scene at 47:22).

5. Margaret added, "Mother's decision to say nothing about it and take the heat for the lack of a formal social season was one of her major, hitherto unknown contributions to Dad's fight to become president in his own right." See Margaret Truman, *Bess W. Truman* (New York: Macmillan, 1986), 329.

6. Testimony of Charles W. Barber, "Second Deficiency Appropriation Bill for 1949, Additional Hearings Before the Subcommittee of the Committee on

Appropriations, House of Representatives, Renovation and Modernization of the Executive Mansion," 81st Cong., 1st sess., H. Doc. 91773, 1949, 4.

7. Oral History Interview with Robert B. Landry.

8. Oral History Interview with *New York Times* photographer George Tames, conducted by Dr. Benedict K. Zebrist, June 11, 1980, §56, Harry S. Truman Library and Museum; Clifton Truman Daniel, *Growing Up with My Grandfather: Memories of Harry S. Truman* (Secaucus, NJ: Carol Publishing Group, 1995), 11.

9. Robert H. Ferrell, ed., *Off the Record: The Private Papers of Harry S. Truman* (New York: Harper & Row, 1980), 146.

10. Margaret Truman, *Harry S. Truman* (New York: William Morrow, 1973), 399.

11. Ibid., 398.

12. Alonzo Fields would recall that "Mr. Winslow . . . thought that steel rods fastened to the beams from the reinforced steel-and-concrete third-floor would sort of hold the [second] floor in suspension." Margaret wrote that the abundance of metal on the second floor was "supposed to hold up the ceilings." It may well have been a little of both. See Alonzo Fields, *My 21 Years in the White House* (New York: Coward-McCann, 1960), 145–46; Margaret Truman, *Bess W. Truman*, 329.

13. Lillian Rogers Parks, with Frances Spatz Leighton, *My Thirty Years Backstairs at the White House* (New York: Fleet Publishing Co., 1961), 23.

14. Richard E. Dougherty, "The White House Made Safe," originally published by *Civil Engineering* magazine and reprinted in *Report on the Commission on the Renovation of the Executive Mansion* (Washington, D.C.: U.S. Government Printing Office, 1952), 97.

15. Untitled paper on the progress of the investigation work, Douglas W. Orr Papers, MSS. 128, box 2, folder J, page 8, New Haven Museum & Historical Society Library.

16. "White House Repair Funds are Approved," *Washington Post*, April 23, 1948.

17. Dorothea Andrews, "White House Architect Plans to Replace Entire 2nd Floor," *Washington Post*, September 30, 1948.

18. Alfred Steinberg, *The Man from Missouri: The Life and Times of Harry S. Truman* (New York: G. P. Putnam's Sons, 1962), 323.

19. Ferrell, ed., *Off the Record*, 150.

20. Paul F. Boller, *Presidential Campaigns* (Oxford University Press, 1996), 271.

21. Steinberg, *The Man from Missouri*, 324.

22. This quote and the anecdote to follow are taken from Hersey's recollection of the train stopping at Norwalk, Connecticut. It appears in the introduction of the book that resulted from *The New Yorker*'s profile. See John Hersey, *Aspects of the Presidency* (New Haven, CT: Ticknor & Fields, 1980), 3.

23. "Memorandum for the President" from H. G. Crim, October 29, 1948, Harry S. Truman Papers, President's Secretary's Files, Harry S. Truman Library and Museum.

24. "Memorandum to the President" from W. E. Reynolds, commissioner of public buildings, October 29, 1948, Harry S. Truman Papers, President's Secretary's Files, Harry S. Truman Library and Museum.

25. William Manchester, *The Glory and the Dream: A Narrative History of America, 1932–1972* (Boston: Little, Brown, 1974), 579.

26. Ferrell, ed., *Off the Record*, 242.

27. *Report of the Commission on the Renovation of the Executive Mansion* (Washington, D.C.: U.S. Government Printing Office, 1952), 39.

28. "Re: White House, Washington, D.C.," letter from Charles B. Spencer to Lorenzo Winslow, November 10, 1948, David H. Stowe Files, "White House [Plans for Renovations]," Harry S. Truman Library and Museum.

29. Ibid.

30. "Remodeling Job at 1600 Pennsylvania Avenue," uncited clipping in the Peggy Watts papers, Harry S. Truman Library and Museum.

31. J. B. West, with Mary Lynn Kotz, *Upstairs at the White House: My Life with the First Ladies* (New York: Coward, McCann & Geohegan, 1973), 102.

32. Ferrell, ed., *Off the Record*, 149.

33. Truman's quotes here come from a dinner he spoke at in January of 1949, remembering the events of that historic November night the previous year. See "Presidential Campaign of 1948," the Harry S. Truman Library and Museum home page, at www.trumanlibrary.org.

34. "The Man," *Time*, January 3, 1949, 11.

35. West, *Upstairs at the White House*, 102.

36. There were apparently no minutes kept of this meeting, but Truman recalled this one comment in 1949 as the opening anecdote to a speech. See "Remarks to the American Society of Civil Engineers," November 2, 1949, document no. 249, Harry S. Truman Library and Museum.

37. West, *Upstairs at the White House*, 102.

38. Ferrell, ed., *Off the Record*, 151.

39. Margaret Truman, *The President's House*, 41–42.

40. Ibid., 41.

41. David McCullough, *Truman* (New York: Simon & Schuster, 1992), 725.

42. Truman uttered these words during a tour of the White House under renovation that he gave to the writer John Hersey on December 16, 1950. See John Hersey, "Profiles, Mr. President: Ghosts in the White House," *The New Yorker*, April 28, 1951, 103–4.

7. THE SLOW MURDER

1. "White House Is Being Closed to Visitors for Safety's Sake," *Washington Post*, November 7, 1948.

2. Milton Lehman, "The White House Shudders," *Collier's*, November 13, 1948, 13.

3. "Address by John R. Steelman, Ph.D., the Assistant to the President of the United States," Fifty-fifth Anniversary Dinner, Columbia Historical Society, Washington, D.C., program, April 12, 1949, Douglas W. Orr Papers, MSS. 128, box 1A, folder S, New Haven Museum & Historical Society Library.

4. Frederick Gutheim, "Rebuilding the White House," *Architectural Record*, June 1949, 117.

5. Scott W. Berg, *Grand Avenues: The Story of the French Visionary Who Designed Washington, D.C.* (New York: Pantheon, 2007), 104.

6. "Address by John R. Steelman."

7. Roland W. Brown, "Age of Wood from Excavations in the District of Colum-

bia and Vicinity," *Records of the Columbia Historical Society, 1953–1956* (Washington, D.C.: Columbia Historical Society, 1959), 353.

8. Gutheim, "Rebuilding the White House," 117.

9. Douglas Orr, "The Reconstruction of the White House," *The National League for Woman's Service Magazine*, August 1950, 10.

10. "Address by John R. Steelman."

11. C. Ford Peatross, ed., *Capitol Drawings: Architectural Designs for Washington, D.C., from the Library of Congress* (Baltimore: Johns Hopkins University Press, 2005), 89.

12. E. John Long, "Repairs Come to the Rescue—Just in the Nick of Time," *Christian Science Monitor*, July 28, 1950.

13. Edmund R. Purves, "A Few Recollections of the White House," Harry S. Truman Papers, Post-Presidential Files, Harry S. Truman Library and Museum, Independence, Missouri, 10.

14. Gutheim, "Rebuilding the White House," 117.

15. Long, "Repairs Come to the Rescue."

16. Oral History Interview with Felix de Weldon, conducted by Jerry N. Hess, January 22, 1969, §40–41, Harry S. Truman Library and Museum.

17. "Address by John R. Steelman."

18. Charles Hurd, *The White House Story* (New York: Hawthorn Books, 1966), 116.

19. "Address by John R. Steelman."

20. Long, "Repairs Come to the Rescue."

21. Untitled paper by Douglas Orr recounting the stages of the structural investigation. See Douglas W. Orr Papers, MSS. 128, box 2, folder J, New Haven Museum & Historical Society Library, 5.

22. John Whitcomb, *Real Life at the White House: Two Hundred Years of Daily Life at America's Most Famous Residence* (New York: Routledge, 2000), 241.

23. Hurd, *The White House Story*, 116.

24. An 1833 fire at Hoban's home incinerated his original drawings for the

White House, but a clue of how structurally inadequate interior brick walls were pops up in a long-forgotten booklet published by the U.S. Government Printing Office in 1903. The book—a congressional record of the renovation work performed for Theodore Roosevelt—includes a photograph taken on the mansion's ground floor in July of 1902, when workmen were digging a pit for a new boiler. There, lurking just behind the right shoulder of a laborer, is one of the original ground-floor piers with the ground fully excavated around and below. Spread footings? None. Directly below the brick pier is a square rubble-work base that looks to extend—at most—a couple of feet into the earth. See "Basement, Excavation for Boiler, July 20, 1902," photo from "Restoration of the White House: Message of the President of the United States Transmitting the Report of the Architects," 57th Cong., 2d sess., Doc. 197, 1903, 47.

25. D. H. Gillette, "November 8, 1948: The President's Household Must Move!" Office of the Commission on the Renovation of the Executive Mansion, November 1, 1949, 1.

26. Richard E. Dougherty, "The White House Made Safe," originally published by *Civil Engineering* magazine and reprinted in the *Report of the Commission on the Renovation of the Executive Mansion* (Washington, D.C.: U.S. Government Printing Office, 1952), 97.

27. Orr, "The Reconstruction of the White House," 11.

28. Testimony of Charles W. Barber, "Second Deficiency Appropriation Bill for 1949, Additional Hearings Before the Subcommittee of the Committee on Appropriations, House of Representatives, Renovation and Modernization of the Executive Mansion," 81st Cong., 1st sess., 1949, H. Doc., 91773 4–5. Barber was not alone in his judgments. Architectural historian Frederick Gutheim came to the same conclusion, writing that the interior-wall footings were so poor as to be "no footings" at all. See "Rebuilding the White House," 116.

29. Gillette, "The President's Household Must Move!" 1.

30. Long, "Repairs Come to the Rescue."

31. *A Monograph of the Work of McKim, Mead & White, 1879–1915* (New York: Architectural Book Publishing Company, 1981), xxii–xxiii.

32. "Restoration of the White House: Message of the President of the United States Transmitting the Report of the Architects," 13, 17–18.

33. Leland M. Roth, *McKim, Mead & White, Architects* (New York: Harper & Row, 1983), 269.

34. The commission report would later conclude not only that "no attempt was

made to replace second floor wooden construction" but that "on the whole, the 1902 renovation corrected only surface matters." See *Report of the Commission on the Renovation of the Executive Mansion*, 33–34. See also Long, "Repairs Come to the Rescue."

35. Roth, *McKim, Mead & White, Architects*, 269.

36. *Report of the Commission on the Renovation of the Executive Mansion*, 33; William Seale, *The President's House: A History*, vol. 2 (Washington, D.C.: White House Historical Association, 1986), 1026.

37. Grace Coolidge, *Grace Coolidge: An Autobiography*, ed. Lawrence E. Wikander and Robert H. Ferrell (Worland, WY: High Plains Publishing Company, 1992), 77.

38. Whitcomb, *Real Life at the White House*, 287.

39. Harry S. Truman, *Where the Buck Stops: The Personal and Private Writings of Harry S. Truman*, ed. Margaret Truman (New York: Warner Books, 1989), 94n.

40. Coolidge, *Grace Coolidge*, 80.

41. This overall analysis relies on accounts that appear in Gutheim, "Rebuilding the White House," 116; Orr, "The Reconstruction of the White House," 10; Seale, *The President's House*, vol. 2, 873.

42. So serious was this mistake from an engineering standpoint that, again and again, it would be faulted as one of the major causes—if not the primary one—of the White House's irreversible collapse. Douglas Orr would state that "the manner of carrying out this alteration was one of the principal causes of the very radical rebuilding required today." As one newspaper article of the time explained it, "Some of the heavy steel roof trusses were footed on the brick inner walls whose foundations were barely adequate to support their own weight . . . a destructive load was thrown onto the crumbling central piers." See Papers of Douglas W. Orr, MSS. 128, box 2, folder J; Long, "Repairs Come to the Rescue."

43. Specifically, engineers determined that the tremendous weight of the house's top floor was "pressing down" on the wooden infrastructure of the second floor. But the two could not now be separated because McKim had removed the north bearing wall of the State Dining Room below. See Bess Furman, *White House Profile* (Indianapolis: Bobbs-Merrill, 1951), 309.

44. The booklet detailing the job survives among Delano's papers at Columbia University in New York. In it, the Office of Public Buildings clearly delineated that "the new work contemplates the carrying of the new roof, third-story, and

second-story ceilings on structural steel supported by the exterior walls *and the interior brick partitions*" (emphasis author's). Advertisement for the roof and third-floor renovation work issued by the Office of Public Buildings and Public Parks of the National Capital, Washington, D.C., November 19, 1926, William Adams Delano Papers, Avery Architectural & Fine Arts Library, Columbia University, New York, 5.

45. Robert H. Ferrell, ed., *Off the Record: The Private Papers of Harry S. Truman* (New York: Harper & Row, 1980), 242.

8. WANTED: HOME FOR PRESIDENT

1. Even the official log of the trip, usually free of much in the way of personal detail, noted that Truman "had just completed a strenuous period of campaigning." Happy as he was that he'd won a second term, Truman was also exhausted. See Log of President Truman's Fifth Trip to Key West, Florida, November 7–21, 1948, compiled by Lt. Comdr. William M. Rigdon, Harry S. Truman Library and Museum, Independence, Missouri.

2. This was reported by Adm. J. J. Manning, then in the employ of John Mc-Shain, the general contractor hired for the White House renovation job. Manning went along on an inspection tour of the house, with Truman in the lead. Outspoken as always, Truman recalled the dark days of 1948, and expressed a fear few guessed he'd felt. See "Observations and Comments Incident to Inspection of the White House with President Truman—December 31, 1949," memorandum from Admiral J. J. Manning to John McShain, January 10, 1950, John McShain Papers, box 159, folder 6, Hagley Museum and Library, Wilmington, Delaware.

3. Harry S. Truman, *Dear Bess: The Letters from Harry to Bess Truman, 1910–1959*, ed. Robert H. Ferrell (New York: W. W. Norton, 1983), 534–35.

4. See, for example, photo no. 59-941-1, November 18, 1948, an incredible riot of baby blue and white curlicues. Harry S. Truman Library and Museum.

5. J. B. West, with Mary Lynn Kotz, *Upstairs at the White House: My Life with the First Ladies* (New York: Coward, McCann & Geoghegan, 1973), 103.

6. Ibid., 104.

7. William Seale, *The President's House: A History*, vol. 2 (Washington, D.C.: White House Historical Association, 1986), 1026.

8. West, *Upstairs at the White House*, 106.

9. Lillian Rogers Parks, with Frances Spatz Leighton, *My Thirty Years Backstairs at the White House* (New York: Fleet Publishing Co., 1961), 294.

10. West, *Upstairs at the White House*, 105.

11. Alonzo Fields, *My 21 Years in the White House* (New York: Coward-McCann, 1960), 149.

12. "B. Altman Company Bill for Care and Storage of Furniture," Minutes of the Commission on the Renovation of the Executive Mansion, June 20, 1950, Harry S. Truman Library and Museum, 12.

13. Ibid., 13.

14. E-mail to author from Maygene Daniels; chief of the Gallery Archives, National Gallery of Art, July 22, 2011; "Bills of B. Altman Co. for Handling, Care and Storage of Furnishings," Minutes of the Commission on the Renovation of the Executive Mansion, June 29, 1950, Harry S. Truman Library and Museum, 4.

15. Parks, *My Thirty Years Backstairs at the White House*, 297.

16. Fields, *My 21 Years in the White House*, 149–50.

17. Parks, *My Thirty Years Backstairs at the White House*, 300.

18. "White House Repairs Uncover Faults Worse Than Expected," *Washington Post*, December 30, 1948.

19. "White House Is Being Closed to Visitors for Safety's Sake," *Washington Post*, November 7, 1948.

20. Letter from Charles B. Spencer to Lorenzo Winslow, November 10, 1948, David H. Stowe Files, Harry S. Truman Library and Museum.

21. Memo to the supervising architect and the chief structural engineer from Charles W. Barber, November 17, 1948, David H. Stowe Files, Harry S. Truman Library and Museum.

22. "A stratum of sand and gravel should be encountered at a depth of about 20 feet," Spencer had written. "Such material should safely support loading of at least 6 tons of square foot, and it is upon this stratum that we recommend that the foundations be placed." Letter from Charles B. Spencer to Lorenzo Winslow, November 10, 1948.

23. Memo to the supervising architect and the chief structural engineer from Charles W. Barber, November 17, 1948.

24. "White House Repairs Uncover Faults Worse Than Expected"; memorandum for President Truman, "Remodeling and Modernization of the Executive

Mansion," December 27, 1948, Harry S. Truman Papers, President's Secretary's Files, Harry S. Truman Library and Museum.

25. Memorandum for President Truman, "Remodeling and Modernization of the Executive Mansion."

26. Bess Furman, "Presidents' Home Called a Wreck," *New York Times*, December 30, 1948.

27. Parks, *My Thirty Years Backstairs at the White House*, 298.

28. Ibid., 297.

29. Ibid., 296.

30. Sara L. Sale, *Bess Wallace Truman* (Lawrence: University Press of Kansas, 2010), 298.

31. Parks, *My Thirty Years Backstairs at the White House*, 297.

9. "THE PEOPLE WANT A NEW BUILDING"

1. Truman would make this characterization in a letter later that summer, but the sentiment could have applied to all of 1949. By the time of the inauguration, the Trumans had already been installed at Blair House, and the White House was empty. See Robert H. Ferrell, ed., *Off the Record: The Private Papers of Harry S. Truman* (New York: Harper & Row, 1980), 161.

2. Marshall Andrews, "White House Is on Verge of Collapse," *Washington Post*, January 30, 1949.

3. J. B. West, with Mary Lynn Kotz, *Upstairs at the White House: My Life with the First Ladies* (New York: Coward, McCann & Geoghegan, 1973), 109–10.

4. William Seale, *The President's House: A History*, vol. 2 (Washington, D.C.: White House Historical Association, 1986), 1026–27.

5. Diary of Lorenzo Winslow, January 11, 1949, Office of the Curator, the White House.

6. For example, Winslow would note on October 17, 1949, that he gave Orr a layout of the second floor for him to show Mrs. Truman and the president. One month later to the day, he would note that the president had approved the plans.

7. "Report of the Commissioner of Public Buildings," February 8, 1949, reprinted in appendix 2, *Report of the Commission on the Renovation of the Executive Mansion* (Washington, D.C.: U.S. Government Printing Office, 1952), 90–94.

8. William P. O'Brien, "Reality and Illusion: The White House and Harry S. Truman," *White House History* 5 (Spring 1999): 8.

9. The full estimate from the PBA chief Reynolds had actually been $5,412,000, but Truman lobbed the $12,000 off for the sake of a round figure. See "Letter to the President of the Senate Transmitting Appropriation Estimate for White House Repairs," February 17, 1949, *The Public Papers of Harry S. Truman* (Washington, D.C.: U.S. Government Printing Office, 1996), 133.

10. Letter from President Truman to Congress, March 25, 1949, Eben A. Ayers Papers, Harry S. Truman Library and Museum, Independence, Missouri.

11. "White House Work Closer to a Start," *New York Times*, March 23, 1949.

12. Hearing on H.R. 3856, "To provide for a commission on the renovation of the Executive Mansion," Committee on Public Works, House of Representatives, 81st Cong., 1st sess., March 30, 1949, 14.

13. Ibid., 18–19, 20–21.

14. Richard L. Lyons, "Rep. Cannon Fought All to Curb Hill Spending," *Washington Post*, May 13, 1964.

15. Clarence Cannon is known to have slugged at least three members of the legislative branch: Senator Kenneth McKellar and Representatives John Phillips and John Taber (the latter's front teeth actually came loose). See "Rep. Cannon Dies; Led Funds Panel," *New York Times*, May 13, 1964.

16. "Rep. Cannon Urges 'New' White House," *Washington Post*, April 16, 1949.

17. Ibid.

18. Given that earlier reports had, in fact, found some cracks in the exterior wall foundations, this statement was not wholly true—but it was true enough for the circumstances, given what was at stake. See "White House Walls Called Excellent," *Washington Post*, April 19, 1949.

19. Letter from Clarence Cannon to President Truman, April 29, 1949, Papers of Harry S. Truman, President's Secretary's Files, Harry S. Truman Library and Museum.

20. "New White House," *Washington Post*, April 17, 1949.

21. West, *Upstairs at the White House*, 106–7.

22. Hearing transcript of H.R. 3856, 20–21.

23. Eleanor Roosevelt, *Eleanor Roosevelt's My Day: Her Acclaimed Columns, 1945–1952*, ed. David Emblidge (New York: Pharos Books, 1990), 168–69.

24. "Letter to the President of the Senate Transmitting Appropriation Estimate for White House Repairs," February 17, 1949, *The Public Papers of Harry S. Truman, 1945–1953* (Washington, D.C.: U.S. Government Printing Office, 1966), 133.

25. Margaret Truman, *Bess W. Truman* (New York: Macmillan, 1986), 338.

26. Sara L. Sale, *Bess Wallace Truman* (Lawrence: University Press of Kansas, 2010), 91–92.

27. Lilian Rixey, "Bess Truman and Her Town," *Life*, July 11, 1949, 95.

28. "Mrs. Truman Opposes Marble White House," *New York Times*, May 25, 1949.

29. Sale, *Bess Wallace Truman*, 91.

30. West, *Upstairs at the White House*, 110.

31. Marie Smith, *Entertaining at the White House* (Washington, D.C.: Acropolis Books, 1967), 223.

32. West, *Upstairs at the White House*, 111.

33. Ibid., 113.

34. Traphes Bryant, with Frances Spatz Leighton, *Dog Days at the White House: The Outrageous Memoirs of the Presidential Kennel Keeper* (New York: Macmillan, 1975), 240.

35. In fact, that is exactly what would happen to J. B. West during the Nixon administration, when agents discovered his other life. The obvious issues of prejudice notwithstanding, homosexuality was seen as a security risk at the time—the man in question being theoretically at the mercy of would-be blackmailers. West "retired" early. See Ronald Kessler, *Inside the White House* (New York: Pocket Books, 1996), 49.

36. Diary of Lorenzo Winslow, January 1 and 29, 1949.

37. Marshall Andrews, "White House Is on Verge of Collapse."

38. Bess Furman, *White House Profile* (Indianapolis: Bobbs-Merrill, 1951), 335.

39. Rabaut would later describe this very incident on the record during a subsequent hearing. See "Second Deficiency Appropriation Bill for 1949, Additional Hearings Before the Subcommittee of the Committee on Appropriations, House of Representatives, Renovation and Modernization of the Executive Mansion," 81st Cong., 1st sess., 1949, H. Doc. 91773, 12.

40. "Two Named to Mansion Remodel Unit," *Washington Post*, April 29, 1949.

41. "White House Walls Called Excellent."

42. "Second Deficiency Appropriation Bill for 1949," 7–8.

43. Ibid., 8.

44. Ibid., 9.

45. "Rep. Cannon Urges 'New' White House."

46. "Second Deficiency Appropriation Bill for 1949," 2.

47. Ibid., 11. As it turned out, Winslow was correct—at least according to Douglas Orr, who would later mention in a speech that building a new White House of marble or granite, or disassembling, then reassembling the existing walls, would come in at 10 percent higher than simply working around them.

48. As a compromise, the House voted two million dollars "to do something about the rickety old White House," the *Washington Post* reported, and handed the mess over to the commission. See "House Wants Commission to Decide on White House," *Washington Post*, June 16, 1949. Eventually, the commission would get all of the money that Truman had asked for.

49. "House Wants Commission to Decide on White House."

10. THE VERDICT

1. *Report of the Commission on the Renovation of the Executive Mansion* (Washington, D.C.: U.S. Government Printing Office, 1952), 49.

2. Debs Myers, "The New White House," *Holiday*, November 1952, 48.

3. "Kenneth Douglas McKellar: A Featured Biography," at www.senate.gov; David McCullough, *Truman* (New York: Simon & Schuster, 1992), 389.

4. "Rabaut, Louis Charles, (1886–1961)," Biographical Directory of the United States Congress, at http://bioguide.congress.gov.

5. "Second Deficiency Appropriation Bill for 1949, Additional Hearings Before the Subcommittee of the Committee on Appropriations, House of Representatives, Renovation and Modernization of the Executive Mansion," 81st Cong., 1st sess., H. Doc. 91773, 1949, 7–8.

6. While the newspapers and the 1952 official report of the commission considered June 3, 1949, to be the group's inaugural gathering, the commission did not begin numbering its meetings until June 15, when the minutes could be kept for the public record. For the purposes of this study, then, the meetings will be numbered as the commission numbered them, with the June 15, 1949, meeting being called its first. "White House Commission Holds Session," *Washington Post*, June 4, 1949; *Report of the Commission on the Renovation of the Executive Mansion*, 23.

7. Minutes of the Commission on the Renovation of the Executive Mansion, June 20, 1949, Harry S. Truman Library and Museum, Independence, Missouri, 7–8.

8. This photo appears in the commission's final report (p. 44), where its caption reads that it was taken on June 3, the date of its first meeting. This date is at variance with the commission's own minutes, however, which indicate a group shot taken on June 20.

9. The anecdote that follows appears in the Diary of Lorenzo Winslow, July 6, 1949, Office of the Curator, the White House.

10. "Glen Edgar Edgerton," *Assembly* (West Point magazine), December 1978, 106.

11. Ibid., 106–7.

12. Bess Furman, "General Arrives to Fix White House," *New York Times*, July 23, 1949.

13. "The President's House," *New York Times*, July 1, 1949.

14. "White House Rebuilding Commission Meets, May Decide on Second Home for President," *New York Times*, June 29, 1949.

15. Minutes of the Commission on the Renovation of the Executive Mansion, July 19, 1949, 1.

16. "House Wants Commission to Decide on White House," *Washington Post*, June 16, 1949.

17. Minutes of the Commission on the Renovation of the Executive Mansion, July 19, 1949.

18. Kenneth Douglas McKellar, "Memoirs by Kenneth Douglas McKellar," unpublished manuscript, 1955, Benjamin L. Hooks Central Library, Memphis, Tennessee, 567–568.

19. Letter from William Adams Delano to Douglas Orr, July 15, 1949, appended to the minutes of the Commission on the Renovation of the Executive Mansion, July 19, 1949, Harry S. Truman Library and Museum.

20. Minutes of the Commission on the Renovation of the Executive Mansion, August 2, 1949, Harry S. Truman Library and Museum, 3.

21. Ibid., 6.

22. Ibid., 4, 6.

23. "White House Saved from Wreckers," *New York Times*, August 3, 1949.

24. Diary of Lorenzo Winslow, August 3, 1949.

25. Untitled typewritten speech of Douglas Orr, November 14, 1952, Douglas W. Orr Papers, MSS. 128, box 2, folder J, New Haven Museum & Historical Society Library.

26. Untitled architectural history of the White House by architect Douglas Orr, Douglas W. Orr Papers, MSS. 128, box 2, folder J, New Haven Museum & Historical Society Library, 11.

11. "SHOOT IT"

1. Steven J. Zaloga, *Target America: The Soviet Union and the Strategic Arms Race, 1945–1964* (Novato, CA: Presidio, 1993), 59; Michael D. Gordin, *Red Cloud at Dawn: Truman, Stalin, and the End of the Atomic Monopoly* (New York: Farrar, Straus and Giroux, 2009), 166. Gordin's account (p. 172) places the tower 170 kilometers (about 105 miles) west of Semipalatinsk. This zone would later become the principal testing ground for Soviet nuclear weapons for the entire Cold War. Between this inaugural detonation and the final burst in 1989, the USSR would explode an astonishing 460 bombs within the Semipalatinsk site, according to the International Atomic Energy Agency.

2. Alfred Steinberg, *The Man from Missouri: The Life and Times of Harry S. Truman* (New York: G. P. Putnam's Sons, 1962), 355–56.

3. Dorothea Andrews, "Dawson Tells How Truman Passes Days," *Washington Post*, November 19, 1949.

4. Margaret Truman, *Harry S. Truman* (New York: William Morrow, 1973),

276; Simon Sebag Montefiore, *Stalin: The Court of the Red Tsar* (London: Weidenfeld & Nicholson, 2003), 441.

5. Margaret Truman, *Harry S. Truman*, 276.

6. Montefiore, *Stalin*, 443.

7. Stephen M. Younger, *The Bomb: A New History* (New York: HarperCollins, 2009), 34.

8. Montefiore, *Stalin*, 446.

9. This description of the layout of Stalin's office is based on numerous period photographs, but mainly on the layout sketched by Faye Emerson Roosevelt at the time she accompanied her husband, Elliott Roosevelt, who interviewed Stalin on December 21, 1946. This interview was subsequently published in *Look*, February 4, 1947.

10. Helen Rappaport, *Joseph Stalin: A Biographical Companion* (Santa Barbara, CA: ABC-Clio, 1999), 267.

11. Zaloga, *Target America*, 58–59.

12. Younger, *The Bomb*, 34.

13. Richard Rhodes, whose books on the history of nuclear weapons are definitive, contends that "the first Soviet bomb core never traveled to Moscow for Stalin to touch, as Soviet-era myths purport, but the project leaders were called there that spring to report." See Richard Rhodes, *Dark Sun: The Making of the Hydrogen Bomb* (New York: Simon & Schuster, 2005), 352.

14. Younger, *The Bomb*, 34.

15. Zaloga, *Target America*, 61.

16. Ibid., 62. Details about Beria's savagery are from Montefiore, *Stalin*, 244, 448–49.

12. THE SHOVEL IN THE EARTH

1. Diary of Lorenzo Winslow, August 7, 1949, Office of the Curator, the White House.

2. William J. Moyer, "The Man Behind the White House Remodeling," *Washington Star Sunday Pictoral Magazine*, December 16, 1951, 14.

3. Winslow had testified that "there is no way we can get out of the tourist problem," nor the continuous repainting that resulted from the scuff marks that visitors left on the walls. Marble was the solution. "Second Deficiency Appropriation Bill for 1949, Additional Hearings Before the Subcommittee of the Committee on Appropriations, House of Representatives, Renovation and Modernization of the Executive Mansion," 81st Cong., 1st sess., 1949, H. Doc. 91773, 3.

4. Barbara G. Carson, "Social Seasons and Rituals of Entertainment," *Our Changing White House*, ed. Wendell Garrett (Boston: Northeastern University Press, 1995), 65.

5. Bess Furman, "White House Going Back to Olden Day," *New York Times*, August 4, 1949, 25. The sole exception to the plan to return the interior to the Federal period, Felix de Weldon would later recall, would be the Lincoln Bedroom, "which had to be Victorian." See Oral History Interview with Felix de Weldon, conducted by Jerry N. Hess, January 22, 1969, §40, Harry S. Truman Library and Museum, Independence, Missouri.

6. John Whitcomb, *Real Life at the White House: Two Hundred Years of Daily Life at America's Most Famous Residence* (New York: Routledge, 2000), 19.

7. "Second Deficiency Appropriation Bill for 1949," 3.

8. Letter from Lorenzo Winslow to Sidney T. Strickland, July 20, 1950, Commission on the Renovation of the Executive Mansion, Harry S. Truman Library and Museum.

9. This exclusionary appraisal would pop up frequently, to justify both items that would be kept and ones that would be discarded. One example of this can be found in the letter from Lorenzo Winslow to William Adams Delano, April 5, 1950, Commission on the Renovation of the Executive Mansion, Harry S. Truman Library and Museum.

10. *Report of the Commission on the Renovation of the Executive Mansion* (Washington, D.C.: U.S. Government Printing Office, 1952), 61.

11. Memorandum from Lorenzo Winslow to Matthew J. Connelly, September 14, 1949, Harry S. Truman Papers, White House Central Files, "White House Renovation," Harry S. Truman Library and Museum.

12. William Seale, *The President's House: A History*, vol. 2 (Washington, D.C.: White House Historical Association, 1986), 1031–32.

13. According to Winslow's notes, the Washington meeting took place on September 22. Delano's patronizing memo to the president was dated the day before. See "Re: The White House," memo from William Adams Delano to

President Truman, September 21, 1949, item 1, Harry S. Truman Papers, President's Secretary's Files, Harry S. Truman Library and Museum.

14. Delano had actually gone down to Washington to press his case with Truman. This letter was waiting for him upon his return. Memorandum from President Truman to William Adams Delano, September 23, 1949, Harry S. Truman Papers, President's Secretary's Files, Harry S. Truman Library and Museum.

15. Seale, *The President's House*, vol. 2, 1032–33.

16. Diary of Lorenzo Winslow, September 2–7, 1949.

17. Diary of Lorenzo Winslow, April 19 and 23, 1949.

18. Diary of Lorenzo Winslow, September 3 and 19, 1949.

19. Diary of Lorenzo Winslow, September 7, 1949.

20. Famed *Titanic* historian Walter Lord described Stead as "a leading British spiritualist, reformer, evangelist and editor, all rolled into one," and in all, "a professional individualist." The circumstances of Stead's death—disputed to this day—conform to the strictures of Edwardian-era gender roles at times of a maritime disaster: with not enough boats for the women and children, the gentlemen patiently and stoically awaited their deaths. See Walter Lord, *A Night to Remember* (New York: Holt, Rinehart and Winston, 1976), 45, 103.

21. Diary of Lorenzo Winslow, November 9, 1949.

22. Matt McDade, "Retiring White House Architect Separates Fiction from Fact," *Washington Post*, May 31, 1953.

23. "General Description of the Work for the Cost-Plus-a-Fixed-Fee Contract, Renovation and Modernization of the Executive Mansion, Washington, D.C.," prepared by the Public Buildings Administration, September 26, 1949, 1, John McShain Papers, box 61, Hagley Museum and Library, Wilmington, Delaware.

24. Untitled press release concerning status of the bidding process, October 11, 1949, Eben A. Ayers Papers, Harry S. Truman Library and Museum.

25. While the usual cost-plus-fixed-fee contract generally reimbursed contractor-incurred costs separately, in the case of the White House contract, the contractor's fee did include a number of overhead costs that the contractor was expected to pay on his own, such as office equipment, traveling expenses, local office rental, and other overhead. See press release from the Commission on the Renovation of the Executive Mansion, November 3, 1949, Eben A. Ayers Papers.

26. "White House Bids Vary by $850,000," *New York Times*, October 29, 1949.

27. "Construction: White House Man," *Time*, November 14, 1949, 98.

28. Letter from the commissioner of public buildings to John McShain, Inc., November 4, 1949, John McShain Papers, box 61, folder 3.

29. Here is what happened. A church official discovered that way back in 1915, McShain's father had used limestone instead of the specified terra-cotta on the exterior trim of a high school he was constructing. Though the substitution had benefited the parish with a longer-lasting building material, the archbishop of Philadelphia apparently considered it a matter of grave dishonesty, and he blackballed John McShain from any further bidding on church contracts. "I was quite shocked to think the Archbishop would hold me responsible for a controversy which he had with my father many years before," McShain later recalled. But the cleric would not budge. See unpublished memoirs of John McShain, John McShain Papers, box 159, folder 3, Hagley Museum and Library, 8.

30. John Gerrity, "He Changed the Face of Washington," *Nation's Business*, January 1952, 44.

31. Ibid.

32. Carl M. Brauer, *The Man Who Built Washington: A Life of John McShain* (Wilmington, DE: Hagley Museum and Library, 1996), 104–5.

33. Author's interview with Sister Pauline McShain, December 13, 2011.

34. V. R. Montanari, "McShain's a Push-Over for Steam Shovels," *Washington Post*, May 16, 1950.

35. Gerrity, "He Changed the Face of Washington," 62.

36. Montanari, "McShain's a Push-Over for Steam Shovels."

37. Brauer, *The Man Who Built Washington*, 104.

38. "Thank you, Mr. Jefferson," 1943 magazine advertisement, author's collection.

39. Letters between John McShain and President Franklin D. Roosevelt, July 6 and 12, 1941, John McShain Papers, box 159, folder 7, Hagley Museum and Library.

40. Author's interview with Sister Pauline McShain, December 13, 2011.

41. Katie Louchheim, "The Authentic Restoration," uncited manuscript, White House Vertical File, Harry S. Truman Library and Museum, 1.

42. Letter from Lorenzo Winslow to Sidney T. Strickland, July 20, 1950, Commission on the Renovation of the Executive Mansion, box 1, Harry S. Truman Library and Museum.

43. Betty C. Monkman, *The White House: Its Historic Furnishings and First Families* (New York: Abbeville Press, 2000), 161.

44. Diary of Lorenzo Winslow, October 20 and 21, 1949.

45. Dorothea Andrews, "3 White House Mantels of Arthur's Time Turn Up Here After Roundabout Search," *Washington Post*, October 25, 1949.

46. There remains some confusion about the date that the work actually began. The *Washington Post* reported that the digging started on December 14, but that seems more likely the date that the paper became aware of the work and reported the story, since there was no ceremonial start to it. General Edgerton's diary clearly states that "S.W.P. Co. digging trenches for underpinning walls near S.W. corner" on December 13. Abbie Rowe's photo of the start of the work (photo no. 58-531-024, Truman Library) also bears the date of December 14, though that is possibly the day he developed his film, or perhaps a cataloging error. The shallowness of the trench that appears in this photo makes clear that the men had been digging only a few minutes when Rowe took this shot, and he would have had to have taken his photograph on the thirteenth to get the view shown here. The author has elected to go with Edgerton's starting date for the account herein. See Gen. Glen E. Edgerton, "Diary of Progress of the Renovation and Remodeling of the Executive Mansion," Office of History, U.S. Army Corps of Engineers, entry of December 13, 1949.

47. Minutes of the Commission on the Renovation of the Executive Mansion, November 29, 1949, Harry S. Truman Library and Museum, 7.

48. Melvin Altshuler, "White House Lawn Signs Stir Up Fuss," *Washington Post*, December 21, 1949.

49. J. B. West, with Mary Lynn Kotz, *Upstairs at the White House: My Life with the First Ladies* (New York: Coward, McCann & Geoghegan, 1973), 107.

13. WRECK IT GENTLY

1. Gen. Glen E. Edgerton, "Diary of Progress of the Renovation and Remodeling of the Executive Mansion," Office of History, U.S. Army Corps of Engineers, entry for January 13, 1950.

2. Anthony Leviero, "Truman Takes Job as Sidewalk Boss," *New York Times*, January 16, 1950.

3. Oral History Interview with James J. Rowley, conducted by Niel M. Johnson, September 20, 1988, §46, Harry S. Truman Library and Museum, Independence, Missouri.

4. "Sketch Showing Area of the White House Grounds to Be Occupied in the Building Operations," hand-drawn map by Lorenzo Winslow on National Park Service map of the executive mansion grounds, April 12, 1949, Harry S. Truman Papers, White House Central Files, Harry S. Truman Library and Museum.

5. "Security Effecting the White House During Its Reconstruction and Renovation," December 2, 1949, Harry S. Truman Papers, White House Central Files, "White House Renovation," Harry S. Truman Library and Museum.

6. Unpublished memoirs of John McShain, John McShain Papers, box 159, folder 3, Hagley Museum and Library, Wilmington, Delaware, 14, 17.

7. Ibid., 24.

8. The inspection sequence to follow, inclusive of quotes, is reconstructed from the recollections of McShain employees Hauck and J. J. Manning, each of whom furnished extensive typewritten versions of this inspection tour to Mc-Shain for his private files on January 10 and January 13, respectively, 1950. See John McShain Papers, box 159, folder 6, Hagley Museum and Library.

9. "General Description of the Work for the Cost-Plus-a-Fixed-Fee Contract, Renovation and Modernization of the Executive Mansion, Washington, D.C.," prepared by the Public Buildings Administration, September 26, 1949, John McShain Papers, box 61, Hagley Museum and Library, 1–2.

10. Delton Lehman, "They're Fixing Up Over at the Trumans'," *Collier's*, October 28, 1950, 61.

11. Ibid.

12. "If a workman selected for the demolition procedure proved to be of too heavy gesture and firm intent, resulting in breakage," the commission's final report read, "he was transferred to be pilot of a wheelbarrow, where the tissues of the arms and legs became of greater importance than the tissues of the brain." See *Report of the Commission on the Renovation of the Executive Mansion* (Washington, D.C.: U.S. Government Printing Office, 1952), 78.

13. Lehman, "They're Fixing Up Over at the Trumans'," 61.

14. Oral History Interview with Jess Larson, conducted by Jerry N. Hess, May 26, 1967, §16, Harry S. Truman Library and Museum.

15. *Report of the Commission on the Renovation of the Executive Mansion*, 60.

16. Letter from Commission on the Renovation of the Executive Mansion to President Truman, August 1, 1950, "Facilities" section, Harry S. Truman Papers, President's Secretary's Files, Harry S. Truman Library and Museum, 2.

17. Diary of Lorenzo Winslow, January 15, 16, 22, and 23, 1950, Office of the Curator, the White House.

18. Leviero, "Truman Takes Job as Sidewalk Boss."

19. "1902 Box with Whiskey Bottle, Coins Found in White House," *Washington Post*, January 7, 1950; "White House 'Cornerstone' Dug Up; Whisky Label, Papers in 1902 Box," *New York Times*, January 7, 1950.

20. Leviero, "Truman Takes Job as Sidewalk Boss."

21. Excerpt accompanying letter from Ray Baker Harris to President Truman, January 16, 1961, Harry S. Truman Papers, Post-Presidential Files, Harry S. Truman Library and Museum.

22. Kenneth Douglas McKellar, "Memoirs by Kenneth Douglas McKellar," unpublished manuscript, 1955, Benjamin L. Hooks Central Library, Memphis, Tennessee, 561–63.

23. Abbie Rowe hurried in, set up his lights, and snapped a photo. Then the men filled the cistern in—with stones and concrete this time, sealing it up. Winslow marked his drawings to show the trouble spot so that no new walls would be built on it. See Edgerton, "Diary of Progress of the Renovation and Remodeling of the Executive Mansion," entry for February 8, 1950.

24. William Seale, *The President's House: A History*, vol. 2 (Washington, D.C.: White House Historical Association, 1986), 1036.

25. J. B. West, with Mary Lynn Kotz, *Upstairs at the White House: My Life with the First Ladies* (New York: Coward, McCann & Geoghegan, 1973), 106–7.

26. Seale, *The President's House*, vol. 2, 1037.

27. "Broken Beam in Room 16, Second Floor," memorandum from executive director Edgerton to project manager Kelley, February 27, 1950, Records of the Committee for the Renovation of the Executive Mansion, folder titled "Material Relating to the Cracked Beam in Miss Margaret Truman's Room," Harry S. Truman Library and Museum.

28. Margaret Truman, *The President's House* (New York: Ballantine Books: 2003), 42.

29. Lehman, "They're Fixing Up Over at the Trumans'," 61. This article mentions the "Lincoln room," which the author construes to mean the room number 223 on Winslow's second-floor plan, the room that Truman first moved Lincoln's furniture down to in 1945, and the room today known as the Lincoln Bedroom.

30. "Disposition of Surplus Material," appendix 9, *Report of the Commission on the Renovation of the Executive Mansion*, 103.

31. Later on, in the summer of 1951, Abbie Rowe would photograph this space. See photo no. 71-461, Harry S. Truman Library and Museum.

32. Lehman, "They're Fixing Up Over at the Trumans'," 36.

33. Douglas Orr, "The Reconstruction of the White House," *The National League for Woman's Service Magazine*, August 1950, 12.

34. The iconic centerpieces consisted of two thousand cubic yards of concrete and three thousand tons of steel. In the end, it would take one thousand creosote-soaked pilings of Douglas fir to hold the whole thing up. Burmister's work on the fair appears in the short biography that accompanies "Foundation Studies for the White House," the article he wrote for the *Columbia Engineering Quarterly*, March 1952.

35. Burmister's explanation continued: "On the contrary, a relatively new art and science was being called upon to predict with accuracy the probable vertical movements of the structure in sequence during the successive stages of reconstruction." See Donald M. Burmister, "Foundation Studies for the White House," reprint from the *Columbia Engineering Quarterly*, March 1952, at http://www.civil.columbia.edu.

36. Not only would Burmister turn out to be right about the gravel layer's solidity; he'd correctly predict the house's settlement to within 1/25th of an inch—and he did all of this from his office in New York. See *Report of the Commission on the Renovation of the Executive Mansion*, 52, 54.

37. Lehman, "They're Fixing Up Over at the Trumans'," 61.

38. Edgerton, "Diary of Progress of the Renovation and Remodeling of the Executive Mansion," entry for January 31, 1950.

39. Lehman, "They're Fixing Up Over at the Trumans'," 61.

40. Letter from Ray Baker Harris to President Truman, January 16, 1961, Papers of Harry S. Truman, Post-Presidential Files, Harry S. Truman Library and Museum.

41. Richard Dougherty, "Interior Decoration and Furnishings at the White House," *Club Dial*, February 1953, 15.

42. *Report of the Commission on the Renovation of the Executive Mansion*, 55. The lateral bracing from the shoring towers can be seen in Abbie Rowe's photos, nos. 71-254 and 71-255, Harry S. Truman Library and Museum.

43. Untitled paper by Douglas Orr, Douglas W. Orr Papers, MSS. 128, box 2, folder J, New Haven Museum & Historical Society Library, 14.

44. Lehman, "They're Fixing Up Over at the Trumans'," 36.

14. "WE ARE NO LONGER AHEAD"

1. Minutes of the Commission on the Renovation of the Executive Mansion, May 8, 1950, Harry S. Truman Library and Museum, Independence, Missouri, 2.

2. Bess Furman, "White House Work Ahead of Schedule," *New York Times*, May 14, 1950.

3. Richard Morris, "Creaky White House Joints Stiffened with Steel Beams," *Washington Post*, June 2, 1950.

4. Untitled paper by Douglas Orr, Douglas W. Orr Papers, MSS. 128, box 2, folder J, the New Haven Museum & Historical Society Library, 14.

5. William Seale, *The President's House: A History*, vol. 2 (Washington, D.C.: White House Historical Association, 1986), 1038.

6. Hugh Sidey, "Standing By Eight Presidents," *Time*, June 21, 2005.

7. David McCullough, *Truman* (New York: Simon & Schuster, 1992), 878.

8. The original figure was expressed in feet: .018. Howard S. Rappleye, from the U.S. Coast and Geodetic Survey, determined the movement on May 24, 1950, and reported it to Edgerton, who recorded in his diary, "Mr. Rappelye [*sic*] reports movement in building viz—NW corner is moving SW, SW corner is moving NW, N face of bldg east of portico moved out .018', N face of bldg west of portico moved in .018'." See Gen. Glen E. Edgerton, "Diary of Progress of the Renovation and Remodeling of the Executive Mansion," Office of History, U.S. Army Corps of Engineers, entry for May 24, 1950.

9. Emilie Tavel, "Within the White House Shell: Historic Moments Pass in Review," *Christian Science Monitor*, July 28, 1950.

10. Bess Furman, "White House Renovation Speeds; Job Is Month Ahead of Schedule," *New York Times*, July 12, 1950.

11. Tavel, "Within the White House Shell: Historic Moments Pass in Review."

12. "'New' White House," *New York Times*, July 12, 1950.

13. "White House Exterior Is Only a Cover for Stripped Interior," *Washington Post*, July 12, 1950.

14. Furman, "White House Renovation Speeds."

15. Tavel, "Within the White House Shell."

16. Letter from President Truman to Ethel Noland, July 20, 1950, Harry S. Truman Papers, President's Secretary's Files, Harry S. Truman Library and Museum.

17. Minutes of the Commission on the Renovation of the Executive Mansion, July 19, 1950, Harry S. Truman Library and Museum, 1. The Bethlehem Steel Company had been awarded the contract for the structural steel on January 30, 1950. Edgerton's diary notes that the first structural steel arrived on June 22, 1950.

18. Richard Dougherty, "Interior Decoration and Furnishings at the White House," *Club Dial*, February 1953, 15.

19. Oral History Interview with Jess Larson, conducted by Jerry N. Hess, May 26, 1967, §20, Harry S. Truman Library and Museum.

20. The window openings were fifty-four inches wide; many of the beams were thirty-six inches thick.

21. Author's interview with Sister Pauline McShain, December 13, 2011.

22. John McShain, Inc., usually had so much work going at the same time that McShain himself simply could not avoid delegating. He had several foremen, but J. Paul Hauck was the best of them—which is why McShain had given the White House job to him. "He trusted him," Sister McShain said. Hauck was "brilliant, honest, and reliable. He knew just what was happening."

23. "The White House Revealed: Photos of the White House Renovation by Abbie Rowe," exhibition catalog, June 15, 2001, Harry S. Truman Library and Museum.

24. Drew Pearson, "Toughest White House Jobs Done," *Washington Post*, September 24, 1950.

25. Minutes of the Commission on the Renovation of the Executive Mansion, August 30, 1950, Harry S. Truman Library and Museum, 3.

26. Minutes of the Commission on the Renovation of the Executive Mansion, August 30, 1950, 2; September 14, 1950, 3.

27. This exchange and the subsequent quotes, unless otherwise noted, are taken from the Minutes of the Commission on the Renovation of the Executive Mansion, August 30, 1950, Harry S. Truman Library and Museum, 3–11.

28. Carl M. Brauer, *The Man Who Built Washington* (Wilmington, DE: Hagley Museum and Library, 1996), 117.

29. "Mr. Orr and Dougherty agree that they should review the specs at once to see if any materials can be cheapened or omitted," Edgerton noted in his diary early in November, suggesting they substitute limestone for granite on the South Portico stairs, and scrap plans for an aluminum catwalk on the roof. See Edgerton, "Diary of Progress of the Renovation and Remodeling of the Executive Mansion," entry for November 6, 1950.

30. This amount would go to the Vermont Marble Company. Minutes of the Commission on the Renovation of the Executive Mansion, August 30, 1950, Harry S. Truman Library and Museum, 15–16. According to the Bureau of Labor Statistics, the average household income in the United States for the year 1950 was five thousand dollars.

31. At length, McShain wrote to Reynolds at the Public Buildings Administration to tell him that finishing the White House by October 1951 was "practically an impossibility." It was partly because of a materials shortage, but mostly because "you find it necessary to extensively revise the drawing and specifications to bring the costs within your budget." See letter from John McShain to Commissioner Reynolds, November 24, 1950, John McShain Papers, box 61, folder 3, Hagley Museum and Library, Wilmington, Delaware.

32. "Steel Frame 90% Up for White House," *New York Times*, October 7, 1950.

15. THE HIDDEN WHITE HOUSE

1. Richard Rhodes, *The Making of the Hydrogen Bomb* (New York: Simon & Schuster, 2005), 241.

2. T. A. Heppenheimer, "How to Detect an Atomic Bomb," *American Heritage of Invention & Technology* 21, no. 4 (Spring 2006); Thomas C. Reed, *At the*

Abyss: An Insider's History of the Cold War (New York: Ballantine Books, 2004), 105–6; Michael S. Goodman, *Spying on the Nuclear Bear* (Stanford, CA: Stanford University Press, 2007), 46–49.

3. William Manchester, *The Glory and the Dream: A Narrative History of America, 1932–1972* (Boston: Little, Brown, 1973), 598; Goodman, *Spying on the Nuclear Bear*, 48.

4. David E. Lilienthal, *The Journals of David E. Lilienthal*, vol. 2, *The Atomic Energy Years, 1945–1950* (New York: Harper & Row, 1964), 570.

5. Jeremy Bernstein, *Oppenheimer: Portrait of an Enigma* (Chicago: Ivan R. Dee, 2004), 98.

6. Manchester, *The Glory and the Dream*, 598.

7. "Text of Truman's Statement," *New York Times*, September 24, 1949.

8. Vermont was an unpleasantly local-sounding name for the detonation of a Soviet nuclear bomb, and it would not last. In a sardonic reference to Joseph Stalin, a young staffer at the Atomic Energy Commission began calling the bomb "Joe 1." The name stuck. See Reed, *At the Abyss*, 17.

9. U.S. Air Force memorandum to Secretary of Defense Louis A. Johnson, November 8, 1949, document 63, Harry S. Truman Papers, President's Secretary's Files, Harry S. Truman Library and Museum, Independence, Missouri.

10. David McCullough, *Truman* (New York: Simon & Schuster, 1992), 775.

11. Richard B. Morris, and Jeffrey B. Morris, *Great Presidential Decisions* (New York: Richardson, Steirman & Black, 1988), 403.

12. Margaret Truman, *Harry S. Truman* (New York: William Morrow, 1973), 455.

13. "Letter from Admiral Dennison," Minutes of the Commission on the Renovation of the Executive Mansion, August 16, 1950, Harry S. Truman Library and Museum, 3.

14. According to Winslow's diary, the Public Buildings Administration became involved on July 27, though he did not mention Reynolds by name. Apparently, that department attempted to gain some measure of supervision over the shelter project, as Winslow complained of a power grab by the PBA. But Winslow would keep control of the drawings, at least, though Public Buildings would get to "supervise and administer construction," according to Dennison's letter of August 1, 1950.

15. Diary of Lorenzo Winslow, August 4, 1950, Office of the Curator, the White House.

16. Diary of Lorenzo Winslow, July 18, 19, and 20, 1950.

17. Diary of Lorenzo Winslow, July 26, 1950.

18. Diary of Lorenzo Winslow, August 15, 1950. Winslow's entry for the sixteenth says only "commission meeting." He apparently made no further notes on the shelter for the remainder of the month, though the pages for August 22–27, 1950, are redacted in the copy the author received from the White House curator.

19. Minutes of the Commission on the Renovation of the Executive Mansion, August 16, 1950, Harry S. Truman Library and Museum, 3.

20. The directions Winslow followed are worth quoting in full from the minutes of the commission's meeting of August 16, 1950. "General Edgerton explained that the work is in addition to, and will be done separately from, the renovation work, but that it affects the renovation work substantially in the basement area. The work to be done consists of strengthening the walls of the basement corridor, increasing the thickness of the floor above it, and thickening the mezzanine floor over the three northeast rooms of the basement." The author's scale estimate of the thickness of the fortifications based on comparisons with the original thickness of the mansion's outer walls.

21. "Utility rooms" appeared in Bess Furman, "White House Renovation Speeds; Job Is Month Ahead of Schedule," *New York Times*, July 12, 1950. This underground area had been created as part of the overall excavation and was slated to be backfilled until Edgerton decided to use it as additional rooms for storage. In the wake of Dennison's memo, Edgerton evidently changed his mind and offered the chambers as part of the shelter complex. See Minutes of the Commission on the Renovation of the Executive Mansion, August 16, 1950, Harry S. Truman Library and Museum, 10.

22. Minutes of the Commission on the Renovation of the Executive Mansion, August 16, 1950, Harry S. Truman Library and Museum, 10.

23. Edgerton had noted in his diary the previous week that "all work on north side . . . shall cease until further notice" because of the "proposed changes." See Gen. Glen E. Edgerton, "Diary of Progress of the Renovation and Remodeling of the Executive Mansion," Office of History, U.S. Army Corps of Engineers, entries for August 7 and 8, 1950.

24. Diary of Lorenzo Winslow, August 4, 1950.

25. Author's emphasis. This quote and the exchange that follows are taken from the Minutes of the Commission on the Renovation of the Executive Mansion, August 30, 1950, Harry S. Truman Library and Museum, 11–13.

26. "White House Traffic Jams Laid to Threat of Atom Bomb," *Washington Post*, October 28, 1945.

27. Kenneth D. Rose, *One Nation Underground* (New York: New York University Press, 2001), 17.

28. Richard Reeves, *Daring Young Men: The Heroism and Triumph of the Berlin Airlift, June 1948–May 1949* (New York: Simon & Schuster, 2010), 77.

29. Robert H. Ferrell, ed., *Off the Record: The Private Papers of Harry S. Truman* (New York: Harper & Row, 1980), 149.

30. "A Report to the National Security Council—NSC 68," April 12, 1950, Harry S. Truman Papers, President's Secretary's Files, Harry S. Truman Library and Museum, 60, 65.

31. Gordon Chaplin, "Underground Washington," *Washington Post Magazine*, September 17, 1978, 22–23.

32. "Air Raid Shelter Built in the White House," *New York Times*, May 20, 1945.

33. Oral History Interview with David H. Stowe, conducted by Niel M. Johnson, June 24, 1989, §76, Harry S. Truman Library and Museum.

34. Winslow revealed these details in the course of congressional testimony in 1946. See "Independent Offices Appropriation Bill, 1947," U.S. Senate Subcommittee of the Committee on Appropriations, transcript of the hearing, Tuesday, February 5, 1946, 189, 191.

35. "A tunnel had been constructed from the East Wing of the White House over to the Treasury Department where there was a deep vault," Stowe recalled many years after the war. "Since it was a tunnel and on an incline," he continued," they could wheel the President, in his wheelchair, into that in the event of necessity." See Oral History Interview with David H. Stowe, §75.

36. Minutes of the Commission on the Renovation of the Executive Mansion, November 16, 1950, Harry S. Truman Library and Museum, 7.

37. Oral History Interview with David H. Stowe, §80.

38. According to Edgerton's diary, the excavation period for the "shelter under East Terrace" began in early February of 1951 and went on for the next

ninety-five days. During this time, workmen excavated a well for drinking water, laid the shelter's sewer line, and installed the blast doors in the basement. Come May, the men began putting in the heavy reinforcing steel—a process that would last for the next two and a half months. McShain began pouring concrete not long after the steel started going in, installing the frame for a second blast door in the basement tunnel and then pouring the shelter's main floor—660 cubic yards of concrete—on July 10. Edgerton noted that the shelter's diesel generator arrived at the end of July and that for the rest of the summer and well into November, workmen waterproofed the underground complex and then backfilled it with earth. See Edgerton, "Diary of Progress on the Renovation and Remodeling of the Executive Mansion," entries for February 2 and 12, March 29, April 20, May 1 and 2, June 15, and July 10, 1951.

39. Minutes of the Commission on the Renovation of the Executive Mansion, November 16, 1950, 5.

40. Ibid.

41. Estimate sheet for "Shelter," marked as page 1, John McShain Papers, box 53, Hagley Museum and Library, Wilmington, Delaware.

42. Author's interview with Sister Pauline McShain, December 13, 2011.

43. "No Atom Shelter for White House, Architect Says," *Washington Post*, January 10, 1950.

44. Tom Vanderbilt, *Survival City: Adventures Among the Ruins of Atomic America* (New York: Princeton Architectural Press, 2002), 129–30.

45. Pat Zacharias, "When Bomb Shelters Were All the Rage," *Detroit News*, April 1, 1999.

46. The most Edgerton would concede was that "some changes in the underground connection with the Treasury Department" were under way. See "Steel Frame 90% Up for White House," *New York Times*, October 7, 1950.

47. "Mr. Kelley said work in the basement has been delayed to some extent because a change was made in the basement corridor, and it became a part of Project 9." The bomb-shelter construction is the only undertaking around this time that would warrant a code name like this. See minutes of the Commission on the Renovation of the Executive Mansion, January 26, 1951, Harry S. Truman Library and Museum, 4. As far as the inspection that Edgerton referenced, OCE likely stood for either the Office of the Corps of Engineers or Office of the Chief of Engineers. In any case, these documents strongly suggest that Project 9 and the White House atomic shelter were one

and the same. See Edgerton, "Diary of Progress on the Renovation and Remodeling of the Executive Mansion," entries for December 8, 1950, and August 24, 1951.

48. Drew Pearson, "Toughest White House Jobs Done," *Washington Post*, September 24, 1950.

49. Later, UPI would peg the shelter's cost at $938,000.

50. During his research visit to the Truman Library in June 2010, the author requested access to copies of Winslow's blueprints for the White House work, inclusive of the basement areas, and was denied permission, based on the fact the drawings had been classified as "records of concern." These restrictions were confirmed in a letter to the author from Sam Rushay, supervisory archivist of the Truman Library, December 29, 2011. The author also submitted a Freedom of Information Act request to the Public Buildings Service—under whose supervision the shelter was built. In a letter dated September 30, 2010, the deputy regional commissioner for the Public Buildings Service stated that no documents pertaining to the protective work on the White House basement or its environs could be located.

51. Ronald Kessler, *In the President's Secret Service* (New York: Crown, 2009), 60.

52. At the time of this writing, a purported set of Winslow's drawings appeared on the Web site of the White House Museum (www.whitehousemuseum.org), a fine enthusiast site, albeit one with no official relationship to the White House. These plans, which appear to be genuine, bear dates in September and December of 1950. That would place them within the period in which Winslow had modified his basement plans to include the shelter construction. For various pertinent details herein, however, the author is relying primarily on a set of plans for the basement mezzanine and the subbasement level discovered in the Vertical File of the Truman Library during his visit there in June 2010. These plans bear the stamp of the Commission on the Renovation of the Executive Mansion and are revised to February 13, 1951, making them the more current.

53. Admiral Dennison's memo of August 1, 1950, makes clear that the shelter included the entry route via the reinforced areas of the White House basement. Edgerton's comments at the August sixteenth commission meeting make it all but certain that the chambers beneath the driveway to the northeast of the mansion would be included, as well. What's more, numerous pieces of evidence make a reasonable case for Winslow's having simply incorporated FDR's old conventional shelter into Truman's new atomic one. The FDR shelter was valuable subterranean space that had gone unused since the end of the war. One transcript from a commission meeting contains a reference to Project 9 taking place beneath the "Hat Box," which is significant. (See Minutes of the

Commission on the Renovation of the Executive Mansion, August 3, 1951, Harry S. Truman Library and Museum, 8.) The Hat Box was the nickname the butlers coined for the East Wing's old cloakroom, which, until its conversion to a movie theater in 1942, occupied the slender protrusion from the mansion known as the East Terrace. Not only did FDR's bomb shelter occupy the underground space directly beneath here; Winslow himself noted in his diary that Truman's shelter was "under the East Terrace." (See Diary of Lorenzo Winslow, August 15, 1950.) If but inadvertently, Abbie Rowe also appears to have furnished evidence for the top secret shelter's location. A photograph (no. 71-426) he took on February 15, 1951, shows that workmen had excavated down to the East Terrace's basement level (again, the site of the old FDR shelter). The men had removed part of a very thick retaining wall and were proceeding to expand the space northward with a new structure of heavy-duty steel-reinforced concrete. This structure is clearly the same one referenced during the Commission's meeting of November 16, 1950, during which Winslow referred to the shelter project as including "the excavation north of the east terrace."

54. Traphes Bryant, with Frances Spatz Leighton, *Dog Days at the White House: The Outrageous Memoirs of the Presidential Kennel Keeper* (New York: Macmillan, 1975), 76.

55. Lillian Rogers Parks, with Frances Spatz Leighton, *My Thirty Years Backstairs at the White House* (New York: Fleet Publishing Co., 1961), 237.

56. Basement Plan, RP-1, revised February 13, 1951, Vertical File, Harry S. Truman Library and Museum.

57. The author has drawn the description of the shelter from McCullough, *Truman*, p. 881. McCullough's cited source for the description is Tubby's diary entry of July 26, 1951. Tubby's papers are currently in the collection of the Sterling Memorial Library at Yale University in New Haven, Connecticut. In an electronic communication on May 28, 2010, Diane E. Kaplan, head of public services, manuscripts, and archives, informed the author that the Tubby collection is officially closed to all researchers until the year 2050.

58. "Truman Digs into Special Fund for $881,000 A-Bomb Shelter," *Washington Post*, April 18, 1951.

59. Oral History Interview with Admiral Robert L. Dennison, conducted by Jerry N. Hess, October 6, 1971, §98, Harry S. Truman Library and Museum.

60. Ibid.

61. Eventually, in the years after Truman left office, a plan known loosely as the Federal Relocation Arc would see the construction of a string of massive under-

ground facilities from Pennsylvania to Virginia, all meant to assure the "continuity of government" in the event of atomic war. These would include the completed Raven Rock Mountain, Mount Weather, Cheyenne Mountain, and the project code-named Greek Island—an underground complex built below the posh Greenbrier Resort in West Virginia and designed to house 535 members of Congress behind a twenty-five-ton steel blast door made by the Mosler Safe Company. See Vanderbilt, *Survival City*, 135, 137, 144–47; N. J. McCamley, *Cold War Secret Nuclear Bunkers* (Barnsley, England: Leo Cooper, 2002), 7–8.

62. Oral History Interview with Admiral Robert L. Dennison, §99.

63. Oral History Interview with General Jess Larson, conducted by Jerry N. Hess, May 26, 1967, §21, Harry S. Truman Library and Museum.

16. TWENTY-SEVEN ROUNDS

1. Alonzo Fields, *My 21 Years in the White House* (New York: Coward-McCann, 1960), 14, 154–55.

2. Alfred Steinberg, *The Man from Missouri: The Life and Times of Harry S. Truman* (New York: G. P. Putnam's Sons, 1962), 345.

3. J. B. West, with Mary Lynn Kotz, *Upstairs at the White House: My Life with the First Ladies* (New York: Coward, McCann & Geoghegan, 1973), 64.

4. Emilie Tavel, "First Family Moves Just Across Street," *Christian Science Monitor*, December 15, 1948.

5. "Dawson Tells How Truman Passes Day," *Washington Post*, November 19, 1949. When the Secret Service learned about this enterprise, the agents apparently decided that it would be easier to curb the president's right to walk than the public's right to watch him, and they began driving Truman to work. He hated the practice immediately. "They wanted to drive me from Blair House to the White House in one of those damn limousines," Truman said. "Can you imagine being *driven* across the street?" See John Whitcomb, *Real Life at the White House: Two Hundred Years of Daily Life at America's Most Famous Residence* (New York: Routledge, 2000), 330.

6. Some accounts put Truman's walking speed at 120 steps per minute, but in this one instance he insisted it was 128. See Harry S. Truman, *The Wit and Wisdom of Harry S. Truman*, ed. Alex Ayers (New York: Meridian, 1998), 164, 168.

7. Margaret Truman, *Harry S. Truman* (New York: William Morrow, 1973), 440–41.

8. Rufus W. Youngblood, *20 Years in the Secret Service: My Life with Five Presidents* (New York: Simon & Schuster, 1973), 32.

9. D. M. Giangreco and Kathryn Moore, *Dear Harry . . . : Truman's Mailroom, 1945–1953* (Mechanicsburg, PA: Stackpole Books, 1999), 431–32; Andrew Tully, *Treasury Agent: The Inside Story* (New York: Simon & Schuster, 1958), 309.

10. Youngblood, *20 Years in the Secret Service*, 33–34.

11. Philip H. Melanson, *The Secret Service: The Hidden History of an Enigmatic Agency* (New York: Barnes & Noble Books, 2004), 293.

12. Lillian Rogers Parks, with Frances Spatz Leighton, *My Thirty Years Backstairs at the White House* (New York: Fleet Publishing Co., 1961), 58.

13. Traphes Bryant, with Frances Spatz Leighton, *Dog Days at the White House: The Outrageous Memoirs of the Presidential Kennel Keeper* (New York: Macmillan, 1975), 79. Truman also believed that it was his duty to get out on the street and commune with the people who had elected him. "A president has to be willing, indeed anxious, to talk to people," he said. See Harry S. Truman, *Where the Buck Stops: The Personal and Private Writings of Harry S. Truman*, ed. Margaret Truman (New York: Warner Books, 1990), 93.

14. Parks, *My Thirty Years Backstairs at the White House*, 300.

15. Tully, *Treasury Agent*, 299.

16. "Nationalist Party of Puerto Rico," Document SJ 100-3, Federal Bureau of Investigation, via Freedom of Information Act request, 1-B.

17. Harry S. Truman, *Where the Buck Stops*, 94.

18. Where not specifically noted, the subsequent re-creation of the gun battle is taken from David McCullough, *Truman* (New York: Simon & Schuster, 1992), 808–11; Youngblood, *20 Years in the Secret Service*, 28–31.

19. McCullough, *Truman*, 809.

20. Most of the accounts of the shooting are vague when it comes to the matter of why Collazo's gun did not initially fire. But Stephen Hunter and John Bainbridge, Jr., in their meticulous account of the incident, make a wholly credible case for the inexperienced Collazo's having activated the safety by mistake. See Stephen Hunter, and John Bainbridge, Jr., *American Gunfight: The Plot to Kill Harry Truman—and the Shoot-out That Stopped It* (New York: Simon & Schuster, 2005), 130–31.

21. West, *Upstairs at the White House*, 116–17.

22. Parks, *My Thirty Years Backstairs at the White House*, 57–58.

23. Fields, *My 21 Years in the White House*, 156.

24. Ronald Kessler, *In the President's Secret Service* (New York: Crown, 2009), 8.

25. Margaret Truman, *Bess W. Truman* (New York: Macmillan, 1986), 361.

26. Later, Reathel Odum, the First Lady's secretary, who'd gone to live with Margaret in New York, broke the news to her.

27. Truman believed that Collazo and Torrasola were "misguided fanatics" and "not really killers." See Harry S. Truman, *Where the Buck Stops*, 94.

28. Ibid.

29. Melanson, *The Secret Service*, 141.

30. Robert H. Ferrell, ed., *Off the Record: The Private Papers of Harry S. Truman* (New York: Harper & Row, 1980), 240.

31. "District Has Sunny, Quiet Holiday," *Washington Post*, November 24, 1950.

32. These were the rooms that General Edgerton had talked about, some of which he'd pledged to incorporate "in connection with the protective project." See Minutes of the Commission on the Renovation of the Executive Mansion, August 16, 1950, Harry S. Truman Library and Museum, 10. See also Abbie Rowe's photo no. 71-401, which shows some of the torn-up earth and what appear to be some of Edgerton's subterranean utility chambers within. Rowe shot this image the day before the Trumans' visit, so it approximates what they likely saw. Actual construction on the shelter had not begun yet because the drawings were not ready. See Minutes of the Commission on the Renovation of the Executive Mansion, November 16, 1950, Harry S. Truman Library and Museum, 2.

17. FURNITURE, RUGS, AND DRAPERIES

1. "B. Altman & Company Department Store Building," landmark designation report, the New York Landmarks Preservation Commission, March 12, 1985, 2.

2. Throughout its long history, B. Altman & Co. gave $500,000 of its profits to charities each year. See Barbara Rudolph, "Debacle on 34th Street," *Time*, December 11, 1989, 77.

3. Betty C. Monkman, *The White House: Its Historic Furnishings and First Families* (New York: Abbeville Press, 2000), 221. Crim had not failed to relate to the commissioners how B. Altman & Co. had been there in the White House's hour of great need (see Minutes of the Commission on the Renovation of the Executive Mansion, June 20, 1950, Harry S. Truman Library and Museum, Independence, Missouri, 12), and it's not a stretch to presume that Crim also did what he could to assure the letter received the commission's full attention.

4. Letter from John S. Burke to the Commission on the Renovation of the Executive Mansion, September 21, 1950, appearing as "9. Furnishings—Proposal of B. Altman & Co." See Minutes of the Commission on the Renovation of the Executive Mansion, September 29, 1950, Harry S. Truman Library and Museum, 8–9.

5. Letter from Charles T. Haight to the Commission on the Renovation of the Executive Mansion, September 21, 1950, appearing as "9. Furnishings—Proposal of B. Altman & Co." See minutes of the Commission on the Renovation of the Executive Mansion, September 29, 1950, 9–10.

6. Letter from John S. Burke to the Commission on the Renovation of the Executive Mansion.

7. E-mail from Jane B. O'Connell to the author, April 26, 2010.

8. Just prior to Burke's letter being received, William Adams Delano had written Douglas Orr to warn him that the scope of the interior-decoration work would be huge and that the commission should select an interior-decorating firm right away (letter from William Adams Delano to Douglas Orr, August 22, 1950, Harry S. Truman Papers, President's Secretary's Files, Harry S. Truman Library and Museum). When that plea yielded nothing, the White House's chief usher weighed in on his own during a commission meeting: "Mr. Crim stated that in view of the fact that the Presidential Family will be moving back to the Executive Mansion in about fifteen months," the minutes read, "he was hopeful that the Commission would be able to decide on the matters concerning interior decoration" (Minutes of the Commission on the Renovation of the Executive Mansion, September 14, 1950, Harry S. Truman Library and Museum, 16). Crim was a bit of a nail-biter anyway, but this time he really had a point. Decorating all of the mansion's rooms and corridors and sitting halls was bound to take a year at least. See also William Seale, *The President's House: A History*, vol. 2 (Washington, D.C.: White House Historical Association, 1986), 1038.

9. On November 29, 1949, after weeks of leading his commission around like Gypsies, McKellar announced that he'd found the group a home—of sorts. "The only space available is in the corridor of the East Wing," the minutes at-

test. McKellar decided to take what he could get, putting in a request for lights, phones, and temporary partitions to be put up. He even requested a rug for the floor, just to make the place a bit more civilized. See Minutes of the Commission on the Renovation of the Executive Mansion, November 29, 1949, 7.

10. Minutes on the Commission on the Renovation of the Executive Mansion, February 17, 1950, 1. The description of the room during an average meeting is based on a group photo of an actual meeting in progress found among the Douglas W. Orr Papers at the New Haven Museum & Historical Society Library. The photo has no credits on the back, but according to the Minutes of the Commission on the Renovation of the Executive Mansion, April 1, 1950 [p. 5, item 5], photographer Abbie Rowe stopped in and took a picture of the group.

11. Minutes of the Commission on the Renovation of the Executive Mansion, September 29, 1950, Harry S. Truman Library and Museum, 11.

12. The deadline was based on the presumption that the commission would award the contract by January, and so the deadline would land in October 1951.

13. Seale, *The President's House*, vol. 2, 1041–42. Haight was referring to far more than the 66 aboveground rooms in the finished house. In his view, even a nook—"a little space with a door and a window"—constituted a room. Haight counted 210 rooms in the new house. The figure of $210,000 was the one Haight gave when Mr. Seale interviewed him for his definitive book, *The President's House*. But accounts of this budget vary. Dougherty later said it was only $200,000 that the commission had set aside for furnishings. The commission's final report fixes the amount at $208,000.

14. "Approximate Cost of Principal Categories of Work," Appendix 9, *Report of the Commission on the Renovation of the Executive Mansion* (Washington, D.C.: United States Government Printing Office, 1952), 101.

15. Seale, *The President's House*, vol. 2, 1042.

16. The commission would end up accepting donations, but only a relative handful of them compared to what it might have had. See Monkman, *The White House*, 222.

17. Why didn't the commission take the time to entertain offers from any other decorators around the country? The official record of this meeting states that "neither the Commission nor its advisors were able to suggest any other possible subcontractor of equal qualifications for this particular work." The statement is, on its face, entirely ludicrous. The more probable reason was that the job was running behind and the commission wanted to get on with it. See

Minutes of the Commission on the Renovation of the Executive Mansion, September 29, 1950, Harry S. Truman Library and Museum, 13; third progress report to President Truman from the Commission on the Renovation of the Executive Mansion, September 6, 1951, Harry S. Truman Papers, President's Secretary's Files, Harry S. Truman Library and Museum.

18. The commission would decide to go with B. Altman on December 14, 1950. The full statement the commission used to dispense with the competitive-bidding process read "The extraordinary nature of this work was recognized in Public Law 119, 81st Congress, 1st Session, which authorized its exception from the usual requirements of competitive bidding. It was found to be impossible to determine and specify in advance the extent and character of that work with sufficient precision to permit competitive bidding on a fixed price basis without large allowances by the bidders for contingent costs, many of which would probably not be incurred." See third progress report to President Truman from the Commission on Renovation of the Executive Mansion, September 6, 1951, Harry S. Truman Papers, President's Secretary's Files, Harry S. Truman Library and Museum.

19. Among the valuable 1902 pieces were the thirteen Louis XVI gilded banquettes by L. Marcotte in the East Room and the Caldwell & Co. light fixtures—the bronze standards in the lobby and, of course, the enormous crystal chandeliers in the Blue Room and the East Room. The handful of accessories that were older included two gilt bronze Russell & LaFarge candelabra, the Hannibal and Minerva mantel clocks (all from 1817), and two oil paintings: Gilbert Stuart's 1797 portrait of George Washington and E. F. Andrews's 1878 portrait of Martha Washington. See Stanley McClure, "A Preliminary Handbook of Historical Information Concerning the White House and Its Furnishings," February 9, 1950, Peggy Watts Papers, Harry S. Truman Library and Museum.

20. John Hersey, *Aspects of the Presidency* (New Haven, CT: Ticknor & Fields, 1980), 93.

21. Marylin Bender, "Did Mrs. Lincoln Sell the Furniture? Mrs. Kennedy's Text May Be Revised," *New York Times*, March 6, 1962.

22. Ford owned theaters in both Washington, D.C., and Baltimore, and it's unclear where the pieces found new homes. See William G. Allman, "Furnishing the Executive Mansion: Nineteenth-Century Washington Sources," in *Our Changing White House*, ed. Wendell Garrett (Boston: Northeastern University Press, 1995), 136, 141, 154.

23. The fate of the legendary Tiffany screen, installed as part of President Arthur's fifteen-thousand-dollar redecoration of the mansion, has been a lively topic ever since its disappearance. While Roosevelt himself is said to have told McKim to take a hammer to it, the screen was actually removed and sold intact. Eventu-

ally, the luminescent masterpiece found a new home at the Belvedere Hotel in Chesapeake Beach, Maryland, which burned to the ground in 1923. See Margaret Truman, *The President's House* (New York: Ballantine Books, 2003), 34.

24. Housekeeper Elizabeth Jaffray, who ruled the backstairs with an iron fist throughout the Taft, Wilson, Harding, and Coolidge administrations, recalled how "fine old-fashioned furniture handed down from the old days" filled those tiny rooms on the top floor. See Elizabeth Jaffray, *Secrets of the White House* (New York: Cosmopolitan Book Corporation, 1927), 122.

25. Grace Coolidge, *Grace Coolidge: An Autobiography*, ed. Laurence E. Wikander and Robert H. Ferrell (Worland, WY: High Plains Publishing Company, 1992), 81–82.

26. Jaffray, *Secrets of the White House*, 122.

27. This inspection trip—actually several of them over a number of days—had taken place since the last meeting, which had been December 19, 1950. The end of 1950 has been chosen as an approximate time frame for the purposes herein. See Minutes of the Commission on the Renovation of the Executive Mansion, January 9, 1951, Harry S. Truman Library and Museum.

28. Undated photograph of the storage room in the National Gallery of Art, Peggy Watts Papers, Harry S. Truman Library and Museum; e-mail to the author from Maygene Daniels, chief of Gallery Archives, the National Gallery of Art, July 22, 2011.

29. Haight harbored few hopes of finding anything of real value in there. Instead, as the commission later reported, "his selection of items to be reused was based on their artistic suitability and the costs of restoration." See Minutes of the Commission on the Renovation of the Executive Mansion, July 17, 1951, Harry S. Truman Library and Museum, 10. Speed was also a consideration. "There is no doubt," the commission declared at the end of January, "that the reconditioning work must be done and we must proceed quickly." See Minutes of the Commission on the Renovation of the Executive Mansion, January 26, 1951, 8–9.

18. THE TOUR

1. *The New Yorker*'s legendary founder and editor, Harold Ross, had originally asked the White House press office for enough face time to allow Hersey to write a profile on "The President as a Human Being." The initial response was lukewarm. The press simply wasn't given that kind of exclusive access in those days, nor did reporters even quote the president directly. Only after Hersey was able to make a personal appeal to Truman and convince him that he should get on the record, for the sake of American history and his own legacy, did the doors finally open. Hersey's articles ran as installments in the magazine

and were later also collected in book form. See John Hersey, *Aspects of the Presidency* (New Haven, CT: Ticknor & Fields, 1980), 4.

2. In response to the demand for reprints, publishing house Alfred A. Knopf rushed the manuscript into book form. *Hiroshima* has yet to go out of print.

3. Americans had already seen any number of articles about the destructive power of the atomic bomb, but Hersey's was the first that allowed them—forced them—to experience its horror through the memories of six of its survivors. As such, it introduced a new set of variables into the country's burgeoning awareness of its postnuclear self: moral uncertainty, guilt, dread. See "Time from Laughter," *New York Times*, August 30, 1946.

4. David McCullough, *Truman* (New York: Simon & Schuster, 1992), 815. The tour would cover everything from the ground floor up; Hersey was not taken into the subterranean levels.

5. Oral History Interview with General Jess Larson, conducted by Jerry N. Hess, May 26, 1967, §17–18, Harry S. Truman Library and Museum, Independence, Missouri.

6. Ibid.

7. Letter from President Truman to Interior Secretary Harold L. Ickes, January 10, 1946, Harry S. Truman Papers, President's Secretary's Files, Harry S. Truman Library and Museum.

8. Letter from President Truman to William Adams Delano, August 25, 1950, Harry S. Truman Papers, President's Secretary's Files, Harry S. Truman Library and Museum.

9. "'Enemies from Within' Senator Joseph R. McCarthy's Accusations of Disloyalty," George Mason University, at www.historymatters.gmu.edu/d/6456.

10. Margaret Truman, *Harry S. Truman* (New York: William Morrow, 1973), 499.

11. In many ways, especially in the face of his inability to end the conflict in Korea, the White House renovation would become Truman's unofficial raison d'être from this point forward. As historian David McCullough has written, "Little else that he was able to accomplish in these last years of his presidency would give him such satisfaction." See McCullough, *Truman*, 876.

12. Also along was William Hassett, Truman's correspondence secretary, whose comments have been omitted here for the sake of brevity. The account of this tour, inclusive of quotes, is drawn from Hersey, *Aspects of the Presidency*, 88–109. This copy appeared originally as "Profiles, Mr. President: Ghosts in the White House," *The New Yorker*, April 28, 1951, 91–96.

13. Truman's exact quote: "Jefferson was long on ingenuity, but he was short on proportions."

14. "Glen Edgar Edgerton," *Assembly* (West Point magazine), December 1978, 106–7.

15. The single known likeness of the man, found among the heirlooms of the Hoban family, would not be discovered until 1957. It was a profile rendered in wax, believed to be the work of an itinerant artist named John Christian Rauschner. The piece is now part of the White House permanent collection.

19. SOMETHING TO REMEMBER YOU BY

1. Quotes and descriptions of the "junk shop" room are drawn from John Hersey, *Aspects of the Presidency* (New Haven, CT: Ticknor & Fields, 1980), 108–9.

2. Milton Lehman, "They're Fixing Up Over at the Trumans'," *Collier's*, October 28, 1950, 36.

3. "White House Timber: Souvenirs Made from Timber Removed from the White House After 112 Years of Service," National Lumber Manufacturers Association, Washington, D.C., undated brochure accompanying chunk of White House roof beam, author's collection.

4. Winslow revealed his anecdote as he addressed the House Committee on Public Works during a tour of the White House on April 3, 1949. See "Quick Repair Set for White House," *New York Times*, April 3, 1949.

5. Ibid.

6. John Whitcomb, *Real Life at the White House: Two Hundred Years of Daily Life at America's Most Famous Residence* (New York: Routledge, 2000), 107.

7. Specifically, they read "From Harry S. Truman, The White House, Washington, D.C." Mechanical pencil, author's collection.

8. Congress was well aware of the potential problem of debris looting even before it passed H.R. 3856, the measure that created the commission in 1949. "I can see where a certain individual could get a barrel of these nails and sell them for $10 apiece for the next forty years," Ohio representative Robert Secrest quipped. See Testimony of L. C. Martin, assistant to the director of the Bureau of the Budget, hearing on H.R. 3856, "To provide for a commission on the renovation of the Executive Mansion," Committee on Public Works, House of Representatives, 81st Cong., 1st sess., March 30, 1949, 12, 19.

9. The quote is from the article, not from McShain directly, though the sentiment was his. See "Construction: White House Man," *Time*, November 14, 1949, 98.

10. "White House Relics May Go to Voters," *Washington Post*, December 1, 1949.

11. Edgerton had realized the scope of the problem early on. Before McShain's workers had even marched into the house with their sledgehammers, the general sent a memo to the commission. "The decisions to be made now," he wrote, "are concerned with the large amounts of wood and fragments which have little or no intrinsic value, but to which a considerable segment of the population attaches sentimental value of a high order." See memorandum from Gen. Glen Edgerton to the commission, November 21, 1949, Exhibit C-13, Minutes of the Commission on the Renovation of the Executive Mansion, November 29, 1949, Harry S. Truman Library and Museum, Independence, Missouri.

12. Burt also suggested stamping presidential footprints onto squares of the old flooring, and ashtrays to be made from melted-down lead pipes. Miscellaneous letters of suggestions regarding use of White House surplus material, Harry S. Truman Papers, Official Files, Harry S. Truman Library and Museum.

13. The commission's tentative plan emerged on January 6, 1950, and would have Truman's approval by February 17. The commission promised "an equitable, nation-wide, nonpartisan, nonsectarian and noncommercial distribution based upon national population quotas." See Lehman, "They're Fixing Up Over at the Trumans'," 61.

14. According to Douglas Orr's recollection, there had originally been *five* classes of surplus, but later the top category—the historic interiors that Winslow had removed—was left out, presumably since the plan was to put all of it back into the mansion. The overall description of the classes of debris herein is taken from "Disposition of Surplus Material," Appendix 9, *Report of the Commission on the Renovation of the Executive Mansion* (Washington, D.C.: U.S. Government Printing Office, 1952), 103–5.

15. The list of potential beneficiaries would come from a questionnaire that the commission would send to Congress in May of 1950, asking each legislator to list whatever museums, libraries, or civic organizations in his district that he felt might be interested in the offer.

16. "White House Will Bury Debris to Foil Vendors," *New York Times*, February 7, 1950. The Class IV debris was the true dregs and the cause of little concern. Wooden fragments were to be burned in the District of Columbia's municipal incinerator. The hole to be dug at Fort Myer was lauded as "as short a haul as possible." See Minutes of the Commission on the Renovation

of the Executive Mansion, August 18, 1949, Harry S. Truman Library and Museum, 3.

17. Letter to the Speaker of the House from Senator Kenneth McKellar, Chairman of the Commission on the Renovation of the Executive Mansion, July 3, 1950, Harry S. Truman Papers, President's Secretary's Files, Harry S. Truman Library and Museum.

18. As McKellar admitted, "the practical problems of administering and financing a program of wide distribution of souvenirs are imposing." See ibid.

19. "Want a White House Souvenir? Commission May Have 'Em," *Washington Post*, March 31, 1949.

20. Emilie Tavel, "Within the White House Shell, Historic Moments Pass in Preview," *Christian Science Monitor*, July 28, 1950.

21. Lehman, "They're Fixing Up Over at the Trumans'."

22. Letter from Jimmy Brown to president Truman, February 17, 1951, Harry S. Truman Papers, Official Files, Miscellaneous Reconstruction Folder, Money for Souvenirs, Harry S. Truman Library and Museum.

23. Letter from Duke H. Baker to the White House, February 1, 1951, ibid. The commission actually *had* burned wood to give away, but "only a few pieces of charred wood are available," it noted. See minutes of the Commission on the Renovation of the Executive Mansion, July 19, 1950, Harry S. Truman Library and Museum, 7.

24. Letter from Margaret V. Bennett to the White House, January 3, 1951, Harry S. Truman Papers, Official Files, Miscellaneous Reconstruction Folder, Harry S. Truman Library and Museum.

25. Anthony Leviero, "Truman Takes Job as Sidewalk Boss," *New York Times*, January 16, 1950.

26. "Anyone Can Buy a Part of the Old White House," *New York Times*, January 13, 1951.

27. "White House Souvenirs to Cost 25 Cents to $100," *Washington Post*, January 13, 1951.

28. Built in 1905, the historic Wainwright Hall is today a hotel for visitors to the base. The site where the shed had been is now tennis courts.

29. Lehman, "They're Fixing Up Over at the Trumans'," 61; "White House Will Bury Debris to Foil Vendors."

30. "Disposition of Surplus Material," 103–5; "Form 2—Application for a Memento of the White House," Commission on the Renovation of the Executive Mansion, Harry S. Truman Library and Museum.

31. Lehman, "They're Fixing Up Over at the Trumans'," 36.

32. *Report of the Commission on the Renovation of the Executive Mansion*, 82.

33. This rare souvenir also turned out to be the most problematic. The sandstone bookends were Kit No. 13, priced at two dollars. Each of the matching blocks measured about four and a half inches square and two inches deep. Owing to Truman's unyielding defense of the White House's outer walls, it's probable that the sandstone originated from a secondary location (steps, possibly, or the old foundations that had lain belowground) or had been damaged in some manner beyond repair. But by May 1951, three months into the souvenir program, the commission had not made or shipped a single set of bookends because the masons had not selected which pieces of stone they were willing to surrender. (See press release concerning the progress of the souvenir distribution, May 18, 1951, Eben A. Ayers Papers, Harry S. Truman Library and Museum.) Bookend buyers were warned to expect a delay of seventy-five days. Then, come August, the commission discontinued the item entirely.

34. Some kits came with small variations in contents, and this figure is the sum of the distribution figures for Kit Nos. 4-A and 4-B. Kit No. 4 was, however, far and away the most popular of the lot, beating out orders of the second-most-popular, Kit No. 1, by some 860 orders. See the fifth and final report concerning the disposition of surplus material, June 30, 1952, Commission on the Renovation of the Executive Mansion, Harry S. Truman Library and Museum.

35. Not only was there nothing illegal about White House debris changing hands behind the scenes; the commission had actually set aside a portion of the souvenirs for congressmen to use as they saw fit. See "White House Souvenirs to Cost 25 Cents to $100." The commission tried to be up front about these transactions, admitting that "special kits" had been offered to "persons who had a close relationship to the renovation project." But this description lay buried in the fine print of the final report. See "Disposition of Surplus Material," 104.

36. Minutes of the Commission on the Renovation of the Executive Mansion, January 26, 1951, Harry S. Truman Library and Museum, 14–15.

37. Dorothy McCardle, "Acheson Heads the Ranks of White House Collectors," *Washington Post*, May 18, 1952.

38. Letter from Donald Dawson to Elenore Dmitrieff, April 5, 1951, Harry S. Truman Papers, White House Central Files, White House Renovation Folder, Harry S. Truman Library and Museum.

39. There's no way to be certain that this was the very same brick that Winslow had found, but it is at least a good possibility. See Cross Reference Sheet filed under Gillette, D. H., Assistant Executive Director, Commission on the Renovation of the Executive Mansion, January 12, 1951, Vertical File, White House Renovation, Harry S. Truman Library and Museum.

40. The group was the Bemidji Civic & Commerce Association. Letter from Les Flewelling to the Honorable Hubert Humphrey, April 7, 1949; letter from Hubert Humphrey to Matthew J. Connelly, May 24, 1949, Harry S. Truman Papers, Official Files, Harry S. Truman Library and Museum.

41. Letter from Walter S. Baring to Matthew Connelly, May 6, 1949, Harry S. Truman Papers, Official Files, Harry S. Truman Library and Museum.

42. Letter from Lorenzo Winslow to Matthew Connelly, June 7, 1949; letter from Lorenzo Winslow to Congressman Harold C. Hagen, April 5, 1949, Harry S. Truman Papers, Official Files, Harry S. Truman Library and Museum.

43. Robert J. Donovan, *Tumultuous Years* (New York: W. W. Norton, 1982), 114–15.

44. David McCullough, *Truman* (New York: Simon & Schuster, 1992), 745.

45. Letter from Mary Ball, office of Clare Magee, to Harry H. Vaughan, August 22, 1951; letter from Harry H. Vaughan to Mary Ball, September 28, 1951; letter from Mary Ball to Harry H. Vaughan, October 2, 1951, Harry S. Truman Papers, Official Files, Harry S. Truman Library and Museum.

46. Hersey, *Aspects of the Presidency*, 109.

47. Oral History Interview with Robert B. Landry, conducted by Hugh A. Ahmann, March 1–2, 1983, §273–74, Harry S. Truman Library and Museum.

48. Quotes here are from Hersey, *Aspects of the Presidency*, 109.

49. Apparently, the commission had initially earmarked the mantel from Margaret's sitting room for shipment to Truman's presidential library, but Truman indicated his wish for the Buffalo Mantel instead. "Memorandum for Mr. Hop-

kins," November 16, 1951, Papers of Harry S. Truman, President's Secretary's Files, Harry S. Truman Library and Museum.

50. Alonzo Fields, *My 21 Years in the White House* (New York: Coward-McCann, 1960), 166, 180.

51. Letter from Lorenzo Winslow to William Adams Delano, April 5, 1950, Commission on the Renovation of the Executive Mansion, Delano Files, Harry S. Truman Library and Museum.

52. Joe Lastelic, "New Buffalo Mantel Ready at White House," *Kansas City Times*, June 30, 1962.

53. Letter from Harry S. Truman to Leslie M. Beals, December 6, 1962, Harry S. Truman Papers, Post-Presidential Files, Harry S. Truman Library and Museum.

54. The memo was dated November 16, 1951, and ordered that the mantel, which had already been placed in storage, be "reserved" for the president. See "Memorandum for Mr. Hopkins," November 16, 1951, Harry S. Truman Papers, President's Secretary's Files, Harry S. Truman Library and Museum.

55. Letter from Gen. Glen Edgerton to Lenna Petty Jenkins, United Daughters of the Confederacy, July 30, 1951, Commission on the Renovation of the Executive Mansion, Harry S. Truman Library and Museum; *Report of the Commission on the Renovation of the Executive Mansion*, 104.

56. In May of 1950, the commission would send a form to every member of Congress, asking each legislator to list any museums, libraries, churches, and civic organizations in his district that both would be deserving of a piece of the mansion—"and would pay handling and transportation costs." Edgerton added these names to a large list and began sending his letters to one institution at a time. See "Disposition of Surplus Material from the White House," memo from the Commission on the Renovation of the Executive Mansion to members of Congress, May 1, 1950, Commission on the Renovation of the Executive Mansion, Harry S. Truman Library and Museum.

57. The commission minutes did not mention this Philadelphia Museum of Art director by name, but it made the message clear: "The Director of that museum had vigorously expressed the opinion some time ago that museums would not be interested in obtaining any of the surplus material from the White House." See Minutes of the Commission on the Renovation of the Executive Mansion, November 29, 1950, Harry S. Truman Library and Museum, 8.

58. "Portions of the old plaster ornament were offered," the commission noted, "but little of the ornament was requested." See "Disposition of Surplus Material," 104; fifth and final report concerning the disposition of surplus material, June 30, 1952, Commission on the Renovation of the Executive Mansion, Harry S. Truman Library and Museum.

59. Minutes of the Commission on the Renovation of the Executive Mansion, August 6, 1952, Harry S. Truman Library and Museum, 4. Even the Smithsonian, that attic of national ephemera, agreed to add just four mantels to its permanent collection; the other five went into the loaner program. Eventually, two of those would be installed at Blair House.

60. Many of the mantels the commission was trying to give away dated from the 1902 renovation. But this was 1951, and those pieces were just forty-nine years old—very likely younger than most of the curators considering whether to accept them into their collections. See letter from Gen. Glen Edgerton to E. R. Hunter, December 26, 1951, Commission on the Renovation of the Executive Mansion, Harry S. Truman Library and Museum.

61. Letter from Gen. Glen Edgerton to Lenna Petty Jenkins.

62. McShain's jackhammers had smashed many of the bricks to pieces, and in the end there were only 200,000 to give away. See Minutes of the Commission on the Renovation of the Executive Mansion, June 20, 1950, Harry S. Truman Museum and Library, 2–3. The 2 percent figure does not include the bricks that were sold as part of Kit No. 11—enough bricks to make a fireplace. There's no telling how many bricks such a kit included, but only sixty-three of them were sold anyway.

63. Minutes of the Commission on the Renovation of the Executive Mansion, August 3, 1951, Harry S. Truman Library and Museum, 16.

64. Author's interview with Simone Monteleone, February 5, 2012.

65. A fairly complete accounting of the dispersal of all Class II material appears in "Disposition of Surplus Material," 104.

66. Author's interview with Sister Pauline McShain, December 13, 2011.

20. "EVERY DOLLAR MUST BE SAVED"

1. The Army-Navy game incident, including McShain's claim of its having only been a joke, is drawn from the minutes of the Commission on the Renovation of the Executive Mansion, January 9, 1951, Harry S. Truman Library and Museum, Independence, Missouri.

2. Letter to W. E. Reynolds from John McShain, November 24, 1950, John McShain Papers, box 61, folder 3, Hagley Museum and Library, Wilmington, Delaware.

3. Philip H. Melanson, *The Secret Service: The Hidden History of an Enigmatic Agency* (New York: Barnes & Noble Books, 2004), 141.

4. Robert H. Ferrell, ed., *Off the Record: The Private Papers of Harry S. Truman* (New York: Harper & Row, 1980), 243.

5. "Lack of drawings has seriously delayed work," Edgerton noted that January. See Gen. Glen Edgerton, "Diary of Progress of the Renovation and Remodeling of the Executive Mansion," Office of History, U.S. Army Corps of Engineers, entry for January 8, 1951.

6. Photo (credit and date unknown) of Haight's presentation. See Douglas W. Orr Papers, MSS. 128, New Haven Museum & Historical Society Library; Minutes of the Commission on the Renovation of the Executive Mansion, February 28, 1951, Harry S. Truman Library and Museum, 6.

7. Richard E. Dougherty, "Interior Decoration and Furnishings at the White House," *Club Dial*, February 1953, 15.

8. Alonzo Fields, *My 21 Years in the White House* (New York: Coward-McCann, 1960), 166.

9. "The President and Mrs. Truman had indicated their preference for the painted finish." See Minutes of the Commission on the Renovation of the Executive Mansion, April 9, 1951, Harry S. Truman Library and Museum, 4.

10. Haight had presented his sketches on February 28, 1951, at which time the Trumans gave their nod. This final vote took place on April 26. Before the painters pried the lids off the paint cans, they slapped a coat of clear shellac on the old oak panels. It would make the paint quick and easy to remove—just in case a future administration changed its mind. See Lucia Brown, "White House Designers Saved Posterity Plenty of Headaches," *Washington Post*, April 9, 1952.

11. "Changes in Retrospect: Harrisburg's Jim Novinger Keeps Active Following a Notable Career," *Construction Dimensions*, August 1978, 28.

12. The men had hammered through the 1902 ceiling in the main hall and discovered the 1817 ceiling entombed above it, its gold trim still glinting in the shadows. The discovery left Truman "delighted," according to West. See J. B.

West, with Mary Lynn Kotz, *Upstairs at the White House: My Life with the First Ladies* (New York: Coward, McCann & Geoghegan, 1973), 108. Abbie Rowe would capture this incredible find in photo no. 58-531-086, Harry S. Truman Library and Museum.

13. West, *Upstairs at the White House*, 108–9.

14. Typewritten draft of an untitled speech by Douglas Orr ("Mr. Chairman and Delegates to Council . . ."), Douglas W. Orr Papers, MSS. 128, box 2, folder J, New Haven Museum & Historical Society Library, 10.

15. "What's Behind Plaster Design," *Christian Science Monitor*, July 28, 1950; "White House Exterior Is Only a Cover for Stripped Interior," *Washington Post*, July 12, 1950. Sometimes Winslow intervened beforehand to simplify the designs that had been taken down, modifying the lavish vines and cartouches of McKim's Renaissance fever dreams to be, as Orr put it, more "American in feeling"—whatever that meant.

16. William J. Moyer, "The Man Behind the White House Remodel," *Washington Sunday Star Pictoral Magazine*, December 16, 1951, 15.

17. Ruth Gmeiner, "Trumans Study White House Colors, President's Shower to Be Blue-Green," *New York World-Telegram and Sun*, May 25, 1951.

18. The debate circled around and around, until Finley finally decided to give his approval of the basket pattern so long as some gold thread was added to it. See Minutes of the Commission on the Renovation of the Executive Mansion, June 19, 1951, and June 29, 1951, Harry S. Truman Library and Museum, 7–8 and 7, respectively.

19. "'Grin,' Little Girl Orders, and the President Obeys," *New York Times*, June 21, 1951.

20. Letter from Douglas Orr to President Truman, June 13, 1951, Harry S. Truman Papers, White House Permanent Files, Harry S. Truman Library and Museum; third progress report to President Truman from the Commission on the Renovation of the Executive Mansion, September 6, 1951, Harry S. Truman Papers, President's Secretary's Files, Harry S. Truman Library and Museum, 2.

21. This amount reflected the total bill for all of the White House's interior stone, which also included slate, granite, and limestone, but Rowe's photos make clear that marble was the stone they used the most of.

22. Milton Lehman, "They're Fixing Up Over at the Trumans'," *Collier's*, October 28, 1950, 37.

23. This amount—$2,995 to be precise—represented the bid amount for both the automatic can washer and the Morse-Boulger incinerator.

24. The Zero Weather Stripping Company would supply "insect screens" for three thousand dollars. See "Contracts and Subcontracts," Appendix 7, *Report of the Commission on the Renovation of the Executive Mansion* (Washington, D.C.: U.S. Government Printing Office, 1952), 102.

25. William Seale, *The President's House: A History*, vol. 2 (Washington, D.C.: White House Historical Association, 1986), 1027.

26. Minutes of the Commission on the Renovation of the Executive Mansion, June 19, 1951, Harry S. Truman Library and Museum, 3–4.

27. Letter from Douglas Orr to President Truman, June 13, 1951, Harry S. Truman Papers, White House Permanent Files, Harry S. Truman Library and Museum.

28. Minutes of the Commission on the Renovation of the Executive Mansion, July 17, 1951, Harry S. Truman Library and Museum, 6.

29. Minutes of the Commission on the Renovation of the Executive Mansion, January 26, 1951, Harry S. Truman Library and Museum, 10.

30. Third progress report to President Truman from the Commission on the Renovation of the Executive Mansion, September 6, 1951, Harry S. Truman Papers, President's Secretary's Files, Harry S. Truman Library and Museum, 3.

31. Minutes of the Commission on the Renovation of the Executive Mansion, June 4, 1951, Harry S. Truman Library and Museum, 5. Crim had already won the battle for the ice-cream machine the previous month: "Matter of ice-cream maker comes up," Edgerton had noted in his diary for March 3, "and Mr. Crim says it must be installed."

32. Minutes of the Commission on the Renovation of the Executive Mansion, June 19, 1951, Harry S. Truman Library and Museum, 12.

21. THE GENERAL'S BURDENS

1. J. B. West, with Mary Lynn Kotz, *Upstairs at the White House: My Life with the First Ladies* (New York: Coward, McCann & Geoghegan, 1973), 120.

2. Dorothea Andrews, "White House Architect Plans to Replace Entire 2nd Floor," *Washington Post*, September 30, 1948.

3. Bryant was speaking in particular of "the vast networking of tunnels and cableways under the White House," which gave the rats boundless nesting area. See Traphes Bryant, with Frances Spatz Leighton, *Dog Days at the White House: The Outrageous Memoirs of the Presidential Kennel Keeper* (New York: Macmillan, 1975), 81.

4. Handwritten note from usher Crim to William J. Hopkins, executive clerk, September 4, 1951, White House Permanent Files, Harry S. Truman Library and Museum, Independence, Missouri.

5. Minutes of the Commission on the Renovation of the Executive Mansion, August 17, 1951, Harry S. Truman Library and Museum, 4–5.

6. "White House Repair Costs Rise," *New York Times*, August 18, 1951.

7. David McCullough, *Truman* (New York: Simon & Schuster, 1992), 837.

8. West, *Upstairs at the White House*, 120.

9. "White House Not Palatial, Senators Told," *Washington Post*, October 8, 1951.

10. "Unusual Jobs Were His Usual Assignments," *K-Stater*, February 1995, 42.

11. Ibid., 42–43.

12. Gen. Glen E. Edgerton "Diary of Progress of the Renovation and Remodeling of the Executive Mansion," Office of History, U.S. Army Corps of Engineers, entries for February 21 and March 12, 1951. Edgerton noted the discussion of a "snow melting proposal" during his 10:00 A.M. meeting on the latter day. Sadly, he gave no further details.

13. Frederick Gutheim, "Rebuilding the White House," *Architectural Record*, June 1949, 182.

14. The play, a hit, was written in 1975 by Samuel Gallu. See "Glen Edgar Edgerton," *Assembly* (West Point magazine), December 1978, 107.

15. Edgerton, "Diary of Progress of the Renovation and Remodeling of the Executive Mansion," entries for March 29 and April 3 and 4, 1951.

16. Ibid., entries for July 11 and 17, 1951.

17. "Inasmuch as these delays were beyond the General Contractor's control," the contractor wrote to the commission, "it is requested that the completion

date of our contract be extended." Letter from John McShain to the General Services Administration, September 8, 1951, John McShain Papers, box 61, folder 3, Hagley Museum and Library, Wilmington, Delaware.

18. Carl M. Brauer, *The Man Who Built Washington: A Life of John McShain* (Wilmington, DE: Hagley Museum and Library, 1996), 102.

19. Ibid., 122.

20. The photo used for this vignette is no. 71-573, November 28, 1951, Harry S. Truman Library and Museum.

21. Author's interview with Sister Pauline McShain, December 13, 2011.

22. Because the commission did not break out the cost of the marble from other types of interior stone in its final accounting, the only figure available is the $247,000 final cost for the category of "Interior Stone and Marble." However, marble was the predominating stone for the interior, and so the comparison is apt enough. See Appendix 6, *Report of the Commission on the Renovation of the Executive Mansion* (Washington, D.C.: U.S. Government Printing Office, 1952), 101.

23. The exact wording from the minutes of the meeting: "Mr. Hauck said he wished to submit to the Commission the seriousness of being too critical of some of the colors of the marble." Minutes of the Commission on the Renovation of the Executive Mansion, September 21, 1951, Harry S. Truman Library and Museum, 5.

24. Ibid.

25. For a while, the commissioners toyed with the idea of firing Hasbrouck and just hiring another contractor. But the next-highest bid would force the commission to cough up another sixty thousand dollars, and there was no money left for that. Hasbrouck would have to do the job somehow.

26. "White House Social Life Still Can't Be Resumed," *New York Times*, October 3, 1951.

27. Elizabeth Maguire, "First Family Plans Thanksgiving in Florida," *Washington Post*, November 14, 1951.

28. Bess Furman, "Symbol Going Back into White House," *New York Times*, October 24, 1951; "White House Wired Again by Same Firm," *Washington Post*, November 11, 1951.

29. William Seale, *The President's House: A History*, vol. 2 (Washington, D.C.: White House Historical Association, 1996), 1044–45.

30. Bess Furman, "The New-Old White House," *New York Times*, October 21, 1951.

31. Betty C. Monkman, *The White House: Its Historic Furnishings and First Families* (New York: Abbeville Press, 2000), 233.

32. The article also noted that a handful of "kind friends" had made some donations to the house. Had the commission decided to actually solicit donations, their number would have been much greater and the interiors the better for it. See Marie McNair, "Space Planning Adds Six Rooms for VIPs," *Washington Post*, October 21, 1951.

33. Minutes of the Commission on the Renovation of the Executive Mansion, of February 28, 1951, Harry S. Truman Library and Museum, 8.

34. Furman, "The New-Old White House"; McNair, "Space Planning Adds Six Rooms for VIPs."

35. To govern the aesthetic decisions about the interiors, the commission established a chain of command. Haight would work under General Edgerton's supervision, "in consultation" with the First Family via usher Crim. Orr and Delano were to be given final say. Nevertheless, as the case with the State Dining Room made clear, the Trumans had a say in the State Floor decorating, too. See Minutes of the Commission on the Renovation of the Executive Mansion, December 19, 1950, and January 9, 1951, Harry S. Truman Library and Museum, 5 and 11, respectively. Monkman, *The White House*, 220; Seale, *The President's House*, vol. 1, 96–97.

36. Oral History Interview with General Jess Larson, conducted by Jerry N. Hess, May 26, 1967, §18–19, Harry S. Truman Library and Museum.

37. Apparently this did not mean that the foyer would have no lantern, but the old piece would be going back up in same shape it had been taken down. This was the plan, anyway, until Truman intervened at the last moment and substituted a chandelier that he liked from the second floor. See "Memorandum for Mr. Hopkins" from General Edgerton, November 16, 1952, Harry S. Truman Papers, President's Secretary's Files, Harry S. Truman Library and Museum; Seale, *The President's House*, vol. 2, 1049.

38. "White House Staff Given Pictures of Blair House," *Washington Post*, December 23, 1951.

22. MISSING PIECES

1. Photographs, GSA Building, Seventh and D SW-001, -002, and -003, District of Columbia Public Library, Washingtoniana Division.

2. The removal of the interiors had taken place between December 13, 1949, and March 23, 1950. Commission chairman Kenneth McKellar had written to Truman on August 1, 1950, to tell him that the old interiors that Winslow had removed from the State Floor were snug in the warehouse: "paneling, trim, mantels, doors and the like." See letter from Senator Kenneth McKellar to President Truman, August 1, 1950, Harry S. Truman Papers, President's Secretary's Files, Harry S. Truman Library and Museum, Independence, Missouri.

3. The paneling that Charles Follen McKim had put in the East Room and the State Dining Room during the 1902 renovations was the work of the New York firm of Herter Brothers, whose long client list included the Guggenheims, the Vanderbilts, and Manhattan's legendary St. Regis Hotel.

4. William Seale, *The President's House: A History*, vol. 2 (Washington, D.C.: White House Historical Association, 1986), 1034.

5. Ibid., 1027.

6. Bess Furman, "White House Work Bars 'Per Centers,'" *New York Times*, August 10, 1949.

7. Typewritten draft of an untitled speech by Douglas Orr ("Mr. Chairman and Delegates to Council . . ."), Douglas W. Orr Papers, MSS. 128, box 2, folder J, New Haven Museum & Historical Society Library, 6.

8. Letter to the Speaker of the House from Commission on the Renovation of the Executive Mansion's chairman, Senator Kenneth McKellar, July 3, 1950, Harry S. Truman Papers, President's Secretary's Files, Harry S. Truman Library and Museum. Shortly after this letter, the commission reported to Truman that McShain's men had completed "the dismantling, packing and storing the interior trim, paneling mantels, doors, decorations, and other similar fixtures [that are] likely to be required for re-use." See second progress report to President Truman from the Commission on the Renovation of the Executive Mansion, August 1, 1950, Harry S. Truman Papers, President's Secretary's Files, Harry S. Truman Library and Museum, 6–7.

9. "White House Will Bury Debris to Foil Vendors," *New York Times*, February 7, 1950; caption of Associated Press wire photo WX17, July 11, 1950, author's collection.

10. It's uncertain if this article ever saw publication, but it was clearly intended for same, and Louchheim was well connected enough among the city's powerful Democrats to have some basis for her assertions. See Katie Louchheim, "The Authentic Restoration," uncited manuscript, White House Vertical File, Harry S. Truman Library and Museum, 2–4.

11. Historian David McCullough has written that items including door frames

and chair rails wound up being hauled away to Forts Myer and Belvoir to be reused as construction material; "a large part" of the interiors wound up "as landfill." See David McCullough, *Truman* (New York: Simon & Schuster, 1992), 880.

12. Oral History Interview with General Jess Larson, conducted by Jerry N. Hess, May 26, 1967, §16, Harry S. Truman Library and Museum.

13. Author's interview with Sister Pauline McShain, December 13, 2011.

14. J. B. West, with Mary Lynn Kotz, *Upstairs at the White House: My Life with the First Ladies* (New York: Coward, McCann & Geoghegan, 1973), 120.

15. Letter from Harry Truman to John McShain, March 16, 1961, Harry S. Truman Papers, Post-Presidential Files, Harry S. Truman Library and Museum. There is an irony here. Truman often preached about the importance of reading history so as not to repeat its mistakes. And he often condemned Charles Follen McKim's 1902 renovation of the White House for Theodore Roosevelt as a "botched job." (See letter from President Truman to Henry C. Smith, July 6, 1949, Harry S. Truman Papers, President's Secretary's Files, Harry S. Truman Library and Museum.) But it wasn't McKim who botched the job; it was Roosevelt. He botched it by failing to give his architect's men enough time to complete a monumentally important task properly. McKim wrote to a friend about Roosevelt's merciless deadline: "With only 90 days ahead of us to get through at least six months work, it is hard to keep from getting rattled." (See Leland M. Roth, *McKim, Mead & White, Architects* [New York: Harper & Row, 1983], 269.) Truman permitted far more time for the job than Theodore Roosevelt had, but he was also repeating Roosevelt's error.

16. According to Douglas Orr's final renovation chronology, the "interior cabinet work" was under way by July 17, 1951, half complete by September 6, and proceeding on the third floor by September 21—which also happens to be the very same day that Winslow agreed to surrender vast quantities of salvaged woodwork, which promptly disappeared.

17. On January 26, 1951, the commission and Knipp agreed on a fee of $281,135 for the "Cabinet & Millworking" subcontract. See third progress report to President Truman from the Commission on the Renovation of the Executive Mansion, September 6, 1951, Harry S. Truman Papers, President's Secretary's Files, Harry S. Truman Library and Museum, 4.

18. The record is unclear as to just how much of the old material went up to Baltimore in total. Edgerton noted on January 17, 1951, that "Knipp hauls another load of lumber to Baltimore," and he gave the figure quoted herein (a board foot is a unit of measurement for lumber that denotes a square footage

area and a thickness of one inch). At the commission meeting on January 26, General Services Administration project manager William Kelley told the commissioners that the material hauled up to Knipp's workshop "includes the State Dining room paneling, doors, etc., as well as the old pine for the ground floor. Shop drawings are now being prepared." See Minutes of the Commission on the Renovation of the Executive Mansion, January 26, 1951, Harry S. Truman Library and Museum, 4.

19. Franklin Knipp had filled his shop with old-world craftsmen who possessed "the skill and patience native sons too often lack for this slow, careful work," one journalist would observe about the firm's restoration of the Rotunda at the University of Virginia, designed by Thomas Jefferson. See Mary H. Cadwalader, "Jefferson's Rotunda: A Classic Restored," *Baltimore Sun*, April 11, 1976.

20. Minutes of the Commission on the Renovation of the Executive Mansion, February 16, 1951, and April 9, 1951, Harry S. Truman Library and Museum, 2 and 7, respectively.

21. Come summer, Edgerton would note continuing delays regarding this time-consuming aspect of the woodwork: "Glazing old sash but have to stop because sash have [sic] not been repaired sufficiently." See Gen. Glen E. Edgerton, "Diary of Progress of the Renovation and Remodeling of the Executive Mansion," Office of History, U.S. Army Corps of Engineers, entry for July 27, 1951.

22. For example, Edgerton noted on July 24, 1951, that Knipp was making "sash replacement in windows."

23. One image in particular shows a worker "cleaning paint off repaired panels." See photo no. 71-510, Harry S. Truman Library and Museum.

24. West, *Upstairs at the White House*, 108. These pieces not only went to the warehouse down on D Street but also filled up much of the long storage shed built on the White House's South Lawn, as Rowe's photo taken on March 7, 1950, shows. See photo no. 71-215, Harry S. Truman Library and Museum.

25. Franklin Knipp would discuss this challenge in his letter to the *Baltimore Sun* of November 28, 1973.

26. Edgerton also complained of "seriously delayed work." See Edgerton, "Diary of Progress of the Renovation and Remodeling of the Executive Mansion," entries for January 8 and 9, 1951.

27. Anne Elizabeth Powell, "President's House," *Preservation*, May/June 1991, 21.

28. Seale, *The President's House*, vol. 2, 1033, 1044, 1049.

29. William P. O'Brien, "Reality and Illusion: The White House and Harry S. Truman," *White House History* 5 (Spring 1999): 12.

30. Minutes of the Commission on the Renovation of the Executive Mansion, September 21, 1951, Harry S. Truman Library and Museum, 9.

31. Seale, *The President's House*, vol. 2, 1046; Powell, "President's House," 26, 30. In addition, as Parks Department historian William P. O'Brien has written, "At the end, in a rush to complete the project before the end of the president's administration, many of the rescued moldings, doors, and other interior ornaments were . . . hauled to dumps." See O'Brien, "Reality and Illusion," 12.

32. According to Seale, "Nearly everything [was] hauled away as landfill in 1951." See Seale, *The President's House*, vol. 2, 1046, 1140, n43.

33. "Disposition of Surplus Material from the White House," Harry S. Truman Papers, President's Secretary's Files, Harry S. Truman Library and Museum, 1.

34. Letter to the Speaker of the House from Commission on the Renovation of the Executive Mansion's chairman, Senator Kenneth McKellar, July 3, 1950, Harry S. Truman Papers, President's Secretary's Files, Harry S. Truman Library and Museum.

35. Since the law permitted the commission to classify anything that had come out of the mansion as it pleased—from Class I "important articles" on down to Class IV "disintegrated, broken, or perishable material"—disposing of Winslow's warehoused interiors would have been an easy matter of declaring a piece unfit, downgrading it to a lower tier, and then disposing of it accordingly. See Powell, "President's House," 26, 30; Seale, *The President's House*, vol. 2, 1044.

36. See "Disposition of Surplus Material," Appendix 9, *Report of the Commission on the Renovation of the Executive Mansion* (Washington, D.C.: U.S. Government Printing Office, 1952), 104; Sean Holton, "White House Is in Washington, Right? Or Is It?" *Orlando Sentinel*, March 26, 1994.

37. Henry Scarupa, "Clement Conger: Curator in the White House 'Kitchen,'" *Baltimore Sun's Sun Magazine*, November 4, 1973, 19.

38. "Disposition of Surplus Material," 105.

39. Author's interview with Kim Holien, February 7, 2012.

40. *Report of the Commission on the Renovation of the Executive Mansion*, 80.

41. On May 16, 1950, Winslow clocked off at noon, took his paramour out to lunch, then drove up to Baltimore to buy a new tire. His diary reflects that he did some shopping and then headed home for dinner. Diary of Lorenzo Winslow, May 16, 1950, Office of the Curator, the White House.

42. Diary of Lorenzo Winslow, July 2–7, 1950.

43. Seale, *The President's House*, vol. 2, 1049.

44. Diary of Lorenzo Winslow, June 25 and August 5, 1950. The Ouija board reference appears in Seale, *The President's House*, vol. 2, 1047.

45. Diary of Lorenzo Winslow, July 29 and August 5, 1950.

46. Scarupa, "Clement Conger," 140.

47. The preceding quote and the subsequent one are taken from Franklin Knipp's letter to the editor of *Sun Magazine*, November 28, 1973, White House Vertical File, Harry S. Truman Library and Museum.

48. Holton, "White House Is in Washington, Right?"

49. The piece had wound up in the lot of mantels given to the Smithsonian, which packed this one into a huge wooden crate labeled "White House." After its discovery, the mantel would become part of a 1989 exhibit at the Smithsonian and then permanently installed in the museum's Ceremonial Court with money donated by Sears. See "FDR Mantelpiece Enshrined," *Kansas City Star*, April 6, 1989.

50. Powell, "President's House," 21.

51. "White House Storage Material," May 13, 1952, Records of the Commission on the Renovation of the Executive Mansion, Harry S. Truman Library and Museum.

23. "A RACE AGAINST TIME"

1. Meticulous as always, Edgerton had taken it upon himself to measure the moisture content of Hasbrouck's subflooring and discovered it to be 100 percent: Hasbrouck had been shipping green lumber. If the moist sleepers were left in place, the parquet on top would eventually buckle and pop out like domino tiles. (See Gen. Glen Edgerton, "Diary of Progress of the Renovation and Remodeling of the Execution Mansion," Office of History, U.S. Army Corps of Engineers, entry for October 12, 1951). Edgerton ordered Hasbrouck

to pry up his flooring and dry it—in a kiln if necessary. See Minutes of the Commission on the Renovation of the Executive Mansion, October 19, 1951, Harry S. Truman Library and Museum, Independence, Missouri, 2–3. Even when Hasbrouck began laying his hardwood again at the end of November, Edgerton noticed that he had only two men on the payroll. "Not enough floor layers," the general lamented, "shortage of floor layers on job." (See Edgerton, "Diary of Progress of the Renovation and Remodeling of the Executive Mansion," entries for November 20, December 10, and December 17, 1951.)

2. Sarah Lundy, "M. Jochum, Redecorated White House," uncited newspaper clipping, Peggy Watts Papers, Harry S. Truman Library and Museum.

3. Truman would later describe in his diary what one of his average mornings had come to be like for him and Bess—or, as he often called her, "the Boss": "The 'Boss' and I had breakfast at 8:30 and about 8:50 I went to the White House office. Since the assault [the assassination attempt] . . . I ride across the street in a car the roof of which will turn a grenade, the windows and sides turn a bullet and the floor will stop a land mine! Behind me in an open car ride six or seven men with automatics and machineguns. The uniformed police stop traffic in every direction." See Robert H. Ferrell, ed., *Off the Record: The Private Papers of Harry S. Truman* (New York: Harper & Row, 1980), 239–240.

4. Edward T. Folliard, "Vivid Colors Mark 'New' White House," *Washington Post*, October 21, 1951.

5. Letter from John McShain to President Truman, January 18, 1952, Harry S. Truman Papers, President's Secretary's Files, Harry S. Truman Library and Museum.

6. Ibid. Apart from McShain's reiteration, no transcript exists of this meeting (letter to the author from Truman Library archivist Randy Sowell, May 2, 2012). The media gave it a brief mention: "Truman Urges Speed-Up in White House Repairs," *New York Times*, January 26, 1952.

7. Letter from John McShain to President Truman, January 28, 1952, Harry S. Truman Papers, President's Secretary's Files, Harry S. Truman Library and Museum.

8. Letter from John McShain to Senator McKellar, September 26, 1952, Harry S. Truman Papers, Official Files, Harry S. Truman Library and Museum.

9. Letter from John McShain to President Truman, January 28, 1952, Harry S. Truman Papers, President's Secretary's Files, Harry S. Truman Library and Museum.

10. Letter from President Truman to John McShain, January 30, 1952, John McShain Papers, box 159, folder 10, Hagley Museum and Library, Wilmington, Delaware.

11. Minutes of the Commission on the Renovation of the Executive Mansion, January 8, 1952, Harry S. Truman Library and Museum, 9.

12. Indeed, McShain had already begun to pay overtime out of his own pocket even before Truman moved the deadline to April 2. According to the commission's minutes, "The McShain Company has authorized and is paying for overtime work the past two Saturdays." See Minutes of the Commission on the Renovation of the Executive Mansion, January 25, 1952, Harry S. Truman Library and Museum, 3.

13. Letter from John McShain to President Truman, January 28, 1952, Harry S. Truman Papers, President's Secretary's Files, Harry S. Truman Library and Museum.

14. "Up to the time I started to supervise the building our record for a concrete pour in one day was 2,250 [cubic] yards," McShain would later write. "The day before Mr. Hauck returned to the job we poured 2,875 yards—a record that stood for the balance of the construction." See unpublished memoirs of John McShain, John McShain Papers, box 159, folder 3, Hagley Museum and Library, 14.

15. V. R. Montanari, "McShain's a Push-Over for Steam Shovels," *Washington Post*, May 16, 1950.

16. John Gerrity, "He Changed the Face of Washington," *Nation's Business*, January 1952, 62.

17. William Kelley of the Public Buildings Administration read McShain's letter into the minutes. "The contractor, Mr. John McShain," he began, "has instructed all subcontractors to conform to a schedule prepared by him." See Minutes of the Commission on the Renovation of the Executive Mansion, February 5, 1952, Harry S. Truman Library and Museum, 2. McShain had not only set new deadlines for all the remaining work—painting, flooring, electrical, mechanical, exterior stone, cleanup—he'd also submitted a progress schedule that subdivided his plan according to floor. The new deadlines stretched like a tight membrane across the months of February and March, starting with the third-floor work and proceeding down through the house. McShain slated the third floor's parquet and painting for completion first. It would allow Charles Haight and Peggy Watts to start hanging curtains the same day, and also trigger B. Altman's own five-week decorating time line for the house. By timing the deadlines according to descending order of the floors, McShain maximized the time that parquet and woodworking subcontractors could devote to the state rooms, where the demand for craftsmanship was at its greatest. McShain's order of business overlooked no exigency. By ordering the painters to finish the third floor by February 6 and slating B. Altman's decorating work to start two days later, for example, McShain had factored in the time needed to let the paint dry.

18. These quotes are the reporters' paraphrases of what Truman said, but they are as close as we have. As John Hersey explained in the foreword to his book *Aspects of the Presidency*, there was "a flat rule of those days which constrained the press from quoting the President directly on any matter." See Merriman Smith, "President Eager for a Bath in 'Solid' White House Tub," *Spokane Daily Chronicle*, February 7, 1952; "White House Work Gains; April Opening Held Likely," *New York Times*, February 17, 1952.

19. "White House Work Gains."

20. Truman would make these comments to a television audience the day after his visit to the Kennedys in January 1961. McShain happened to see the former president still slinging mud at his company and wrote a letter requesting the former president to set the record straight. Truman replied with a note that, while not an apology, did tell McShain that "your reputation, which has always been excellent, is not the point at issue and should not be questioned." Letter from John McShain to Harry S. Truman, January 24, 1961, and letter from Harry S. Truman to John McShain, March 16, 1961, Harry S. Truman Papers, Post-Presidential Files, Harry S. Truman Library and Museum.

21. The minutes of the February 5, 1952, meeting reveal that McShain essentially bought the assurances of his subcontractors' adherence to his schedule with the promise of overtime.

22. The plaque was a stone tablet engraved with the names of the twenty-two men central to the renovation effort. Letter from John McShain to Senator McKellar, September 26, 1952. Senator McKellar declined McShain's offer of the thirty thousand dollars for overtime work.

23. Historian Carl Brauer points out that this figure—McShain's own—was likely exaggerated. Even so, there can be no doubt that McShain went above and beyond what he'd been legally stipulated to do on the White House job. See Carl M. Brauer, *The Man Who Built Washington* (Wilmington, DE: Hagley Museum and Library, 1996), 123.

24. Author's interview with Sister Pauline McShain, December 13, 2011.

25. "He wanted to go home," Pauline McShain recalls, "but the White House was everything to him. He spent a lot of time at the Hay-Adams." Ibid.

26. Letter from John McShain to President Truman, October 17, 1952, Harry S. Truman Papers, Official Files, Harry S. Truman Library and Museum.

27. "'Moving Day' at White House Hints Trumans' Early Return," *Washington Post*, March 14, 1952.

28. Letter from John McShain to President Truman, February 15, 1952, Harry S. Truman Papers, President's Secretary's Files, Harry S. Truman Library and Museum. Despite the ironclad schedule, some of the deadlines—specifically those for the flooring and interior woodwork—did creep back by a couple of days. See Minutes of the Commission on the Renovation of the Executive Mansion, February 18, 1952, Harry S. Truman Library and Museum, 2.

29. Letter from President Truman to John McShain, February 18, 1952, John McShain Papers, box 159, folder 10, Hagley Museum and Library.

30. "Trumans Planning Receptions in May," *New York Times*, February 20, 1952.

31. The White House Social Office bluffed while it could, but, after her arrival, Queen Juliana herself revealed the entire plan. During her official toast to the president, she said, "We wanted to come and you wanted us to come . . . and you even wanted us to come to the White House in its new state." See "Toasts of the President and Queen Juliana," April 2, 1952, document 47, the Public Papers of the Presidents: Harry S. Truman, Harry S. Truman Library and Museum.

32. David McCullough, *Truman* (New York: Simon & Schuster, 1992), 511.

33. Edgerton, "Diary of Progress of Renovation and Remodeling of the Executive Mansion," entry for February 25, 1952.

34. Dorothy McCardle, "1600 Pennsylvania Avenue Gets Ready for Juliana, Trumans' Moving Day," *Washington Post*, March 9, 1952.

35. John McShain had already put the muscle on Haight personally and assured the commission "he is confident he can complete the installation." Letter from John McShain to President Truman, March 6, 1952, Harry S. Truman Papers, President's Secretary's Files, Harry S. Truman Library and Museum.

36. Margaret Truman, *Bess W. Truman* (New York: Macmillan, 1986), 382.

37. Margaret Truman, *First Ladies* (New York: Fawcett Books, 1995), 34.

38. J. B. West, with Mary Lynn Kotz, *Upstairs at the White House: My Life with the First Ladies* (New York: Coward, McCann & Geoghegan, 1973), 121.

39. Minutes of the Commission on the Renovation of the Executive Mansion, January 26, 1951, Harry S. Truman Library and Museum, 9.

40. West, *Upstairs at the White House*, 130.

41. Lillian Rogers Parks, with Frances Spatz Leighton, *My Thirty Years Backstairs at the White House* (New York: Fleet Publishing Co., 1961), 38.

42. Margaret Truman, *The President's House* (New York: Ballantine Books, 2003), 212.

43. "Several Saw Engraving on Bathtub," *Washington Post*, January 2, 1953.

24. OPEN HOUSE

1. Alonzo Fields, *My 21 Years in the White House* (New York: Coward-McCann, 1960), 166.

2. Ibid., 179.

3. There had been precious little room for engraving, but somehow Yale had managed to fit "Harry S. Truman, President of the United States of America" on one side and "The White House—1952" on the other.

4. Robert H. Ferrell, ed., *Off the Record: The Private Papers of Harry S. Truman* (New York, Harper & Row, 1980), 246.

5. Edward T. Folliard, "First Family Moves into White House," *Washington Post*, March 28, 1952.

6. "'Moving Day' at White House Hints Trumans' Early Return," *Washington Post*, March 14, 1952.

7. "Rebuilt White House Will Be Ready for 3-Day Stay of Juliana in April," *New York Times*, March 15, 1952.

8. Lillian Rogers Parks, with Frances Spatz Leighton, *My Thirty Years Backstairs at the White House* (New York: Fleet Publishing Co., 1961), 297.

9. J. B. West, with Mary Lynn Kotz, *Upstairs at the White House: My Life with the First Ladies* (New York: Coward, McCann & Geoghegan, 1973), 122.

10. Truman had already decided not to run, though he'd made no announcement as yet. He might have given it a shot, but ultimately he threw in the towel because of his wife. A few months earlier, Bess Truman told him flat out that another term would hurt her and kill him. "That warning shook dad to the depths of his soul," Margaret said. So it was that Harry Truman planned the end of his political career. See Margaret Truman, *Bess W. Truman* (New York: Macmillan, 1986), 381.

11. This exchange is taken from two very similar but separate accounts: West, *Upstairs at the White House*, 122; Jean Reiff, "1000 Officials and Wives Tour Reconstructed White House," *Washington Post*, March 24, 1952.

12. Telegram from Congressman Rabaut to President Truman, March 23, 1952, Harry S. Truman Papers, Official Files, Harry S. Truman Library and Museum, Independence, Missouri.

13. When the commissioners met formally in the East Wing, they noted that "a small amount of work remains to be done." See Minutes of the Commission on the Renovation of the Executive Mansion, March 27, 1952, Harry S. Truman Library and Museum, 2–3.

14. *Report of the Commission on the Renovation of the Executive Mansion* (Washington, D.C.: U.S. Government Printing Office, 1952), 70.

15. Fields, *My 21 Years in the White House*, 166, 180.

16. Lucia Brown, "White House Designers Saved Posterity Plenty of Headaches," *Washington Post*, April 9, 1952.

17. Merriman Smith, "Penthouse Solarium to Give White House a Tropical Touch," *Washington Post*, February 24, 1952.

18. Fields, *My 21 Years in the White House*, 166.

19. A Gallup Poll conducted between February 9 and 14, 1952, had yielded the 22 percent approval rating. By the time Truman was ready to leave office that December, the number would climb to 32 percent. See "Performance Ratings for President Truman, 1945–1952," Roper Center for Public Opinion Research, University of Connecticut at Storrs.

20. Ferrell, ed., *Off the Record*, 246.

21. Room counts are a rather slippery statistic when it comes to the White House, and many sources do not agree. White House historian William Seale places the mansion's aboveground figure at 54, but the author has chosen to use J. B. West's tally of 66 here. The total figure of 132 includes the basement rooms, and the number comes from the final report of the commission.

22. The quote is from an uncited article titled "Fit for a President," Peggy Watts Papers, Harry S. Truman Library and Museum.

23. Letter from President Truman to Douglas Orr, April 18, 1952, Douglas

W. Orr Papers, MSS. 128, box 1A, folder *S*, New Haven Museum & Historical Society Library.

24. Back in 1949, the renovation was supposed to have cost $5 million, even though Congress had wound up appropriating $5.4 million, a figure it bumped to $5.5 million just before the work began. When the commission had run out of cash late in 1951, Congress had kicked in another $261,000. That put the final tab at $5,761,000, a figure the tourist guides rounded to $5.8 million.

25. Margaret Truman, *Bess W. Truman*, 382.

26. Ferrell, ed., *Off the Record*, 246.

27. Letter from President Truman to Senator McKellar, March 28, 1952, Harry S. Truman Papers, Official Files, Harry S. Truman Library and Museum.

28. Letter from President Truman to Richard Dougherty, April 12, 1952, Harry S. Truman Papers, Official Files, Harry S. Truman Library and Museum.

29. The head was facing toward the talons clutching spears (the symbol of war) instead of those holding the olive branch. It would take a special executive order to get the seal repaired.

30. "It will take at least two months to find things," Truman wrote on his third day. "I don't know where my shirts, socks, neckties, underwear are packed. My study looks like an atomic explosion had taken place." See letter from President Truman to Charles Sawyer, March 30, 1952, Harry S. Truman Papers, President's Secretary's Files, Harry S. Truman Library and Museum.

31. Ferrell, ed., *Off the Record*, 256.

32. Henry Scarupa, "Clement Conger: Curator in the White House 'Kitchen,'" *Baltimore Sun*'s *Sun Magazine*, November 4, 1973, 14.

33. The man's name was Frederic N. Whitley, and his total pay was "not expected to exceed $500," according to the Minutes of the Commission on the Renovation of the Executive Mansion, July 19, 1950, Harry S. Truman Library and Museum, 10.

34. The incident regarding the fireplace is drawn from Margaret Truman, *Bess W. Truman*, 395.

35. Parks, *My Thirty Years Backstairs at the White House*, 36–38.

36. Ibid., 36, 310.

37. West, *Upstairs at the White House*, 121.

38. Margaret Truman, *Harry S. Truman* (New York: William Morrow, 1973), 538.

39. West, *Upstairs at the White House*, 122–23.

40. William P. O'Brien, "Reality and Illusion: The White House and Harry S. Truman," *White House History* 5 (Spring 1999): 4.

41. As Truman himself would later explain, "There was no question but that the interior was in danger of imminent collapse and it was not possible to consider an archeological restoration." See letter from Harry S. Truman to Stewart Alsop, November 3, 1965, Harry S. Truman Papers, Post-Presidential Files, Harry S. Truman Library and Museum.

42. Senator McKellar, the commission's chairman, addressed this point specifically in the memoirs he would write two years before his death. "It was necessary to rebuild and reconstruct the White House," he said, ". . . so as to have a building for the occupancy of our Presidents that would be entirely safe and have every modern convenience." See Kenneth Douglas McKellar, "Memoirs by Kenneth Douglas McKellar," unpublished manuscript, 1955, Benjamin L. Hooks Central Library, Memphis, Tennessee, 565.

43. This was the gospel that Lorenzo Winslow had learned in May 1949 during his visit to Colonial Williamsburg, where the Governor's Palace—burned to oblivion in 1781—had undergone a "faithful reconstruction" in 1934 and been accepted as the original. (See "Governor's Palace" at www.history.org.) Orr, too, seemed to believe that sincerity of intent was enough to forgive curatorial shortcomings. Aware that B. Altman had mixed together a casserole of the mansion's handful of historic furnishings with cheap, valueless knockoffs, Orr still praised Haight's interiors for having "given the remodeling an authenticity which was formerly lacking." (See letter from Douglas Orr to William Adams Delano, April 1952, William Adams Delano Papers, Avery Architectural & Fine Arts Library, Columbia University, New York.) Much of the public would have agreed. Georgetown socialite Katie Louchheim— praising what she called "this new-authentic White House"—thrilled to the idea that enthused that "future sightseers will have a difficult time detecting which plaster, panels and ceilings are new and which are old." Were she making this statement today, Louchheim might as well argue that plastic fruit is just as good as the real thing, so long as it's all arranged nicely in the serving bowl. See Katie Louchheim, "The Authentic Restoration," uncited manuscript, White House Vertical File, Harry S. Truman Library and Museum.

44. Alice Winchester, editorial, *The Magazine Antiques*, July 1952, 31.

EPILOGUE

1. Margaret Truman, *Bess W. Truman* (New York: Macmillan, 1986), 383.

2. Bess Furman, "Juliana and Bernhard Welcomed in Washington," *New York Times*, April 3, 1952.

3. "Toasts of the President and Queen Juliana," April 2, 1952, document 47, the Public Papers of the Presidents: Harry S. Truman, Harry S. Truman Library and Museum, Independence, Missouri.

4. Kenneth Douglas McKellar, "Memoirs by Kenneth Douglas McKellar," unpublished manuscript, 1955, Benjamin L. Hooks Central Library, Memphis, Tennessee, 569–70.

5. With the exception of two fine-print mentions buried in the book's appendixes, McShain's name was nowhere to be seen. It was as though the White House had renovated itself.

6. *Report of the Commission on the Renovation of the Executive Mansion* (Washington, D.C.: U.S. Government Printing Office, 1952), 55, 59, 65. As if to salt the wound further, the book also failed to acknowledge the gift of a beautiful desk that John McShain had given to President Truman, even as the other donations—invariably, ones received from the bluebloods of Georgetown and Park Avenue—received gracious nods.

7. Letter from John McShain to General Edgerton, October 6, 1952; letter from John McShain to President Truman c/o Matthew Connelly, October 17, 1952, Harry S. Truman Papers, Official Files, Harry S. Truman Library and Museum.

8. Letter from John McShain to President Truman, September 30, 1952, Harry S. Truman Papers, Official Files, Harry S. Truman Library and Museum.

9. Letter from John McShain to Senator McKellar, September 26, 1952, Harry S. Truman Papers, Official Files, Harry S. Truman Library and Museum.

10. Whoever had blackballed McShain had planned the maneuver well: Ten thousand volumes had already been printed and four hundred mailed out by the time McShain received his copy, creating the highly convenient excuse that it was too late to take corrective measures. In a chilly response to his general contractor, Edgerton claimed that a "readable and attractive" book like the *Report of the Commission* "does not lend itself well to the inclusion of all the factual material." (See letter from General Edgerton to John McShain, October 3, 1952, Harry S. Truman Papers, Official Files, Harry S. Truman Library

and Museum.) Orr took this excuse a step further when he told McShain that the book had included only those names that were "necessary for clarification of context," whatever that was supposed to mean. (See letter from Douglas Orr to John McShain, September 30, 1952, Harry S. Truman Papers, Official Files, Harry S. Truman Library and Museum.)

11. "The course of events during the last two and one-half years has convinced me," McShain told Edgerton, "that our association on the White House has meant little, if anything, to you." See letters from John McShain to General Edgerton, October 3 and 6, 1952, Harry S. Truman Papers, Official Files, Harry S. Truman Library and Museum.

12. Author's interview with Sister Pauline McShain, December 13, 2011.

13. Even Peggy Watts, Haight's assistant on the decorating job, had saved a newspaper clipping that read "Much of the new White House, like an iceberg, is below the surface, underfoot and out of sight." See "Remodeling Job at 1600 Pennsylvania Avenue," uncited clipping in the Peggy Watts Papers, Harry S. Truman Library and Museum.

14. Gen. Glen E. Edgerton "Diary of Progress of the Renovation and Remodeling of the Executive Mansion," Office of History, U.S. Army Corps of Engineers, entry for August 24, 1951.

15. Chalmers M. Roberts, "Secret U.S. Plan Would Spread Agencies 50 Miles Around D.C.," *Washington Post*, July 28, 1950.

16. Oral History Interview with Adm. Robert L. Dennison, conducted by Jerry N. Hess, October 6, 1971, §99, Harry S. Truman Library and Museum.

17. Philip H. Melanson, *The Secret Service: The Hidden History of an Enigmatic Agency* (New York: Barnes & Noble Books, 2004), 140.

18. David McCullough, *Truman* (New York: Simon & Schuster, 1992), 881.

19. McCullough, *Truman*, 881; Melanson, *The Secret Service*, 140.

20. "Public Rooms of White House Seen by 5544 on Reopening," *Washington Post*, April 23, 1952.

21. Letter from John S. Burke to William Adams Delano, April 1, 1952, William Adams Delano Papers, Avery Architectural & Fine Arts Library, Columbia University, New York.

22. "White House Fabrics Put on Display Here," *New York Times*, March 29,

1952; Minutes of the Commission on the Renovation of the Executive Mansion, March 24, 1951, Harry S. Truman Library and Museum, 6.

23. Margaret Truman, *The President's House* (New York: Ballantine Books, 2003), 43.

24. "Truman Loses on Renovating White House," *Washington Post*, June 25, 1952.

25. Margaret Truman, *First Ladies* (New York: Fawcett Books, 1995), 34.

26. "Performance Ratings for President Truman, 1945–1952," Roper Center for Public Opinion, University of Connecticut at Storrs.

27. Margaret Truman, *Bess W. Truman*, 385.

28. Ibid., 378.

29. Margaret Truman, *Harry S. Truman* (New York: William Morrow, 1973), 558.

30. The Trumans would always see the White House "more or less as a temporary government residence." See J. B. West, with Mary Lynn Kotz, *Upstairs at the White House: My Life with the First Ladies* (New York: Coward, McCann & Geoghegan, 1973), 126.

31. Ibid.

32. Lillian Rogers Parks, with Frances Spatz Leighton, *My Thirty Years Backstairs at the White House* (New York: Fleet Publishing Co., 1961), 333–34; Alfred Steinberg, *The Man from Missouri: The Life and Times of Harry S. Truman* (New York: G. P. Putnam's Sons, 1962), 421.

33. Unless otherwise noted, the account of Truman's tour of the house, inclusive of quotes, is taken from the following: "White House Tour: Music by Truman," *New York Times*, May 4, 1952; Jean Reiff and Thomas Winship, "White House TV Tour Take [*sic*] by Truman," *Washington Post*, May 4, 1952; typewritten transcript of the tour, President's Secretary's Files, Harry S. Truman Library and Museum.

34. Sara L. Sale, *Bess Wallace Truman* (Lawrence: University Press of Kansas, 2010), 102.

35. McCullough, *Truman*, 887.

36. The sequence with Bourgholtzer, including details and quotes, is taken

from NBC's Web-archived footage of the May 2, 1952, tour. See http://video .msnbc.msn.com/nightly-news/39619222#39619222.

37. Truman later corrected this portion of his own commentary in a letter to Junius B. Wood, August 14, 1952: "I have the exact information on the Minerva clock from the archives of the White House. It was not purchased for Thomas Jefferson by Monroe but was bought by Monroe himself when he was President. The bill in payment of the purchase was approved May 4, 1818 by Monroe himself." See document 229, "Letter to Junius B. Wood on the Minerva Clock and Other Antique White House Furnishings," at www.trumanlibrary .org/publicpapers/index.php.

INDEX